# Dodge Aries Plymouth Reliant Automotive Repair Manual

## by Larry Warren and John H Haynes
Member of the Guild of Motoring Writers

**Models covered:**
All Dodge Aries and Plymouth Reliant models
1981 through 1989

ABCDE
FGHIJ
KLMNO
PQRS

**Haynes Publishing Group**
Sparkford Nr Yeovil
Somerset BA22 7JJ England

**Haynes North America, Inc**
861 Lawrence Drive
Newbury Park
California 91320 USA

## Acknowledgements
We are grateful to the Chrysler Corporation for assistance with technical information and certain illustrations. Technical writers who contributed to this project include Robert Maddox and Jay Storer.

**A book in the Haynes Automotive Repair Manual Series**

**Printed in the U.S.A.**

**ISBN 1 56392 228 2**

**Library of Congress Catalog Card Number 96-77662**

While every attempt is made to ensure that the information in this manual is correct, no liability can be accepted by the authors or publishers for loss, damage or injury caused by any errors in, or omissions from, the information given.

96-320

# Contents

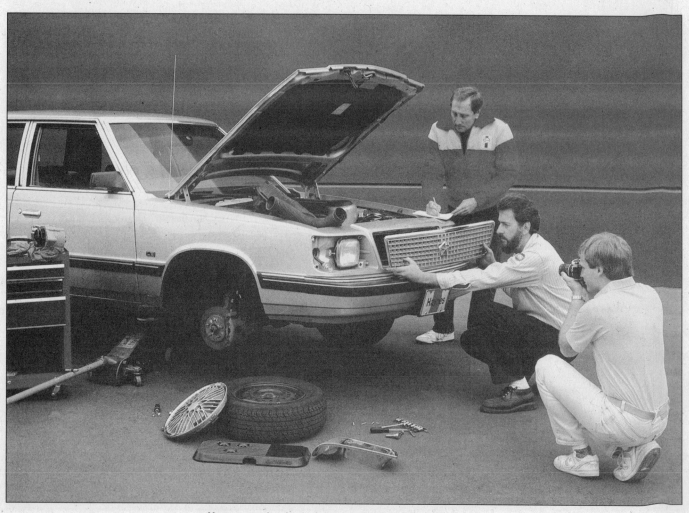

**Haynes mechanic, author and photographer with K-car**

# About this manual

## Its purpose

The purpose of this manual is to help you get the best value from your vehicle. It can do so in several ways. It can help you decide what work must be done, even if you choose to have it done by a dealer service department or a repair shop; it provides information and procedures for routine maintenance and servicing; and it offers diagnostic and repair procedures to follow when trouble occurs.

We hope you use the manual to tackle the work yourself. For many simpler jobs, doing it yourself may be quicker than arranging an appointment to get the vehicle into a shop and making the trips to leave it and pick it up. More importantly, a lot of money can be saved by avoiding the expense the shop must pass on to you to cover its labor and overhead costs. An added benefit is the sense of satisfaction and accomplishment that you feel after doing the job yourself.

## Using the manual

The manual is divided into Chapters. Each Chapter is divided into numbered Sections, which are headed in bold type between horizontal lines. Each Section consists of consecutively numbered paragraphs.

At the beginning of each numbered Section you will be referred to any illustrations which apply to the procedures in that Section. The reference numbers used in illustration captions pinpoint the pertinent Section and the Step within that Section. That is, illustration 3.2 means the illustration refers to Section 3 and Step (or paragraph) 2 within that Section.

Procedures, once described in the text, are not normally repeated. When it's necessary to refer to another Chapter, the reference will be given as Chapter and Section number. Cross references given without use of the word "Chapter" apply to Sections and/or paragraphs in the same Chapter. For example, "see Section 8" means in the same Chapter.

References to the left or right side of the vehicle assume you are sitting in the driver's seat, facing forward.

Even though we have prepared this manual with extreme care, neither the publisher nor the author can accept responsibility for any errors in, or omissions from, the information given.

**NOTE**

A **Note** provides information necessary to properly complete a procedure or information which will make the procedure easier to understand.

**CAUTION**

A **Caution** provides a special procedure or special steps which must be taken while completing the procedure where the Caution is found. Not heeding a Caution can result in damage to the assembly being worked on.

**WARNING**

A **Warning** provides a special procedure or special steps which must be taken while completing the procedure where the Warning is found. Not heeding a Warning can result in personal injury.

# Introduction to the Dodge Aries and Plymouth Reliant models

These models are available in two-door coupe, four-door sedan and station wagon body styles.

Transversely mounted inline four-cylinder engines, equipped with carburetors or electronic fuel injection are used. The engine drives the front wheels through either a four- or five-speed manual or a three-speed automatic transaxle via independent driveaxles.

The fully independent front suspension consists of coil spring/strut units, control arms and a stabilizer bar. The rear suspension uses shock absorbers, coil springs, a solid axle with integral trailing arms and a track bar (Panhard rod).

The steering gear is of the rack-and-pinion type, with power assist as an option.

The braking system is vacuum assisted and features disc brakes at the front and self-adjusting drums at the rear.

# Vehicle identification numbers

Modifications are a continuing and unpublicized process in vehicle manufacturing. Since spare parts manuals and lists are compiled on a numerical basis, the individual vehicle numbers are essential to correctly identify the component required.

## *Vehicle Identification Number (VIN)*

The Vehicle Identification Number (VIN), which appears on the Vehicle Certificate of Title and Registration, is also embossed on a gray plate located on the upper left (driver's side) corner of the dashboard, near the windshield **(see illustration)**. The VIN tells you when and where a vehicle was manufactured, its country of origin, make, type, passenger safety system, line, series, body style, engine and assembly plant.

## *Body Code Plate*

The body code plate, which is located on the left (driver's side) firewall, wheel housing or the upper radiator support **(see illustration)**, provides more specific information about the vehicle - type of engine, transaxle, paint, etc. - to which it's attached.

## *Engine Identification Number (EIN)*

On four-cylinder engines, the Engine Identification Number (EIN) is stamped into a machined boss on the engine block. On 2.2L and 2.5L engines it is stamped into the left end of the engine block, just about the transaxle bellhousing **(see illustration)**. On 2.6L engines, the number is on the radiator side of the of the block, between the core plug and the transaxle end of the block **(see illustration)**.

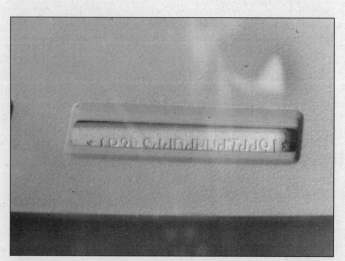

The Vehicle Identification Number (VIN) is visible from the outside of the vehicle, through the driver's side of the windshield

The Body Code Plate is located on the driver's side of the firewall, the wheel housing or the upper radiator support (shown) - it provides information about the type of engine, transaxle, paint etc. of the model to which it is attached

Location of the engine identification number on
2.2L and 2.5L engines

Location of the engine serial number on the 2.6L engine

Location of the engine identification number on the 2.6L engine

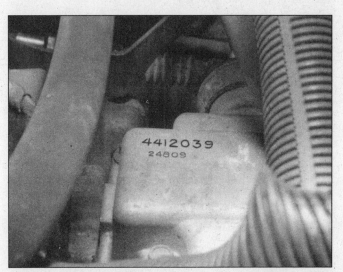

The Transaxle Identification Number (TIN) is stamped into a flat
spot on top of the transaxle housing

## Engine Serial Number

In addition the EIN, a serial number, which is sometimes required when buying replacement parts, is also stamped into the block. On 2.2L and 2.5L engines, it is located just below the EIN on the block. On the 2.6L engine, it is located on the right-rear side of the engine block, adjacent to the exhaust manifold stud (firewall side of the vehicle) **(see illustration)**.

## Transaxle Identification Number (TIN)

The Transaxle Identification Number (TIN) is stamped on a boss located on top of the transaxle housing **(see illustration)**.

## Transaxle Serial Number

Besides the TIN, the transaxle also has a serial number which you'll need to reference when buying transaxle parts. On manual transaxles, the serial number is embossed on a metal tag attached to the front side of the transaxle; on automatic transaxles, the serial number is located on a pad just above the oil pan at the rear of the transaxle.

# Buying parts

Replacement parts are available from many sources, which generally fall into one of two categories - authorized dealer parts departments and independent retail auto parts stores. Our advice concerning these parts is as follows:

*Retail auto parts stores:* Good auto parts stores will stock frequently needed components which wear out relatively fast, such as clutch components, exhaust systems, brake parts, tune-up parts, etc. These stores often supply new or reconditioned parts on an exchange basis, which can save a considerable amount of money. Discount auto parts stores are often very good places to buy materials and parts needed for general vehicle maintenance such as oil, grease, filters, spark plugs, belts, touch-up paint, bulbs, etc. They also usually sell tools and general accessories, have convenient hours, charge lower prices and can often be found not far from home.

*Authorized dealer parts department:* This is the best source for parts which are unique to the vehicle and not generally available elsewhere (such as major engine parts, transmission parts, trim pieces, etc.).

*Warranty information:* If the vehicle is still covered under warranty, be sure that any replacement parts purchased - regardless of the source - do not invalidate the warranty!

To be sure of obtaining the correct parts, have engine and chassis numbers available and, if possible, take the old parts along for positive identification.

# Maintenance techniques, tools and working facilities

## Maintenance techniques

There are a number of techniques involved in maintenance and repair that will be referred to throughout this manual. Application of these techniques will enable the home mechanic to be more efficient, better organized and capable of performing the various tasks properly, which will ensure that the repair job is thorough and complete.

## Fasteners

Fasteners are nuts, bolts, studs and screws used to hold two or more parts together. There are a few things to keep in mind when working with fasteners. Almost all of them use a locking device of some type, either a lockwasher, locknut, locking tab or thread adhesive. All threaded fasteners should be clean and straight, with undamaged threads and undamaged corners on the hex head where the wrench fits. Develop the habit of replacing all damaged nuts and bolts with new ones. Special locknuts with nylon or fiber inserts can only be used once. If they are removed, they lose their locking ability and must be replaced with new ones.

Rusted nuts and bolts should be treated with a penetrating fluid to ease removal and prevent breakage. Some mechanics use turpentine in a spout-type oil can, which works quite well. After applying the rust penetrant, let it work for a few minutes before trying to loosen the nut or bolt. Badly rusted fasteners may have to be chiseled or sawed off or removed with a special nut breaker, available at tool stores.

If a bolt or stud breaks off in an assembly, it can be drilled and removed with a special tool commonly available for this purpose. Most automotive machine shops can perform this task, as well as other repair procedures, such as the repair of threaded holes that have been stripped out.

Flat washers and lockwashers, when removed from an assembly, should always be replaced exactly as removed. Replace any damaged washers with new ones. Never use a lockwasher on any soft metal surface (such as aluminum), thin sheet metal or plastic.

## Fastener sizes

For a number of reasons, automobile manufacturers are making wider and wider use of metric fasteners. Therefore, it is important to be able to tell the difference between standard (sometimes called U.S. or SAE) and metric hardware, since they cannot be interchanged.

All bolts, whether standard or metric, are sized according to diameter, thread pitch and length. For example, a standard 1/2 - 13 x 1 bolt is 1/2 inch in diameter, has 13 threads per inch and is 1 inch long. An M12 - 1.75 x 25 metric bolt is 12 mm in diameter, has a thread pitch of 1.75 mm (the distance between threads) and is 25 mm long. The two bolts are nearly identical, and easily confused, but they are not interchangeable.

In addition to the differences in diameter, thread pitch and length, metric and standard bolts can also be distinguished by examining the bolt heads. To begin with, the distance across the flats on a standard bolt head is measured in inches, while the same dimension on a metric bolt is sized in millimeters (the same is true for nuts). As a result, a standard wrench should not be used on a metric bolt and a metric wrench should not be used on a standard bolt. Also, most standard bolts have slashes radiating out from the center of the head to denote the grade or strength of the bolt, which is an indication of the amount of torque that can be applied to it. The greater the number of slashes, the greater the strength of the bolt. Grades 0 through 5 are commonly used on automobiles. Metric bolts have a property class (grade) number, rather than a slash, molded into their heads to indicate bolt strength. In this case, the higher the number, the stronger the bolt. Property class numbers 8.8, 9.8 and 10.9 are commonly used on automobiles.

Strength markings can also be used to distinguish standard hex nuts from metric hex nuts. Many standard nuts have dots stamped into one side, while metric nuts are marked with a number. The greater the number of dots, or the higher the number, the greater the strength of the nut.

Metric studs are also marked on their ends according to property class (grade). Larger studs are numbered (the same as metric bolts), while smaller studs carry a geometric code to denote grade.

**Grade 1 or 2**     **Grade 5**     **Grade 8**

4.6   4.8   5.8   8.8   9.8   10.9

**Bolt strength markings (top - standard/SAE/USS; bottom - metric)**

| Grade | Identification |
|---|---|
| Hex Nut Grade 5 | 3 Dots |
| Hex Nut Grade 8 | 6 Dots |

**Standard hex nut strength markings**

| Class | Identification |
|---|---|
| Hex Nut Property Class 9 | Arabic 9 |
| Hex Nut Property Class 10 | Arabic 10 |

**Metric hex nut strength markings**

CLASS 10.9     CLASS 9.8     CLASS 8.8

**Metric stud strength markings**

It should be noted that many fasteners, especially Grades 0 through 2, have no distinguishing marks on them. When such is the case, the only way to determine whether it is standard or metric is to measure the thread pitch or compare it to a known fastener of the same size.

Standard fasteners are often referred to as SAE, as opposed to metric. However, it should be noted that SAE technically refers to a non-metric fine thread fastener only. Coarse thread non-metric fasteners are referred to as USS sizes.

Since fasteners of the same size (both standard and metric) may have different strength ratings, be sure to reinstall any bolts, studs or nuts removed from your vehicle in their original locations. Also, when replacing a fastener with a new one, make sure that the new one has a strength rating equal to or greater than the original.

## Tightening sequences and procedures

Most threaded fasteners should be tightened to a specific torque value (torque is the twisting force applied to a threaded component such as a nut or bolt). Overtightening the fastener can weaken it and cause it to break, while undertightening can cause it to eventually come loose. Bolts, screws and studs, depending on the material they are made of and their thread diameters, have specific torque values, many of which are noted in the Specifications at the beginning of each Chapter. Be sure to follow the torque recommendations closely. For fasteners not assigned a specific torque, a general torque value chart is presented here as a guide. These torque values are for dry (unlubricated) fasteners threaded into steel or cast iron (not aluminum). As was previously mentioned, the size and grade of a fastener determine the amount of torque that can safely be applied to it. The figures listed

| Metric thread sizes | Ft-lbs | Nm |
|---|---|---|
| M-6 | 6 to 9 | 9 to 12 |
| M-8 | 14 to 21 | 19 to 28 |
| M-10 | 28 to 40 | 38 to 54 |
| M-12 | 50 to 71 | 68 to 96 |
| M-14 | 80 to 140 | 109 to 154 |
| **Pipe thread sizes** | | |
| 1/8 | 5 to 8 | 7 to 10 |
| 1/4 | 12 to 18 | 17 to 24 |
| 3/8 | 22 to 33 | 30 to 44 |
| 1/2 | 25 to 35 | 34 to 47 |
| **U.S. thread sizes** | | |
| 1/4 - 20 | 6 to 9 | 9 to 12 |
| 5/16 - 18 | 12 to 18 | 17 to 24 |
| 5/16 - 24 | 14 to 20 | 19 to 27 |
| 3/8 - 16 | 22 to 32 | 30 to 43 |
| 3/8 - 24 | 27 to 38 | 37 to 51 |
| 7/16 - 14 | 40 to 55 | 55 to 74 |
| 7/16 - 20 | 40 to 60 | 55 to 81 |
| 1/2 - 13 | 55 to 80 | 75 to 108 |

**Standard (SAE and USS) bolt dimensions/grade marks**

    *G*   Grade marks (bolt strength)
    *L*   Length (in inches)
    *T*   Thread pitch (number of threads per inch)
    *D*   Nominal diameter (in inches)

**Metric bolt dimensions/grade marks**

    *P*   Property class (bolt strength)
    *L*   Length (in millimeters)
    *T*   Thread pitch (distance between threads in millimeters)
    *D*   Diameter

here are approximate for Grade 2 and Grade 3 fasteners. Higher grades can tolerate higher torque values.

Fasteners laid out in a pattern, such as cylinder head bolts, oil pan bolts, differential cover bolts, etc., must be loosened or tightened in sequence to avoid warping the component. This sequence will normally be shown in the appropriate Chapter. If a specific pattern is not given, the following procedures can be used to prevent warping.

Initially, the bolts or nuts should be assembled finger-tight only. Next, they should be tightened one full turn each, in a criss-cross or diagonal pattern. After each one has been tightened one full turn, return to the first one and tighten them all one-half turn, following the same pattern. Finally, tighten each of them one-quarter turn at a time until each fastener has been tightened to the proper torque. To loosen and remove the fasteners, the procedure would be reversed.

## Component disassembly

Component disassembly should be done with care and purpose to help ensure that the parts go back together properly. Always keep track of the sequence in which parts are removed. Make note of special characteristics or marks on parts that can be installed more than one way, such as a grooved thrust washer on a shaft. It is a good idea to lay the disassembled parts out on a clean surface in the order that they were removed. It may also be helpful to make sketches or take instant photos of components before removal.

When removing fasteners from a component, keep track of their locations. Sometimes threading a bolt back in a part, or putting the washers and nut back on a stud, can prevent mix-ups later. If nuts and bolts cannot be returned to their original locations, they should be kept in a compartmented box or a series of small boxes. A cupcake or muffin tin is ideal for this purpose, since each cavity can hold the bolts and nuts from a particular area (i.e. oil pan bolts, valve cover bolts, engine mount bolts, etc.). A pan of this type is especially helpful when working on assemblies with very small parts, such as the carburetor, alternator, valve train or interior dash and trim pieces. The cavities can be marked with paint or tape to identify the contents.

Whenever wiring looms, harnesses or connectors are separated, it is a good idea to identify the two halves with numbered pieces of masking tape so they can be easily reconnected.

## Gasket sealing surfaces

Throughout any vehicle, gaskets are used to seal the mating surfaces between two parts and keep lubricants, fluids, vacuum or pressure contained in an assembly.

Many times these gaskets are coated with a liquid or paste-type gasket sealing compound before assembly. Age, heat and pressure can sometimes cause the two parts to stick together so tightly that they are very difficult to separate. Often, the assembly can be loosened by striking it with a soft-face hammer near the mating surfaces. A regular hammer can be used if a block of wood is placed between the hammer and the part. Do not hammer on cast parts or parts that could be easily damaged. With any particularly stubborn part, always recheck to make sure that every fastener has been removed.

Avoid using a screwdriver or bar to pry apart an assembly, as they can easily mar the gasket sealing surfaces of the parts, which must remain smooth. If prying is absolutely necessary, use an old broom handle, but keep in mind that extra clean up will be necessary if the wood splinters.

After the parts are separated, the old gasket must be carefully scraped off and the gasket surfaces cleaned. Stubborn gasket material can be soaked with rust penetrant or treated with a special chemical to soften it so it can be easily scraped off. A scraper can be fashioned from a piece of copper tubing by flattening and sharpening one end. Copper is recommended because it is usually softer than the surfaces to be scraped, which reduces the chance of gouging the part. Some gaskets can be removed with a wire brush, but regardless of the method used, the mating surfaces must be left clean and smooth. If for some reason the gasket surface is gouged, then a gasket sealer thick enough to fill scratches will have to be used during reassembly of the components. For most applications, a non-drying (or semi-drying) gasket sealer should be used.

## Hose removal tips

**Warning:** *If the vehicle is equipped with air conditioning, do not disconnect any of the A/C hoses without first having the system depressurized by a dealer service department or a service station.*

Hose removal precautions closely parallel gasket removal precautions. Avoid scratching or gouging the surface that the hose mates against or the connection may leak. This is especially true for radiator hoses. Because of various chemical reactions, the rubber in hoses can bond itself to the metal spigot that the hose fits over. To remove a hose, first loosen the hose clamps that secure it to the spigot. Then, with slip-joint pliers, grab the hose at the clamp and rotate it around the spigot. Work it back and forth until it is completely free, then pull it off. Silicone or other lubricants will ease removal if they can be applied between the hose and the outside of the spigot. Apply the same lubricant to the inside of the hose and the outside of the spigot to simplify installation.

As a last resort (and if the hose is to be replaced with a new one anyway), the rubber can be slit with a knife and the hose peeled from the spigot. If this must be done, be careful that the metal connection is not damaged.

If a hose clamp is broken or damaged, do not reuse it. Wire-type clamps usually weaken with age, so it is a good idea to replace them with screw-type clamps whenever a hose is removed.

## Tools

A selection of good tools is a basic requirement for anyone who plans to maintain and repair his or her own vehicle. For the owner who has few tools, the initial investment might seem high, but when compared to the spiraling costs of professional auto maintenance and repair, it is a wise one.

**Micrometer set**

**Dial indicator set**

Dial caliper

Hand-operated vacuum pump

Timing light

Compression gauge with spark plug hole adapter

Damper/steering wheel puller

General purpose puller

Hydraulic lifter removal tool

Valve spring compressor

Valve spring compressor

Ridge reamer

Piston ring groove cleaning tool

Ring removal/installation tool

**Ring compressor**

**Cylinder hone**

**Brake hold-down spring tool**

**Brake cylinder hone**

**Clutch plate alignment tool**

**Tap and die set**

To help the owner decide which tools are needed to perform the tasks detailed in this manual, the following tool lists are offered: *Maintenance and minor repair, Repair/overhaul* and *Special.*

The newcomer to practical mechanics should start off with the *maintenance and minor repair* tool kit, which is adequate for the simpler jobs performed on a vehicle. Then, as confidence and experience grow, the owner can tackle more difficult tasks, buying additional tools as they are needed. Eventually the basic kit will be expanded into the *repair and overhaul* tool set. Over a period of time, the experienced do-it-yourselfer will assemble a tool set complete enough for most repair and overhaul procedures and will add tools from the special category when it is felt that the expense is justified by the frequency of use.

## Maintenance and minor repair tool kit

The tools in this list should be considered the minimum required for performance of routine maintenance, servicing and minor repair work. We recommend the purchase of combination wrenches (box-end and open-end combined in one wrench). While more expensive than open end wrenches, they offer the advantages of both types of wrench.

*Combination wrench set (1/4-inch to 1 inch or 6 mm to 19 mm)*
*Adjustable wrench, 8 inch*
*Spark plug wrench with rubber insert*
*Spark plug gap adjusting tool*
*Feeler gauge set*
*Brake bleeder wrench*
*Standard screwdriver (5/16-inch x 6 inch)*
*Phillips screwdriver (No. 2 x 6 inch)*
*Combination pliers - 6 inch*
*Hacksaw and assortment of blades*
*Tire pressure gauge*
*Grease gun*

*Oil can*
*Fine emery cloth*
*Wire brush*
*Battery post and cable cleaning tool*
*Oil filter wrench*
*Funnel (medium size)*
*Safety goggles*
*Jackstands (2)*
*Drain pan*

**Note:** *If basic tune-ups are going to be part of routine maintenance, it will be necessary to purchase a good quality stroboscopic timing light and combination tachometer/dwell meter. Although they are included in the list of special tools, it is mentioned here because they are absolutely necessary for tuning most vehicles properly.*

## Repair and overhaul tool set

These tools are essential for anyone who plans to perform major repairs and are in addition to those in the maintenance and minor repair tool kit. Included is a comprehensive set of sockets which, though expensive, are invaluable because of their versatility, especially when various extensions and drives are available. We recommend the 1/2-inch drive over the 3/8-inch drive. Although the larger drive is bulky and more expensive, it has the capacity of accepting a very wide range of large sockets. Ideally, however, the mechanic should have a 3/8-inch drive set and a 1/2-inch drive set.

*Socket set(s)*
*Reversible ratchet*
*Extension - 10 inch*
*Universal joint*
*Torque wrench (same size drive as sockets)*
*Ball peen hammer - 8 ounce*
*Soft-face hammer (plastic/rubber)*
*Standard screwdriver (1/4-inch x 6 inch)*

*Standard screwdriver (stubby - 5/16-inch)*
*Phillips screwdriver (No. 3 x 8 inch)*
*Phillips screwdriver (stubby - No. 2)*
*Pliers - vise grip*
*Pliers - lineman's*
*Pliers - needle nose*
*Pliers - snap-ring (internal and external)*
*Cold chisel - 1/2-inch*
*Scribe*
*Scraper (made from flattened copper tubing)*
*Centerpunch*
*Pin punches (1/16, 1/8, 3/16-inch)*
*Steel rule/straightedge - 12 inch*
*Allen wrench set (1/8 to 3/8-inch or 4 mm to 10 mm)*
*A selection of files*
*Wire brush (large)*
*Jackstands (second set)*
*Jack (scissor or hydraulic type)*

**Note:** *Another tool which is often useful is an electric drill with a chuck capacity of 3/8-inch and a set of good quality drill bits.*

## Special tools

The tools in this list include those which are not used regularly, are expensive to buy, or which need to be used in accordance with their manufacturer's instructions. Unless these tools will be used frequently, it is not very economical to purchase many of them. A consideration would be to split the cost and use between yourself and a friend or friends. In addition, most of these tools can be obtained from a tool rental shop on a temporary basis.

This list primarily contains only those tools and instruments widely available to the public, and not those special tools produced by the vehicle manufacturer for distribution to dealer service departments. Occasionally, references to the manufacturer's special tools are included in the text of this manual. Generally, an alternative method of doing the job without the special tool is offered. However, sometimes there is no alternative to their use. Where this is the case, and the tool cannot be purchased or borrowed, the work should be turned over to the dealer service department or an automotive repair shop.

*Valve spring compressor*
*Piston ring groove cleaning tool*
*Piston ring compressor*
*Piston ring installation tool*
*Cylinder compression gauge*
*Cylinder ridge reamer*
*Cylinder surfacing hone*
*Cylinder bore gauge*
*Micrometers and/or dial calipers*
*Hydraulic lifter removal tool*
*Balljoint separator*
*Universal-type puller*
*Impact screwdriver*
*Dial indicator set*
*Stroboscopic timing light (inductive pick-up)*
*Hand operated vacuum/pressure pump*
*Tachometer/dwell meter*
*Universal electrical multimeter*
*Cable hoist*
*Brake spring removal and installation tools*
*Floor jack*

## Buying tools

For the do-it-yourselfer who is just starting to get involved in vehicle maintenance and repair, there are a number of options available when purchasing tools. If maintenance and minor repair is the extent of the work to be done, the purchase of individual tools is satisfactory. If, on the other hand, extensive work is planned, it would be a good idea

to purchase a modest tool set from one of the large retail chain stores. A set can usually be bought at a substantial savings over the individual tool prices, and they often come with a tool box. As additional tools are needed, add-on sets, individual tools and a larger tool box can be purchased to expand the tool selection. Building a tool set gradually allows the cost of the tools to be spread over a longer period of time and gives the mechanic the freedom to choose only those tools that will actually be used.

Tool stores will often be the only source of some of the special tools that are needed, but regardless of where tools are bought, try to avoid cheap ones, especially when buying screwdrivers and sockets, because they won't last very long. The expense involved in replacing cheap tools will eventually be greater than the initial cost of quality tools.

## Care and maintenance of tools

Good tools are expensive, so it makes sense to treat them with respect. Keep them clean and in usable condition and store them properly when not in use. Always wipe off any dirt, grease or metal chips before putting them away. Never leave tools lying around in the work area. Upon completion of a job, always check closely under the hood for tools that may have been left there so they won't get lost during a test drive.

Some tools, such as screwdrivers, pliers, wrenches and sockets, can be hung on a panel mounted on the garage or workshop wall, while others should be kept in a tool box or tray. Measuring instruments, gauges, meters, etc. must be carefully stored where they cannot be damaged by weather or impact from other tools.

When tools are used with care and stored properly, they will last a very long time. Even with the best of care, though, tools will wear out if used frequently. When a tool is damaged or worn out, replace it. Subsequent jobs will be safer and more enjoyable if you do.

## Working facilities

Not to be overlooked when discussing tools is the workshop. If anything more than routine maintenance is to be carried out, some sort of suitable work area is essential.

It is understood, and appreciated, that many home mechanics do not have a good workshop or garage available, and end up removing an engine or doing major repairs outside. It is recommended, however, that the overhaul or repair be completed under the cover of a roof.

A clean, flat workbench or table of comfortable working height is an absolute necessity. The workbench should be equipped with a vise that has a jaw opening of at least four inches.

As mentioned previously, some clean, dry storage space is also required for tools, as well as the lubricants, fluids, cleaning solvents, etc. which soon become necessary.

Sometimes waste oil and fluids, drained from the engine or cooling system during normal maintenance or repairs, present a disposal problem. To avoid pouring them on the ground or into a sewage system, pour the used fluids into large containers, seal them with caps and take them to an authorized disposal site or recycling center. Plastic jugs, such as old antifreeze containers, are ideal for this purpose.

Always keep a supply of old newspapers and clean rags available. Old towels are excellent for mopping up spills. Many mechanics use rolls of paper towels for most work because they are readily available and disposable. To help keep the area under the vehicle clean, a large cardboard box can be cut open and flattened to protect the garage or shop floor.

Whenever working over a painted surface, such as when leaning over a fender to service something under the hood, always cover it with an old blanket or bedspread to protect the finish. Vinyl covered pads, made especially for this purpose, are available at auto parts stores.

# Jacking and towing

## Jacking

The jack supplied with the vehicle should be used only for raising the vehicle when changing a tire or placing jackstands under the frame. **Warning:** *Never work under the vehicle or start the engine when this jack is being used as the only means of support.*

The vehicles covered by this manual are supplied with a scissors-type jack which mates with a locator pin in the rocker panel flange **(see illustration)**.

The vehicle should be on level ground with the wheels blocked and the transaxle in Park (automatic) or Neutral (manual). If a tire is being changed, loosen the lug nuts one-half turn and leave them in place until the wheel is raised off the ground. Make sure no one is in the vehicle as it's being raised off the ground.

Place the jack under the side of the vehicle at the locating pin nearest the wheel to be changed . If you're using a floor jack, place it beneath the crossmember at the front or rear **(see illustration). Caution:** *Never place the jack under the rear trailing arms.* Operate the jack with a slow, smooth motion until the wheel is raised off the ground. If you're using jackstands, position them beneath the support points along the front or rear rocker panel flange. Remove the lug nuts, pull off the wheel, install the spare and thread the lug nuts back on with the beveled sides facing in. Tighten them snugly, but wait until the vehicle is lowered to tighten them completely.

Lower the vehicle, remove the jack and tighten the lug nuts (if loosened or removed) in a criss-cross pattern. If possible, tighten them with a torque wrench (see Chapter 1 for the torque figures). If you don't have access to a torque wrench, have the nuts checked by a service station or repair shop as soon as possible. Retighten the lug nuts after 500 miles.

If the vehicle is equipped with a temporary spare tire, remember that it is intended only for temporary use until the regular tire can be repaired. Do not exceed the maximum speed that the tire is rated for.

## Towing

Manual transaxle equipped models can be towed at legal highway speeds with all four wheels on the ground and the shift lever in Neutral. While towing, the parking brake must be released and the transaxle must be in Neutral. The steering must be unlocked (ignition switch in the OFF position). Don't exceed 50 mph (35 mph on rough roads).

Models with automatic transaxles shouldn't be towed with all four wheels on the ground - instead, the vehicle should be towed from the

**JACK LOCATOR PIN**

**Jack lifting points**

**There's a jack locator pin like this (arrow) near each wheel - when raising the vehicle with the standard scissor-type jack, make sure the jack head is securely engaged with the pin nearest the wheel you're raising**

rear with the front wheels placed on a dolly. **Caution:** *Don't use the hook loops under the vehicle for towing (they're intended only for use as tie-downs).*

The best way to tow any vehicle is with a flatbed tow truck. In this case, pull the vehicle onto the truck towards the front, using the J-hooks at the front suspension control arms with the points turned down.

Safety is a major consideration while towing and all applicable state and local laws must be obeyed. A safety chain system must be used at all times. Remember that power steering and power brakes will not work with the engine off.

**Frame lifting locations**

▨ DRIVE ON HOIST

▦ FRAME CONTACT HOIST

▥ TWIN POST HOIST

▩ FLOOR JACK

# Booster battery (jump) starting

Observe these precautions when using a booster battery to start a vehicle:

a) *Before connecting the booster battery, make sure the ignition switch is in the Off position.*
b) *Turn off the lights, heater and other electrical loads.*
c) *Your eyes should be shielded. Safety goggles are a good idea.*
d) *Make sure the booster battery is the same voltage as the dead one in the vehicle.*
e) *The two vehicles MUST NOT TOUCH each other!*
f) *Make sure the transaxle is in Neutral (manual) or Park (automatic).*
g) *If the booster battery is not a maintenance-free type, remove the vent caps and lay a cloth over the vent holes.*

Connect the red jumper cable to the positive (+) terminals of each battery **(see illustration)**.

Connect one end of the black jumper cable to the negative (-) terminal of the booster battery. The other end of this cable should be connected to a good ground on the vehicle to be started, such as a bolt or bracket on the body.

Start the engine using the booster battery, then, with the engine running at idle speed, disconnect the jumper cables in the reverse order of connection.

**Make the booster battery cable connections in the numerical order shown (note that the negative cable of the booster battery is NOT attached to the negative terminal of the dead battery)**

# Automotive chemicals and lubricants

A number of automotive chemicals and lubricants are available for use during vehicle maintenance and repair. They include a wide variety of products ranging from cleaning solvents and degreasers to lubricants and protective sprays for rubber, plastic and vinyl.

## Cleaners

**Carburetor cleaner and choke cleaner** is a strong solvent for gum, varnish and carbon. Most carburetor cleaners leave a dry-type lubricant film which will not harden or gum up. Because of this film it is not recommended for use on electrical components.

**Brake system cleaner** is used to remove grease and brake fluid from the brake system, where clean surfaces are absolutely necessary. It leaves no residue and often eliminates brake squeal caused by contaminants.

**Electrical cleaner** removes oxidation, corrosion and carbon deposits from electrical contacts, restoring full current flow. It can also be used to clean spark plugs, carburetor jets, voltage regulators and other parts where an oil-free surface is desired.

**Demoisturants** remove water and moisture from electrical components such as alternators, voltage regulators, electrical connectors and fuse blocks. They are non-conductive, non-corrosive and non-flammable.

**Degreasers** are heavy-duty solvents used to remove grease from the outside of the engine and from chassis components. They can be sprayed or brushed on and, depending on the type, are rinsed off either with water or solvent.

## Lubricants

**Motor oil** is the lubricant formulated for use in engines. It normally contains a wide variety of additives to prevent corrosion and reduce foaming and wear. Motor oil comes in various weights (viscosity ratings) from 5 to 80. The recommended weight of the oil depends on the season, temperature and the demands on the engine. Light oil is used in cold climates and under light load conditions. Heavy oil is used in hot climates and where high loads are encountered. Multi-viscosity oils are designed to have characteristics of both light and heavy oils and are available in a number of weights from 5W-20 to 20W-50.

**Gear oil** is designed to be used in differentials, manual transmissions and other areas where high-temperature lubrication is required.

**Chassis and wheel bearing grease** is a heavy grease used where increased loads and friction are encountered, such as for wheel bearings, balljoints, tie-rod ends and universal joints.

**High-temperature wheel bearing grease** is designed to withstand the extreme temperatures encountered by wheel bearings in disc brake equipped vehicles. It usually contains molybdenum disulfide (moly), which is a dry-type lubricant.

**White grease** is a heavy grease for metal-to-metal applications where water is a problem. White grease stays soft under both low and high temperatures (usually from -100 to +190-degrees F), and will not wash off or dilute in the presence of water.

**Assembly lube** is a special extreme pressure lubricant, usually containing moly, used to lubricate high-load parts (such as main and rod bearings and cam lobes) for initial start-up of a new engine. The assembly lube lubricates the parts without being squeezed out or washed away until the engine oiling system begins to function.

**Silicone lubricants** are used to protect rubber, plastic, vinyl and nylon parts.

**Graphite lubricants** are used where oils cannot be used due to contamination problems, such as in locks. The dry graphite will lubricate metal parts while remaining uncontaminated by dirt, water, oil or acids. It is electrically conductive and will not foul electrical contacts in locks such as the ignition switch.

**Moly penetrants** loosen and lubricate frozen, rusted and corroded fasteners and prevent future rusting or freezing.

**Heat-sink grease** is a special electrically non-conductive grease that is used for mounting electronic ignition modules where it is essential that heat is transferred away from the module.

## Sealants

**RTV sealant** is one of the most widely used gasket compounds. Made from silicone, RTV is air curing, it seals, bonds, waterproofs, fills surface irregularities, remains flexible, doesn't shrink, is relatively easy to remove, and is used as a supplementary sealer with almost all low and medium temperature gaskets.

**Anaerobic sealant** is much like RTV in that it can be used either to seal gaskets or to form gaskets by itself. It remains flexible, is solvent resistant and fills surface imperfections. The difference between an anaerobic sealant and an RTV-type sealant is in the curing. RTV cures when exposed to air, while an anaerobic sealant cures only in the absence of air. This means that an anaerobic sealant cures only after the assembly of parts, sealing them together.

**Thread and pipe sealant** is used for sealing hydraulic and pneumatic fittings and vacuum lines. It is usually made from a Teflon compound, and comes in a spray, a paint-on liquid and as a wrap-around tape.

## Chemicals

**Anti-seize compound** prevents seizing, galling, cold welding, rust and corrosion in fasteners. High-temperature ant-seize, usually made with copper and graphite lubricants, is used for exhaust system and exhaust manifold bolts.

**Anaerobic locking compounds** are used to keep fasteners from vibrating or working loose and cure only after installation, in the absence of air. Medium strength locking compound is used for small nuts, bolts and screws that may be removed later. High-strength locking compound is for large nuts, bolts and studs which aren't removed on a regular basis.

**Oil additives** range from viscosity index improvers to chemical treatments that claim to reduce internal engine friction. It should be noted that most oil manufacturers caution against using additives with their oils.

**Gas additives** perform several functions, depending on their chemical makeup. They usually contain solvents that help dissolve gum and varnish that build up on carburetor, fuel injection and intake parts. They also serve to break down carbon deposits that form on the inside surfaces of the combustion chambers. Some additives contain upper cylinder lubricants for valves and piston rings, and others contain chemicals to remove condensation from the gas tank.

## Miscellaneous

**Brake fluid** is specially formulated hydraulic fluid that can withstand the heat and pressure encountered in brake systems. Care must be taken so this fluid does not come in contact with painted surfaces or plastics. An opened container should always be resealed to prevent contamination by water or dirt.

**Weatherstrip adhesive** is used to bond weatherstripping around doors, windows and trunk lids. It is sometimes used to attach trim pieces.

**Undercoating** is a petroleum-based, tar-like substance that is designed to protect metal surfaces on the underside of the vehicle from corrosion. It also acts as a sound-deadening agent by insulating the bottom of the vehicle.

**Waxes and polishes** are used to help protect painted and plated surfaces from the weather. Different types of paint may require the use of different types of wax and polish. Some polishes utilize a chemical or abrasive cleaner to help remove the top layer of oxidized (dull) paint on older vehicles. In recent years many non-wax polishes that contain a wide variety of chemicals such as polymers and silicones have been introduced. These non-wax polishes are usually easier to apply and last longer than conventional waxes and polishes.

# Conversion factors

## Length (distance)

| | | | | | |
|---|---|---|---|---|---|
| Inches (in) | X | 25.4 = Millimetres (mm) | X | 0.0394 | = Inches (in) |
| Feet (ft) | X | 0.305 = Metres (m) | X | 3.281 | = Feet (ft) |
| Miles | X | 1.609 = Kilometres (km) | X | 0.621 | = Miles |

## Volume (capacity)

| | | | | | |
|---|---|---|---|---|---|
| Cubic inches (cu in; in$^3$) | X | 16.387 = Cubic centimetres (cc; cm$^3$) | X | 0.061 | = Cubic inches (cu in; in$^3$) |
| Imperial pints (Imp pt) | X | 0.568 = Litres (l) | X | 1.76 | = Imperial pints (Imp pt) |
| Imperial quarts (Imp qt) | X | 1.137 = Litres (l) | X | 0.88 | = Imperial quarts (Imp qt) |
| Imperial quarts (Imp qt) | X | 1.201 = US quarts (US qt) | X | 0.833 | = Imperial quarts (Imp qt) |
| US quarts (US qt) | X | 0.946 = Litres (l) | X | 1.057 | = US quarts (US qt) |
| Imperial gallons (Imp gal) | X | 4.546 = Litres (l) | X | 0.22 | = Imperial gallons (Imp gal) |
| Imperial gallons (Imp gal) | X | 1.201 = US gallons (US gal) | X | 0.833 | = Imperial gallons (Imp gal) |
| US gallons (US gal) | X | 3.785 = Litres (l) | X | 0.264 | = US gallons (US gal) |

## Mass (weight)

| | | | | | |
|---|---|---|---|---|---|
| Ounces (oz) | X | 28.35 = Grams (g) | X | 0.035 | Ounces (oz) |
| Pounds (lb) | X | 0.454 = Kilograms (kg) | X | 2.205 | = Pounds (lb) |

## Force

| | | | | | |
|---|---|---|---|---|---|
| Ounces-force (ozf; oz) | X | 0.278 = Newtons (N) | X | 3.6 | = Ounces-force (ozf; oz) |
| Pounds-force (lbf; lb) | X | 4.448 = Newtons (N) | X | 0.225 | = Pounds-force (lbf; lb) |
| Newtons (N) | X | 0.1 = Kilograms-force (kgf; kg) | X | 9.81 | = Newtons (N) |

## Pressure

| | | | | | |
|---|---|---|---|---|---|
| Pounds-force per square inch (psi; lbf/in$^2$; lb/in$^2$) | X | 0.070 = Kilograms-force per square centimetre (kgf/cm$^2$; kg/cm$^2$) | X | 14.223 | = Pounds-force per square inch (psi; lbf/in$^2$; lb/in$^2$) |
| Pounds-force per square inch (psi; lbf/in$^2$; lb/in$^2$) | X | 0.068 = Atmospheres (atm) | X | 14.696 | = Pounds-force per square inch (psi; lbf/in$^2$; lb/in$^2$) |
| Pounds-force per square inch (psi; lbf/in$^2$; lb/in$^2$) | X | 0.069 = Bars | X | 14.5 | = Pounds-force per square inch (psi; lbf/in$^2$; lb/in$^2$) |
| Pounds-force per square inch (psi; lbf/in$^2$; lb/in$^2$) | X | 6.895 = Kilopascals (kPa) | X | 0.145 | = Pounds-force per square inch (psi; lbf/in$^2$; lb/in$^2$) |
| Kilopascals (kPa) | X | 0.01 = Kilograms-force per square centimetre (kgf/cm$^2$; kg/cm$^2$) | X | 98.1 | = Kilopascals (kPa) |

## Torque (moment of force)

| | | | | | |
|---|---|---|---|---|---|
| Pounds-force inches (lbf in; lb in) | X | 1.152 = Kilograms-force centimetre (kgf cm; kg cm) | X | 0.868 | = Pounds-force inches (lbf in; lb in) |
| Pounds-force inches (lbf in; lb in) | X | 0.113 = Newton metres (Nm) | X | 8.85 | = Pounds-force inches (lbf in; lb in) |
| Pounds-force inches (lbf in; lb in) | X | 0.083 = Pounds-force feet (lbf ft; lb ft) | X | 12 | = Pounds-force inches (lbf in; lb in) |
| Pounds-force feet (lbf ft; lb ft) | X | 0.138 = Kilograms-force metres (kgf m; kg m) | X | 7.233 | = Pounds-force feet (lbf ft; lb ft) |
| Pounds-force feet (lbf ft; lb ft) | X | 1.356 = Newton metres (Nm) | X | 0.738 | = Pounds-force feet (lbf ft; lb ft) |
| Newton metres (Nm) | X | 0.102 = Kilograms-force metres (kgf m; kg m) | X | 9.804 | = Newton metres (Nm) |

## Power

| | | | | | |
|---|---|---|---|---|---|
| Horsepower (hp) | X | 745.7 = Watts (W) | X | 0.0013 | = Horsepower (hp) |

## Velocity (speed)

| | | | | | |
|---|---|---|---|---|---|
| Miles per hour (miles/hr; mph) | X | 1.609 = Kilometres per hour (km/hr; kph) | X | 0.621 | = Miles per hour (miles/hr; mph) |

## Fuel consumption*

| | | | | | |
|---|---|---|---|---|---|
| Miles per gallon, Imperial (mpg) | X | 0.354 = Kilometres per litre (km/l) | X | 2.825 | = Miles per gallon, Imperial (mpg) |
| Miles per gallon, US (mpg) | X | 0.425 = Kilometres per litre (km/l) | X | 2.352 | = Miles per gallon, US (mpg) |

## Temperature

Degrees Fahrenheit = (°C x 1.8) + 32

Degrees Celsius (Degrees Centigrade; °C) = (°F - 32) x 0.56

*It is common practice to convert from miles per gallon (mpg) to litres/100 kilometres (l/100km), where mpg (Imperial) x l/100 km = 282 and mpg (US) x l/100 km = 235

# Safety first!

Regardless of how enthusiastic you may be about getting on with the job at hand, take the time to ensure that your safety is not jeopardized. A moment's lack of attention can result in an accident, as can failure to observe certain simple safety precautions. The possibility of an accident will always exist, and the following points should not be considered a comprehensive list of all dangers. Rather, they are intended to make you aware of the risks and to encourage a safety conscious approach to all work you carry out on your vehicle.

## Essential DOs and DON'Ts

**DON'T** rely on a jack when working under the vehicle. Always use approved jackstands to support the weight of the vehicle and place them under the recommended lift or support points.

**DON'T** attempt to loosen extremely tight fasteners (i.e. wheel lug nuts) while the vehicle is on a jack - it may fall.

**DON'T** start the engine without first making sure that the transmission is in Neutral (or Park where applicable) and the parking brake is set.

**DON'T** remove the radiator cap from a hot cooling system - let it cool or cover it with a cloth and release the pressure gradually.

**DON'T** attempt to drain the engine oil until you are sure it has cooled to the point that it will not burn you.

**DON'T** touch any part of the engine or exhaust system until it has cooled sufficiently to avoid burns.

**DON'T** siphon toxic liquids such as gasoline, antifreeze and brake fluid by mouth, or allow them to remain on your skin.

**DON'T** inhale brake lining dust - it is potentially hazardous (see *Asbestos* below).

**DON'T** allow spilled oil or grease to remain on the floor - wipe it up before someone slips on it.

**DON'T** use loose fitting wrenches or other tools which may slip and cause injury.

**DON'T** push on wrenches when loosening or tightening nuts or bolts. Always try to pull the wrench toward you. If the situation calls for pushing the wrench away, push with an open hand to avoid scraped knuckles if the wrench should slip.

**DON'T** attempt to lift a heavy component alone - get someone to help you.

**DON'T** rush or take unsafe shortcuts to finish a job.

**DON'T** allow children or animals in or around the vehicle while you are working on it.

**DO** wear eye protection when using power tools such as a drill, sander, bench grinder, etc. and when working under a vehicle.

**DO** keep loose clothing and long hair well out of the way of moving parts.

**DO** make sure that any hoist used has a safe working load rating adequate for the job.

**DO** get someone to check on you periodically when working alone on a vehicle.

**DO** carry out work in a logical sequence and make sure that everything is correctly assembled and tightened.

**DO** keep chemicals and fluids tightly capped and out of the reach of children and pets.

**DO** remember that your vehicle's safety affects that of yourself and others. If in doubt on any point, get professional advice.

## Asbestos

Certain friction, insulating, sealing, and other products - such as brake linings, brake bands, clutch linings, torque converters, gaskets, etc. - contain asbestos. Extreme care must be taken to avoid inhalation of dust from such products, since it is hazardous to health. If in doubt, assume that they do contain asbestos.

## Fire

Remember at all times that gasoline is highly flammable. Never smoke or have any kind of open flame around when working on a vehicle. But the risk does not end there. A spark caused by an electrical short circuit, by two metal surfaces contacting each other, or even by static electricity built up in your body under certain conditions, can ignite gasoline vapors, which in a confined space are highly explosive. Do not, under any circumstances, use gasoline for cleaning parts. Use an approved safety solvent.

Always disconnect the battery ground (-) cable at the battery before working on any part of the fuel system or electrical system. Never risk spilling fuel on a hot engine or exhaust component. It is strongly recommended that a fire extinguisher suitable for use on fuel and electrical fires be kept handy in the garage or workshop at all times. Never try to extinguish a fuel or electrical fire with water.

## Fumes

Certain fumes are highly toxic and can quickly cause unconsciousness and even death if inhaled to any extent. Gasoline vapor falls into this category, as do the vapors from some cleaning solvents. Any draining or pouring of such volatile fluids should be done in a well ventilated area.

When using cleaning fluids and solvents, read the instructions on the container carefully. Never use materials from unmarked containers.

Never run the engine in an enclosed space, such as a garage. Exhaust fumes contain carbon monoxide, which is extremely poisonous. If you need to run the engine, always do so in the open air, or at least have the rear of the vehicle outside the work area.

If you are fortunate enough to have the use of an inspection pit, never drain or pour gasoline and never run the engine while the vehicle is over the pit. The fumes, being heavier than air, will concentrate in the pit with possibly lethal results.

## The battery

Never create a spark or allow a bare light bulb near a battery. They normally give off a certain amount of hydrogen gas, which is highly explosive.

Always disconnect the battery ground (-) cable at the battery before working on the fuel or electrical systems.

If possible, loosen the filler caps or cover when charging the battery from an external source (this does not apply to sealed or maintenance-free batteries). Do not charge at an excessive rate or the battery may burst.

Take care when adding water to a non maintenance-free battery and when carrying a battery. The electrolyte, even when diluted, is very corrosive and should not be allowed to contact clothing or skin.

Always wear eye protection when cleaning the battery to prevent the caustic deposits from entering your eyes.

## Household current

When using an electric power tool, inspection light, etc., which operates on household current, always make sure that the tool is correctly connected to its plug and that, where necessary, it is properly grounded. Do not use such items in damp conditions and, again, do not create a spark or apply excessive heat in the vicinity of fuel or fuel vapor.

## Secondary ignition system voltage

A severe electric shock can result from touching certain parts of the ignition system (such as the spark plug wires) when the engine is running or being cranked, particularly if components are damp or the insulation is defective. In the case of an electronic ignition system, the secondary system voltage is much higher and could prove fatal.

# Troubleshooting

## Contents

This section provides an easy reference guide to the more common problems which may occur during the operation of your vehicle. These problems and their possible causes are grouped under headings denoting various components or systems, such as Engine, Cooling system, etc. They also refer you to the chapter and/or section which deals with the problem.

Remember that successful troubleshooting is not a mysterious black art practiced only by professional mechanics. It is simply the result of the right knowledge combined with an intelligent, systematic approach to the problem. Always work by a process of elimination, starting with the simplest solution and working through to the most complex - and never overlook the obvious. Anyone can run the gas tank dry or leave the lights on overnight, so don't assume that you are exempt from such oversights.

Finally, always establish a clear idea of why a problem has occurred and take steps to ensure that it doesn't happen again. If the electrical system fails because of a poor connection, check the other connections in the system to make sure that they don't fail as well. If a particular fuse continues to blow, find out why - don't just replace one fuse after another. Remember, failure of a small component can often be indicative of potential failure or incorrect functioning of a more important component or system.

## Engine

### 1  Engine will not rotate when attempting to start

1   Battery terminal connections loose or corroded (Chapter 1).
2   Battery discharged or faulty (Chapter 1).
3   Automatic transaxle not completely engaged in Park (Chapter 7) or clutch not completely depressed (Chapter 8).
4   Broken, loose or disconnected wiring in the starting circuit (Chapters 5 and 12).
5   Starter motor pinion jammed in flywheel ring gear (Chapter 5).
6   Starter solenoid faulty (Chapter 5).
7   Starter motor faulty (Chapter 5).
8   Ignition switch faulty (Chapter 12).
9   Starter pinion or flywheel teeth worn or broken (Chapter 5).

### 2  Engine rotates but will not start

1   Fuel tank empty.
2   Battery discharged (engine rotates slowly) (Chapter 5).
3   Battery terminal connections loose or corroded (Chapter 1).
4   Leaking fuel injector, fuel pump, pressure regulator, etc. (Chapter 4).
5   Clogged fuel filter (Chapter 1) or fuel not reaching carburetor or fuel injection system (Chapter 4).
6   Ignition components damp or damaged (Chapter 5).
7   Worn, faulty or incorrectly gapped spark plugs (Chapter 1).
8   Broken, loose or disconnected wiring in the starting circuit (Chapter 5).
9   Loose distributor is changing ignition timing (Chapter 1).
10  Broken, loose or disconnected wires at the ignition coil or faulty coil (Chapter 5).
11  Broken or stripped timing belt or chain.

### 3  Engine hard to start when cold

1   Battery discharged or low (Chapter 1).
2   Carburetor choke inoperative or faulty fuel injection system (Chapter 4).
3   Distributor rotor carbon tracked (Chapter 5).

### 4  Engine hard to start when hot

1   Air filter clogged (Chapter 1).
2   Fuel not reaching the carburetor or fuel injection system (Chapter 4).
3   Corroded battery connections, especially ground (Chapter 1).

### 5  Starter motor noisy or excessively rough in engagement

1   Pinion or flywheel gear teeth worn or broken (Chapter 5).
2   Starter motor mounting bolts loose or missing (Chapter 5).

### 6  Engine starts but stops immediately

1   Loose or faulty electrical connections at distributor, coil or alternator (Chapter 5).
2   Insufficient fuel reaching the carburetor or fuel injector (Chapters 1 and 4).
3   Vacuum leak at the gasket between the intake manifold or carburetor/fuel injection throttle body (Chapters 1 and 4).

### 7  Oil puddle under engine

1   Oil pan gasket and/or oil pan drain bolt washer leaking (Chapter 2).
2   Oil pressure sending unit leaking (Chapter 2).
3   Valve covers leaking (Chapter 2).
4   Engine oil seals leaking (Chapter 2).
5   Oil pump housing leaking (Chapter 2).

### 8  Engine lopes while idling or idles erratically

1   Vacuum leakage (Chapters 2 and 4).
2   Leaking EGR valve (Chapter 6).
3   Air filter clogged (Chapter 1).
4   Fuel pump not delivering sufficient fuel to the carburetor or fuel injection system (Chapter 4).
5   Leaking head gasket (Chapter 2).
6   Timing belt and/or pulleys worn (Chapter 2).
7   Camshaft lobes worn (Chapter 2).
8   Automatic Idle Speed (AIS) motor defective (Chapter 4)

### 9  Engine misses at idle speed

1   Spark plugs worn or not gapped properly (Chapter 1).
2   Faulty spark plug wires (Chapter 1).
3   Vacuum leaks (Chapter 1).
4   Incorrect ignition timing (Chapter 1).
5   Uneven or low compression (Chapter 2).

### 10  Engine misses throughout driving speed range

1   Fuel filter clogged and/or impurities in the fuel system (Chapter 1).
2   Low fuel output at the injector (Chapter 4).
3   Faulty or incorrectly gapped spark plugs (Chapter 1).
4   Incorrect ignition timing (Chapter 5).
5   Cracked distributor cap, disconnected distributor wires or damaged distributor components (Chapters 1 and 5).
6   Faulty spark plug wires (Chapters 1 or 5).
7   Faulty emission system components (Chapter 6).
8   Low or uneven cylinder compression pressures (Chapter 2).
9   Weak or faulty ignition system (Chapter 5).
10  Vacuum leak at the carburetor/fuel injection throttle body, intake manifold, or vacuum hoses (Chapter 4).

### 11  Engine stumbles on acceleration

1   Spark plugs fouled (Chapter 1).
2   Spark plug wire(s) faulty.
3   Carburetor or fuel injection system needs adjustment or repair (Chapter 4).
4   Fuel filter clogged (Chapters 1 and 4).
5   Incorrect ignition timing (Chapter 1).
6   Intake manifold air leak (Chapters 2 and 4).

### 12   Engine surges while holding accelerator steady

1   Intake air leak (Chapter 4).
2   Fuel pump faulty (Chapter 4).
3   Loose fuel injector wire harness connectors (Chapter 4).
4   Defective ECU (Chapter 6).

### 13   Engine stalls

1   Fuel filter clogged and/or water and impurities in the fuel system (Chapters 1 and 4).
2   Distributor components damp or damaged (Chapter 5).
3   Faulty emissions system components (Chapter 6).
4   Faulty or incorrectly gapped spark plugs (Chapter 1).
5   Faulty spark plug wires (Chapter 1).
6   Vacuum leak in the carburetor/fuel injection system, intake manifold or vacuum hoses (Chapters 2 and 4).
7   Idle speed too low (Chapter 1).

### 14   Engine lacks power

1   Incorrect ignition timing (Chapter 5).
2   Excessive play in distributor shaft (Chapter 5).
3   Worn rotor, distributor cap or wires (Chapters 1 and 5).
4   Faulty or incorrectly gapped spark plugs (Chapter 1).
5   Carburetor or fuel injection system out of adjustment or malfunctioning (Chapter 4).
6   Faulty coil (Chapter 5).
7   Brakes binding (Chapter 9).
8   Automatic transaxle fluid level incorrect (Chapter 1).
9   Clutch slipping (Chapter 8).
10   Fuel filter clogged and/or impurities in the fuel system (Chapters 1 and 4).
11   Emission control system not functioning properly (Chapter 6).
12   Low or uneven cylinder compression pressures (Chapter 2).

### 15   Engine backfires

1   Emission control system not functioning properly (Chapter 6).
2   Ignition timing incorrect (Chapter 1).
3   Faulty secondary ignition system (cracked spark plug insulator, faulty plug wires, distributor cap and/or rotor) (Chapters 1 and 5).
4   Carburetor or fuel injection system in need of adjustment or malfunctioning (Chapter 4).
5   Vacuum leak at carburetor/throttle body or fuel injector, intake manifold, air control valve or vacuum hoses (Chapters 2 and 4).

### 16   Pinging or knocking engine sounds during acceleration or uphill

1   Incorrect grade of fuel.
2   Ignition timing incorrect (Chapter 1).
3   Carburetor or fuel injection system in need of adjustment or repair (Chapter 4).
4   Improper or damaged spark plugs or wires (Chapter 1).
5   Worn or damaged distributor components (Chapter 5).
6   Faulty emission system (Chapter 6).
7   Vacuum leak (Chapters 2 and 4).

### 17   Engine runs with oil pressure light on

1   Low oil level (Chapter 1).
2   Idle rpm below specification (Chapter 1).

3   Short in wiring circuit (Chapter 12).
4   Faulty oil pressure sender (Chapter 2).
5   Worn engine bearings and/or oil pump (Chapter 2).

### 18   Engine diesels (continues to run) after switching off

1   Excessive engine operating temperature (Chapter 3).
2   Idle speed too high (Chapter 1).

## Engine electrical system

### 19   Battery will not hold a charge

1   Alternator drivebelt defective or not adjusted properly (Chapter 1).
2   Battery electrolyte level low (Chapter 1).
3   Battery terminals loose or corroded (Chapter 1).
4   Alternator not charging properly (Chapter 5).
5   Loose, broken or faulty wiring in the charging circuit (Chapter 5).
6   Short in vehicle wiring (Chapter 12).
7   Internally defective battery (Chapters 1 and 5).

### 20   Alternator light fails to go out

1   Faulty alternator or charging circuit (Chapter 5).
2   Alternator drivebelt defective or out of adjustment (Chapter 1).
3   Alternator voltage regulator inoperative (Chapter 5).

### 21   Alternator light fails to come on when key is turned on

1   Light bulb defective (Chapter 12).
2   Fault in the printed circuit, dash wiring or bulb holder (Chapter 12).

## Fuel system

### 22   Excessive fuel consumption

1   Dirty or clogged air filter element (Chapter 1).
2   Incorrectly set ignition timing (Chapter 1).
3   Emissions system not functioning properly (Chapter 6).
4   Carburetor or fuel injection system malfunctioning (Chapter 4).
5   Low tire pressure or incorrect tire size (Chapter 1).

### 23   Fuel leakage and/or fuel odor

1   Leaking fuel feed or return line (Chapters 1 and 4).
2   Tank overfilled.
3   Evaporative canister filter clogged (Chapters 1 and 6).
4   Carburetor or fuel injection system malfunctioning (Chapter 4).

## Cooling system

### 24   Overheating

1   Insufficient coolant in system (Chapter 1).
2   Water pump drivebelt defective or out of adjustment (Chapter 1).
3   Radiator core blocked or grille restricted (Chapter 3).

4    Thermostat faulty (Chapter 3).
5    Electric cooling fan blades broken or cracked (Chapter 3).
6    Radiator cap not maintaining proper pressure (Chapter 3).
7    Ignition timing incorrect (Chapter 5).

## 25  Overcooling

1    Faulty thermostat (Chapter 3).
2    Inaccurate temperature gauge sending unit (Chapter 3)

## 26  External coolant leakage

1    Deteriorated/damaged hoses; loose clamps (Chapters 1 and 3).
2    Water pump seal defective (Chapter 3).
3    Leakage from radiator core or coolant reservoir bottle (Chapter 3).
4    Engine drain or water jacket core plugs leaking (Chapter 2).

## 27  Internal coolant leakage

1    Leaking cylinder head gasket (Chapter 2).
2    Cracked cylinder bore or cylinder head (Chapter 2).

## 28  Coolant loss

1    Too much coolant in system (Chapter 1).
2    Coolant boiling away because of overheating (Chapter 3).
3    Internal or external leakage (Chapter 3).
4    Faulty radiator cap (Chapter 3).

## 29  Poor coolant circulation

1    Inoperative water pump (Chapter 3).
2    Restriction in cooling system (Chapters 1 and 3).
3    Water pump drivebelt defective/out of adjustment (Chapter 1).
4    Thermostat sticking (Chapter 3).

## Clutch

## 30  Clutch pedal travels to floor - no pressure or very little resistance

Clutch cable broken (Chapter 8).

## 31  Unable to select gears

1    Faulty transaxle (Chapter 7).
2    Faulty clutch disc (Chapter 8).
3    Fork and bearing not assembled properly (Chapter 8).
4    Faulty pressure plate (Chapter 8).
5    Pressure plate-to-flywheel bolts loose (Chapter 8).

## 32  Clutch slips (engine speed increases with no increase in vehicle speed)

1    Clutch plate worn (Chapter 8).
2    Clutch plate is oil soaked by leaking rear main seal (Chapters 2

and 8).
3    Warped pressure plate or flywheel (Chapter 8).
4    Weak diaphragm spring (Chapter 8).
5    Clutch plate overheated. Allow to cool.

## 33  Grabbing (chattering) as clutch is engaged

1    Oil on clutch plate lining, burned or glazed facings (Chapter 8).
2    Worn or loose engine or transaxle mounts (Chapters 2 and 7).
3    Worn splines on clutch plate hub (Chapter 8).
4    Warped pressure plate or flywheel (Chapter 8).
5    Glazed clutch disc, flywheel or pressure plate (Chapter 8).

## 34  Transaxle rattling (clicking)

1    Release fork loose (Chapter 8).
2    Clutch plate damper spring failure (Chapter 8).

## 35  Noise in clutch area

1    Fork shaft improperly installed (Chapter 8).
2    Faulty bearing (Chapter 8).

## 36  Clutch pedal stays on floor

1    Broken release bearing or fork (Chapter 8).
2    Clutch cable broken (Chapter 8)

## 37  High pedal effort

1    Pressure plate faulty (Chapter 8).
2    Damaged or binding clutch cable (Chapter 8).

## Manual transaxle

## 38  Knocking noise at low speeds

1    Worn driveaxle constant velocity (CV) joints (Chapter 8).
2    Worn side gear shaft counterbore in differential case (Chapter 7A).*

## 39  Noise most pronounced when turning

Differential gear noise (Chapter 7A).*

## 40  Clunk on acceleration or deceleration

1    Loose engine or transaxle mounts (Chapters 2 and 7A).
2    Worn differential pinion shaft in case.*
3    Worn axleshaft counterbore in differential case (Chapter 7A).*
4    Worn or damaged driveaxle inboard CV joints (Chapter 8).

## 41  Clicking noise in turns

Worn or damaged outboard CV joint (Chapter 8).

## 42   Vibration

1   Rough wheel bearing (Chapters 1 and 10).
2   Damaged driveaxle (Chapter 8).
3   Out-of-round tires (Chapter 1).
4   Tire out of balance (Chapters 1 and 10).
5   Worn CV joint (Chapter 8).

## 43   Noisy in neutral with engine running

1   Damaged input gear bearing (Chapter 7A).*
2   Damaged clutch release bearing (Chapter 8).

## 44   Noisy in one particular gear

1   Damaged or worn constant-mesh gears (Chapter 7A).*
2   Damaged or worn synchronizers (Chapter 7A).*
3   Bent reverse fork (Chapter 7A).*
4   Damaged fourth speed gear or output gear (Chapter 7A).*
5   Worn or damaged reverse idler gear or idler bushing (Chapter 7A).*

## 45   Noisy in all gears

1   Insufficient lubricant (Chapter 7A).
2   Damaged or worn bearings (Chapter 7A).*
3   Worn or damaged input gear shaft and/or output gear shaft (Chapter 7A).*

## 46   Slips out of gear

1   Worn or improperly adjusted linkage (Chapter 7A).
2   Transaxle loose on engine (Chapter 7A).
3   Shift linkage does not work freely, binds (Chapter 7A).
4   Input gear bearing retainer broken or loose (Chapter 7A).*
5   Dirt between clutch cover and engine housing (Chapter 7A).
6   Worn shift fork (Chapter 7A).*

## 47   Leaks lubricant

1   Axleshaft seals worn (Chapter 7A).
2   Excessive amount of lubricant in transaxle (Chapters 1 and 7A).
3   Loose or broken input gear shaft bearing retainer (Chapter 7A).*
4   Input gear bearing retainer O-ring and/or lip seal damaged (Chapter 7A).*

## 48   Locked in second gear

Lock pin or interlock pin missing (Chapter 7A).*

*Although the corrective action necessary to remedy the symptoms described is beyond the scope of the home mechanic, the above information should be helpful in isolating the cause of the condition so that the owner can communicate clearly with a professional mechanic.*

### Automatic transaxle

**Note:** *Due to the complexity of the automatic transaxle, it is difficult for the home mechanic to properly diagnose and service this component. For problems other than the following, the vehicle should be taken to a dealer service department, transmission shop or other automotive repair facility.*

## 49   Fluid leakage

1   Automatic transmission fluid is a deep red color. Fluid leaks should not be confused with engine oil, which can easily be blown onto the transaxle by air flow.
2   To pinpoint a leak, first remove all built-up dirt and grime from the transaxle housing with degreasing agents and/or steam cleaning. Then drive the vehicle at low speeds so air flow will not blow the leak far from its source. Raise the vehicle and determine where the leak is coming from. Common areas of leakage are:
    a) *Pan (Chapters 1 and 7)*
    b) *Dipstick tube (Chapters 1 and 7)*
    c) *Transaxle oil lines (Chapter 7)*
    d) *Speed sensor (Chapter 7)*

## 50   Transaxle fluid brown or has a burned smell

Transaxle fluid burned (Chapter 1).

## 51   General shift mechanism problems

1   Chapter 7, Part B, deals with checking and adjusting the shift linkage on automatic transaxles. Common problems which may be attributed to poorly adjusted linkage are:
    a) *Engine starting in gears other than Park or Neutral.*
    b) *Indicator on shifter pointing to a gear other than the one actually being used.*
    c) *Vehicle moves when in Park.*
2   Refer to Chapter 7B for the shift linkage adjustment procedure.

## 52   Transaxle will not downshift with accelerator pedal pressed to the floor

Throttle Valve (TV) cable out of adjustment (Chapter 7B).

## 53   Engine will start in gears other than Park or Neutral

Neutral start switch malfunctioning (Chapter 7B).

## 54   Transaxle slips, shifts roughly, is noisy or has no drive in forward or reverse gears

There are many probable causes for the above problems, but the home mechanic should be concerned with only one possibility - fluid level. Before taking the vehicle to a repair shop, check the level and condition of the fluid as described in Chapter 1. Correct the fluid level as necessary or change the fluid and filter if needed. If the problem persists, have a professional diagnose the cause.

### Driveaxles

## 55   Clicking noise in turns

Worn or damaged outboard CV joint (Chapter 8).

## 56   Shudder or vibration during acceleration

1   Excessive toe-in (Chapter 10).

2    Worn or damaged inboard or outboard CV joints (Chapter 8).
3    Sticking inboard CV joint assembly (Chapter 8).

## 57   Vibration at highway speeds

1    Out-of-balance front wheels and/or tires (Chapters 1 and 10).
2    Out-of-round front tires (Chapters 1 and 10).
3    Worn CV joint(s) (Chapter 8).

## Brakes

**Note:** *Before assuming that a brake problem exists, make sure that:*
   *a) The tires are in good condition and properly inflated (Chapter 1).*
   *b) The front end alignment is correct (Chapter 10).*
   *c) The vehicle is not loaded with weight in an unequal manner.*

## 58   Vehicle pulls to one side during braking

1    Incorrect tire pressures (Chapter 1).
2    Front end out of line (have the front end aligned).
3    Front or rear tires not matched to one another.
4    Restricted brake lines or hoses (Chapter 9).
5    Malfunctioning caliper or drum brake assembly (Chapter 9).
6    Loose suspension parts (Chapter 10).
7    Grease, oil or brake fluid on disc or drum (Chapter 9).
8    Excessive wear of brake shoe or pad material or disc/drum on one side.

## 59   Noise (high-pitched squeal when the brakes are applied)

1    Front disc brake pads worn out. The noise comes from the wear sensor rubbing against the disc (does not apply to all vehicles). Replace pads with new ones immediately (Chapter 9).
2    Incorrectly installed new pads (many require an anti-squeal compound on the backing plates).

## 60   Brake roughness or chatter (pedal pulsates)

1    Excessive lateral runout (Chapter 9).
2    Uneven pad wear (Chapter 9).
3    Defective disc (Chapter 9).

## 61   Excessive brake pedal effort required to stop vehicle

1    Malfunctioning power brake booster (Chapter 9).
2    Partial system failure (Chapter 9).
3    Excessively worn pads or shoes (Chapter 9).
4    Piston in caliper or wheel cylinder stuck or sluggish (Chapter 9).
5    Brake pads or shoes contaminated with oil or grease (Chapter 9).
6    New pads or shoes installed and not yet seated. It will take a while for the new material to seat against the disc or drum.

## 62   Excessive brake pedal travel

1    Partial brake system failure (Chapter 9).
2    Insufficient fluid in master cylinder (Chapters 1 and 9).
3    Air trapped in system (Chapters 1 and 9).

## 63   Dragging brakes

1    Incorrect adjustment of brake light switch (Chapter 9).
2    Master cylinder pistons not returning correctly (Chapter 9).
3    Restricted brake lines or hoses (Chapters 1 and 9).
4    Incorrect parking brake adjustment (Chapter 9).

## 64   Grabbing or uneven braking action

1    Malfunction of proportioning valve (Chapter 9).
2    Malfunction of power brake booster unit (Chapter 9).
3    Binding brake pedal mechanism (Chapter 9).

## 65   Brake pedal feels spongy when depressed

1    Air in hydraulic lines (Chapter 9).
2    Master cylinder mounting bolts loose (Chapter 9).
3    Master cylinder defective (Chapter 9).

## 66   Brake pedal travels to the floor with little resistance

1    Little or no fluid in the master cylinder reservoir caused by leaking caliper piston(s) (Chapter 9).
2    Loose, damaged or disconnected brake lines (Chapter 9).

## 67   Parking brake does not hold

Parking brake linkage improperly adjusted (Chapters 1 and 9).

## Suspension and steering systems

**Note:** *Before attempting to diagnose the suspension and steering systems, perform the following preliminary checks:*
   *a) Tires for wrong pressure and uneven wear.*
   *b) Steering universal joints from the column to the steering gear for loose connectors or wear.*
   *c) Front and rear suspension and the steering gear assembly for loose or damaged parts.*
   *d) Out-of-round or out-of-balance tires, bent rims and loose and/or rough wheel bearings.*

## 68   Vehicle pulls to one side

1    Mismatched or uneven tires (Chapter 10).
2    Broken or sagging springs (Chapter 10).
3    Wheel alignment (Chapter 10).
4    Front brake dragging (Chapter 9).

## 69   Abnormal or excessive tire wear

1    Wheel alignment (Chapter 10).
2    Sagging or broken springs (Chapter 10).
3    Tire out of balance (Chapter 10).
4    Worn strut damper (Chapter 10).
5    Overloaded vehicle.
6    Tires not rotated regularly.

## 70   Wheel makes a thumping noise

1    Blister or bump on tire (Chapter 10).
2    Improper strut damper action (Chapter 10).

## 71  Shimmy, shake or vibration

1   Tire or wheel out-of-balance or out-of-round (Chapter 10).
2   Loose or worn wheel bearings (Chapters 1, 8 and 10).
3   Worn tie-rod ends (Chapter 10).
4   Worn lower balljoints (Chapters 1 and 10).
5   Excessive wheel runout (Chapter 10).
6   Blister or bump on tire (Chapter 10).

## 72  Hard steering

1   Lack of lubrication at balljoints, tie-rod ends and steering gear assembly (Chapter 10).
2   Front wheel alignment (Chapter 10).
3   Low tire pressure(s) (Chapters 1 and 10).

## 73  Poor returnability of steering to center

1   Lack of lubrication at balljoints and tie-rod ends (Chapter 10).
2   Binding in balljoints (Chapter 10).
3   Binding in steering column (Chapter 10).
4   Lack of lubricant in steering gear assembly (Chapter 10).
5   Front wheel alignment (Chapter 10).

## 74  Abnormal noise at the front end

1   Lack of lubrication at balljoints and tie-rod ends (Chapters 1 and 10).
2   Damaged strut mounting (Chapter 10).
3   Worn control arm bushings or tie-rod ends (Chapter 10).
4   Loose stabilizer bar (Chapter 10).
5   Loose wheel nuts (Chapters 1 and 10).
6   Loose suspension bolts (Chapter 10).

## 75  Wander or poor steering stability

1   Mismatched or uneven tires (Chapter 10).
2   Lack of lubrication at balljoints and tie-rod ends (Chapters 1 and 10).
3   Worn strut assemblies (Chapter 10).
4   Loose stabilizer bar (Chapter 10).
5   Broken or sagging springs (Chapter 10).
6   Wheel alignment (Chapter 10).

## 76  Erratic steering when braking

1   Wheel bearings worn (Chapter 10).
2   Broken or sagging springs (Chapter 10).
3   Leaking wheel cylinder or caliper (Chapter 10).
4   Warped discs or drums (Chapter 10).

## 77  Excessive pitching and/or rolling around corners or during braking

1   Loose stabilizer bar (Chapter 10).

2   Worn strut dampers or mounts (Chapter 10).
3   Broken or sagging springs (Chapter 10).
4   Overloaded vehicle.

## 78  Suspension bottoms

1   Overloaded vehicle.
2   Worn strut dampers (Chapter 10).
3   Incorrect, broken or sagging springs (Chapter 10).

## 79  Cupped tires

1   Front or rear wheels out of alignment (Chapter 10).
2   Worn strut dampers or shock absorbers (Chapter 10).
3   Wheel bearings worn (Chapter 10).
4   Excessive tire or wheel runout (Chapter 10).
5   Worn balljoints (Chapter 10).

## 80  Excessive tire wear on outside edge

1   Inflation pressures incorrect (Chapter 1).
2   Excessive speed in turns.
3   Front end alignment incorrect (excessive toe-in). Have professionally aligned.
4   Suspension arm bent or twisted (Chapter 10).

## 81  Excessive tire wear on inside edge

1   Inflation pressures incorrect (Chapter 1).
2   Front end alignment incorrect (toe-out). Have professionally aligned.
3   Loose or damaged steering components (Chapter 10).

## 82  Tire tread worn in one place

1   Tires out of balance.
2   Damaged or buckled wheel. Inspect and replace if necessary.
3   Defective tire (Chapter 1).

## 83  Excessive play or looseness in steering system

1   Wheel bearing(s) worn (Chapter 10).
2   Tie-rod end loose (Chapter 10).
3   Steering gear loose (Chapter 10).
4   Worn or loose steering intermediate shaft (Chapter 10).

## 84  Rattling or clicking noise in steering gear

1   Insufficient or improper lubricant in steering gear assembly (Chapter 10).
2   Steering gear attachment loose (Chapter 10).

# Chapter 1
# Tune-up and routine maintenance

## Contents

## Specifications

### Recommended lubricants and fluids

Engine oil
  Type .......................................................... API SG or SG/CD multigrade and fuel efficient oil
  Viscosity .................................................. See accompaning chart

**For best fuel economy and cold starting, select the lowest SAE viscosity grade for the expected temperature range**

1-a3 HAYNES

## ...mmended lubricants and fluids (continued)

| | |
|---|---|
| ...al transaxle lubricant | |
| ...986 and earlier models | DEXRON II automatic transmission fluid (do not use gear oil) |
| 1987 and later models | SAE 5W30 engine oil |
| Automatic transaxle fluid | DEXRON II automatic transmission fluid |
| Differential lubricant (1991 and 1982 automatic transaxle only) | DEXRON II automatic transmission fluid |
| Power steering fluid | Mopar 4-253 power steering fluid or equivalent |
| Brake fluid | DOT 3 brake fluid |
| Engine coolant | 50/50 mixture of ethylene glycol-based antifreeze and water |
| Transaxle shift linkage grease | NLGI no. 2 chassis grease |
| Clutch linkage grease | NLGI no. 2 chassis grease |
| Parking brake mechanism grease | White lithium-based grease NLGI no. 2 |
| Chassis lubrication grease | NLGI no. 2 EP grease |
| Rear wheel bearing grease | NLGI no. 2 EP high-temperature wheel bearing grease |
| Manual steering gear lubricant | API GL-4 SAE 90W gear oil |
| Steering shaft seal | NLGI no. 2 EP grease |
| Hood, door and trunk/liftgate hinge lubricant | Engine oil |
| Door hinge and check-spring grease | NLGI no. 2 multi-purpose grease |
| Key lock cylinder lubricant | Graphite spray |
| Hood latch assembly lubricant | Mopar Lubriplate or equivalent |
| Door latch striker lubricant | Mopar Door Ease no. 3744859 or equivalent |

## Capacities*

| | |
|---|---|
| Engine oil (including filter) - all models | 4.5 qts |
| Automatic transaxle | |
| Drain and refill | 4.0 qts |
| Dry fill (including torque converter) | 8.9 qts |
| Manual transaxle | 2.3 qts |
| Cooling system | 9.0 qts |

*All capacities approximate. Add as necessary to bring to appropriate level.*

## Brakes

| | |
|---|---|
| Disc brake pad wear limit (including metal shoe) | 5/16 inch |
| Drum brake shoe lining wear limit | 1/16 inch |

## Ignition system

| | |
|---|---|
| Spark plug type | |
| 1981 through 1985 | Champion RN14YC or equivalent |
| 1886 through 1989 | Champion RN12YC or equivalent |
| Spark plug gap | |
| 2.2L and 2.5L engines | 0.035 inch |
| 2.6L engine | |
| US | 0.040 inch |
| Canada | 0.035 inch |
| Spark plug wire resistance | |
| Minimum | 3,000 ohms per foot |
| Maximum | 7200 ohms per foot |
| Ignition timing | See the *Vehicle Emissions Control Information* label in the engine compartment |
| Firing order | 1-3-4-2 |

Cylinder location and distributor rotation

## Drivebelt deflection

| | |
|---|---|
| Alternator | |
| New | 1/8 inch |
| Used | 1/4 inch |
| Power steering pump | |
| New | 1/4 inch |
| Used | 7/16 inch |
| Water pump | |
| New | 1/8 inch |
| Used | 1/4 inch |
| Air conditioning compressor | |
| New | 5/16 inch |
| Used | 7/16 inch |

## Automatic transaxle band adjustment

Kickdown band
| | |
|---|---|
| 1981 ..................................................... | Tighten to 72 in-lbs, then back off 2 turns |
| 1982 ..................................................... | Tighten to 72 in-lbs, then back off 2-1/2 turns |
| 1983 ..................................................... | Tighten to 72 in-lbs, then back off 2-3/4 turns |
| 1984 and later ........................................ | Tighten to 72 in-lbs, then back off 2-1/2 turns |
| Low-Reverse band ..................................... | Tighten to 41 in-lbs, then back off 3-1/2 turns |

## Valve clearance (hot) (2.6L engine only)

| | |
|---|---|
| Intake ..................................................... | 0.006 inch |
| Exhaust .................................................. | 0.010 inch |
| Jet valve.................................................. | 0.006 inch |

## Torque specifications

| | **Ft-lbs** (unless otherwise indicated) |
|---|---|
| Carburetor mounting bolts/nuts ..................... | 17 |
| Throttle body mounting bolts/nuts .................. | 175 in-lbs |
| Spark plugs............................................... | 26 |
| Wheel lug nuts | |
| 1983 and earlier models........................... | 80 |
| 1984 and later models.............................. | 95 |
| Automatic transaxle | |
| Pan bolts .............................................. | 170 in-lbs |
| Filter-to-valve body screws ...................... | 40 in-lbs |
| Kickdown band adjusting screw locknut ........ | 35 |
| Low-Reverse band adjusting screw locknut | |
| 1981 and 1982 ...................................... | 20 |
| 1983 and later........................................ | 120 in-lbs |

**1**

**Typical engine compartment underside components**

| | | | | | |
|---|---|---|---|---|---|
| 1 | Alternator | 6 | Left driveaxle | 11 | Lower control arm |
| 2 | Fuel pump | 7 | Outer driveaxle CV boot | 12 | Control arm grease fitting |
| 3 | Oil filter | 8 | Sway bar | 13 | Inner driveaxle CV boot |
| 4 | Oil pan | 9 | Catalytic converter | 14 | Brake caliper |
| 5 | Transaxle pan | 10 | Oil drain plug | 15 | Brake hose |

**Engine compartment components -
carbureted 2.2L engine shown,
others similar**

1   Ignition coil
2   Oil filler cap
3   Vent module
4   PCV valve
5   Air filter housing
6   Brake fluid reservoir
7   Voltage regulator and engine relays
8   Battery
9   Spark control computer
10  Coolant reservoir
11  Radiator cap
12  Fan shroud
13  Fan motor
14  Fan connector
15  Engine oil dipstick
16  Engine oil filter
17  Air conditioner compressor
18  Charcoal canister location

**Typical rear underside components**

| | | | | | |
|---|---|---|---|---|---|
| 1 | Muffler | 4 | Shock absorber | 6 | Parking brake cable |
| 2 | Fuel lines | 5 | Fuel tank | 7 | Exhaust system hanger |
| 3 | Fuel filler hose | | | | |

# 1 Chrysler K-car model Maintenance schedule

The following maintenance intervals are based on the assumption that the vehicle owner will be doing the maintenance or service work, as opposed to having a dealer service department do the work. Although the time/mileage intervals are loosely based on factory recommendations, most have been shortened to ensure, for example, that such items as lubricants and fluids are checked/changed at intervals that promote maximum engine/driveline service life. Also, subject to the preference of the individual owner interested in keeping his or her vehicle in peak condition at all times, and with the vehicle's ultimate resale in mind, many of the maintenance procedures may be performed more often than recommended in the following schedule. We encourage such owner initiative.

## Every 250 miles or weekly, whichever comes first

Check the engine oil level; add oil as necessary (see Section 4)

Check the engine coolant level; add coolant as necessary (see Section 4)

Check the windshield washer fluid level (see Section 4)

Check the battery electrolyte level (see Section 4)

Check the brake fluid level (see Section 4)

Check the tires and tire pressures (see Section 5)
Check the automatic transaxle fluid level (see Section 6)
Check the power steering fluid level (see Section 7)
Check the wiper blade condition (see Section 9)
Check the operation of all lights
Check the horn operation

## Every 3,000 miles or 3 months, whichever comes first

Change the engine oil and filter (see Section 8)*

## Every 7,500 miles or 6 months, whichever comes first

Check and clean the battery (see Section 10)
Rotate the tires (see Section 11)
Check the manual transaxle lubricant level (see Section 12)
Check the differential lubricant level (1982 and earlier automatic transaxle models only) (see Section 13)
Add combustion chamber conditioner to the engine (Canadian leaded fuel models only) (see Section 14)

## Every 15,000 miles or 12 months, whichever comes first

Check and adjust if necessary, the valve clearance (2.6L engine only) (see Section 15)
Lubricate the front suspension and steering balljoints (see Section 16)*

## Every 25,000 miles or 18 months, whichever comes first

Replace the fuel filter (see Section 17)
Replace the spark plugs (see Section 18)
Check the condition of the primary ignition wires and spark plug wires (see Section 19)
Check the distributor cap and rotor (see Section 19)
Check the drivebelts (see Section 20)
Replace the air filter element (see Section 21)*
Replace the PCV valve (see Section 22)
Check the EGR system components for proper operation (see Section 23)

## Every 30,000 miles or 24 months, whichever comes first

Check the condition of all vacuum hoses and connections (see Section 24)
Check the operation of the carburetor choke (see Section 25)
Check the carburetor/fuel injection throttle body mounting nut/bolt torque (see Section 26)
Check the operation of the heated air intake system (see Section 27)
Check the fuel system hoses and connections for leaks and damage (see Section 28)

Check the cooling system hoses and connections for leaks and damage (see Section 29)
Check the exhaust pipes and hangers (see Section 30)
Check for freeplay in the steering linkage and balljoints (see Section 31)
Lubricate the steering shaft seal (see Section 32)
Check and service the rear wheel bearings (see Section 33)*
Check the brakes (see Section 34)*
Check the parking brake operation (see Section 34)
Drain and replace the engine coolant (see Section 35)
Check and adjust if necessary, the ignition timing (see Section 36)
Change the manual transaxle lubricant (see Section 37)*
Change the differential lubricant (1982 and earlier automatic transaxle models only) (see Section 38)*
Change the automatic transaxle fluid and filter (see Section 39)*
Adjust the automatic transaxle bands (see Section 40)*
Check the driveaxle boots (see Section 41)*
Check the fuel evaporative emission system hoses and connections (see Section 42)
Check the operation of the seat belts (see Section 43)

## Every 50,000 miles or 60 months, whichever comes first

Replace the oxygen sensor (Chapter 6)

*This item is affected by "severe" operating conditions as described below. If the vehicle in question is operated under "severe" conditions, perform all maintenance procedures marked with an asterisk (*) at the following intervals:*

## Every 2,000 miles

Change the engine oil and filter
Check the driveaxle, suspension and steering boots

## Every 9,000 miles

Check the brakes
Service the rear wheel bearings

## Every 15,000 miles

Replace the air filter element
Lubricate the tie-rod ends
Change the automatic transaxle fluid and filter
Adjust the automatic transaxle bands
Change the manual transaxle lubricant and clean the pan magnet
*Consider the conditions "severe" if most driving is done . . .*
In dusty areas
Towing a trailer
Idling for extended periods and/or low-speed operation
When outside temperatures remain below freezing and most trips are less than four miles
In heavy city traffic where outside temperatures regularly reach 90-degrees F or higher

## 2  Introduction

This Chapter is designed to help the home mechanic maintain the Chrysler K-car models with the goals of maximum performance, economy, safety and reliability in mind.

Included is a master maintenance schedule, followed by procedures dealing specifically with each item on the schedule. Visual checks, adjustments, component replacement and other helpful items are included. Refer to the accompanying illustrations of the engine compartment and the underside of the vehicle for the locations of various components.

Adhering to the mileage/time maintenance schedule and following the step-by-step procedures, which is simply a preventive maintenance program, will result in maximum reliability and vehicle service life. Keep in mind that it's a comprehensive program - maintaining some items but not others at the specified intervals will not produce the same results.

As you service the vehicle, you'll discover that many of the procedures can - and should - be grouped together because of the nature of the particular procedure you're performing or because of the close proximity of two otherwise unrelated components to one another.

For example, if the vehicle is raised, you should inspect the exhaust, suspension, steering and fuel systems while you're under the vehicle. When you're rotating the tires, it makes good sense to check the brakes, since the wheels are already removed. Finally, let's suppose you have to borrow or rent a torque wrench. Even if you only need it to tighten the spark plugs, you might as well check the torque of as many critical fasteners as time allows.

The first step in this maintenance program is to prepare yourself before the actual work begins. Read through all the procedures you're planning to do, then gather up all the parts and tools needed. If it looks like you might run into problems during a particular job, seek advice from a mechanic or an experienced do-it-yourselfer.

## 3  Tune-up general information

The term "tune-up" is used in this manual to represent a combination of individual operations rather than one specific procedure.

If, from the time the vehicle is new, the routine maintenance schedule is followed closely and frequent checks are made of fluid levels and high wear items, as suggested throughout this manual, the engine will be kept in relatively good running condition and the need for additional work will be minimized.

More likely than not, however, there will be times when the engine is running poorly due to lack of regular maintenance. This is even more likely if a used vehicle, which hasn't received regular and frequent maintenance checks, is purchased. In such cases, an engine tune-up will be needed outside of the regular routine maintenance intervals.

The first step in any tune-up or diagnostic procedure to help correct a poor running engine is a cylinder compression check. A compression check (see Chapter 2, Part C) will help determine the condition of internal engine components and should be used as a guide for tune-up and repair procedures. For instance, if a compression check indicates serious internal engine wear, a conventional tune-up will not improve the performance of the engine and would be a waste of time and money. Because of its importance, the compression check should be done by someone with the right equipment and the knowledge to use it properly.

The following procedures are those most often needed to bring a generally poor running engine back into a proper state of tune:

### Minor tune-up

*Check all engine related fluids (see Section 4)*
*Clean, inspect and test the battery (see Section 10)*
*Replace the spark plugs (see Section 18)*
*Inspect the distributor cap and rotor (see Section 19)*
*Inspect the spark plug and coil wires (see Section 19)*
*Check and adjust the drivebelts (see Section 20)*

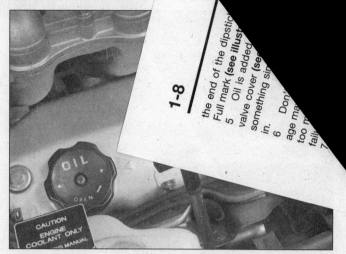

**4.4a  The engine oil dipstick is located on the front (radiator side) of the engine**

*Check the air filter (see Section 21)*
*Check the PCV valve (see Section 22)*
*Check all underhood hoses (see Section 24)*
*Check the cooling system (see Section 29)*
*Check and adjust the ignition timing (see Section 36)*

### Major tune-up

*All items listed under Minor tune-up plus . . .*
*Adjust the valves (2.6L engine only) (see Section 15)*
*Replace the air filter (see Section 21)*
*Replace the distributor cap and rotor (see Section 19)*
*Replace the spark plug wires (see Section 18)*
*Check the EGR system (see Section 23)*
*Check the fuel system (see Section 28)*
*Check the ignition system (see Chapter 5)*
*Check the charging system (see Chapter 5)*

## 4  Fluid level checks (every 250 miles or weekly)

**Note:** *The following are fluid level checks to be done on a 250-mile or weekly basis. Additional fluid level checks can be found in specific maintenance procedures which follow. Regardless of the intervals, develop the habit of checking under the vehicle periodically for evidence of fluid leaks.*

1  Fluids are an essential part of the lubrication, cooling, brake and window washer systems. Because the fluids gradually become depleted and/or contaminated during normal operation of the vehicle, they must be replenished periodically. *See Recommended lubricants and fluids* at the beginning of this Chapter before adding fluid to any of the following components. **Note:** *The vehicle must be on level ground when fluid levels are checked.*

### Engine oil

*Refer to illustrations 4.4a, 4.4b and 4.5*

2  The engine oil level is checked with a dipstick which is located on the front (radiator) side of the engine block. The dipstick extends through a tube and into the oil pan at the bottom of the engine.

3  The oil level should be checked before the vehicle has been driven, or about 15 minutes after the engine has been shut off. If the oil is checked immediately after driving the vehicle, some of the oil will remain in the upper engine components, resulting in an inaccurate reading on the dipstick.

4  Pull the dipstick out of the tube **(see illustration)** and wipe all the oil off the end with a clean rag or paper towel. Insert the clean dipstick all the way back into the tube, then pull it out again. Note the oil level at

...k. Add oil as necessary to keep the level at the
...ration).

...to the engine after removing a cap located on the
... **illustration**). The cap may be marked "Engine oil" or
...milar. A funnel may help reduce spills as the oil is poured

... allow the level to drop below the Add mark or engine dam-
... occur. On the other hand, don't overfill the engine by adding
... much oil - it may result in oil fouled spark plugs, oil leaks or seal
...ures.

Checking the oil level is an important preventive maintenance step. A consistently low oil level indicates oil leakage through damaged seals, defective gaskets or past worn rings or valve guides. If the oil looks milky in color or has water droplets in it, the block may be cracked. The engine should be checked immediately. The condition of the oil should also be checked. Each time you check the oil level, slide your thumb and index finger up the dipstick before wiping off the oil. If you see small dirt or metal particles clinging to the dipstick, the oil should be changed (see Section 8).

## Engine coolant

Refer to illustrations 4.8 and 4.12

**Warning:** *Do not allow antifreeze to come in contact with your skin or painted surfaces of the vehicle. Flush contaminated areas immediately with plenty of water. Don't store new coolant or leave old coolant lying around where it's accessible to children or pets - they're attracted by its sweet smell. Ingestion of even a small amount of coolant can be fatal! Wipe up garage floor and drip pan spills immediately. Keep antifreeze containers covered and repair cooling system leaks as soon as they're noticed.*

8    All vehicles covered by this manual are equipped with a pressurized coolant recovery system, which makes coolant level checks very easy. A coolant reservoir attached to the inner fender panel or the radiator itself is connected by a hose to the radiator filler neck **(see illustration)**. As the engine warms up, some coolant escapes through a valve in the radiator cap and travels through the hose into the reservoir. As the engine cools, the coolant is automatically drawn back into the cooling system to maintain the correct level.

9    The coolant level should be checked when the engine is at normal operating temperature. Simply note the fluid level in the reservoir - it should be at or near the MAX mark.

10    The coolant level can also be checked by removing the radiator cap. **Warning:** *Don't remove the cap to check the coolant level when the engine is warm! Wait until the engine has cooled, then wrap a thick cloth around the cap and turn it to the first stop. If any steam escapes from the cap, allow the engine to cool further, then remove the cap and check the level in the radiator.*

11    If only a small amount of coolant is required to bring the system

**4.4b  The oil level should be between the ADD and FULL marks on the dipstick - if it isn't, add enough oil to bring the level up to or near the Full mark (it takes one quart to raise the level from the Add to Full mark)**

up to the proper level, regular water can be used. However, to maintain the proper antifreeze/water mixture in the system, both should be mixed together to replenish a low level. High-quality antifreeze/coolant should be mixed with water in the proportion specified on the antifreeze container.

12    Coolant should be added to the reservoir after removing the cap **(see illustration)**.

13    As the coolant level is checked, note the condition of the coolant as well. It should be relatively clear. If it's brown or rust colored, the system should be drained, flushed and refilled (see Section 35).

14    If the coolant level drops consistently, there may be a leak in the system. Check the radiator, hoses, filler cap, drain plugs and water pump (see Section 35). If no leaks are noted, have the radiator filler cap pressure tested by a service station.

## Windshield washer fluid

Refer to illustration 4.15

15    The fluid for the windshield washer system is stored in a plastic reservoir. The level inside each reservoir should be maintained about one inch below the filler cap. The reservoir is accessible after opening the hood **(see illustration)**.

16    In milder climates, plain water can be used in the reservoir, but it should be kept no more than two-thirds full to allow for expansion if the water freezes. In colder climates, use windshield washer system antifreeze, available at any auto parts store, to lower the freezing point of the fluid. Mix the antifreeze with water in accordance with the manufacturer's directions on the container. **Caution:** *Don't use cooling system antifreeze - it'll damage the vehicle's paint. To help prevent icing in cold weather, warm the windshield with the defroster before using the washer.*

**4.5  Turn the oil filler cap counterclockwise to remove it**

**4.8  Make sure the coolant level in the reservoir is between the MIN and MAX marks - if it's below the MIN mark, add more coolant mixture or water**

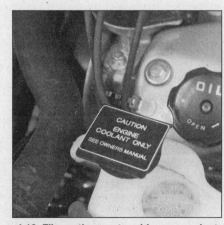

**4.12  Flip up the cap to add more coolant to the reservoir**

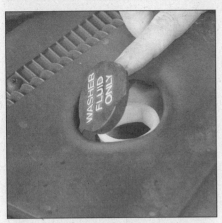

**4.15  The windshield washer reservoir is mounted in the cavity between the windshield and the engine compartment**

**4.19  Remove the cell caps to check the water level in the battery - if the level is low add distilled water only**

**4.22  The brake fluid reservoir should be kept at or near the bottom of the rings inside the reservoir filler neck**

## Battery electrolyte

*Refer to illustration 4.19*

**Warning:** *Certain precautions must be followed when checking or servicing a battery. Hydrogen gas, which is highly flammable, is produced in the cells, so keep lighted tobacco, open flames, bare light bulbs and sparks away from the battery. The electrolyte inside the battery is dilute sulfuric acid, which can burn skin and cause serious injury if splashed in your eyes (wear safety glasses). It'll also ruin clothes and painted surfaces. Remove all metal jewelry which could contact the positive battery terminal and a grounded metal source, causing a direct short.*

17   Vehicles equipped with a maintenance-free battery require no maintenance - the battery case is sealed and has no removable caps for adding water.

18   If a maintenance-type battery is installed, the caps on top of the battery should be removed periodically to check for a low electrolyte level. This check is more critical during warm summer months.

19   Remove each of the caps and add distilled water to bring the level in each cell to the split ring in the filler opening **(see illustration)**.

20   At the same time the battery water level is checked, the overall condition of the battery and related components should be noted. See Section 10 for complete battery check and maintenance procedures.

## Brake fluid

*Refer to illustration 4.22*

21   The brake master cylinder is located on the driver's side of the engine compartment firewall.

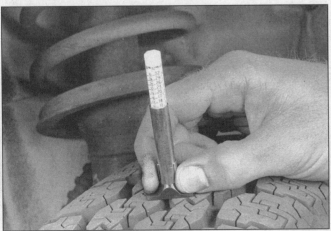

**5.2  Use a tire tread depth indicator to monitor tire wear - they are available at auto parts stores and service stations and cost very little**

22   Before removing the cap(s) to check the fluid, use a rag to clean all dirt off the top of the reservoir. If any foreign matter enters the master cylinder when the caps are removed, blockage in the brake system lines can occur. Also, make sure all painted surfaces around the master cylinder are covered, since brake fluid will ruin paint. The level should be maintained at the bottom of the rings in the neck of the reservoir (there are actually two separate reservoirs, so be sure to check both of them) **(see illustration)**.

23   If additional fluid is necessary to bring the level up, carefully pour new, clean brake fluid into the master cylinder. Be careful not to spill the fluid on painted surfaces. Be sure the specified fluid is used; mixing different types of brake fluid can cause damage to the system. See *Recommended lubricants and fluids* at the beginning of this Chapter or your owner's manual.

24   At this time the fluid and the master cylinder can be inspected for contamination. Normally the brake hydraulic system won't need periodic draining and refilling, but if rust deposits, dirt particles or water droplets are seen in the fluid, the system should be dismantled, cleaned and refilled with fresh fluid.

25   Reinstall the master cylinder caps.

26   The brake fluid in the master cylinder will drop slightly as the brake shoes or pads at each wheel wear down during normal operation. If the master cylinder requires repeated replenishing to keep the level up, it's an indication of leaks in the brake system which should be corrected immediately. Check all brake lines and connections, along with the wheel cylinders and calipers (see Chapter 9 for more information).

27   If you discover one or both reservoirs empty or nearly empty, the brake system should be bled (see Chapter 9).

---

### 5   Tire and tire pressure checks (every 250 miles or weekly)

*Refer to illustrations 5.2, 5.3, 5.4a, 5.4b and 5.8*

1   Periodic inspection of the tires may spare you the inconvenience of being stranded with a flat tire. It can also provide you with vital information regarding possible problems in the steering and suspension systems before major damage occurs.

2   The original tires on this vehicle are equipped with 1/2-inch wide bands that will appear when tread depth reaches 1/16-inch (when the tires are worn out). Tread wear can be monitored with a simple, inexpensive device known as a tread depth indicator **(see illustration)**.

3   Note any abnormal tread wear **(see illustration)**. Tread pattern irregularities such as cupping, flat spots and more wear on one side than the other are indications of front end alignment and/or balance problems. If any of these conditions are noted, take the vehicle to a tire shop or service station to correct the problem.

**1**

UNDERINFLATION

INCORRECT TOE-IN OR EXTREME CAMBER

CUPPING

UNDERINFLATION AND/OR MECHANICAL
IRREGULARITIES SUCH AS OUT-OF-BALANCE
CONDITION OF WHEEL AND/OR TIRE, AND BENT
OR DAMAGED WHEEL.
POSSIBLE LOOSE OR WORN STEERING TIE-ROD
OR STEERING IDLER ARM.
POSSIBLE LOOSE, DAMAGED OR WORN FRONT
SUSPENSION PARTS.

OVERINFLATION

FEATHERING DUE TO MISALIGNMENT

1-b HAYNES

**5.3  This chart will help you determine the condition of the tires, the probable cause(s) of abnormal wear
and the corrective action necessary**

4     Look closely for cuts, punctures and embedded nails or tacks. Sometimes a tire will hold air pressure for a short time or leak down very slowly after a nail has embedded itself in the tread. If a slow leak persists, check the valve stem core to make sure it's tight **(see illustration)**. Examine the tread for an object that may have embedded itself in the tire or for a "plug" that may have begun to leak (radial tire punctures are repaired with a plug that's installed in a puncture). If a puncture is suspected, it can be easily verified by spraying a solution of soapy water onto the puncture area **(see illustration)**. The soapy solution will bubble if there's a leak. Unless the puncture is unusually large, a tire shop or service station can usually repair the tire.

5     Carefully inspect the inner sidewall of each tire for evidence of brake fluid leakage. If you see any, inspect the brakes immediately.

6     Correct air pressure adds miles to the lifespan of the tires, improves mileage and enhances overall ride quality. Tire pressure cannot be accurately estimated by looking at a tire, especially if it's a radial. A tire pressure gauge is essential. Keep an accurate gauge in the vehicle. The pressure gauges attached to the nozzles of air hoses at gas stations are often inaccurate.

7     Always check tire pressure when the tires are cold. Cold, in this case, means the vehicle has not been driven over a mile in the three hours preceding a tire pressure check. A pressure rise of four to eight pounds is not uncommon once the tires are warm.

8     Unscrew the valve cap protruding from the wheel or hubcap and push the gauge firmly onto the valve stem **(see illustration)**. Note the reading on the gauge and compare the figure to the recommended tire pressure shown on the placard on the driver's side door pillar. Be sure to reinstall the valve cap to keep dirt and moisture out of the valve stem mechanism. Check all four tires and, if necessary, add enough air to bring them up to the recommended pressure.

9     Don't forget to keep the spare tire inflated to the specified pressure (refer to your owner's manual or the tire sidewall). Note that the pressure recommended for the compact spare is higher than for the tires on the vehicle.

**5.4a  If a tire loses air on a steady basis, check the valve core first to make sure it's snug (special inexpensive wrenches are commonly available at auto parts stores)**

**5.4b  If the valve core is tight, raise the corner of the vehicle with the low tire and spray a soapy water solution onto the tread as the tire is turned slowly - leaks will cause small bubbles to appear**

**5.8  To extend the life of the tires, check the air pressure at least once a week with an accurate gauge (don't forget the spare!)**

**6.3  The automatic transaxle fluid is checked by removing the dipstick on the transaxle case - don't confuse it with the engine oil dipstick**

## 6  Automatic transaxle fluid level check (every 250 miles or weekly)

*Refer to illustrations 6.3 and 6.4*

1    The fluid inside the transaxle should be at normal operating temperature to get an accurate reading on the dipstick. This is done by driving the vehicle for several miles, making frequent starts and stops to allow the transaxle to shift through all gears.

2    Park the vehicle on a level surface, place the gear selector lever in Park and leave the engine running.

3    Remove the transaxle dipstick **(see illustration)** and wipe all the fluid from the end with a clean rag.

4    Push the dipstick back into the transaxle until the cap seats completely. Remove the dipstick again and note the fluid on the end. The level should be in the area marked Hot (between the two upper holes in the dipstick) **(see illustration)**. If the fluid isn't hot (temperature about 100-degrees F), the level should be in the area marked Warm (between the two lower holes).

5    If the fluid level is at or below the Add mark on the dipstick, add enough fluid to raise the level to within the marks indicated for the appropriate temperature. Fluid should be added directly into the dipstick hole, using a funnel to prevent spills.

6    Do not overfill the transaxle. Never allow the fluid level to go above the upper hole on the dipstick - it could cause internal transaxle

damage. The best way to prevent overfilling is to add fluid a little at a time, driving the vehicle and checking the level between additions.

7    Use only the transaxle fluid specified by the manufacturer. This information can be found in the *Recommended lubricants and fluids* Section at the beginning of this Chapter.

8    The condition of the fluid should also be checked along with the level. If it's a dark reddish-brown color, or if it smells burned, it should be changed. If you're in doubt about the condition of the fluid, purchase some new fluid and compare the two for color and smell.

## 7  Power steering fluid level check (every 250 miles or weekly)

*Refer to illustrations 7.2 and 7.5*

1    Unlike manual steering, the power steering system relies on fluid which may, over a period of time, require replenishing.

2    The reservoir for the power steering pump is located on the rear side of the engine on the passenger's side of the engine compartment **(see illustration)**.

3    The power steering fluid level can be checked with the engine cold.

4    With the engine off, use a rag to clean the reservoir cap and the area around the cap. This will help prevent foreign material from falling into the reservoir when the cap is removed.

5    Turn and pull out the reservoir cap, which has a dipstick attached to it. Remove the fluid at the bottom of the dipstick with a clean rag. Reinstall the cap to get a fluid level reading. Remove the cap again and note the fluid level. It should be at the Full Cold mark on the dipstick **(see illustration)**. If the engine is warm, the level can be checked on the other side of the dipstick.

6    If additional fluid is required, pour the specified type directly into the reservoir using a funnel to prevent spills.

7    If the reservoir requires frequent fluid additions, all power steering hoses, hose connections, the power steering pump and the steering box should be carefully checked for leaks.

## 8  Engine oil and filter change (every 3,000 miles or 3 months)

*Refer to illustrations 8.3, 8.9, 8.14 and 8.19*

1    Frequent oil changes are the most important preventive maintenance procedures that can be done by the home mechanic. When engine oil ages, it gets diluted and contaminated, which ultimately leads to premature engine wear.

2    Although some sources recommend oil filter changes every other oil change, a new filter should be installed every time the oil is changed.

3    Gather together all necessary tools and materials before beginning this procedure **(see illustration)**. **Note:** *To avoid rounding off the corners of the drain plug, use a six-point socket.*

**6.4  Check the fluid with the transaxle at normal operating temperature - the level should be kept in the HOT range (between the two upper holes or marks)**

**7.2  The power steering fluid reservoir is located at the front of the engine, near the passenger's side of the firewall**

**7.5  The power steering dipstick is marked on both sides for checking the fluid cold (as shown) or hot**

4    In addition, you should have plenty of clean rags and newspapers handy to mop up any spills. Access to the underside of the vehicle is greatly improved if it can be lifted on a hoist, driven onto ramps or supported by jackstands. **Warning:** *Don't work under a vehicle that is supported only by a jack!*

5    If this is your first oil change on the vehicle, crawl underneath it and familiarize yourself with the locations of the oil drain plug and the oil filter. Since the engine and exhaust components will be warm during the actual work, it's a good idea to figure out any potential problems beforehand.

6    Allow the engine to warm up to normal operating temperature. If oil or tools are needed, use the warm-up time to gather everything necessary for the job. The correct type of oil to buy for your application can be found in the *Recommended lubricants and fluids* Section at the beginning of this Chapter.

7    With the engine oil warm (warm oil will drain better and more built-up sludge will be removed with it), raise the vehicle and support it securely on jackstands. They should be placed under the portions of the body designated as hoisting and jacking points (see *Jacking and towing* at the front of this manual).

8    Move all necessary tools, rags and newspapers under the vehicle. Place the drain pan under the drain plug. Keep in mind that the oil will initially flow from the engine with some force, so position the pan accordingly.

9    Being careful not to touch any of the hot exhaust components, use the breaker bar and socket to remove the drain plug near the bottom of the oil pan **(see illustration)**. Depending on how hot the oil is, you may want to wear gloves while unscrewing the plug the final few turns.

10    Allow the oil to drain into the pan. It may be necessary to move the pan further under the engine as the oil flow reduces to a trickle.

11    After all the oil has drained, clean the plug thoroughly with a rag. Small metal particles may cling to it and would immediately contaminate the new oil.

12    Clean the area around the oil pan opening and reinstall the plug. Tighten it securely.

13    Move the drain pan into position under the oil filter.

14    Now use the filter wrench to loosen the oil filter **(see illustration)**. Chain or metal band-type filter wrenches may distort the filter canister, but don't worry about it - the filter will be discarded anyway.

15    Sometimes the oil filter is on so tight it cannot be loosened, or it's positioned in an area inaccessible with a conventional filter wrench. Other type of tools, which fit over the end of the filter and turned with a ratchet/breaker bar, are available and may be better suited for removing the filter. If the filter is extremely tight, position the filter wrench near the threaded end of the filter, close to the engine.

16    Completely unscrew the old filter. Be careful, it's full of oil. Empty the old oil inside the filter into the drain pan.

17    Compare the old filter with the new one to make sure they're identical.

**8.3  These tools are required when changing the engine oil and filter**

1    **Drain pan** - *It should be fairly shallow in depth, but wide to prevent spills*

2    **Rubber gloves** - *When removing the drain plug and filter, you will get oil on your hands (the gloves will prevent burns)*

3    **Breaker bar** - *Sometimes the oil drain plug is tight, and a long breaker bar is needed to loosen it*

4    **Socket** - *To be used with the breaker bar or a ratchet (must be the correct size to fit the drain plug - six-point preferred)*

5    **Filter wrench** - *This is a metal band-type wrench, which requires clearance around the filter to be effective*

6    **Filter wrench** - *This type fits on the bottom of he filter and can be turned with a ratchet or breaker bar (different-size wrenches are available for different types of filters)*

18    Use a clean rag to remove all oil, dirt and sludge from the area where the oil filter mounts on the engine. Check the old filter to make sure the rubber gasket isn't stuck to the engine mounting surface.

19    Apply a light coat of oil to the rubber gasket on the new oil filter **(see illustration)**.

20    Attach the new filter to the engine following the tightening directions printed on the filter canister or packing box. Most filter

**8.9  To avoid rounding off the corners, use the correct size box-end wrench or a six-point socket to remove the engine oil drain plug**

**8.14  The oil filter is usually on very tight and normally will require a special wrench for removal - DO NOT use the wrench to tighten the filter!**

**8.19 Lubricate the oil filter gasket with clean engine oil before installing the filter on the engine**

**9.4 Use a small screwdriver to press the release lever, then slide the wiper assembly off the arm in the direction shown**

**9.5 Squeeze in on the tabs, then slide the element out of the wiper assembly**

manufacturers recommend against using a filter wrench due to the possibility of overtightening and damaging the canister.

21   Remove all tools and materials from under the vehicle, being careful not to spill the oil in the drain pan. Lower the vehicle off the jackstands.

22   Move to the engine compartment and locate the oil filler cap on the engine.

23   If the filler opening is obstructed, use a funnel when adding oil.

24   Pour the specified amount of new oil into the engine. Wait a few minutes to allow the oil to drain to the pan, then check the level on the dipstick (see Section 4 if necessary). If the oil level is at or above the Add mark, start the engine and allow the new oil to circulate.

25   Run the engine for only about a minute, then shut it off. Immediately look under the vehicle and check for leaks at the oil pan drain plug and around the oil filter. If either one is leaking, tighten with a bit more force.

26   With the new oil circulated and the filter now completely full, recheck the level on the dipstick. If necessary, add enough oil to bring the level to the Full mark on the dipstick.

27   During the first few trips after an oil change, make it a point to check for leaks and keep a close watch on the oil level.

28   The old oil drained from the engine cannot be reused in its present state and should be disposed of. Oil reclamation centers, auto repair shops and gas stations will normally accept the oil. After the oil has cooled, it should be drained into containers (plastic bottles with screw-on tops are preferred) for transport to a disposal site.

## 9   Wiper blade inspection and replacement (every 7,500 miles or 6 months)

*Refer to illustrations 9.4 and 9.5*

1   The windshield wiper blade elements should be checked periodically for cracks and deterioration.

2   To gain access to the wiper blades, turn on the ignition switch and cycle the wipers to a position on the windshield where the work can be performed, then turn off the ignition.

3   Lift the wiper blade assembly away from the glass.

4   Press the release button and slide the wiper off the pin **(see illustration)**.

5   Use needle-nose pliers to squeeze the tabs, then slide the element out of the frame **(see illustration)**.

6   Slide the new element into the frame until it locks.

7   Installation is the reverse of removal.

## 10   Battery check, maintenance and charging (every 7,500 miles or 6 months)

*Refer to illustrations 10.1, 10.5, 10.6a, 10.6b, 10.7a and 10.7b*

1   A routine preventive maintenance program for the battery in your vehicle is the only way to ensure quick and reliable starts. But before

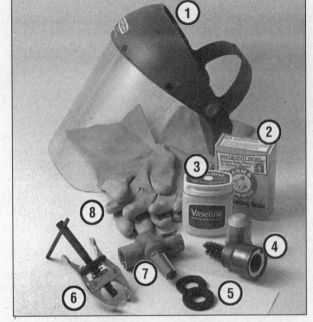

**10.1 Tools and materials required for battery maintenance**

1   *Face shield/safety goggles* - When removing corrosion with a brush, the acidic particles can easily fly up into your eyes

2   *Baking soda* - A solution of baking soda and water can be used to neutralize corrosion

3   *Petroleum jelly* - A layer of this on the battery posts will help prevent corrosion

4   *Battery post/cable cleaner* - This wire brush cleaning tool will remove all traces of corrosion from the battery posts and cable clamps

5   *Treated felt washers* - Placing one of these on each post, directly under the cable clamps, will help prevent corrosion

6   *Puller* - Sometimes the cable clamps are very difficult to pull off the posts, even after the nut/bolt has been completely loosened. This tool pulls the clamp straight up and off the post without damage

7   *Battery post/cable cleaner* - Here is another cleaning tool which is a slightly different version of Number 4 above, but it does the same thing

8   *Rubber gloves* - Another safety item to consider when servicing the battery; remember that's acid inside the battery!

performing any battery maintenance, make sure that you have the proper equipment necessary to work safely around the battery **(see illustration)**.

**10.5  The battery is secured by a clamp at the base (arrow) - make sure the nut is tight**

**10.6a  Battery terminal corrosion usually appears as light, fluffy powder**

2    There are also several precautions that should be taken whenever battery maintenance is performed. Before servicing the battery, always turn the engine and all accessories off and disconnect the cable from the negative terminal of the battery.

3    The battery produces hydrogen gas, which is both flammable and explosive. Never create a spark, smoke or light a match around the battery. Always charge the battery in a ventilated area.

4    Electrolyte contains poisonous and corrosive sulfuric acid. Do not allow it to get in your eyes, on your skin on your clothes. Never ingest it. Wear protective safety glasses when working near the battery. Keep children away from the battery.

5    Note the external condition of the battery. If the positive terminal and cable clamp on your vehicle's battery is equipped with a rubber protector, make sure that it's not torn or damaged. It should completely cover the terminal. Look for any corroded or loose connections, cracks in the case or cover or loose hold-down clamps **(see illustration)**. Also check the entire length of each cable for cracks and frayed conductors.

6    If corrosion, which looks like white, fluffy deposits **(see illustration)** is evident, particularly around the terminals, the battery should be removed for cleaning. Loosen the cable clamp nuts with a wrench, being careful to remove the negative cable first, and slide them off the terminals **(see illustration)**. Then disconnect the hold-down clamp nuts, remove the clamp and lift the battery from the engine compartment.

7    Clean the cable clamps thoroughly with a battery brush or a terminal cleaner and a solution of warm water and baking soda **(see**

**illustration)**. Wash the terminals and the top of the battery case with the same solution but make sure that the solution doesn't get into the battery. When cleaning the cables, terminals and battery top, wear safety goggles and rubber gloves to prevent any solution from coming in contact with your eyes or hands. Wear old clothes too - even diluted, sulfuric acid splashed onto clothes will burn holes in them. If the terminals have been extensively corroded, clean them up with a terminal cleaner **(see illustration)**. Thoroughly wash all cleaned areas with plain water.

8    Before reinstalling the battery in the engine compartment, inspect the plastic battery carrier. If it's dirty or covered with corrosion, remove it and clean it in the same solution of warm water and baking soda. Inspect the metal brackets which support the carrier to make sure that they are not covered with corrosion. If they are, wash them off. If corrosion is extensive, sand the brackets down to bare metal and spray them with a zinc-based primer (available in spray cans at auto paint and body supply stores).

9    Reinstall the battery carrier and the battery back into the engine compartment. Make sure that no parts or wires are laying on the carrier during installation of the battery.

10   Install a pair of specially treated felt washers around the terminals (available at auto parts stores), then coat the terminals and the cable clamps with petroleum jelly or grease to prevent further corrosion. Install the cable clamps and tighten the nuts, being careful to install the negative cable last.

11   Install the hold-down clamp and nuts. Tighten the nuts only enough to hold the battery firmly in place. Overtightening these nuts can crack the battery case.

**10.6b  Remove the cable from a battery post with a wrench - sometimes special battery pliers are required for this procedure if corrosion has caused deterioration of the nut hex (always remove the ground cable first and hook it up last!)**

**10.7a  When cleaning the cable clamps, all corrosion must be removed (the inside of the clamp is tapered to match the taper on the post, so don't remove too much material)**

**10.7b  Regardless of the type of tool used on the battery posts, a clean, shiny surface should be the result**

11.2 The recommended tire rotation pattern for these models

## Charging

12  Remove all of the cell caps (if equipped) and cover the holes with a clean cloth to prevent spattering electrolyte. Disconnect the negative battery cable and hook the battery charger leads to the battery posts (positive to positive, negative to negative), then plug in the charger. Make sure it is set at 12 volts if it has a selector switch.

13  If you're using a charger with a rate higher than two amps, check the battery regularly during charging to make sure it doesn't overheat. If you're using a trickle charger, you can safely let the battery charge overnight after you've checked it regularly for the first couple of hours.

14  If the battery has removable cell caps, measure the specific gravity with a hydrometer every hour during the last few hours of the charging cycle. Hydrometers are available inexpensively from auto parts stores - follow the instructions that come with the hydrometer. Consider the battery charged when there's no change in the specific gravity reading for two hours and the electrolyte in the cells is gassing (bubbling) freely. The specific gravity reading from each cell should be very close to the others. If not, the battery probably has a bad cell(s).

15  Some batteries with sealed tops have built-in hydrometers on the top that indicate the state of charge by the color displayed in the hydrometer window. Normally, a bright-colored hydrometer indicates a full charge and a dark hydrometer indicates the battery still needs charging. Check the battery manufacturer's instructions to be sure you know what the colors mean.

16  If the battery has a sealed top and no built-in hydrometer, you can hook up a digital voltmeter across the battery terminals to check the charge. A fully charged battery should read 12.6 volts or higher.

17  Further information on the battery and jump starting can be found in Chapter 5 and at the front of this manual.

## 11  Tire rotation (every 7,500 miles or 6 months)

*Refer to illustration 11.2*

1  The tires should be rotated at the specified intervals and whenever uneven wear is noticed. Since the vehicle will be raised and the tires removed anyway, this is a good time to check the brakes (see Section 34) and/or repack the rear wheel bearings (see Section 33). Read over the appropriate Section if other work will be done at the

13.2 On 1982 and earlier models with an automatic transaxle, the differential lubricant is checked by removing the fill plug

12.3 Use a small screwdriver to pry the rubber fill plug out of the transaxle

same time.

2  The rotation pattern depends on whether or not the spare is included in the rotation (**see illustration**).

3  See the information in *Jacking and towing* at the front of this manual for the proper procedures to follow when raising the vehicle and changing a tire; however, if the brakes are to be checked, don't apply the parking brake as stated. Make sure the tires are blocked to prevent the vehicle from rolling.

4  Preferably, the entire vehicle should be raised at the same time. This can be done on a hoist or by jacking up each corner of the vehicle and lowering it onto jackstands. Always use four jackstands and make sure the vehicle is safely supported.

5  After the tire rotation, check and adjust the tire pressures as necessary and be sure to check wheel lug nut torque.

## 12  Manual transaxle lubricant level check (every 7,500 miles or 6 months)

*Refer to illustration 12.3*

1  Manual transaxles don't have a dipstick. The lubricant level is checked by removing a rubber plug from the side of the transaxle case. Check the lubricant level with the engine cold.

2  Locate the plug and use a rag to clean it and the surrounding area. It may be necessary to remove the left inner fenderwell cover for access to the plug.

3  Pry the plug out with a small screwdriver (**see illustration**). If lubricant immediately starts leaking out, insert the plug back into the transaxle - the lubricant level is full. If lubricant doesn't leak out, completely remove the plug and use a finger to feel the lubricant level. The lubricant level should be even with the bottom of the plug hole.

4  If the transaxle requires additional lubricant, use a funnel with a rubber tube or a syringe to pour or squeeze the recommended lubricant into the plug hole to restore the level. **Caution:** *Use only the specified transaxle lubricant - see* Recommended lubricants and fluids *at the beginning of this Chapter.*

5  Push the plug securely back into the transaxle. Drive the vehicle and check for leaks around the plug.

## 13  Differential lubricant level check (1982 and earlier automatic transaxle models only) (every 7,500 miles or 6 months)

*Refer to illustration 13.2*

1  On these models the differential lubricant must be checked separately from the transaxle. Raise the vehicle and support it securely on jackstands.

2  Remove the differential fill plug (**see illustration**).

**15.7 There should be a slight drag as the feeler gauge is pulled between the jet valve adjusting screw and the valve stem**

**15.12 To make sure the adjusting screw doesn't move when the locknut is tightened, use a box-end wrench and have a good grip on the screwdriver**

3    The lubricant level should be even with the bottom of the filler hole.

4    If the level is low, add the specified lubricant with a syringe or pump and install the plug.

## 14    Combustion chamber conditioner application (Canadian leaded fuel models only) (every 7,500 miles or 6 months)

1    At the specified intervals, combustion chamber conditioner (see *Recommended lubricants and fluids* at the beginning of this Chapter) must be sprayed into the carburetor or fuel injection throttle body to help prevent the buildup of deposits in the combustion chamber and on the valves.

2    Remove the carburetor or throttle body inlet hose.

3    With the engine idling at normal operating temperature, the transaxle in Park (automatic) or Neutral (manual) and the parking brake applied, spray a can of the specified conditioner into the carburetor or fuel injection throttle body opening.

4    Reattach the hose to the air inlet.

## 15    Valve clearance check and adjustment (2.6L engine only) (every 15,000 miles or 12 months)

*Refer to illustrations 15.7 and 15.12*

**Warning:** *Disconnect the fan motor or negative battery cable when working in the vicinity of the fan.*

1    The valve clearances must be checked and adjusted at the specified intervals with the engine at normal operating temperature.

2    Remove the air cleaner assembly (see Chapter 4).

3    Remove the valve cover (see Chapter 2).

4    Place the number one piston at Top Dead Center (TDC) on the compression stroke (see Chapter 2). The number one cylinder rocker arms (closest to the timing chain end of the engine) should be loose (able to move up and down slightly) and the camshaft should be facing away from the rocker arms.

5    With the crankshaft in this position, the number one cylinder jet valve (if equipped), intake and exhaust clearances can be checked and adjusted. **Note:** *Some engines are not equipped with jet valves (small valves next to the intake valve rocker arms which are actuated by extensions of the intake valve rocker arms). If you're not sure whether or not the engine is equipped with jet valves,* **see illustration 15.7.**

6    First adjust the jet valve - if equipped - (if the engine is not equipped with jet valves, loosen the intake adjusting screw two turns and proceed to Step 9). Make sure the intake valve adjusting screw has been backed off two full turns, then loosen the locknut on the jet valve adjusting screw.

7    Turn the jet valve adjusting screw counterclockwise and insert the appropriate size feeler gauge (see this Chapter's Specifications) between the valve stem and adjusting screw. Carefully tighten the adjusting screw until you can feel a slight drag on the feeler gauge as you withdraw it from between the stem and adjusting screw **(see illustration).**

8    Since the jet valve spring is relatively weak, use special care not to force the jet valve open. Be particularly careful if the adjusting screw is hard to turn. Hold the adjusting screw with a screwdriver (to keep it from turning) and tighten the locknut. Recheck the clearance to make sure it hasn't changed.

9    Next, check and adjust the intake valve clearance. Insert the appropriate size feeler gauge between the intake valve stem and the adjusting screw. Carefully tighten the adjusting screw until you can feel a slight drag as you withdraw it from between the stem and adjusting screw.

10    Hold the adjusting screw with a screwdriver (to keep it from turning) and tighten the locknut. Recheck the clearance to make sure it hasn't changed.

11    Loosen the locknut on the exhaust valve adjusting screw. Turn the adjusting screw counterclockwise and insert the appropriate size feeler gauge between the valve stem and the adjusting screw. Carefully tighten the adjusting screw until you can feel a slight drag on the feeler gauge as you withdraw it from between the stem and adjusting screw.

12    Hold the adjusting screw with a screwdriver (to keep it from turning) and tighten the locknut **(see illustration).** Recheck the clearance to make sure it hasn't changed.

13    Rotate the crankshaft to position each of the remaining pistons at TDC on the compression stroke (see Chapter 2) and adjust the valves for each cylinder. Only adjust the valves for the cylinder that's at TDC. Always adjust the jet valve first.

14    Install the valve cover and the air cleaner assembly.

## 16    Chassis lubrication (every 15,000 miles or 12 months)

*Refer to illustrations 16.1 and 16.6*

1    A grease gun and a cartridge filled with the proper grease (see *Recommended lubricants and fluids*), graphite spray and an oil can filled with engine oil will be required to lubricate the chassis components **(see illustration).** Occasionally, on later model vehicles, plugs will be installed rather than grease fittings. If so, grease fittings will have to be purchased and installed.

2    Look under the vehicle and see if grease fittings or plugs are installed. If there are plugs, remove them with a wrench and buy grease fittings which will thread into the component. A dealer parts department or auto parts store will be able to supply the correct fittings. Straight and angled fittings are available.

**16.1  Materials required for chassis and body lubrication**

*1   Engine oil* - *Light engine oil in a can like this can be used for door and hood hinges*
*2   Graphite spray* - *Used to lubricate lock cylinders*
*3   Grease* - *Grease, in a variety of types and weights, is available for use in a grease gun. Check the Specifications for your requirements*
*4   Grease gun* - *A common grease gun, shown here with a detachable hose and nozzle, is needed for chassis lubrication. After use, clean it thoroughly*

3    For easier access under the vehicle, raise it with a jack and place jackstands under the portions of the body designated as hoisting and jacking points front and rear (see *Jacking and towing* at the front of this manual). Make sure it's securely supported by the stands.
4    Before beginning, force a little grease out of the nozzle to remove any dirt from the end of the gun. Wipe the nozzle clean with a rag.
5    With the grease gun and plenty of clean rags, crawl under the vehicle and begin lubricating the components.
6    Wipe the suspension balljoint grease fitting clean and push the nozzle firmly over it **(see illustration)**. Operate the lever on the grease gun to force grease into the component. The balljoints should be lubricated until the rubber seal is firm to the touch. Don't pump too much grease into the fitting as it could rupture the seal. For all other suspension and steering components, continue pumping grease into the fitting until it oozes out of the joint between the two components. If grease escapes around the grease gun nozzle, the fitting is clogged or the nozzle is not completely seated on the fitting. Resecure the gun nozzle to the fitting and try again. If necessary, replace the fitting with a new one.
7    Wipe the excess grease from the components and the grease fitting. Repeat the procedure for the remaining fittings.
8    Lubricate the sliding contact and pivot points of the manual transaxle shift linkage with the specified grease. While you're under the vehicle, clean and lubricate the parking brake cable along with the cable guides and levers. This can be done by smearing some of the chassis grease onto the cable and related parts with your fingers. Lubricate the clutch adjuster and cable, as well as the cable positioner, with a thin film of multi-purpose grease.
9    Lower the vehicle to the ground.
10    Open the hood and smear a little chassis grease on the hood latch mechanism. Have an assistant pull the hood release lever from inside the vehicle as you lubricate the cable at the latch.
11    Lubricate all the hinges (door, hood, etc.) with the recommended lubricant to keep them in proper working order.

**16.6  Pump the grease into the balljoint fitting until the rubber seal is firm**

**17.1a  2.2L carbureted engine fuel filter details**

12    The key lock cylinders can be lubricated with spray-on graphite or silicone lubricant which is available at auto parts stores.
13    Lubricate the door weatherstripping with silicone spray. This will reduce chafing and retard wear.

**17   Fuel filter replacement
(every 25,000 miles or 18 months)**

*Refer to illustrations 17.1a, 17.1b and 17.10*
**Warning:** *Gasoline is extremely flammable, so take extra precautions when you work on any part of the fuel system. Don't smoke or allow open flames or bare light bulbs near the work area, and don't work in a garage where a natural gas-type appliance (such as a water heater or clothes dryer) with a pilot light is present. If you spill any fuel on your skin, rinse it off immediately with soap and water. When you perform any kind of work on the fuel system, wear safety glasses and have a Class B type fire extinguisher on hand.*
**Caution:** *The electric cooling fan on some models can activate at any time, even when the ignition switch is in the Off position. Disconnect the negative battery cable when working in the vicinity of the fan.*

*Carbureted models*

1    The fuel filter is a disposable unit and is located between the fuel pump and the carburetor **(see illustrations)**.

**17.1b  On 2.6L engines, the fuel filter (arrow) is mounted near the carburetor**

2      This job is best done with the engine cold (after sitting at least three hours). You will need pliers to loosen and slide back the fuel line clamps, the correct replacement filter and some clean rags.
3      Place the rags under the filter to catch any fuel that is spilled as the fuel line is disconnected.
4      Slide back the clamps, pull the hoses off and remove the filter. On 2.6L engines it will be necessary to detach the mounting bracket.
5      Push the hoses onto the new filter and install the clamps.
6      Connect the battery.

## Fuel-injected models

7      Depressurize the fuel system (see Chapter 4).
8      The fuel filter is a disposable canister type and is located in the fuel line under the right rear of the vehicle, adjacent to the fuel tank.
9      Raise the rear of the vehicle and support it securely on jackstands.

**18.2  Tools required for changing spark plugs**

1   *Spark plug socket - This will have special padding inside to protect the spark plug's porcelain insulator*
2   *Torque wrench - Although not mandatory, using this tool is the best way to ensure the plugs are tightened properly*
3   *Ratchet - Standard hand tool to fit the spark plug socket*
4   *Extension - Depending on model and accessories, you may need special extensions and universal joints to reach one or more of the plugs*
5   *Spark plug gap gauge - This gauge for checking the gap comes in a variety of styles. Make sure the gap for your engine is included*

**17.10  Fuel-injected engine fuel filter details**

10      Loosen the screw clamps and detach the hoses **(see illustration)**.
11      Wrap a cloth around the fuel filter to catch the residual fuel (which may still be under slight pressure) and disconnect the hoses. It's a good idea to tie rags around your wrists to keep fuel from running down your arms.
12      Remove the bracket mounting bolt and detach the filter from the vehicle; hold your finger over the outlet to keep the residual fuel from running out.
13      Place the new filter in position, install the mounting bolt and tighten it securely. If the hoses are damaged or deteriorated, install new ones along with the new filter.
14      Connect the hoses and install the screw clamps securely.
15      Start the engine and check carefully for leaks at the hose connections.

## 18   Spark plug check and replacement (every 25,000 miles or 18 months)

*Refer to illustrations 18.2, 18.5a, 18.5b, 18.7, 18.9 and 18.11*
**Warning:** *Before beginning work, disconnect the negative battery cable to prevent the electric cooling fan from coming on.*
1      The spark plugs are located on the front side of the engine, facing the radiator.
2      In most cases the tools necessary for spark plug replacement include a spark plug socket which fits onto a ratchet (this special socket will be padded inside to protect the porcelain insulators on the

**18.5a  Spark plug manufacturers recommend using a wire-type gauge when checking the gap - if the wire does not slide between the electrodes with a slight drag, adjustment is required**

**18.5b To change the gap, bend the side electrode only, as indicated by the arrows, and be very careful not to crack or chip the porcelain insulator surrounding the center electrode**

**18.7 Pull on the spark plug wire boot and twist it back-and-forth to remove it**

new plugs), various extensions and a feeler gauge to check and adjust the spark plug gap **(see illustration)**. A special plug wire removal tool is available for separating the wire boot from the spark plug, but it isn't absolutely necessary. Since these engines are equipped with an aluminum cylinder head, a torque wrench should be used for tightening the spark plugs.

3    The best approach when replacing the spark plugs is to purchase the new spark plugs beforehand, adjust them to the proper gap and then replace each plug one at a time. When buying the new spark plugs, be sure to obtain the correct plug for your specific engine. This information can be found on the Vehicle Emissions Control Information label located under the hood, in the factory owner's manual or in the Specifications at the front of this Chapter. If differences exist between the sources, purchase the spark plug type specified on the VECI label as it was printed for your specific engine.

4    Allow the engine to cool completely before attempting to remove any of the plugs. During this cooling off time, each of the new spark plugs can be inspected for defects and the gaps can be checked.

5    The gap is checked by inserting the proper thickness gauge between the electrodes at the tip of the plug **(see illustration)**. The gap between the electrodes should be as specified on the VECI label in the engine compartment. The wire should touch each of the electrodes. If the gap is incorrect, use the adjuster on the thickness gauge body to bend the curved side electrode slightly until the proper gap is obtained

**(see illustration)**. Also, at this time check for cracks in the spark plug body (if any are found, the plug should not be used). If the side electrode is not exactly over the center one, use the adjuster to align the two.

6    Cover the front of the vehicle to prevent damage to the paint.

7    With the engine cool, remove the spark plug wire from one spark plug. Pull only on the boot at the end of the wire; don't pull on the wire. Use a twisting motion to free the boot and wire from the plug. A plug wire removal tool (mentioned earlier) should be used if available **(see illustration)**.

8    If compressed air is available, use it to blow any dirt or foreign material away from the spark plug area. A common bicycle pump will also work. The idea here is to eliminate the possibility of material falling into the cylinder through the plug hole as the spark plug is removed.

9    Now place the spark plug socket over the plug and remove it from the engine by turning it in a counterclockwise direction **(see illustration)**.

10    Compare the spark plug with the chart on the inside back cover of this manual to get an indication of the overall running condition of the engine.

11    Thread one of the new plugs into the hole, tightening it as much as possible by hand. **Caution:** *Be extremely careful - these engines have aluminum cylinder heads, which means the spark plug hole threads can be stripped easily. It may be a good idea to slip a short length of rubber hose over the end of the plug to use as a tool to thread it into place. The hose will grip the plug well enough to turn it, but will start to slip on the plug if the plug begins to cross-thread in the hole - this will prevent damaged threads and the accompanying costs involved in repairing them* **(see illustration)**.

12    Attach the plug wire to the new spark plug, again using a twisting motion on the boot until it's seated on the spark plug.

13    Repeat the above procedure for the remaining spark plugs, replacing them one at a time to prevent mixing up the spark plug wires.

**18.9 Use a ratchet and short extension to remove the spark plugs**

**18.11 A length of 3/16-inch ID rubber hose will save time and prevent damaged threads when installing the spark plugs**

**19.7a After removing the splash shield, loosen the two screws (arrows) and lift the distributor cap off (2.2L and 2.5L engines)**

## 19   Spark plug wire, distributor cap and rotor check and replacement (every 25,000 miles or 18 months)

*Refer to illustrations 19.7a, 19.7b, 19.9 and 19.10*

1    The spark plug wires should be checked at the recommended intervals or whenever new spark plugs are installed.

2    The wires should be inspected one at a time to prevent mixing up the order which is essential for proper engine operation.

3    Disconnect the plug wire from the spark plug. A removal tool can be used for this, or you can grab the rubber boot, twist slightly and then pull the wire free. Don't pull on the wire itself, only on the rubber boot.

4    Check inside the boot for corrosion, which will look like a white, crusty powder (don't mistake the white dielectric grease used on some plug wire boots for corrosion).

5    Now push the wire and boot back onto the end of the spark plug. It should be a tight fit on the plug end. If not, remove the wire and use a pair of pliers to carefully crimp the metal connector inside the wire boot until the fit is snug.

6    Now, using a cloth, clean each wire along its entire length. Remove all built-up dirt and grease. As this is done, inspect for burned areas, cracks and any other form of damage. Bend the wires in several places to ensure that the conductive material inside hasn't hardened. Repeat the procedure for the remaining wires (don't forget the distributor cap-to-coil wire).

7    Remove the distributor cap splash shield and check the wires at the cap, making sure they aren't loose and that the wires and boots aren't cracked or damaged. **Note:** *Don't attempt to pull the wires off the cap - they're retained on the inside by wire clips. The manufacturer doesn't recommend removing the wires from the cap for inspection because this could damage the integrity of the boot seal. If the wires appear to be damaged, replace them with new ones.* Remove the distributor cap, release the wire clips with a pair of pliers and remove the wires **(see illustrations)**. Insert the new wires into the cap while squeezing the boots to release any trapped air as you push them into place. Continue pushing until you feel the wire clips snap into position.

8    A visual check of the spark plug wires can also be made. In a darkened garage (make sure there is ventilation), start the engine and look at each plug wire. Be careful not to come into contact with any moving engine parts. If there's a crack in the insulation, you'll see arcing or a small spark at the damaged area.

9    Remove the distributor cap with the wires attached and check the cap for cracks, carbon tracks and other damage. Examine the terminals inside the cap for corrosion (slight corrosion can be removed with a pocket knife) **(see illustration)**.

10    Check the rotor (now visible on the end of the distributor shaft) for cracks and a secure fit on the shaft. Make sure the terminals aren't burned, corroded or pitted excessively. A small fine file can be used to restore the rotor terminals **(see illustration)**.

11    If new spark plug wires are needed, purchase a complete pre-cut

**19.7b When replacing the spark plug wires, use a pair of pliers to compress the wire retaining clips inside the distributor cap before pulling the wires out**

set for your particular engine. The terminals and rubber boots should already be installed on the wires. Replace the wires one at a time to avoid mixing up the firing order and make sure the terminals are securely seated in the distributor cap and on the spark plugs.

## 20   Drivebelt check, adjustment and replacement (every 25,000 miles or 18 months)

*Refer to illustrations 20.3, 20.4, 20.5a and 20.5b*
**Warning:** *The electric cooling fan on some models can activate at any time, even when the ignition switch is in the Off position. Disconnect the negative battery cable when working in the vicinity of the fan.*

1    The drivebelts, or V-belts as they are sometimes called, at the front of the engine, play an important role in the overall operation of the vehicle and its components. Due to their function and material makeup, the belts are prone to failure after a period of time and should be inspected and adjusted periodically to prevent major damage.

**19.9 Shown here are some of the common defects to look for when inspecting the distributor cap (if in doubt about its condition, install a new one)**

19.10 The ignition rotor should be checked for wear and corrosion as indicated here (if in doubt about its condition, buy a new one)

INSUFFICIENT SPRING TENSION

CRACKS

ROTOR TIP CORRODED

EVIDENCE OF PHYSICAL CONTACT WITH CAP

1-AC HAYNES

RULER

BELT DEFLECTION

STRAIGHT EDGE

MAKE SURE RULER IS PERPENDICULAR TO STRAIGHT EDGE

1-S HAYNES

20.4 Measuring drivebelt deflection with a straightedge and ruler

STREAKED SIDEWALL

FRAYING

CRACKS

SEPARATION

GLAZING

OIL SOAKED

TENSILE BREAK

1-R HAYNES

20.3 Here are some of the more common problems associated with drivebelts (check the belts very carefully to prevent an untimely breakdown)

1

2    The number of belts used on a particular engine depends on the accessories installed. Drivebelts are used to turn the alternator, power steering pump, water pump and air conditioning compressor. Depending on the pulley arrangement, a single belt may be used for more than one of these components. Some later models use a serpentine drivebelt in place of multiple V-belts. A serpentine belt requires no adjustment, as this is taken care of by a tensioner.
3    With the engine off, open the hood and locate the various belts at the front of the engine. Using your fingers (and a flashlight if necessary), examine the belts. Check for cracks and separation of the plies. Look for contamination by grease or oil and glazed areas, which give

the belt a shiny appearance. Both sides of each belt should be inspected, which means you'll have to twist them to check the underside **(see illustration)**.
4    The tightness of each belt is checked by pushing on it at a distance halfway between the pulleys **(see illustration)**. Apply about 10 pounds of force with your thumb and see how much the belt moves down (deflects). Refer to this Chapter's Specifications for the amount of deflection allowed in each belt.
5    If adjustment is necessary, it's done by moving the belt-driven accessory on the bracket **(see illustrations)**.

LOCKING NUT

ADJUSTING NUT

TC AND Z-F PUMP

LOCKING SCREW

REAR SUPPORT BRACKET

LOCKING NUT

S-PUMP

LOCKING SCREWS

SQUARE OPENING

PIVOT NUT

ADJUSTING SCREW

20.5a Typical 2.2L and 2.5L engine drivebelt adjustment details

PIVOT SCREW

IDLER BRACKET PIVOT SCREW

LOCKING NUT (T-BOLT)

**20.5b  Typical 2.6L engine drivebelt details**

**21.3a  2.2L carbureted engine air cleaner details - The wing nuts must be removed and the clips disengaged to access the air filter element - when reinstalling, tighten the wing nuts in the order shown**

6    For each component, there's a locking bolt and a pivot bolt or nut. Both must be loosened slightly to move the component.

7    After the two bolts have been loosened, move the component away from the engine (to tighten the belt) or toward the engine (to loosen the belt). Many accessories are equipped with a square hole designed to accept a 3/8-inch or 1/2-inch square drive breaker bar. The bar can be used to lever the component and tension the drivebelt. Hold the accessory in position and check the belt tension. If it's correct, tighten the two bolts until snug, then recheck the tension. If it's all right, tighten the two bolts completely.

8    To adjust the alternator drivebelt, loosen the pivot nut and the locking screw or T-bolt locknut, then turn the adjusting bolt to tension the belt.

9    It may be necessary to use some sort of prybar to move a component while the belt is adjusted. If this must be done, be very careful not to damage the component being moved, or the part being pried against.

10   Run the engine for about 15 minutes, then recheck the belt tension.

## 21   Air filter replacement (every 25,000 miles or 18 months)

1    At the specified intervals, the air filter element and (if equipped) crankcase ventilation filter should be replaced.

2    The air filter element is located in a housing on top of or adjacent to the engine.

## Carbureted models

*Refer to illustrations 21.3a and 21.3b*

3    Referring to the accompanying illustrations, remove the nuts (if equipped, detach the clips, remove the cover, then lift the element and remove the ventilation filter **(see illustrations)**.

4    Installation is the reverse of removal.

## Models with Throttle Body Injection (TBI)

*Refer to illustrations 21.5 and 21.6*

5    Remove the screws and lift off the cover **(see illustration)**.

6    Lift the element out **(see illustration)**.

7    Be careful not to drop anything down into the throttle body or air cleaner assembly. Clean the inside of the housing with a rag.

**21.3b  2.6L engine air cleaner details**

**21.5  A socket and extension are required to remove the air cleaner cover on later TBI models**

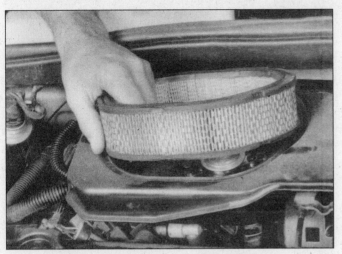

**21.6  Lift the element out of the housing**

**22.2a  2.2L carbureted engine PCV valve details**

8    Pull the crankcase ventilation filter (if equipped) out of the housing. Wash the crankcase filter in solvent and oil it lightly before reinstalling.

9    Place the new filter element in position and install the cover. Be sure to tighten any hose clamps which were loosened or removed.

## 22  Positive Crankcase Ventilation (PCV) valve check and replacement (every 25,000 miles or 18 months)

*Refer to illustrations 22.2a, 22.2b and 22.2c*

1    The PCV valve on 2.6L engines is located in the rubber hose connected to the valve cover, or on 2.2L models, in a vent module adjacent to it.

2    With the engine idling at normal operating temperature, pull the valve (with the hose attached) from the rubber fitting **(see illustrations)**.

3    Place your finger over the valve opening. If there's no vacuum at the valve, check for a plugged hose, manifold port or valve. Replace any plugged or deteriorated hoses.

4    Turn off the engine and shake the PCV valve, listening for a rattle. If the valve doesn't rattle, replace it with a new one.

5    To replace the valve, pull it from the end of the hose, noting its installed position and direction.

6    When purchasing a replacement PCV valve, make sure it's for your particular vehicle and engine size. Compare the old valve with the new one to make sure they're the same. On 2.2L carbureted engines, part of PCV valve maintenance involves detaching the vent module from the valve cover and washing it out with solvent. Pour a small amount of oil into the module, shaking to distribute it, then reinstall the module.

7    Push the valve into the end of the hose or vent module until it's seated.

8    Inspect the rubber fitting for damage and replace it with a new one if necessary.

9    Push the PCV valve and hose securely into position.

## 23  Exhaust Gas Recirculation (EGR) system check (every 25,000 miles or 18 months)

### 2.2L and 2.5L engines

*Refer to illustration 23.2*

1    The EGR valve is located on the intake manifold, adjacent to the carburetor or throttle body.

2    Check the EGR valve hose and pipe for damage and leaks **(see illustration)**.

**22.2b  2.6L engine PCV valve location details**

**22.2c  Pull the PCV valve out of the fitting**

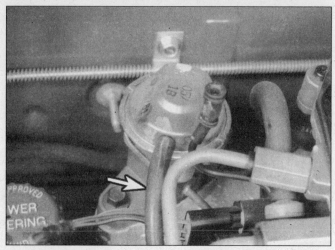

**23.2  Inspect the rubber hose on the EGR valve (arrow) for hardening and cracks**

**25.3  The choke plate (arrow) is located in the carburetor throat and should be closed when the engine is cold**

3    With the engine idling at normal operating temperature, watch the stem under the valve for movement and increase the engine speed to approximately 2,500 rpm.

4    The stem should move up and down as the engine speed changes, indicating that the EGR system is operating properly.

### 2.6L engine

5    These models use two EGR valves. The sub EGR valve is located at the base of the carburetor and is operated by the carburetor linkage. The dual EGR valve bolts to the intake manifold and is controlled by engine vacuum.

6    Check the sub EGR valve linkage to make sure it's securely connected and inspect the dual EGR valve vacuum hoses

7    See Chapter 6 for more information on the EGR system.

## 24   Underhood hose check and replacement (every 30,000 miles or 24 months)

**Warning:** *Replacement of air conditioning hoses must be left to a dealer service department or air conditioning shop equipped to depressurize the system safely. Never remove air conditioning components or hoses until the system has been depressurized.*

### General

1    High temperatures under the hood can cause the deterioration of the rubber and plastic hoses used for engine, accessory and emission systems operation. Periodic inspection should be made for cracks, loose clamps, material hardening and leaks.

2    Information specific to the cooling system hoses can be found in Section 29.

3    Some, but not all, hoses use clamps to secure the hoses to fittings. Where clamps are used, check to be sure they haven't lost their tension, allowing the hose to leak. Where clamps are not used, make sure the hose hasn't expanded and/or hardened where it slips over the fitting, allowing it to leak.

### Vacuum hoses

4    It's quite common for vacuum hoses, especially those in the emissions system, to be color coded or identified by colored stripes molded into the hose. Various systems require hoses with different wall thickness, collapse resistance and temperature resistance. When replacing hoses, make sure the new ones are made of the same material.

5    Often the only effective way to check a hose is to remove it completely from the vehicle. Where more than one hose is removed, be sure to label the hoses and their attaching points to insure proper reattachment.

6    When checking vacuum hoses, be sure to include any plastic T-fittings in the check. Check the fittings for cracks and the hose where it fits over the fitting for enlargement, which could cause leakage.

7    A small piece of vacuum hose (1/4-inch inside diameter) can be used as a stethoscope to detect vacuum leaks. Hold one end of the hose to your ear and probe around vacuum hoses and fittings, listening for the "hissing" sound characteristic of a vacuum leak. **Warning:** *When probing with the vacuum hose stethoscope, be careful not to allow your body or the hose to come into contact with moving engine components such as the drivebelt, cooling fan, etc.*

### Fuel hose

**Warning:** *Gasoline is extremely flammable, so take extra precautions when you work on any part of the fuel system. Don't smoke or allow open flames or bare light bulbs near the work area, and don't work in a garage where a natural gas-type appliance (such as a water heater or clothes dryer) with a pilot light is present. If you spill any fuel on your skin, rinse it off immediately with soap and water. When you perform any kind of work on the fuel system, wear safety glasses and have a Class B type fire extinguisher on hand. Before working on any part of the fuel system, relieve the fuel system pressure (see Chapter 4).*

8    Check all rubber fuel hoses for damage and deterioration. Check especially for cracks in areas where the hose bends and just before clamping points, such as where a hose attaches to the carburetor or throttle body.

9    High quality fuel line, specifically designed for fuel systems, should be used for fuel line replacement. **Warning:** *Never use vacuum line, clear plastic tubing or water hose for fuel lines.*

10   Spring-type clamps are commonly used on fuel lines. These clamps often lose their tension over a period of time, and can be "sprung" during the removal process. Therefore it is recommended that all spring-type clamps be replaced with screw clamps whenever a hose is replaced.

### Metal lines

11   Sections of metal line are often used for fuel line between the fuel pump and carburetor or throttle body. Check carefully to be sure the line has not been bent and crimped and that cracks have not started in the line.

12   If a section of metal fuel line must be replaced, only seamless steel tubing should be used, since copper and aluminum tubing do not have the strength necessary to withstand normal engine operating vibration.

13   Check the metal brake lines where they enter the master cylinder and brake proportioning unit (if used) for cracks in the lines or loose fittings. Any sign of brake fluid leakage calls for an immediate thorough inspection of the brake system.

**25.8a  Apply the solvent to the choke shaft in the areas indicated by arrows**

**25.8b  On 2.2L engines, apply the solvent to the link between the choke shaft, thermostat and sealing block**

**26.4  Fuel injection throttle body bolt locations (arrows) - upper arrows point to the rear bolts, which are not visible**

## 25  Carburetor choke check and cleaning (every 30,000 miles or 24 months)

**Warning:** *Disconnect the fan motor or negative battery when working in the vicinity of the fan.*

### Check

*Refer to illustration 25.3*

1  The choke operates only when the engine is cold, so this check should be performed before the engine is started for the day.

2  Expose the top of the carburetor by taking off the top of the air cleaner assembly or the inlet air duct. If any vacuum hoses must be disconnected, make sure you tag the hoses for reinstallation in their original positions. Place the top plate and wing nut aside, out of the way of moving engine components.

3  Look at the center of the air cleaner housing. You will notice a flat plate at the carburetor opening **(see illustration)**.

4  Press the accelerator to the floor. The plate should close completely. Start the engine while you watch the plate at the carburetor. Don't position your face near the carburetor, as the engine could backfire, causing serious burns. When the engine starts, the choke plate should open slightly.

5  Allow the engine to continue running at idle speed. As the engine

warms up to operating temperature, the plate should slowly open, allowing more air to enter through the top of carburetor.

6  After a few minutes, the choke plate should be fully open to the vertical position. Tap the accelerator to make sure the fast idle cam disengages.

7  You'll notice that the engine speed corresponds with the plate opening. With the plate fully closed, the engine should run at fast idle speed. As the plate opens and the throttle is moved to disengage the fast idle cam, the engine speed should decrease.

### Cleaning

*Refer to illustrations 25.8a and 25.8b*

8  With the engine off, use aerosol carburetor solvent (available at auto parts stores) to clean the contact surfaces of the choke plate shaft where it passes through the carburetor body. Also clean the idle cam and link mechanism **(see illustrations)**.

9  Refer to Chapter 4 for specific information on adjusting and servicing the choke components.

## 26  Carburetor/fuel injection throttle body mounting bolt/nut torque check (every 30,000 miles or 24 months)

*Refer to illustration 26.4*

1  The carburetor or fuel injection throttle body is attached to the intake manifold by bolts or nuts. These can sometimes work loose during normal engine operation and cause a vacuum leak.

2  To properly tighten the mounting bolts or nuts, a torque wrench is necessary. If you do not own one, they can usually be rented on a daily basis.

3  Remove the air cleaner assembly.

4  Locate the mounting bolts at the base of the throttle body **(see illustration)**. Decide what special tools or adapters will be necessary, if any, to tighten the bolts with a socket and the torque wrench.

5  Tighten the bolts to the torque listed in this Chapter's Specifications. Do not overtighten the bolts, as the threads may strip.

6  If you suspect a vacuum leak exists at the bottom of the throttle body, obtain a short length of rubber hose. Start the engine and place one end of the hose next to your ear as you probe around the base of the carburetor or throttle body with the other end. You should hear a hissing sound if a leak exists.

7  If, after the bolts/nuts are properly tightened, a vacuum leak still exists, the carburetor or throttle body must be removed and a new gasket installed. See Chapter 4 for more information.

8  After tightening the bolts/nuts, reinstall the air cleaner housing.

**28.6  Check the fuel tank hoses for damage and deterioration**

## 27   Heated inlet air system check (every 30,000 miles or 24 months)

1    Carbureted and TBI-equipped models are equipped with a heated inlet air cleaner which draws air to the carburetor or fuel injection throttle body from different locations, depending on engine temperature.

2    This is a simple visual check; however, the outside air duct must be removed.

3    Locate the vacuum air control valve in the air cleaner assembly. It's located inside the air cleaner duct fitting, where you removed the outside air duct from. Make sure the flexible heat duct under the air cleaner is securely attached and undamaged.

4    The check should be done when the engine and outside air are cold (less than 65-degrees F). Start the engine and look through the duct fitting at the valve (which should move up to the "heat on" position). With the valve up, air cannot enter through the end of the duct fitting, but instead enters the air cleaner through the heat duct attached to the exhaust manifold.

5    As the engine warms up to operating temperature, the valve should move down to the "heat off" position to allow air through the duct fitting. Depending on outside air temperature, this may take 10 to 15 minutes. To speed up the check you can reconnect the outside air duct, drive the vehicle and then check to see if the valve has moved down.

6    If the air cleaner isn't operating properly, see Chapter 4 for more information.

## 28   Fuel system check (every 30,000 miles or 24 months)

*Refer to illustration 28.6*

**Warning:** *Gasoline is extremely flammable, so take extra precautions when you work on any part of the fuel system. Don't smoke or allow open flames or bare light bulbs near the work area, and don't work in a garage where a natural gas-type appliance (such as a water heater or clothes dryer) with a pilot light is present. If you spill any fuel on your skin, rinse it off immediately with soap and water. When you perform any kind of work on the fuel system, wear safety glasses and have a Class B type fire extinguisher on hand.*

1    On fuel injected models the fuel system is under pressure even when the engine is off. Consequently, the fuel system must be depressurized (see Chapter 4) whenever it is worked on. Even after depressurization, if any fuel lines are disconnected for servicing, be prepared to catch some fuel as it spurts out. Plug all disconnected fuel lines immediately to prevent the tank from emptying itself.

2    The fuel system is most easily checked with the vehicle raised on a hoist where the components on the underside are readily visible and accessible.

3    If the smell of gasoline is noticed while driving, or after the vehicle has been parked in the sun, the fuel system should be thoroughly inspected immediately.

4    Remove the gas tank cap and check for damage, corrosion and a proper sealing imprint on the gasket. Replace the cap with a new one if necessary.

5    Inspect the gas tank and filler neck for punctures, cracks and other damage. The connection between the filler neck and the tank is especially critical. Sometimes a rubber filler neck will leak due to loose clamps or deteriorated rubber; problems a home mechanic can usually rectify. **Warning:** *Do not, under any circumstances, try to repair a fuel tank yourself (except to replace rubber components). A welding torch or any open flame can easily cause the fuel vapors to explode if the proper precautions are not taken.*

6    Carefully check all rubber hoses and metal lines leading away from the fuel tank. Check for loose connections, deteriorated hoses, crimped lines and damage of any kind **(see illustration)**. Follow the lines up to the front of the vehicle, carefully inspecting them all the way. Repair or replace damaged sections as necessary (see Chapter 4).

## 29   Cooling system check (every 30,000 miles or 24 months)

*Refer to illustration 29.4*

**Warning:** *The electric cooling fan on some models can activate at any time, even when the ignition switch is in the Off position. Disconnect the fan motor or the negative battery cable when working in the vicinity of the fan.*

1    Many major engine failures can be attributed to a faulty cooling system. If the vehicle is equipped with an automatic transaxle, the cooling system is also used to cool the transaxle fluid.

2    The cooling system should be checked with the engine cold. Do this before the vehicle is driven for the day or after it has been shut off for three or four hours.

3    Remove the radiator cap and thoroughly clean the cap (inside and out) with water. Also clean the filler neck on the radiator. All traces of corrosion should be removed.

4    Carefully check the upper and lower radiator hoses along with the smaller diameter heater hoses. Inspect the entire length of each hose, replacing any that are cracked, swollen or deteriorated. Cracks may become more apparent when a hose is squeezed **(see illustration)**.

5    Also check that all hose connections are tight. A leak in the cooling system will usually show up as white or rust-colored deposits on the areas adjoining the leak.

6    Use compressed air or a soft brush to remove bugs, leaves, and other debris from the front of the radiator or air conditioning condenser. Be careful not to damage the delicate cooling fins, or cut yourself on them.

7    Finally, have the cap and system pressure tested. If you do not have a pressure tester, most gas stations and repair shops will do this for a minimal charge.

## 30   Exhaust system check (every 30,000 miles or 24 months)

1    With the engine cold (at least three hours after the vehicle has been driven), check the complete exhaust system from its starting point at the engine to the end of the tailpipe. This should be done on a hoist where unrestricted access is available.

2    Check the pipes and connections for signs of leakage and/or corrosion indicating a potential failure. Make sure that all brackets and hangers are in good condition and tight.

3    At the same time, inspect the underside of the body for holes, corrosion and open seams which may allow exhaust gases to enter the passenger compartment. Seal all body openings with silicone sealant or body putty.

4    Rattles and other noises can often be traced to the exhaust

ALWAYS CHECK FOR CHAFED OR BURNED AREAS THAT MAY CAUSE AN UNTIMELY AND COSTLY FAILURE.

SOFT HOSE INDICATES INSIDE DETERIORATION. THIS DETERIORATION CAN CONTAMINATE THE COOLING SYSTEM AND CAUSE PARTICLES TO CLOG THE RADIATOR.

HARDENED HOSE CAN FAIL AT ANY TIME. TIGHTENING HOSE CLAMPS WILL NOT SEAL THE CONNECTION OR STOP LEAKS.

SWOLLEN HOSE OR OIL SOAKED ENDS INDICATE DANGER AND POSSIBLE FAILURE FROM OIL OR GREASE CONTAMINATION. SQUEEZE THE HOSE TO LOCATE CRACKS AND BREAKS THAT CAUSE LEAKS.

1-m HAYNES

**29.4  Hoses, like drivebelts, have a habit of failing at the worst possible time - to prevent the inconvenience of a blown radiator or heater hose, inspect them carefully as shown here**

**31.4  With the vehicle weight resting on the suspension, try to move the balljoint grease fittings with your fingers - if the fittings can be moved easily, the balljoints are worn and must be replaced**

**31.3  This leaking fluid (arrow) indicates a defective seal, which means the shock absorber must be replaced**

system, especially the mounts and hangers. Try to move the pipes, muffler and catalytic converter. If the components can come into contact with the body, secure the exhaust system with new mounts.

5    This is also an ideal time to check the running condition of the engine by inspecting the very end of the tailpipe. The exhaust deposits here are an indication of engine state-of-tune. If the pipe is black and sooty or coated with white deposits, the engine may be in need of a tune-up (including a thorough fuel system inspection and adjustment).

## 31  Steering and suspension check (every 30,000 miles or 24 months)

*Refer to illustrations 31.3 and 31.4*

1    Whenever the front of the vehicle is raised for service it is a good idea to visually check the suspension and steering components for wear and damage.

2    Indications of wear and damage include excessive play in the steering wheel before the front wheels react, excessive lean around corners, body movement over rough roads or binding at some point as the steering wheel is turned.

3    Before the vehicle is raised for inspection, test the shock absorbers by pushing down to rock the vehicle at each corner. If it does not come back to a level position within one or two bounces, the shocks are worn and should be replaced. As this is done, check for squeaks and unusual noises from the suspension components. Check the shock absorbers for fluid leakage **(see illustration)**. Information on shock absorbers and suspension components can be found in Chapter 10.

4    Check the balljoints for wear by grasping the grease fittings securely and attempting to move them **(see illustration)**. If the grease fittings move easily, the balljoints are worn and must be replaced with new ones.

5    Now raise the front end of the vehicle and support it securely with jackstands placed under the jacking and hoisting points (see *Jacking and towing* at the front of this manual). Because of the work to be done, the vehicle must be stable and safely supported.

6    Check the driveaxle/hub nuts for the correct torque.

7    Crawl under the vehicle and check for loose bolts, broken or disconnected parts and deteriorated rubber bushings on all suspension and steering components. Look for grease or fluid leaking from around the steering gear boots. Check the power steering hoses and connections for leaks. Check the steering joints for wear.

8    Have an assistant turn the steering wheel from side-to-side and check the steering components for free movement, chafing and binding. If the wheels don't respond to the movement of the steering wheel, try to determine where the slack is located.

1

**33.1 Tools and materials needed for rear wheel bearing maintenance**

1   *Hammer* - A common hammer will do just fine
2   *Grease* - High-temperature grease that is formulated specially for wheel bearings should be used
3   *Wood block* - If you have a scrap piece of 2x4, it can be used to drive the new seal into the hub
4   *Needle-nose pliers* - Used to straighten and remove the cotter pin in the spindle
5   *Torque wrench* - This is very important in this procedure; if the bearing is too tight, the wheel won't turn freely - if it's too loose, the wheel will "wobble" on the spindle. Either way, it could mean extensive damage
6   *Screwdriver* - Used to remove the seal from the hub (a long screwdriver is preferred)
7   *Socket/breaker bar* - Needed to loosen the nut on the spindle if it's extremely tight
8   *Brush* - Together with some clean solvent, this will be used to remove old grease from the hub and spindle

## 32   Steering shaft seal lubrication (1985 and earlier models only) (every 30,000 miles or 24 months)

1   The steering shaft seal protects the steering shaft at the point where it passes through the firewall. The inner circumference of the seal should be lubricated with grease at the specified interval or if the shaft makes noise or sticks in the seal when turned.
2   Raise the vehicle and support it securely on jackstands.
3   Peel back the upper edge of the seal and apply a light coat of the specified grease where it contacts the steering shaft.
4   Lower the vehicle.

## 33   Rear wheel bearing check, repack and adjustment (every 30,000 or 24 months)

*Refer to illustrations 33.1, 33.7, 33.8, 33.14 and 33.26*
1   In most cases the rear wheel bearings won't need servicing until the brake shoes are changed. However, the bearings should be checked whenever the rear of the vehicle is raised for any reason. Several items, including a torque wrench and special grease, are required for this procedure **(see illustration)**.
2   With the vehicle securely supported on jackstands, spin each wheel and check for noise, rolling resistance and freeplay.

**33.7 An exploded view of the rear brake drum/hub and bearing components**

3   Grasp the top of each tire with one hand and the bottom with the other. Move the wheel in-and-out on the spindle. If there's any noticeable movement, the bearings should be checked and then repacked with grease or replaced if necessary.
4   Remove the wheel.
5   Pry the grease cap out of the hub with a screwdriver or hammer and chisel.
6   Straighten the bent ends of the cotter pin, then pull the cotter pin out of the lock. Discard the cotter pin and use a new one during reassembly.
7   Remove the lock and the hub nut from the end of the spindle **(see illustration)**.
8   Pull the brake drum/hub assembly out slightly, then push it back into its original position. This should force the outer bearing and washer off the spindle enough so they can be removed **(see illustration)**.
9   Pull the brake drum/hub assembly off the spindle. If it does not come off easily, back off the adjuster as described in the drum brake shoe replacement procedure in Chapter 9.
10   Use a screwdriver to pry the dust seal out of the rear of the hub. As this is done, note how the seal is installed.
11   Remove the inner wheel bearing from the hub.
12   Use solvent to remove all traces of old grease from the bearings, hub and spindle. A small brush may prove helpful; however, make sure no bristles from the brush embed themselves inside the bearing rollers. Allow the parts to air dry.
13   Carefully inspect the bearings for cracks, heat discoloration, worn rollers, etc. check the bearing races inside the hub for wear and damage. If the bearing races are defective, the hubs should be taken to a machine shop with the facilities to remove the old races and press new ones in. Note that the bearings and races come as matched sets - old bearings should never be installed on new races and vice-versa.
14   Use high-temperature wheel bearing grease to pack the bearings. Work the grease completely into the bearings, forcing it between the rollers, cone and cage from the back side **(see illustration)**.
15   Apply a thin coat of grease to the spindle at the outer bearing seat, inner bearing seat, shoulder and seal seat.
16   Put a small quantity of grease on the inner side of each bearing race inside the hub. Using your finger, form a dam at these points to provide extra grease availability and to keep thinned grease from flowing out of the bearing.
17   Place the grease-packed inner bearing into the rear of the hub and put a little more grease on the outer side of the bearing.
18   Place a new dust seal over the inner bearing and tap the seal evenly into place with a hammer and block of wood until it's flush with the hub.
19   Carefully place the drum/hub assembly on the spindle and push

**33.8 Pull the brake drum/hub out slightly to dislodge the outer wheel bearing, then remove the washer and bearing**

**33.14 Work the grease into each bearing from the large diameter side until it's forced out of the small diameter side**

**33.26 Tap the grease cap into place with a large punch and a hammer (work around the outer edge)**

the grease-packed outer bearing into position.

20   Install the washer and nut. Tighten the nut only slightly (no more than 12 ft-lbs of torque).

21   Spin the drum/hub in a forward direction to seat the bearings and remove any grease or burrs which could cause excessive bearing play later.

22   Verify that the tightness of the nut is still approximately 12 ft-lbs.

23   Loosen the nut until it's just loose, no more.

24   Using your hand (not a wrench of any kind), tighten the nut until it's snug. Install the lock and a new cotter pin through the hole in the spindle and lock. If the lock slots don't line up, remove the lock and rotate it to another position.

25   Bend the ends of the cotter pin until they're flat against the nut. Cut off any extra length which could interfere with the grease cap.

26   Install the grease cap, tapping it into place with a hammer **(see illustration)**.

27   Install the wheel and tighten the lug nuts.

28   Grasp the top and bottom of the tire and check the bearings in the manner described earlier in this Section.

29   Lower the vehicle.

## 34   Brake system check (every 30,000 miles or 24 months)

1   The brakes should be inspected every time the wheels are removed or whenever a defect is suspected. Indications of a potential brake system problem include the vehicle pulling to one side when the brake pedal is depressed, noises coming from the brakes when they are applied, excessive brake pedal travel, pulsating pedal and leakage of fluid, usually seen on the inside of the tire or wheel.

### Disc brakes

*Refer to illustration 34.5*

2   Disc brakes can be visually checked without removing any parts except the wheels.

3   Raise the vehicle and place it securely on jackstands. Remove the wheels (see *Jacking and towing* at the front of this manual if necessary).

4   Now visible is the disc brake caliper which contains the pads. There is an outer brake pad and an inner pad. Both should be checked for wear.

5   Note the pad thickness by looking at each end of the caliper and through the inspection hole in the caliper body **(see illustration)**. If the combined thickness of the pad lining and metal shoe is 5/16-inch or less, the pads should be replaced.

6   Since it'll be difficult, if not impossible, to measure the exact thickness of the pad, if you're in doubt as to the pad quality, remove them for further inspection or replacement. See Chapter 9 for disc

**34.5 There's an inspection hole like this in each caliper - by looking through the hole you can determine the thickness of the remaining friction material on both the inner and outer pads**

brake pad replacement.

7   Before installing the wheels, check for leakage around the brake hose connections leading to the caliper and for damaged brake hoses (cracks, leaks, chafed areas, etc.). Replace the hoses or fittings as necessary (see Chapter 9).

8   Also check the disc for score marks, wear and burned spots. If these conditions exist, the hub/disc assembly should be removed for servicing (see Chapter 9).

### Drum brakes

*Refer to illustrations 34.13 and 34.15*

9   Raise the vehicle and support it securely on jackstands. Block the front tires to prevent the vehicle from rolling; however, don't apply the parking brake or it will lock the drums in place.

10   Remove the wheels, referring to *Jacking and towing* at the front of this manual if necessary.

11   Remove the brake drum as described in Section 33.

12   With the drum removed, carefully clean off any accumulations of dirt and dust using brake system cleaner. **Warning:** *Don't blow the dust out with compressed air and don't inhale any of it (it may contain asbestos, which is harmful to your health).*

13   Note the thickness of the lining material on both front and rear brake shoes. If the material has worn away to within 1/8-inch of the recessed rivets or metal backing, the shoes should be replaced **(see**

1

illustration). The shoes should also be replaced if they're cracked, glazed (shiny areas), or covered with brake fluid.

14    Make sure all the brake assembly springs are connected and in good condition.

15    Check the brake components for signs of fluid leakage. Carefully pry back the rubber cups on the wheel cylinder located at the top of the brake shoes (see illustration). Any leakage here is an indication that the wheel cylinders should be overhauled immediately (see Chapter 9). Also, check all hoses and connections for signs of leakage.

16    Wipe the inside of the drum with a clean rag and denatured alcohol or brake cleaner. Again, be careful not to breathe the dangerous asbestos dust.

17    Check the inside of the drum for cracks, score marks, deep scratches and "hard spots" which will appear as small discolored areas. If imperfections cannot be removed with fine emery cloth, the drum must be taken to an automotive machine shop for resurfacing.

18    Repeat the procedure for the remaining wheel. If the inspection reveals that all parts are in good condition, reinstall the brake drums. Install the wheels and lower the vehicle to the ground.

### Parking brake

19    The parking brake is operated by a foot pedal and locks the rear brake system. The easiest, and perhaps most obvious method of periodically checking the operation of the parking brake assembly is to stop the vehicle on a steep hill with the parking brake set and the transmission in Neutral. If the parking brake cannot prevent the vehicle from rolling, adjust it (see Chapter 9).

### Drum brake adjustment (1982 and earlier models)

*Refer to illustration 34.24*

20    The drum brakes on these models are not self-adjusting so the last step of brake inspection is adjustment.

21    Raise the vehicle and support it securely on jackstands.

22    Remove the rubber plug from the adjustment access hole in the backing plate.

23    Release the parking brake and if necessary, back off the cable adjuster so the cable is slack.

24    Insert a thin screwdriver through the hole in the backing plate and move the adjuster wheel down (left side) or up (right side) until the tire can't rotate, then back off the adjuster ten clicks (see illustration).

25    Repeat the adjustment on the opposite wheel.

26    Install the plugs in the backing plate holes and apply RTV sealant around the plugs and the return spring openings.

27    Adjust the parking brake cable (see Chapter 9).

28    Lower the vehicle.

---

### 35   Cooling system servicing (draining, flushing and refilling) (every 30,000 or 24 months)

---

**Warning:** *Do not allow engine coolant (antifreeze) to come in contact with your skin or painted surfaces of the vehicle. Rinse off spills immediately with plenty of water. Antifreeze is highly toxic if ingested. Never leave antifreeze lying around in an open container or in puddles on the floor; children and pets are attracted by it's sweet smell and may drink it. Check with local authorities about disposing of used antifreeze. Many communities have collection centers which will see that antifreeze is disposed of safely.*

1    Periodically, the cooling system should be drained, flushed and refilled to replenish the antifreeze mixture and prevent formation of rust and corrosion, which can impair the performance of the cooling system and cause engine damage. When the cooling system is serviced, all hoses and the radiator cap should be checked and replaced, if necessary.

### Draining

*Refer to illustrations 35.5a and 35.5b*

2    At the same time the cooling system is serviced, all hoses and the

**34.13  If the lining is bonded to the brake shoe, measure the lining thickness from the outer surface to the metal shoe, as shown here; if the lining is riveted to the shoe, measure from the lining outer surface to the rivet head**

**34.15  Use a small screwdriver to carefully pry the boot away from the cylinder and check for fluid leakage**

**34.24  Use a thin screwdriver to carefully turn the brake adjuster wheel**

**35.5a  The drain fitting (arrow) is located at the bottom of the radiator**

**35.5b  To allow the system on fuel-injected engines to drain, remove the vacuum switch or bleeder plug (shown here) located on the thermostat housing**

radiator cap should be inspected and replaced if faulty (see Section 29).

3    With the engine cold, remove the radiator cap and set the heater control to Heat (Max).

4    Move a large container under the radiator to catch the coolant mixture as it's drained.

5    Open the drain fitting at the bottom of the radiator **(see illustration)**. Remove the vacuum switch or bleeder plug from the top of the thermostat housing on fuel-injected engines **(see illustration)**.

6    Disconnect the coolant reservoir hose, remove the reservoir and flush it with clean water.

7    Place a hose (a common garden hose is fine) in the radiator filler neck at the top of the radiator and flush the system until the water runs clear at all drain points.

**36.2  Tools needed to check and adjust the ignition timing**

1    **Vacuum plugs** - *Vacuum hoses will, in most cases, have to be disconnected and plugged. Molded plugs in various shapes and sizes are available for this*

2    **Inductive pick-up timing light -** *Flashes a bright, concentrated beam of light when the number one spark plug fires. Connect the leads according to the instructions supplied with the light*

3    **Distributor wrench** - *On some models, the hold-down bolt for the distributor is difficult to reach and turn with conventional wrenches or sockets. A special wrench like this must be used*

## Flushing

8    In severe cases of contamination or clogging of the radiator, remove it (see Chapter 3) and reverse flush it. This involves inserting the hose in the bottom radiator outlet to allow the clean water to run against the normal flow, draining through the top. A radiator repair shop should be consulted if further cleaning or repair is necessary.

9    Where the coolant is regularly drained and the system refilled with the correct antifreeze mixture there should be no need to employ chemical cleaners or descalers.

## Refilling

10   Install the coolant reservoir, reconnect the hoses and close the drain fitting.

11   Add coolant to the radiator. On fuel-injected engines, add coolant until it reaches the bottom of the threaded bleeder plug hole in the thermostat housing. Reinstall the plug or vacuum switch in the hole and tighten it securely. Continue adding coolant to the radiator until it reaches the radiator cap seat.

12   Add coolant to the reservoir until the level is between the MIN and MAX marks.

13   Run the engine until normal operating temperature is reached and, with the engine idling, add coolant up the correct level.

14   Always refill the system with a mixture of antifreeze and water in the proportion called for on the antifreeze container or in you owner's manual. Chapter 3 also contains information on antifreeze mixtures.

15   Keep a close watch on the coolant level and the various cooling system hoses during the first few miles of driving. Tighten the hose clamps and add more coolant mixture as necessary.

## 36   Ignition timing check and adjustment (every 30,000 miles or 24 months)

*Refer to illustrations 36.2, 36.5a, 36.5b and 36.12*

1    All vehicles are equipped with a Vehicle Emissions Control Information label inside the engine compartment. The label contains important ignition timing specifications and the proper timing procedure for your specific vehicle. If the information on the emissions label is different from the information included in this Section, follow the procedure on the label.

2    At the specified intervals, or when the distributor has been removed, the ignition timing must be checked and adjusted if necessary. Tools required for this procedure include an inductive pick-up timing light, a tachometer and a distributor wrench **(see illustration)**.

3    Before you check the timing, make sure the engine is at normal operating temperature.

4    Connect a timing light in accordance with the manufacturer's

**36.5a  The bellhousing window (2.2L and 2.5L engines) allows you to view the flywheel/driveplate notch (arrow) - mark this notch and the mark along side it on the window that corresponds to the number of degrees specified on the Vehicle Emissions Control Information label in the engine compartment**

**36.5b  On 2.6L four-cylinder engines, the timing marks are attached to the front of the engine and the crankshaft pulley has a groove in it for reference**

**36.12  On fuel-injected models, unplug the coolant sensor connector (arrow) before checking the ignition timing**

instructions. Usually, the light must be connected to the battery and the number one spark plug in some fashion. The number one spark plug wire or terminal should be marked at the distributor; trace it back to the spark plug and attach the timing light lead near the plug. **Caution:** *If an inductive pick-up timing light isn't available, don't puncture the spark plug wire to attach the timing light pick-up lead. Instead, use an adapter between the spark plug and plug wire. If the insulation on the plug wire is damaged, the secondary voltage will jump to ground at the damaged point and the engine will misfire.*

5      Locate the timing marks at the window in the transaxle bellhousing or front of the engine **(see illustrations)**.

6      Locate the notched groove across the flywheel/driveplate. It may be necessary to have an assistant temporarily turn the ignition on and off in short bursts without starting the engine in order to bring the groove into a position where it can easily be cleaned and marked. **Warning:** *Stay clear of all moving engine components when the engine is turned over in this manner.*

7      Use white chalk or paint to mark the groove in the flywheel **(see illustration 36.5a)**. Also, mark the number corresponding to the number of degrees specified on the Vehicle Emissions Control Information label in the engine compartment.

8      Connect a tachometer to the engine, setting the selector to the correct cylinder position.

9      Make sure the wiring for the timing light is clear of all moving engine components, then start the engine.

10      On 2.6L engines, disconnect the vacuum hose from the distributor and plug it.

11      On 2.2L carbureted engines, disconnect and plug the vacuum hose at the Spark Control Computer. If equipped with a carburetor switch, connect a jumper between the switch and a good ground.

12      On fuel-injected engines, disconnect the coolant temperature sensor connector (located on the thermostat housing) **(see illustration)**.

13      Aim the timing light at the marks, again being careful not to come into contact with moving parts. The marks you made should appear stationary. If the marks are in alignment, the timing is correct. If the marks are not aligned, turn off the engine.

14      Loosen the hold-down bolt at the base of the distributor. Loosen the bolt only slightly, just enough to turn the distributor (see Chapter 5).

15      Now restart the engine and turn the distributor very slowly until the timing marks are aligned.

16      Shut off the engine and tighten the distributor bolt, being careful not to move the distributor.

17      Start the engine and recheck the timing to make sure the marks are still in alignment. Reconnect the vacuum hoses or coolant temperature sensor.

## 37   Manual transaxle lubricant change (every 30,000 or 24 months)

1      Raise the front of the vehicle and support it securely on jackstands. Apply the parking brake.

2      If the transaxle is equipped with a drain plug, remove plug and drain fluid into a suitable container.

3      If not equipped with a drain plug, draw the fluid out through the fill plug opening with a suction syringe.

4      Replace the drain plug, if equipped, and tighten securely.

5      Fill the transaxle with the recommended lubricant (see *Recommended lubricants and fluids* at the beginning of this Chapter) until the level is at the bottom edge of the filler plug. Drive the vehicle and check the cover for leaks.

## 38   Differential lubricant change (1982 and earlier automatic transaxle models only) (every 30,000 miles or 24 months)

1      Raise the front of the vehicle and support it securely on jackstands.

2      Remove the differential fill plug (see Section 13).

3      Use a suction pump to remove the lubricant through the fill plug hole.

4      Fill the differential with the specified lubricant until the level is just below the fill hole and install the plug.

5      Lower the vehicle.

**39.3  Use a soft-face hammer to break the gasket seal at the corner of the pan so the fluid will drain out**

**39.4  A Torx-head tool may be required for removing the filter screws**

**39.8  Apply a 1/8-inch diameter bead of RTV sealant and install the pan before the sealant dries**

**40.7  Hold the screw so it can't turn and tighten the locknut with a box-end wrench**

## 39   Automatic transaxle fluid and filter change (every 30,000 miles or 24 months)

*Refer to illustrations 39.3, 39.4 and 39.8*

1   The automatic transaxle fluid and filter should be changed, the magnet cleaned and the bands adjusted at the recommended intervals.

2   Raise the front of the vehicle and support it securely on jack-stands. Apply the parking brake.

3   Position a container under the transaxle fluid pan. Loosen the pan bolts. Completely remove the bolts along the rear of the pan. Tap the corner of the pan **(see illustration)** to break the seal and allow the fluid to drain into the container (the remaining bolts will prevent the pan from separating from the transaxle). Remove the remaining bolts and detach the pan.

4   Remove the filter screws and detach the filter (a special Torx bit may be required for the screws) **(see illustration)**.

5   Refer to Section 40 and adjust the bands before proceeding with the fluid change.

6   Install the new gasket and filter. Tighten the filter screws securely.

7   Carefully remove all traces of old sealant from the pan and transaxle body (don't nick or gouge the sealing surfaces). Clean the magnet in the pan with a clean, lint-free cloth.

8   Apply a 1/8-inch bead of RTV sealant to the pan sealing surface and position it on the transaxle **(see illustration)**. Install the bolts and tighten them to the torque listed in this Chapter's Specifications following a criss-cross pattern. Work up to the final torque in three or four steps.

9   Lower the vehicle and add three quarts of the specified fluid (see Recommended lubricants and fluids at the beginning of this Chapter) to the transaxle. Start the engine and allow it to idle for at least two minutes, then move the shift lever through each of the gear positions, ending in Park or Neutral. Check for fluid leakage around the pan.

10   Add more fluid until the level is between the Add and Full marks. Add fluid a little at a time until it is (be careful not to overfill it).

11   Make sure the dipstick is seated completely or dirt could get into the transaxle.

## 40   Automatic transaxle band adjustment (three-speed models only) (every 30,000 miles or 24 months)

1   The transaxle bands should be adjusted when specified in the maintenance schedule or at the time of a fluid and filter change (see Section 39).

### Kickdown band

*Refer to illustration 40.7*

2   The kickdown band adjustment screw is located at the top left side of the transaxle case.

3   On some models the accelerator cable may interfere with band adjustment. If so, mark its position and then remove the accelerator cable adjustment bolt. Move the cable away from the band adjustment screw.

4   Loosen the locknut approximately five turns.

5   Make sure the adjusting screw turns freely.

6   Tighten the adjusting screw to the specified torque, then back the adjusting screw off the specified number of turns (see the Specifications Section at the beginning of this Chapter).

7   Hold the screw in position and tighten the locknut securely **(see illustration)**.

40.9  Low-Reverse band pressure plug location (arrow)

40.10  Insert feeler gauges between the Low-Reverse band end to measure wear - if the gap is less than 0.080-inch, a new band is needed

## Low-Reverse band

*Refer to illustrations 40.9, 40.10, 40.11a, 40.11b, 40.12, 40.13 and 40.15*

8    To gain access to the Low-Reverse band, the transaxle pan must be removed (see Section 39).

9    To determine if the band is worn excessively, remove the Low-Reverse pressure plug from the transaxle case **(see illustration)** and apply 30 psi of air pressure to the port.

10    Measure the gap between the band ends **(see illustration)**. It should be 0.080-inch minimum. If it's less than that, the band should be replaced with a new one.

11    To proceed with adjustment, pry off the parking rod E-clip and remove the rod **(see illustrations)**.

12    Loosen the locknut approximately five turns **(see illustration)**.

13    Use an inch-pound torque wrench to tighten the adjusting screw to the specified torque **(see illustration)**, then back the screw off the specified number of turns (see the Specifications Section at the beginning of this Chapter).

14    Hold the adjusting screw in position and tighten the locknut securely.

15    Push the shift pawl in the transaxle case to the rear and reinstall the parking rod **(see illustration)**.

16    Install the pan and refill the transaxle (see Section 39).

40.11a  Use a screwdriver to pry off the parking rod E-clip . . .

40.11b  . . . then lower the rod from the transaxle

40.12  Loosen the locknut the specified number of turns

**40.13  It may be necessary to use a universal joint between the socket and extension when tightening the Low-Reverse band adjusting screw**

**41.15  Push the shift pawl with your finger before inserting the parking rod**

## 41   Driveaxle boot check (every 30,000 miles or 24 months)

*Refer to illustration 41.3*

1    If the driveaxle boots are damaged or deteriorated, serious and costly damage can occur to the CV joints the boots are designed to protect. The boots should be inspected very carefully at the recommended intervals.

2    Raise the front of the vehicle and support it securely on jackstands (see *Jacking and towing* at the front of this manual if necessary).

3    Crawl under the vehicle and check the four driveaxle boots (two on each driveaxle) very carefully for cracks, tears, holes, deteriorated

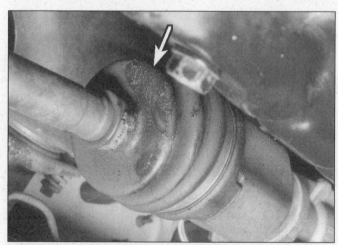

**41.3  Push on the boot to check for damage and look for signs of grease (arrow) indicating a leak**

rubber and loose or missing clamps **(see illustration)**. If the boots are dirty, wipe them clean before beginning the inspection.

4    If damage or deterioration is evident, replace the boots with new ones and check the CV joints for damage (see Chapter 8).

## 42   Evaporative emissions control system check (every 30,000 miles or 24 months)

1    The function of the evaporative emissions control system is to draw fuel vapors from the gas tank and fuel system, store them in a charcoal canister and route them to the intake manifold during normal engine operation.

2    The most common symptom of a fault in the evaporative emissions system is a strong fuel odor in the engine compartment. If a fuel odor is detected, inspect the charcoal canister, located in the engine compartment on the passenger's side, behind the headlight. Check the canister and all hoses for damage and deterioration.

3    The evaporative emissions control system is explained in more detail in Chapter 6.

## 43   Seat belt check (every 30,000 miles or 24 months)

1    Check the seat belts, buckles, latch plates and guide loops for obvious damage and signs of wear.

2    See if the seat belt reminder light comes on when the key is turned to the Run or Start positions. A chime should also sound.

3    The seat belts are designed to lock up during a sudden stop or impact, yet allow free movement during normal driving. Make sure the retractors return the belt against your chest while driving and rewind the belt fully when the buckle is unlatched.

4    If any of the above checks reveal problems with the seat belt system, replace parts as necessary.

# Notes

**2A-2**

**Oil pump**
Outer rotor-to...
Standar...
Servi...
Outer...

# Chapter 2 Part A
# 2.2L and 2.5L four-cylinder engines

## Contents

**2A**

## Specifications

### General

| | |
|---|---|
| Firing order | 1-3-4-2 |
| Cylinder numbers (drivebelt end-to-transaxle end) | 1-2-3-4 |
| Bore and stroke | |
| 2.2L | 3.44 x 3.62 inches |
| 2.5L | 3.44 x 4.09 inches |
| Displacement | |
| 2.2L | 135 cubic inches |
| 2.5L | 153 cubic inches |

### Camshaft

| | |
|---|---|
| Endplay | 0.005 to 0.013 inch |
| Runout | 0.0004 inch |
| Journal diameter | |
| Standard | 1.375 to 1.376 inch |
| Oversize | 1.395 to 1.396 inch |
| Lobe wear (maximum) | |
| 1984 and earlier | 0.005 inch |
| 1985 on | 0.010 inch |

### Cylinder head

| | |
|---|---|
| Warpage limit | 0.004 inch |

### Intake/exhaust manifolds

| | |
|---|---|
| Warpage limit | 0.008 inch per foot of manifold length |

**Cylinder location and distributor rotation**

...housing clearance

  ...d ............................................................ 0.010 inch

  ...ce limit .................................................... 0.014 inch

...rotor thickness

  1985 and earlier

    Standard ...................................................... 0.826 to 0.827 inch

    Service limit................................................... 0.825 inch

  1986 on

    Standard ...................................................... 0.944 to 0.945 inch

    Service limit................................................... 0.9435 inch

Inner rotor-to-outer rotor tip clearance

  1985 and earlier

    Standard ...................................................... 0.010 inch

    Service limit................................................... 0.010 inch

  1986 on

    Standard ...................................................... 0.004 inch

    Service limit................................................... 0.008 inch

Inner and outer rotor-to-housing clearance

  Standard .......................................................... 0.001 to 0.003 inch

  Service limit ..................................................... 0.0035 inch

Pump cover flatness

  1985 and earlier

    Standard ...................................................... 0.010 inch maximum

    Service limit................................................... 0.015 inch

  1986 on

    Standard ...................................................... 0.002 inch maximum

    Service limit................................................... 0.003 inch

Relief spring free length ........................................ 1.95 inch

## Torque specifications

**Ft-lbs** (unless otherwise indicated)

Camshaft bearing cap bolts

  1987 and earlier.............................................. 165 in-lbs

  1988 on ........................................................... 215 in-lbs

Valve cover bolts/nuts .......................................... 105 in-lbs

Timing belt tensioner bolt .................................... 45

Camshaft sprocket bolt ........................................ 65

Crankshaft pulley Torx head bolts........................ 250 in-lbs

Crankshaft pulley center bolt................................ 50

Cylinder head bolts - engine cold *(use the tightening sequence shown in Section 12)*

  1985 and earlier

    Step 1............................................................ 30

    Step 2............................................................ 45

    Step 3............................................................ 45

    Step 4............................................................ Tighten an additional 1/4-turn

  1986 on

    Step 1............................................................ 45

    Step 2............................................................ 65

    Step 3............................................................ 65

    Step 4............................................................ Tighten an additional 1/4-turn

Driveplate-to-crankshaft bolts

  M10 ................................................................. 70

  M12 ................................................................. 100

Flywheel-to-crankshaft bolts

  1985 and earlier.............................................. 65

  1986 on ........................................................... 70

Crankshaft front oil seal housing bolts ................ 105 in-lbs

Intake/exhaust manifold nuts/bolts ... ................. 16

Intermediate shaft oil seal housing bolts ............ 105 in-lbs

Intermediate shaft sprocket bolt.......................... 65

Oil pan-to-engine block fasteners

  M8 ................................................................... 16

  M6 ................................................................... 105 in-lbs

Oil pick-up tube-to-oil pump housing bolt ........... 16

Oil pump mounting bolts ...................................... 21

Oil pump cover bolts ............................................ 105 in-lbs

Oil pan drain plug ................................................ 20

Rear main oil seal housing bolts.......................... 105 in-lbs

Timing belt cover bolts ........................................ 40 in-lbs

Water pump hub bolt............................................ 21

3.6  Use a felt tip marker or chalk to mark the distributor housing directly beneath the number one spark plug wire terminal

## 1  General information

This Part of Chapter 2 is devoted to in-vehicle repair procedures for the 2.2L and 2.5L engines. All information concerning engine removal and installation and engine block and cylinder head overhaul can be found in Part C of this Chapter.

The following repair procedures are based on the assumption that the engine is installed in the vehicle. If the engine has been removed from the vehicle and mounted on a stand, many of the steps outlined in this Part of Chapter 2 will not apply.

The Specifications included in this Part of Chapter 2 apply only to the procedures contained in this Part. Part C of Chapter 2 contains the Specifications necessary for cylinder head and engine block rebuilding.

## 2  Repair operations possible with the engine in the vehicle

Many major repair operations can be accomplished without removing the engine from the vehicle.

Clean the engine compartment and the exterior of the engine with some type of degreaser before any work is done. It will make the job easier and help keep dirt out of the internal areas of the engine.

Depending on the components involved, it may be helpful to remove the hood to improve access to the engine as repairs are performed (refer to Chapter 11 if necessary). Cover the fenders to prevent damage to the paint. Special pads are available, but an old bedspread or blanket will also work.

If vacuum, exhaust, oil or coolant leaks develop, indicating a need for gasket or seal replacement, the repairs can generally be made with

3.8  When you're bringing the number one piston to TDC, look at the timing mark on the flywheel/driveplate through the opening in the bellhousing, and align the mark with the 0-degree mark on the bellhousing - you may have to remove a plug from the bellhousing to see the flywheel

the engine in the vehicle. The intake and exhaust manifold gaskets, oil pan gasket, crankshaft oil seals and cylinder head gasket are all accessible with the engine in place.

Exterior engine components, such as the intake and exhaust manifolds, the oil pan (and the oil pump), the water pump, the starter motor, the alternator, the distributor and the fuel system components can be removed for repair with the engine in place.

Since the cylinder head can be removed without pulling the engine, camshaft and valve component servicing can also be accomplished with the engine in the vehicle. Replacement of the timing belt and sprockets is also possible with the engine in the vehicle.

In extreme cases caused by a lack of necessary equipment, repair or replacement of piston rings, pistons, connecting rods and rod bearings is possible with the engine in the vehicle. However, this practice is not recommended because of the cleaning and preparation work that must be done to the components involved.

## 3  Top Dead Center (TDC) for number one piston - locating

*Refer to illustrations 3.6 and 3.8*

**Note:** *The following procedure is based on the assumption that the spark plug wires and distributor are correctly installed. If you are trying to locate TDC to install the distributor correctly, piston position must be determined by feeling for compression at the number one spark plug hole, then aligning the ignition timing marks as described in Step 8. In the event of timing belt breakage, remove the timing belt cover and align the marks on the camshaft sprocket as shown in illustration 6.19, then align the mark on the flywheel with the correct mark on the timing scale as directed in Step 4.*

1    Top Dead Center (TDC) is the highest point in the cylinder that each piston reaches as it travels up-and-down when the crankshaft turns. Each piston reaches TDC on the compression stroke and again on the exhaust stroke, but TDC generally refers to piston position on the compression stroke.

2    Positioning the piston(s) at TDC is an essential part of many procedures such as camshaft and timing belt/sprocket removal and distributor removal.

3    Before beginning this procedure, be sure to place the transmission in Neutral and apply the parking brake or block the rear wheels. Also, disable the ignition system by detaching the coil wire from the center terminal of the distributor cap and grounding it on the block with a jumper wire. Remove the spark plugs (see Chapter 1).

4    In order to bring any piston to TDC, the crankshaft must be turned using one of the methods outlined below. When looking at the front of the engine, normal crankshaft rotation is clockwise.

a) *The preferred method is to turn the crankshaft with a socket and ratchet attached to the bolt threaded into the front of the crankshaft.*

b) *A remote starter switch, which may save some time, can also be used. Follow the instructions included with the switch. Once the piston is close to TDC, use a socket and ratchet as described in the previous paragraph.*

c) *If an assistant is available to turn the ignition switch to the Start position in short bursts, you can get the piston close to TDC without a remote starter switch. Make sure your assistant is out of the vehicle, away from the ignition switch, then use a socket and ratchet as described in Paragraph a) to complete the procedure.*

5    Note the position of the terminal for the number one spark plug wire on the distributor cap. If the terminal isn't marked, follow the plug wire from the number one cylinder spark plug to the cap.

6    Use a felt-tip pen or chalk to make a mark on the distributor body directly under the terminal **(see illustration)**.

7    Detach the cap from the distributor and set it aside (see Chapter 1 if necessary).

8    Locate the round window in the bellhousing. You'll see the timing increments on the edge of the window. Turn the crankshaft (see Step 4) until the TDC mark (zero) on the edge of the bellhousing is aligned with the groove in the flywheel **(see illustration)**.

9     Look at the distributor rotor - it should be pointing directly at the mark you made on the distributor body. If the rotor is pointing at the mark, go to Step 12. If it isn't, go to Step 10.

10    If the rotor is 180-degrees off, the number one piston is at TDC on the exhaust stroke.

11    To get the piston to TDC on the .compression stroke, turn the crankshaft one complete turn (360-degrees) clockwise. The rotor should now be pointing at the mark on the distributor. When the rotor is pointing at the number one spark plug wire terminal in the distributor cap and the ignition timing marks are aligned, the number one piston is at TDC on the compression stroke.

12    After the number one piston has been positioned at TDC on the compression stroke, TDC for any of the remaining pistons can be located by turning the crankshaft and following the firing order. Mark the remaining spark plug wire terminal locations on the distributor body just like you did for the number one terminal, then number the marks to correspond with the cylinder numbers. As you turn the crank-shaft, the rotor will also turn. When it's pointing directly at one of the marks on the distributor, the piston for that particular cylinder is at TDC on the compression stroke.

---

## 4     Valve cover - removal and installation

---

### *Removal*

*Refer to illustrations 4.4a, 4.4b, 4.5 and 4.6*

1     Detach the cable from the negative battery terminal.

2     Detach the accelerator cable from the cable bracket.

3     Wipe off the valve cover thoroughly to prevent debris from falling onto the exposed cylinder head or camshaft/valve train assembly.

4     Remove the upper half of the timing belt cover (see Section 6). Remove the valve cover bolts **(see illustrations)**.

5     Carefully lift off the valve cover and gasket. If the gasket is stuck to the cylinder head, use a putty knife or flat-bladed screwdriver to remove it **(see illustration)**. Set the cover aside.

6     If the vehicle is fuel-injected, you'll note a "curtain" (baffle for enhancing air/oil separation) under the valve cover. If you're simply replacing a leaking valve cover gasket, you don't need to remove the curtain. If you want to adjust the valves or service the camshaft assem-bly or cylinder head, remove the curtain **(see illustration)**. Don't lose the two small rubber "bumpers" which act as cushions between the curtain and the valve cover.

### *Installation*

*Refer to illustrations 4.9a and 4.9b*

7     Make sure the gasket mating surfaces of the cylinder head and the valve cover are clean. **Note:** *Chrysler Corporation states that all*

**4.4a  Typical valve cover and related components**

**4.4b  Remove the valve cover bolts (arrows)**

*1989 and 1990 vehicles equipped with a 2.2L or 2.5L engine must have the valve cover changed if it continues to leak oil. The updated valve cover uses RTV sealant instead of a gasket. The new cover also includes all new bolts (shorter length) and washers. The parts are only available at a dealer parts department.*

8     If the engine is equipped with a curtain (and it has been removed),

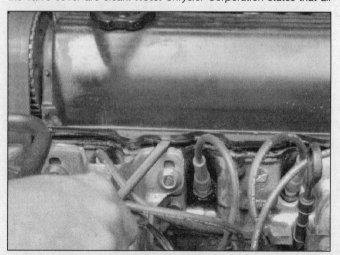

**4.5  Carefully pry the valve cover off the cylinder head - be careful not to bend the rails, which could cause oil leaks later on**

**4.6  Lift the curtain off the cylinder head**

**4.9a  Use a small pair of pliers to pull the tabs (arrows) through the housing, insuring the seal is flush against the valve**

**4.9b  Apply a small amount of RTV sealant to the corners of the cylinder head to prevent oil leaks**

install it now, manifold side first, with the cutouts over the cam towers and contacting the cylinder head floor, then press the opposite (distributor) side into position below the gasket mating surface. Be sure to install the rubber bumpers on top of the curtain.

9    Install new gaskets on the valve cover **(see illustration 12.8a)**. Install the molded rubber gaskets to the ends of the cover by pushing the tabs through the slots in the cover **(see illustration)**. Apply a 1/8-inch wide bead of RTV sealant to the cylinder head rail in the area indicated **(see illustration)**. Install the cover and bolts and tighten the bolts to the torque listed in this Chapter's Specifications.

10    The remainder of installation is the reverse of removal.

## 5    Intake/exhaust manifold - removal and installation

**Warning:** *Gasoline is extremely flammable, so take extra precautions when you work on any part of the fuel system. Don't smoke or allow open flames or bare light bulbs near the work area, and don't work in a garage where a natural gas-type appliance (such as a water heater or clothes dryer) with a pilot light is present. If you spill any fuel on your skin, rinse it off immediately with soap and water. When you perform any kind of work on the fuel system, wear safety glasses and have a Class B type fire extinguisher on hand.*
**Note:** *On these models the throttle body assembly and intake manifold must be removed as a unit before the exhaust manifold can be removed.*

### Removal

*Refer to illustrations 5.15a, 5.15b and 5.18*

1    Relieve the fuel system pressure (see Chapter 4).
2    Detach the cable from the negative battery terminal.
3    Drain the cooling system (see Chapter 1).
4    Remove the air cleaner and the air heater hose (see Chapter 4).
5    Clearly label and detach all vacuum lines, electrical wiring and fuel lines.
6    Detach the accelerator cable from the throttle linkage (see Chapter 4).
7    Loosen the power steering pump (if equipped) and remove the drivebelt (see Chapter 1).
8    Detach the power brake vacuum hose from the intake manifold.
9    If you're working on a Canadian model engine, remove the coupling hose from the air injection tube.
10    Remove the water hoses from the coolant crossover lines.
11    Raise the front of the vehicle and support it securely on jackstands. Detach the exhaust pipe from the exhaust manifold.
12    Remove the power steering pump (if equipped) and set it aside (see Chapter 10).
13    Remove the intake manifold support bracket and detach the EGR tube from the exhaust manifold.
14    If you're working on a Canadian model with a 2.2L engine, remove the air injection tube assembly.
15    Remove the intake manifold fasteners **(see illustrations)**.

**5.15a  Intake and exhaust manifold bolt locations**

**5.15b  Intake manifold fasteners (2.2L engine shown)**

**5.18  Exhaust manifold fasteners (2.2L engine shown)**

**6.3  Crankshaft and water pump pulley - exploded view**

16   Lower the vehicle.

17   If you're working on a TBI engine:

a) *Remove the throttle body and the intake manifold as a single assembly.*

b) *Detach the throttle body and gasket from the intake manifold (see Chapter 4) after the unit is on the bench.*

18   Remove the exhaust manifold nuts **(see illustration)** and detach the exhaust manifold. Discard the old gaskets and clean all gasket mating surfaces.

19   Clean the manifolds with solvent and dry them with compressed air.

20   Check the mating surfaces of the manifolds for flatness with a precision straightedge and feeler gauges. Refer to this Chapter's Specifications for the warpage limit.

21   Inspect the manifolds for cracks and distortion.

22   If the manifolds are cracked or warped, replace them or see if they can be resurfaced/repaired at an automotive machine shop.

## Installation

23   If you're replacing either manifold, transfer the studs from the old manifold to the new one.

24   When working on a TBI engine:

a) *Apply a thin coat of gasket sealant to the manifold sides of the new gaskets and place them in position on the manifolds.*

b) *Place the exhaust manifold in position on the cylinder head and install the nuts. Starting at the center, tighten the nuts in a criss-cross pattern until the torque listed in this Chapter's Specifications is reached.*

c) *Position the intake manifold on the head.*

d) *Raise the vehicle and support it securely on jackstands.*

e) *Working under the vehicle, install the intake manifold bolts finger tight. Starting at the center and working out in both directions, tighten the bolts in a criss-cross pattern until the torque listed in this Chapter's Specifications is reached.*

25   The remainder of the installation procedure is the reverse of removal.

## 6   Timing belt and sprockets - removal, inspection and installation

### Timing belt removal

*Refer to illustrations 6.3, 6.4, 6.5, 6.6a, 6.6b, 6.6c, 6.6d, 6.7, 6.8a, 6.8b and 6.8c*

1   Position the number one piston at TDC on the compression stroke (see Section 3), then detach the cable from the negative battery terminal.

**6.4  Raise the vehicle and detach the right inner splash shield to remove the crankshaft pulley**

**6.5  Remove the four Torx head bolts (arrows) from the crankshaft pulley**

6.6a Remove the two bolts (arrows) that secure the timing belt upper cover to the valve cover

6.6b Remove the bolts from the timing belt lower cover (arrows) - the third bolt is located behind the water pump

2   Remove all accessory drivebelts (see Chapter 1).

3   Remove the bolts and detach the water pump pulley **(see illustration)**.

4   Raise the vehicle, support it securely on jackstands and remove the right inner splash shield **(see illustration)**.

5   Remove the crankshaft pulley bolts **(see illustration)**. Remove the crankshaft pulley.

6   Remove the screws and nuts holding the timing belt cover to the cylinder head and block **(see illustrations)**. Remove both halves of the timing belt cover. Also remove the engine mount closest to the cover **(see illustration)**. Use a block of wood and a floor jack positioned under the transaxle to keep the engine level while the engine mount is removed.

7   Check to make sure the number one piston is still at Top Dead Center on the compression stroke. The marks on the crankshaft and intermediate shaft sprocket will be aligned **(see illustration)** and the arrows on the camshaft sprocket will line up with the bearing cap parting line **(see illustration 6.19)**.

8   Use a wrench to loosen the center bolt of the belt tensioner, releasing the tension from the timing belt. Remove the belt and the ten-

6.6c Remove the fasteners and detach the two halves of the timing belt cover

6.6d Remove the bolts (arrows) and separate the engine mount from the chassis (the rear bolt is hidden from view)

6.7 If you have correctly positioned the number one piston at TDC, the marks on the crankshaft and intermediate shaft sprockets will be aligned

6.8a  Loosen the tensioner locking bolt and remove the tensioner

6.8b  Remove the bolts (arrows) and the air conditioning compressor bracket from the engine

sioner (see illustrations). Note: *If the engine is equipped with air conditioning, remove the air conditioning compressor (see Chapter 3) and the bracket* (see illustration).

### Timing belt, tensioner and sprocket inspection

*Refer to illustration 6.10*

9    Rotate the tensioner pulley by hand and move it side-to-side to detect roughness and excessive play. Replace it if it doesn't turn smoothly or if play is noted.

10    Inspect the timing belt for cracks, wear, signs of stretching, ply separation and damaged or missing teeth. Look for contamination by oil, gasoline, coolant and other liquids, which could damage the belt (see illustration). Replace the belt if it's worn or damaged. **Note:** *Unless the engine has very low mileage, it's common practice to replace the timing belt with a new one every time it's removed. Don't reinstall the original belt unless it's in like-new condition. Never reinstall a belt in questionable condition.*

11    Visually inspect the sprockets for wear and damage. If any of the sprockets are damaged or worn, replace them.

12    Inspect the area directly below each sprocket for leaking engine oil. If there is oil below a sprocket, the seal behind that sprocket is leaking and must be replaced (see Sections 7, 8 and 9).

6.8c  Timing belt and related components

6.10 Carefully inspect the timing bolt for the conditions shown here

6.13 A pin spanner (or homemade substitute like the one shown here) will hold the intermediate shaft sprocket while the bolt is loosened

## Sprocket removal and installation

*Refer to illustrations 6.13, 6.14, 6.16 and 6.19*

13   Remove the intermediate shaft sprocket bolt while holding the sprocket with a pin spanner or a homemade substitute **(see illustration)**. Pull the sprocket off the shaft.

14   Remove the bolt and use a puller to remove the crankshaft sprocket **(see illustration)**.

15   Hold the camshaft sprocket as described in Step 13 and remove the bolt, then detach the sprocket from the cam.

16   Make sure the Woodruff keys are in place, then install the crankshaft and intermediate shaft sprockets. Turn the shafts until the marks are aligned **(see illustration)**.

17   Install the crankshaft sprocket bolt, lock the crankshaft to keep it from rotating and tighten the bolt to the torque listed in this Chapter's Specifications.

18   Install the intermediate shaft sprocket bolt and tighten it to the torque listed in this Chapter's Specifications. Double-check to make sure the marks are aligned as shown in **illustration 6.16**.

19   Install the camshaft sprocket and bolt. Tighten the bolt to the torque listed in this Chapter's Specifications. The triangles on the sprocket hub must align with the camshaft bearing cap parting line **(see illustration)**.

## Timing belt installation

*Refer to illustrations 6.23 and 6.25*

20   When installing the timing belt, the marks on the sprockets MUST BE ALIGNED as described in Steps 16 and 19.

21   Install the timing belt without turning any of the sprockets.

22   Install the tensioner pulley with the bolt finger tight.

6.14 Use a puller to get the crankshaft sprocket off

6.16 Use a straight edge to make sure the marks (dimples) line up with the centers of the sprocket bolt holes

6.19 The small hole must be at the top (arrow) and the triangles on the camshaft sprocket must be aligned with the bearing cap parting lines (arrows)

**6.23  Use a ruler to measure timing belt deflection**

**6.25  To check the camshaft timing when the timing belt is installed, bring the number one piston to TDC on the compression stroke and verify the small hole in the camshaft sprocket is aligned with the hole in the cover**

**7.2  Wrap tape around the end of a small screwdriver and pry the seal out of the housing**

23    With the help of an assistant, apply tension to the timing belt and temporarily tighten the tensioner bolt. Measure the deflection of the belt half-way between the camshaft sprocket and tensioner pulley. Adjust the tensioner until belt deflection is approximately 5/16-inch **(see illustration)**.

24    Turn the crankshaft two complete revolutions in a clockwise direction (viewed from the front). This will align the belt on the pulleys. Recheck the belt deflection and tighten the tensioner pulley. **Note:** *When tightening the tensioner, use two wrenches. One wrench must keep the large hex surface in a stationary position (adjusted position) while the other wrench tightens the smaller bolt (locking bolt).*

25    Recheck the camshaft timing mark with the timing belt cover installed and the number one piston at TDC on the compression stroke. The small hole in the camshaft sprocket must be centered in the timing belt cover hole **(see illustration)**.

26    The remainder of installation is the reverse of removal.

## 7    Camshaft oil seal - replacement

*Refer to illustrations 7.2 and 7.5*

1    Remove the timing belt and camshaft sprocket (see Section 6).

2    Wrap the tip of a small screwdriver with tape and use it to carefully pry out the seal. Don't nick or scratch the camshaft journal or

the new seal will leak **(see illustration)**.

3    Thoroughly clean and inspect the seal bore and the seal journal on the camshaft. Both must be clean and smooth. Use emery cloth or 400-grit sandpaper to remove small burrs.

4    If a groove has been worn into the journal on the camshaft (from contact with the seal lip), installing a new seal probably won't stop the leak. Such wear normally indicates the camshaft or the bearing surfaces in the caps are worn. It's probably time to overhaul the cylinder head (see Chapter 2, Part E) or replace the head or camshaft.

5    Coat the lip of the new seal with clean engine oil or multi-purpose grease and carefully tap the seal into place with a large socket or piece of pipe and a hammer. If you don't have a socket as large in diameter as the seal, tap around the outer edge of the seal with the large end of a punch **(see illustration)**.

6    Install the camshaft sprocket and timing belt (see Section 6).

7    Start the engine and check for oil leaks.

## 8    Intermediate shaft oil seal - replacement

*Refer to illustrations 8.3 and 8.7*

1    Drain the engine oil (see Chapter 1).

2    Remove the timing belt and intermediate shaft sprocket (see Section 6).

**7.5  If you don't have a socket large enough to drive in the new seal, tap around the outer edge with the large end of the punch**

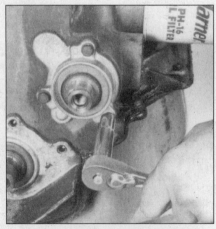

**8.3  Remove the bolts and detach the seal housing**

**8.7  Using a soft-face hammer, carefully tap the new seal into the housing**

9.5 **Remove the bolts and detach the housing/seal assembly**

9.9 **Tap the new crankshaft oil seal into the housing with a soft-face hammer**

3    Remove the oil seal housing **(see illustration)**.
4    Pry the old seal out of the housing with a screwdriver (wrap the tip of the screwdriver with tape). Make sure you don't scratch the seal bore.
5    Thoroughly clean and inspect the seal bore and the seal journal on the intermediate shaft. Both must be clean and smooth. Remove small burrs with emery cloth or 400-grit sandpaper.
6    If a groove has been worn in the seal journal (from contact with the seal lip), installing a new seal probably won't stop the leak. Such wear normally indicates the intermediate shaft or shaft bearing surfaces in the engine block are worn. It's probably time to overhaul the engine (see Chapter 2, Part C).
7    Using a soft-face hammer, carefully tap the new seal into the housing **(see illustration)**.
8    Coat the lip of the seal with clean engine oil or multi-purpose grease and install the housing and seal on the front of the engine block. Make sure you don't damage the seal lip. Install the housing bolts and tighten them to the torque listed in this Chapter's Specifications.
9    Install the intermediate shaft sprocket and the timing belt (see Section 6).
10    Check the engine oil level and add oil, if necessary (see Chapter 1).
11    Start the engine and check for oil leaks.

## 9   Crankshaft front oil seal - replacement

*Refer to illustrations 9.5 and 9.9*
1    Drain the engine oil (see Chapter 1).
2    Remove the timing belt and crankshaft sprocket (see Section 6).
3    Raise the front of the vehicle and support it securely on jackstands.
4    Remove the oil pan (see Section 13). **Note:** *It is possible to remove the seal without removing the oil pan, if a special seal puller tool is used.*
5    Working underneath the vehicle, remove the bolts and detach the

oil seal housing **(see illustration)**.
6    Use a punch and hammer to drive the old seal out of the housing. Make sure you don't damage the seal bore. To prevent this, wrap the tip of the punch with tape.
7    Thoroughly clean the seal bore in the housing and the seal journal on the end of the crankshaft. Remove small burrs with emery cloth or 400-grit sandpaper.
8    If a groove has been worn in the seal journal on the crankshaft (from contact with the seal lip), installing a new seal probably won't stop the leak. Such wear normally indicates the crankshaft and/or the main bearings are excessively worn. It's probably time to overhaul the engine (see Chapter 2, Part C).
9    Apply a thin coat of RTV sealant to the surface of the seal bore, lay the housing on a clean, flat work surface, position the new seal in the bore and tap it into place with a soft-face hammer **(see illustration)**. Make sure the seal lip faces the proper direction (towards the engine).
10    Lubricate the seal lip with multi-purpose grease and apply a 1 mm wide bead of anaerobic gasket sealant to the engine block mating surface of the seal housing. Position the housing on the engine. Install the retaining bolts and tighten them to the torque listed in this Chapter's Specifications.
11    Reinstall the crankshaft sprocket, timing belt and related components.
12    Install the oil pan (see Section 13).
13    Check the engine oil level and add oil, if necessary (see Chapter 1).
14    Start the engine, let it warm up and check for leaks.

## 10   Camshaft and hydraulic lash adjusters/rocker arms - removal, inspection and installation

**Note:** *It is possible to remove the rocker arms and lash adjusters without removing the camshaft (see Section 11 for details)*

### Removal
*Refer to illustrations 10.3, 10.5, 10.6 and 10.8*
1    Remove the valve cover (see Section 4).
2    Remove the timing belt cover, timing belt and camshaft sprocket (see Section 6). **Note:** *If you want to save time by not removing and installing the timing belt, you can unfasten the camshaft sprocket and suspend it out of the way - with the belt still attached - on a piece of wire. Be sure the wire maintains tension on the belt so it won't disengage any of the sprockets.*
3    The camshaft rides on five bearings. Each bearing cap is held by two fasteners. On some engines, the bearing caps are numbered from 1 to 5, beginning at the drivebelt end of the engine **(see illustration)**.

**10.3  The camshaft bearing caps are numbered from 1 to 5 (arrow) so they don't get mixed up - if the caps aren't numbered, mark them (they must be reinstalled in their original positions)**

**Note:** *All numbers face either the spark plug or manifold side of the engine. This is to ensure you install the caps facing the right direction.*

4     On some engines, the bearing caps aren't numbered. If this is the case, you must mark them before removal. Be sure to put the marks on the same ends of all the caps to prevent incorrect orientation of the caps during installation.

5     Also mark the rocker arms **(see illustration)** to ensure they're installed in the same position during reassembly.

6     Remove the bolts from all the bearing caps **(see illustration)** except cap numbers 2 and 4. Next, loosen each of the four fasteners on 2 and 4 a little at a time to relieve valve spring tension evenly until the caps are loose. If any of the caps stick, gently tap them with a soft-face hammer. **Caution:** *Failure to follow this procedure exactly as described could tilt the camshaft in the housing, which could damage the housing or bend the camshaft.*

7     Lift out the camshaft, wipe it off with a clean shop towel and set it aside.

8     Lift out each rocker arm and lash adjuster **(see illustration)**, wipe them off and set them aside in labeled plastic bags or an egg carton.

### Inspection

*Refer to illustrations 10.9 and 10.12*

9     To check camshaft endplay:
a)  *Install the camshaft and secure it with caps 1 and 5.*

**10.5  Mark the rocker arms and lash adjusters before removing them**

b)  *Mount a dial indicator on the head (see illustration).*
c)  *Using a large screwdriver as a lever at the opposite end, move the camshaft forward-and-backward and note the dial indicator reading.*
d)  *Compare the reading with the endplay listed in this Chapter's Specifications.*
e)  *If the indicated reading is higher, either the camshaft or the head is worn. Replace parts as necessary.*

10    To check camshaft runout:
a)  *Support the camshaft with a pair of V-blocks and attach a dial indicator with the stem resting against the center bearing journal on the camshaft.*
b)  *Rotate the camshaft and note the indicated runout.*
c)  *Compare the results to the camshaft runout listed in this Chapter's Specifications.*
d)  *If the indicated runout exceeds the specified runout, replace the camshaft.*

11    Check the camshaft bearing journals and caps for scoring and signs of wear. If they are worn, replace the cylinder head with a new or rebuilt unit. Measure the journals on the camshaft with a micrometer, comparing your readings with this Chapter's Specifications. If the diameter of any of the journals is out of specification, replace the camshaft. **Note:** *When servicing the camshaft or cylinder head, it is necessary to be certain that oversized camshafts are used only with oversized journals. Cylinder heads with oversized journals can be iden-*

**10.6  Remove the bolts (arrows) from the camshaft bearing caps**

**10.8  The lash adjusters should slide out easily if they aren't coated with varnish**

**10.9 To check camshaft endplay, set up a dial indicator like this, with gauge plunger touching the nose of the camshaft - pry the camshaft back-and-forth and note the reading on the dial indicator**

**10.12 Measure the height of the camshaft lobes at the wear zone and unworn area, then subtract the wear zone measurement from the unworn area measurement to get the actual wear - compare the wear to the limit listed in this Chapter's Specifications**

tified by green paint on the tops of the camshaft bearing caps and OS/J stamped to the rear of the oil gallery plug on the air pump end of the cylinder head. Camshafts with oversized journals are identified by green paint on the barrel of the shaft and OS/J stamped on the end of the shaft.

12  Check the cam lobes for wear:

a) *Check the toe and ramp areas of each cam lobe for score marks and uneven wear. Also check for flaking and pitting.*

b) *If there's wear on the toe or the ramp, replace the camshaft, but first try to find the cause of the wear. Check the lash adjusters, look for abrasive substances in the oil and inspect the oil pump and oil passages for blockage. Lobe wear is usually caused by inadequate lubrication or dirty oil.*

c) *Using a micrometer, calculate the lobe wear* **(see illustration)**. *If the lobe wear is greater than listed in this Chapter's Specifications, replace the camshaft.*

13  Inspect the rocker arms and hydraulic lash adjusters for wear, galling and pitting of the contact surfaces.

14  If any of the conditions described above are noted, the cylinder head is probably getting insufficient lubrication or dirty oil, so make sure you track down the cause of this problem (low oil level, low oil pump capacity, clogged oil passage, etc.) before installing a new head, camshaft or followers.

## Installation

*Refer to illustrations 10.17, 10.20 and 10.21*

15  Thoroughly clean the camshaft, the bearing surfaces in the head and caps, the rocker arms and hydraulic lash adjusters. Remove all sludge and dirt. Wipe off all components with a clean, lint-free cloth.

16  Lubricate the lash adjuster and the contact surfaces on the top of the rocker arms with assembly lube or moly-base grease. Install the lash adjusters and rocker arms, making sure you put them in their original locations.

17  Lubricate the camshaft bearing surfaces in the head and the bearing journals and lobes on the camshaft with assembly lube or moly-base grease. Carefully lower the camshaft into position with the lobes for the number one cylinder pointing away from the rocker arms **(see illustration)**. **Caution:** *Failure to adequately lubricate the camshaft and related components can cause serious damage to bearing and friction surfaces during the first few seconds after engine start-up, when the oil pressure is low or nonexistent.*

18  Apply a thin coat of assembly lube or moly-base grease to the bearing surfaces of the camshaft bearing caps and install the caps in their original locations.

19  Install the bolts for bearing caps 2 and 4. Gradually tighten all four fasteners - 1/4-turn at a time - until the camshaft is drawn down and seated in the bearing saddles. Don't tighten the fasteners completely at this time.

20  Apply anaerobic-type sealant to the contact surfaces of bearing caps 1 and 5 **(see illustration)**.

21  Install bearing caps 3 and 5 **(see illustration)** and tighten the fasteners the same way you did for caps 2 and 4.

**10.17 Install the camshaft with the lobes pointing away from the number one cylinder intake and exhaust valves**

**10.20 Apply anaerobic-type gasket sealant to the dark areas only on the front and rear camshaft bearing caps**

**10.21 Apply RTV sealant to the outer circumference of the camshaft rear plug before installing the number 5 cap**

**11.4 This is what the air hose adapter that threads into the spark plug hole looks like - they're commonly available from auto parts stores**

**11.5 Using this tool, the valve springs can be depressed and the rocker arms removed without removing the camshaft - this is also the preferred type of spring compressor to use when removing the valve keepers**

22 Install a new oil seal on the front of the camshaft, then install bearing cap 1. Don't tighten the fasteners completely at this time.

23 Remove any excess sealant from the two end bearing caps.

24 Working in a criss-cross pattern, tighten the fasteners for bearing caps 2 and 4 to the torque listed in this Chapter's Specifications. Then tighten the fasteners for bearing caps 3 and 5 the same way. Finally, tighten the fasteners for bearing cap 1.

25 Install the camshaft sprocket, timing belt, timing belt cover and related components (see Section 6). If you suspended the camshaft sprocket out of the way and didn't disturb the timing belt or sprockets, the valve timing should still be correct. Rotate the camshaft as necessary to reattach the sprocket to the camshaft. If the valve timing was disturbed, align the sprockets and install the belt as described in Section 6.

26 Remove the spark plugs and rotate the crankshaft by hand to make sure the valve timing is correct. After two revolutions, the timing marks on the sprockets should still be aligned. If they're not, re-index the timing belt to the sprockets (see Section 6). **Note:** *If you feel resistance while rotating the crankshaft, stop immediately and check the valve timing by referring to Section 6.*

## 11 Valve springs, retainers and seals - replacement

*Refer to illustrations 11.4, 11.5, 11.9, 11.15 and 11.17*

**Note:** *Broken valve springs and defective valve stem seals can be replaced without removing the cylinder heads. Two special tools and a compressed air source are normally required to perform this operation, so read through this Section carefully and rent or buy the tools before beginning the job. If compressed air isn't available, a length of nylon rope can be used to keep the valves from falling into the cylinder during this procedure.*

1 Refer to Section 4 and remove the valve cover.

2 Remove the spark plug from the cylinder which has the defective component. If all of the valve stem seals are being replaced, all of the spark plugs should be removed.

3 Turn the crankshaft until the piston in the affected cylinder is at top dead center on the compression stroke (see Section 3 for instructions). If you're replacing all of the valve stem seals, begin with cylinder number one and work on the valves for one cylinder at a time. Move from cylinder-to-cylinder following the firing order sequence (see the Specifications).

4 Thread an adapter into the spark plug hole and connect an air hose from a compressed air source to it **(see illustration)**. Most auto parts stores can supply the air hose adapter. **Note:** *Many cylinder compression gauges utilize a screw-in fitting that may work with your*

air hose quick-disconnect fitting.

5 Depress the valve spring with a valve spring compressor (Chrysler tool no. 4682, or equivalent) **(see illustration)** and remove the rocker arm for the valve with the defective part. If all of the valve stem seals are being replaced, all of the rocker arms should be removed.

6 Apply compressed air to the cylinder. **Warning:** *The piston may be forced down by compressed air, causing the crankshaft to turn suddenly. If the wrench used when positioning the number one piston at TDC is still attached to the bolt in the crankshaft nose, it could cause damage or injury when the crankshaft moves.*

7 The valves should be held in place by the air pressure. If the valve faces or seats are in poor condition, leaks may prevent air pressure from retaining the valves - refer to the alternative procedure below.

8 If you don't have access to compressed air, an alternative method can be used. Position the piston at a point approximately 45-degrees before TDC on the compression stroke, then feed a long piece of nylon rope through the spark plug hole until it fills the combustion chamber. Be sure to leave the end of the rope hanging out of the engine so it can be removed easily. Use a large ratchet and socket to rotate the crankshaft in the normal direction of rotation until slight resistance is felt.

9 Stuff shop rags into the cylinder head holes above and below the valves to prevent parts and tools from falling into the engine, then use a valve spring compressor to compress the spring. Remove the keepers with small needle-nose pliers or a magnet. **Note:** *A couple of different types of tools are available for compressing the valve springs with the head in place. One type, shown here, grips the lower spring coils and presses on the retainer as the knob is turned, while the other type utilizes the rocker arm assembly for leverage. Both types work very well, although the lever type is usually less expensive* **(see accompanying illustration and illustration 11.5).**

10 Remove the spring retainer, shield and valve spring, then remove the umbrella-type guide seal. **Note:** *If air pressure fails to hold the valve in the closed position during this operation, the valve face or seat is probably damaged. If so, the cylinder head will have to be removed for additional repair operations.*

11 Wrap a rubber band or tape around the top of the valve stem so the valve won't fall into the combustion chamber, then release the air pressure. **Note:** *If a rope was used instead of air pressure, turn the crankshaft slightly in the direction opposite normal rotation.*

12 Inspect the valve stem for damage. Rotate the valve in the guide and check the end for eccentric movement, which would indicate that the valve is bent.

13 Move the valve up-and-down in the guide and make sure it doesn't bind. If the valve stem binds, either the valve is bent or the guide is damaged. In either case, the head will have to be removed for repair.

**11.9  If the special tool isn't available, use a screw-type spring compressor - remove the keepers with a magnet or needle-nose pliers**

**11.15  Be sure to note if there are differences in the intake and exhaust valve stem seals.  Use a special stem seal tool or a deep socket to install the new seal(s)**

**11.17  Apply a small dab of grease to each keeper before installation to hold it in place on the valve stem until the spring compressor is released**

14    Reapply air pressure to the cylinder to retain the valve in the closed position, then remove the tape or rubber band from the valve stem. If a rope was used instead of air pressure, rotate the crankshaft in the normal direction of rotation until slight resistance is felt.

15    Lubricate the valve stem with engine oil and install a new guide seal **(see illustration)**.

16    Install the spring(s) in position over the valve.

17    Install the valve spring retainer. Compress the valve spring and carefully position the keepers in the groove. Apply a small dab of grease to the inside of each keeper to hold it in place **(see illustration)**.

18    Remove the pressure from the spring tool and make sure the

keepers are seated.

19    Disconnect the air hose and remove the adapter from the spark plug hole. If a rope was used in place of air pressure, pull it out of the cylinder.

20    Refer to Section 10 and install the rocker arm(s).

21    Install the spark plug(s) and hook up the wire(s).

22    Refer to Section 4 and install the valve cover.

23    Start and run the engine, then check for oil leaks and unusual sounds coming from the valve cover area.

## 12   Cylinder head - removal and installation

**Caution:** *Allow the engine to cool completely before beginning this procedure.*

### Removal

*Refer to illustrations 12.8a, 12.8b and 12.9*

1     Position the number one piston at Top Dead Center (see Section 3):

2     Disconnect the negative cable from the battery.

3     Drain the cooling system and remove the spark plugs (see Chapter 1).

4     Remove the intake/exhaust manifold (see Section 5). **Note:** *If you're only replacing the cylinder head gasket, it isn't necessary to remove the manifolds. If you leave the manifolds attached, you may need an assistant to help lift the head off the engine.*

5     Remove the distributor (see Chapter 5), including the cap and wires.

6     Remove the timing belt (see Section 6).

7     Remove the valve cover (see Section 4).

8     Loosen the head bolts in 1/4-turn increments until they can be removed by hand. Follow the recommended sequence to avoid warping the head **(see illustrations)**.

9     Lift the head off the engine. If resistance is felt, don't pry between the head and block gasket mating surfaces - damage to the mating

**12.8a  Exploded view of the cylinder head and related components - 2.2L engine shown, 2.5L similar**

BUMPERS

TBI GASKET ONE PIECE "RIBBON TYPE"

CURTAIN

HEAD BOLTS

ROCKER ARM (ROLLER FOLLOWER)

VALVE STEM SEAL

LOCKS

HYDRAULIC LASH ADJUSTER

SPRING

VALVE GUIDE

VALVE SEAT

SEAL

**12.8b  Loosen the head bolts 1/4-turn at a time, in the sequence shown, until they can be removed by hand**

2A

**12.9 If the cylinder head is difficult to remove, pry only on the protrusions located on the side of the cylinder head as this will not damage the cylinder head surface**

**12.12 Use a gasket scraper to remove the old head gasket**

**12.14 A die should be use to remove sealant and corrosion from the head bolt threads prior to installation**

**12.15 When you put the new head gasket in position on the engine block, be sure it's right side up and facing the right direction - the holes in the gasket must match the passage in the block for coolant and oil to circulate properly**

**12.16 Cylinder head bolt TIGHTENING sequence**

surfaces will result. Instead, pry against the casting protrusions on the sides of the cylinder head **(see illustration)**. Set the head on blocks of wood to prevent damage to the gasket sealing surfaces.

10    Cylinder head disassembly and inspection procedures are covered in detail in Chapter 2, Part C. It's a good idea to have the head checked for warpage, even if you're just replacing the gasket.

## Installation

*Refer to illustrations 12.12, 12.14, 12.15 and 12.16*

11    The mating surfaces of the cylinder head and block must be perfectly clean when the head is installed.

12    Use a gasket scraper to remove all traces of carbon and old gasket material **(see illustration)**, then clean the mating surfaces with lacquer thinner or acetone. If there's oil on the mating surfaces when the head is installed, the gasket may not seal correctly and leaks may develop. When working on the block, stuff the cylinders with clean shop rags to keep out debris. Use a vacuum cleaner to remove material that falls into the cylinders. Since the head is made of aluminum, aggressive scraping can cause damage. Be extra careful not to nick or gouge the mating surfaces with the scraper.

13    Check the block and head mating surfaces for nicks, deep scratches and other damage. If damage is slight, it can be removed with a file; if it's excessive, machining may be the only alternative.

14    Use a tap of the correct size to chase the threads in the head bolt holes. Mount each head bolt in a vise and run a die down the threads to remove corrosion and restore the threads **(see illustration)**. Dirt,

corrosion, sealant and damaged threads will affect torque readings.

15    Place a new gasket on the block **(see illustration)** and set the cylinder head in position.

16    Install the bolts. They must be tightened in four steps, following a specific sequence **(see illustration)**, to the torque listed in this Chapter's Specifications.

17    Reinstall the timing belt (see Section 6).

18    Reinstall the remaining parts in the reverse order of removal.

19    Be sure to refill the cooling system and check all fluid levels.

20    Rotate the crankshaft clockwise slowly by hand through two complete revolutions. Recheck the camshaft timing marks (see Section 6).

21    Start the engine and check the ignition timing (see Chapter 1).

22    Run the engine until normal operating temperature is reached. Check for leaks and proper operation.

## 13    Oil pan - removal and installation

*Refer to illustrations 13.4, 13.8a and 13.8b*

**Note:** *The following procedure is based on the assumption that the engine is in the vehicle.*

## Removal

1    Warm up the engine, then drain the oil and replace the oil filter (see Chapter 1).

2    Detach the cable from the negative battery terminal.

3    Raise the vehicle and support it securely on jackstands.

4    Remove the bolts securing the oil pan to the engine block **(see illustration)**.

5    Tap on the pan with a soft-face hammer to break the gasket seal, then detach the oil pan from the engine. Don't pry between the block and oil pan mating surfaces.

6    Using a gasket scraper, remove all traces of old gasket and/or

13.4  Remove the bolts (arrows) from the oil pan

13.8b  Apply a continuous 1/8-inch wide bead of RTV sealant to the oil pan, then install the pan

13.8a  Install the new oil pan end seals and hold them in place with a bead of RTV sealant as shown here

14.3  Oil pump drive shaft alignment

sealant from the engine block and oil pan. Remove the seals from each end of the engine block or oil pan. Clean the mating surfaces with lacquer thinner or acetone. Make sure the threaded bolt holes in the block are clean.

7    Clean the oil pan with solvent and dry it thoroughly. Check the gasket flanges for distortion, particularly around the bolt holes. If

14.5a  Engine oil pump pick-up mounting details

necessary, place the pan on a block of wood and use a hammer to flatten and restore the gasket surfaces.

## Installation

8    Install new seals in the retainers at the front and rear of the engine block (see illustration). Apply a 1/8-inch wide bead of RTV sealant to the oil pan gasket surfaces. Continue the bead across the end seals. Make sure the sealant is applied to the inside of the bolt holes (see illustration). Note: *1989 engines are equipped with side gaskets as well as end gaskets. Use RTV sealant to retain the side gaskets in place, and apply a dab of sealant at the junction of the side and end gaskets.*
9    Carefully place the oil pan in position.
10   Install the bolts and tighten them in 1/4-turn increments to the torque listed in this Chapter's Specifications. Start with the bolts closest to the center of the pan and work out in a spiral pattern. Don't overtighten them or leakage may occur. Note that some 2.2L engines have bolts with different diameters, which require different torque values.
11   Add oil, run the engine and check for oil leaks.

## 14   Oil pump - removal, inspection and installation

### Removal

*Refer to illustrations 14.3, 14.5a, 14.5b and 14.5c*
1    Position the number one piston at Top Dead Center on the compression stroke (see Section 3).
2    Remove the distributor (see Chapter 5).
3    Check to see that the oil pump shaft slot is parallel to the center line of the crankshaft (see illustration).
4    Remove the oil pan (see Section 13).
5    Remove the oil pump mounting bolts. If equipped, also remove the brace bolt (see illustrations).
6    Remove the oil pump assembly.

**14.5b  Oil pump and related components - exploded view**

**14.5c  Oil pump mounting bolts (arrows)**

## Inspection

*Refer to illustrations 14.8, 14.9, 14.10, 14.11, 14.12 and 14.13*

7      Remove the bolts and lift off the oil pump cover.

8      Check the rotor endplay with feeler gauges and a straightedge **(see illustration)**.

9      Remove the outer rotor and measure its thickness **(see illustration)**.

10      Check the clearance between the inner and outer rotor tips with feeler gauges **(see illustration)**.

11      Measure the outer rotor-to-pump body clearance **(see illustration)**.

12      Check the oil pump cover for warpage with feeler gauges and a straightedge **(see illustration)**.

13      Remove the cotter pin and cup, then extract the spring and oil pump relief valve from the pump housing **(see illustration)**. Measure the free length of the oil pressure relief valve spring.

14      Compare the measurements to the oil pump Specifications at the beginning of this Chapter. If any of them are outside the limits, replace the pump.

15      Install the rotor with the large chamfered edge facing toward the pump body. Install the oil pressure relief valve and spring assembly. Install the pump cover and tighten the bolts to the torque listed in this Chapter's Specifications.

## Installation

*Refer to illustration 14.18*

16      Apply a thin coat of RTV sealant to the mating surface of the pump and place the pump in position. Rotate it back-and-forth a little to ensure there's positive contact between the pump and the engine block.

17      Coat the threads of the mounting bolts with sealant and, while holding the pump securely in place, install the bolts. Tighten them to the torque listed in this Chapter's Specifications.

**14.8  Check the rotor endplay by placing a precision straightedge across the pump housing like this and inserting feeler gauges between the rotor face and the straightedge**

**14.9  Measure the thickness of the oil pump rotor with a micrometer**

**14.10  Check the inner rotor-to-outer rotor tip clearance with feeler gauges**

**14.11 Check the outer rotor-to-pump body clearance with feeler gauge**

18   Install a new O-ring in the oil pump pick-up opening **(see illustration)**.
19   Carefully work the pick-up tube into the pump, install the retaining bolt and tighten it to the torque listed in this Chapter's Specifications.
20   Install the brace bolt and tighten it securely.
21   Install the oil pan (see Section 13).

## 15   Flywheel/driveplate - removal and installation

### *Removal*

*Refer to illustrations 15.3a and 15.3b*

1   Raise the vehicle and support it securely on jackstands, then refer to Chapter 7 and remove the transaxle. If it's leaking, now would be a very good time to replace the front pump seal/O-ring (automatic transaxle only).
2   Remove the pressure plate and clutch disc (see Chapter 8) (manual transaxle equipped vehicles). Now is a good time to check/replace the clutch components and pilot bearing.
3   Remove the bolts that secure the flywheel/driveplate to the crankshaft **(see illustrations)**. If the crankshaft turns, wedge a screwdriver in the ring gear teeth to jam the flywheel.

**14.12 Check the oil pump cover for warpage with a straightedge and feeler gauge**

**14.13 Oil pressure relief valve components - exploded view**

**14.18 Before attaching the oil pick-up tube assembly, lubricate the new O-ring and install it in the oil pump**

**15.3a Flywheel and related components - exploded view**

**15.3b  If the bolts are arranged in a staggered pattern, it isn't necessary to mark the crankshaft and flywheel (note the two bolts [arrows] are spaced much farther apart than the others - if they aren't spaced like this, be sure to mark the relationship of the flywheel to the crankshaft**

4    Remove the flywheel/driveplate from the crankshaft. Since the flywheel is fairly heavy, be sure to support it while removing the last bolt.
5    Clean the flywheel to remove grease and oil. Inspect the surface for cracks, rivet grooves, burned areas and score marks. Light scoring can be removed with emery cloth. Check for cracked and broken ring gear teeth. Lay the flywheel on a flat surface and use a straightedge to check for warpage.
6    Clean and inspect the mating surfaces of the flywheel/driveplate and the crankshaft. If the crankshaft rear seal is leaking, replace it before reinstalling the flywheel/driveplate.

**16.4  Carefully pry the seal from the retainer**

### Installation

7    Position the flywheel/driveplate against the crankshaft. Be sure to align the marks made during removal. Note that some engines have an alignment dowel or staggered bolt holes to ensure correct installation. Before installing the bolts, apply thread locking compound to the threads.
8    Wedge a screwdriver through in the ring gear teeth to keep the flywheel/driveplate from turning as you tighten the bolts to the torque listed in this Chapter's Specifications.
9    The remainder of installation is the reverse of the removal procedure.

**17.4a  Details of the engine mounts (typical)**

**17.4b Remove the bolts and nuts (arrows) that hold the rear strut onto the crossmember and the engine**

## 16   Rear main oil seal - replacement

*Refer to illustration 16.4*
1    Remove the transaxle (see Chapter 7).
2    If the vehicle has a manual transaxle, remove the clutch and fly-wheel (see Chapter 8 and Section 15 of this Chapter).
3    If the vehicle has an automatic transaxle, remove the driveplate (see Section 15).
4    Pry the oil seal from the retainer with a screwdriver **(see illustration)**. Be careful not to nick or scratch the crankshaft or the seal retainer bore. Thoroughly clean the seal bore in the seal housing with a shop towel. Remove all traces of oil and dirt.
5    Lubricate the lips of the new seal with engine oil or multi-purpose grease. Install the seal over the end of the crankshaft (make sure the lips of the seal point toward the engine) and carefully tap it into place with a plastic hammer.
6    Install the driveplate or flywheel (see Section 15) and clutch (see Chapter 8).
7    Install the transaxle (see Chapter 7).

**17.4c An exploded view of the front engine mount**

## 17   Engine mounts - check, replacement and adjustment

*Refer to illustrations 17.4a, 17.4b, 17.4c, 17.4d, 17.4e and 17.15*
1    Engine mounts seldom require attention, but broken or deterio-rated mounts should be replaced immediately or the added strain placed on the driveline components may cause damage or wear.

### Check

2    During the check, the engine must be raised slightly to remove the weight from the mounts.
3    Raise the vehicle and support it securely on jackstands, then position a jack under the engine oil pan. Place a large block of wood between the jack head and the oil pan, then carefully raise the engine just enough to take the weight off the mounts. **Warning:** *DO NOT place any part of your body under the engine when it's supported only by a jack!*
4    Check the mount insulators **(see illustrations)** to see if the rubber is cracked, hardened or separated from the metal plates. Sometimes the rubber will split right down the center.
5    Check for relative movement between the mount plates and the engine or frame (use a large screwdriver or prybar to attempt to move the mounts). If movement is noted, lower the engine and tighten the mount fasteners.
6    Rubber preservative should be applied to the insulators to slow deterioration.

**17.4d An exploded view of the right engine mount**

**17.4e An exploded view of the left engine mount**

## Replacement

7    Disconnect the negative battery cable from the battery, then raise the vehicle and support it securely on jackstands (if not already done).

8    Remove the fasteners and detach the insulator from the frame bracket.

9    Raise the engine slightly with a jack or hoist. Remove the insulator-to-engine bolts and detach the insulator.

10    Installation is the reverse of removal. Use thread locking compound on the mount bolts and be sure to tighten them securely.

## Adjustment

11    The right and left engine mounts are adjustable to allow drivetrain movement in relation to driveaxle assembly length (see Chapter 8).

12    Always adjust the insulators when:

  a) *You service the driveaxles.*
  b) *The vehicle sustains front end structural damage.*
  c) *You replace an insulator.*

13    Remove the load on the engine mounts by carefully supporting the engine and transaxle assembly with a floor jack.

14    Loosen the right insulator vertical fasteners and the front engine mount bracket-to-front crossmember bolts and nuts.

15    The left engine mount insulator is sleeved over the shaft and long support bolt **(see illustration)** to provide lateral movement adjustment.

**17.15  Cutaway of the left insulator sleeve assembly**

16    Pry the engine right or left as required to achieve the proper driveaxle length (see Chapter 8).

17    Tighten the right engine mount insulator vertical bolts securely, tighten the front engine mount bolts and nuts securely and center the left engine mount insulator.

18    Recheck the driveaxle length.

# Chapter 2 Part B
# 2.6L four-cylinder engine

## Contents

**2B**

## Specifications

### General

| | |
|---|---|
| Firing order | 1-3-4-2 |
| Cylinder numbers (drivebelt end-to-transaxle end) | 1-2-3-4 |
| Bore and stroke | 3.59 X 3.86 inches |
| Displacement | 156 cubic inches |

**Cylinder location and distributor rotation**

### Camshaft

| | |
|---|---|
| Endplay | 0.004 to 0.008 inch |
| Runout | 0.03 inch |
| Journal diameter | 1.339 inches |
| Bearing journal oil clearance | 0.002 to 0.004 inch |
| Lobe wear (maximum) | 0.020 inch |

### Cylinder head

| | |
|---|---|
| Warpage limit | 0.002 inch |

### Intake/exhaust manifold

| | |
|---|---|
| Warpage limit | 0.006 inch per foot of manifold length |

### Oil pump

| | |
|---|---|
| Drive gear-to-bearing clearance | 0.0008 to 0.0020 inch |
| Driven gear-to-bearing clearance | 0.0008 to 0.0020 inch |
| Drive gear-to-housing clearance | 0.0043 to 0.0059 inch |
| Driven gear-to-housing clearance | 0.0043 to 0.0059 inch |
| Drive gear endplay | 0.0020 to 0.0043 inch |
| Driven gear endplay | 0.0016 to 0.0039 inch |
| Relief spring free length | 1.85 inches |

## Torque specifications

| | Ft-lbs (unless otherwise indicated) |
|---|---|
| Balance shaft chain guides **(see illustration 9.8)** | |
|     Chain guide A bolts | 156 in-lbs |
|     Chain guide B bolts | |
|         Bolt A | 12 in-lbs |
|         Bolt B | 14 |
|     Chain guide C bolts | 156 in-lbs |
| Balance shaft sprocket bolt | 25 |
| Camshaft bearing cap bolts | 160 in-lbs |
| Camshaft sprocket bolt | 40 |
| Carburetor air heater mounting bolts **(see illustration 8.9)** | |
|     A | 100 in-lbs |
|     B | 80 in-lbs |
| Crankshaft sprocket bolt | 87 |
| Cylinder head bolts (use the tightening sequence shown in Section 14) | |
|     First step (engine cold) | 34 |
|     Second step (engine cold) | 69 |
|     Third step (engine hot) | 75 |
| Driveplate-to-crankshaft bolts | 50 |
| Engine mount - front **(see illustration 19.1b)** | |
|     A | 40 |
|     B | 45 |
| Engine mount - right **(see illustration 19.1a)** | |
|     A | 250 in-lbs |
|     B and C | 75 in-lbs |
| Exhaust manifold heat cowl screws | 80 in-lbs |
| Exhaust manifold nuts | 150 in-lbs |
| Flywheel-to-crankshaft bolts | 60 |
| Intake manifold bolts | 150 in-lbs |
| Oil pan-to-engine block fasteners | 60 in-lbs |
| Oil pick-up tube bolt(s) | 50 in-lbs |
| Oil pump cover bolts | 71 in-lbs |
| Oil pump mounting bolts | 71 in-lbs |
| Oil pump sprocket bolt | 25 |
| Rear main oil seal housing bolts | 105 in-lbs |
| Timing chain cover bolts | 160 in-lbs |
| Timing chain guides bolts | 156 in-lbs |
| Valve cover bolts/nuts | 53 in-lbs |

## 1   General information

This Part of Chapter 2 is devoted to in-vehicle repair procedures for the 2.6L engine. All information concerning engine removal and installation and engine block and cylinder head overhaul can be found in Part C of this Chapter.

The following repair procedures are based on the assumption that the engine is installed in the vehicle. If the engine has been removed from the vehicle and mounted on a stand, many of the steps outlined in this Part of Chapter 2 will not apply.

The Specifications included in this Part of Chapter 2 apply only to the procedures contained in this Part. Part C of Chapter 2 contains the Specifications necessary for cylinder head and engine block rebuilding.

The 2.6 liter engine is an inline vertical four, with a chain-driven overhead camshaft and a balance shaft counterbalancing system which cancels the engine's power pulses and produces relatively vibration-free operation. The crankshaft rides in five renewable insert-type main bearings, with the center bearing (the thrust bearing) assigned the additional task of controlling crankshaft endplay.

The pistons have two compression rings and one oil control ring. The semi-floating piston pins are press fitted into the small end of the connecting rod. The connecting rod big ends are also equipped with renewable insert-type plain bearings.

The engine is liquid-cooled, utilizing a centrifugal impeller-type pump, driven by a belt from the camshaft, to circulate coolant around the cylinders and combustion chambers and through the intake manifold.

Lubrication is handled by a gear-type oil pump mounted on the front of the engine under the timing chain cover. It is driven by the balance shaft chain. The oil is filtered continuously by a cartridge-type filter mounted on the radiator side of the engine.

## 2   Repair operations possible with the engine in the vehicle

Many major repair operations can be accomplished without removing the engine from the vehicle.

Clean the engine compartment and the exterior of the engine with some type of degreaser before any work is done. It will make the job easier and help keep dirt out of the internal areas of the engine.

Depending on the components involved, it may be helpful to remove the hood to improve access to the engine as repairs are performed (refer to Chapter 11 if necessary). Cover the fenders to prevent damage to the paint. Special pads are available, but an old bedspread or blanket will also work.

If vacuum, exhaust, oil or coolant leaks develop, indicating a need for gasket or seal replacement, the repairs can generally be made with the engine in the vehicle. The intake and exhaust manifold gaskets, oil pan gasket, crankshaft oil seals and cylinder head gasket are all accessible with the engine in place.

Exterior engine components, such as the intake and exhaust manifolds, the oil pan, the water pump, the starter motor, the alternator, the distributor and the fuel system components can be removed for repair with the engine in place.

Since the cylinder head can be removed without pulling the engine, camshaft and valve component servicing can also be accom-

**3.1 Align the notch in the pulley with the 0 on the timing plate, then check to see if the distributor rotor is pointing to the number 1 cylinder; if not, the camshaft is 180-degrees out of time (number 4 is at TDC) - the crankshaft will have to rotated 360-degrees**

**4.4 Remove the carburetor brace bolts (arrows) and lift the brace from the engine**

plished with the engine in the vehicle. Replacement of the timing chain and sprockets is also possible with the engine in the vehicle.

In extreme cases caused by a lack of necessary equipment, repair or replacement of piston rings, pistons, connecting rods and rod bearings is possible with the engine in the vehicle. However, this practice is not recommended because of the cleaning and preparation work that must be done to the components involved.

## 3   Top Dead Center (TDC) for number one piston - locating

*Refer to illustration 3.1*

This procedure is essentially the same as for the 2.2L/2.5L engine. Refer to Part A, Section 3 and follow the procedure outlined there, except use the **accompanying illustration**.

## 4   Valve cover - removal and installation

### *Removal*

*Refer to illustrations 4.4, 4.9a and 4.9b*

1    Detach the cable from the negative battery terminal.

2    Remove the water pump pulley cover from the valve cover (see Chapter 3).
3    Remove the air cleaner inlet hose and housing assembly from the carburetor and the top of the valve cover (see Chapter 4).
4    Remove the bolts from the carburetor/valve cover brace **(see illustration)** and lift the brace from the engine.
5    Remove the distributor cap and wires from the cylinder head (see Chapter 1). Be sure to mark each wire for correct installation.
6    Remove any fuel lines or vent lines from the carburetor or fuel filter that will interfere with the removal of the valve cover.
7    Disconnect any electrical connections from the carburetor that will interfere with the removal of the valve cover.
8    Wipe off the valve cover thoroughly to prevent debris from falling onto the exposed cylinder head or camshaft/valve train assembly.
9    Remove the valve cover bolts **(see illustrations)**.
10   Carefully lift off the valve cover and gasket. If the gasket is stuck to the cylinder head, tap it with a rubber mallet to break the seal. Do not pry between the cover and cylinder head or you'll damage the gasket mating surfaces.

### *Installation*

*Refer to illustration 4.13*

11   Use a gasket scraper to remove all traces of old gasket material from the gasket mating surfaces of the cylinder head and the valve cover. Clean the surfaces with a rag soaked in lacquer thinner or acetone.
12   Be sure to install the semi-circular seal (camshaft plug) on top of

**4.9a An exploded view of the valve cover and related components**

**4.9b Remove the two bolts (arrows) from the valve cover and lift the cover off the engine**

**2B**

**4.13 Apply a small amount of RTV sealant to the corners of the cylinder head next to the camshaft bearing cap**

**5.3 Remove the rocker arm assembly bolts (arrows)**

the cylinder head near the camshaft sprocket. Apply beads of RTV sealant to the points where the seal meets the valve cover mating surfaces.

13   Install a new gasket onto the valve cover. Install the molded rubber gasket onto the cover by pushing the new gasket into the slot that circles the valve cover perimeter. Apply beads of RTV sealant where the cylinder head and camshaft bearing cap meet **(see illustration)**. Wait five minutes or so and let the RTV "set-up" (slightly harden) and then install the cover and bolts and tighten them to the torque listed in this Chapter's Specifications.

14   The remainder of installation is the reverse of removal.

## 5   Rocker arm assembly - removal, inspection and installation

**Note 1:** *The camshaft bearing caps are removed together with the rocker arm assembly. To prevent the water-pump end of the camshaft*

*from popping up (from timing-chain tension) after the assembly is removed, have an assistant hold the water-pump end of the camshaft down, then reinstall the main bearing cap on that end to hold it in place until reassembly.*

**Note 2:** *While the camshaft bearing caps are off, inspect them, as well as the camshaft bearing journals, as described in Section 13.*

### Removal

*Refer to illustration 5.3*

1   Remove the valve cover (see Section 4).

2   Position the number one piston at Top Dead Center (see Section 3).

3   Have an assistant hold down the water-pump end of the camshaft, then loosen the camshaft bearing cap bolts 1/4-turn at a time each until the spring pressure is relieved **(see illustration)**. Do not remove the bolts.

4   Lift the rocker arms and shaft assembly from the cylinder head. Reinstall the bearing cap at the water-pump end to hold the camshaft in place.

**5.5 An exploded vie of the rockers arms and shafts (typical)**

5.6 Check the contact faces and adjusting screw tips (arrows)

5.7 Back off the adjusters until they only protrude 1 mm (0.040 in)

5.8a Install the rocker shafts into the front bearing cap

## Inspection

*Refer to illustrations 5.5 and 5.6*

5    If you wish to disassemble and inspect the rocker arm assemblies (a good idea as long as you have them off), remove the retaining bolts and slip the rocker arms, springs and bearing caps off the shafts **(see illustration)**. Keep the parts in order so you can reassemble them in the same positions.

6    Thoroughly clean the parts and inspect them for wear and damage. Check the rocker arm faces that contact the camshaft and the adjusting screw tips **(see illustration)**. Check the surfaces of the shafts that the rocker arms ride on, as well as the bearing surfaces inside the rocker arms, for scoring and excessive wear. Replace any parts that are damaged or excessively worn. Also, make sure the oil holes in the shafts are not plugged.

## Installation

*Refer to illustrations 5.7, 5.8a and 5.8b*

7    Loosen the locknuts and back off the adjusters until they only protrude 1 mm (0.040-inch) **(see illustration)**.

8    Lubricate all components with assembly lube or engine oil and reassemble the shafts. When installing the rocker arms, shafts and springs, note the markings and the difference between the left and right side parts **(see illustration)**. Place the marks in the end of the shaft directly in line with the marks on the caps **(see illustration)** to keep them aligned until they are ready to be installed onto the cylinder head.

9    Position the rocker arm assemblies on the cylinder head and install the mounting bolts finger tight. **Note:** *Check the numbered markings on the caps to make sure the caps are in the correct numerical sequence.*

10    Tighten the camshaft bearing cap bolts as described in Section 13.

11    Adjust the valve clearances (cold) as described in Chapter 1.

12    Temporarily install the valve cover and run the engine until it is fully warmed up.

13    Readjust the valves while the engine is still warm (see Chapter 1).

14    Reinstall the remaining parts in the reverse order of removal.

15    Run the engine and check for oil leaks and proper operation.

## 6    Valve springs, retainers and seals - replacement

**Note:** *The jet valve is mounted directly beside each intake valve. Refer to Chapter 2, Part C for the jet valve servicing procedure.*

This procedure is essentially the same as for the 2.2L/2.5L engine. Refer to Part A Section 11 and follow the procedure outlined there.

5.8b Be sure the mating mark on the cap is aligned with the mating mark on the shaft

## 7    Intake manifold - removal and installation

*Refer to illustration 7.11*

**Warning:** *Gasoline is extremely flammable, so take extra precautions when you work on any part of the fuel system. Don't smoke or allow open flames or bare light bulbs near the work area, and don't work in a garage where a natural gas-type appliance (such as a water heater or clothes dryer) with a pilot light is present. If you spill any fuel on your skin, rinse it off immediately with soap and water. When you perform any kind of work on the fuel system, wear safety glasses and have a Class B type fire extinguisher on hand.*

## Removal

1    Detach the cable from the negative battery terminal.

2    Drain the cooling system (see Chapter 1).

3    Remove the air cleaner (see Chapter 4).

4    Clearly label, then detach all vacuum lines, electrical wiring and fuel lines.

5    Detach the accelerator cable from the throttle linkage (see Chapter 4).

6    Remove the drivebelts (see Chapter 1).

7    Remove the carburetor from the intake manifold (see Chapter 4).

8    Remove the coolant hoses from the intake manifold.

9    Disconnect the fuel inlet line at the fuel filter (see Chapter 4).

10    Remove the fuel pump and fuel filter and lay them aside (see Chapter 4).

**7.11  An exploded view of the intake manifold**

11    Remove the intake manifold bolts **(see illustration)** and remove the manifold from the engine.

## Installation

12    Clean the manifold with solvent and dry them with compressed air. **Warning:** *Wear eye protection!*

13    Check the mating surfaces of the manifold for flatness with a precision straightedge and feeler gauges. Refer to this Chapter's Specifications for the warpage limit.

14    Inspect the manifold for cracks and distortion.

15    If the manifold is cracked or warped, replace it or see if it can be resurfaced/repaired at an automotive machine shop.

16    Check carefully for any stripped or broken intake manifold bolts. Replace any defective bolts with new parts.

17    Using a scraper, remove all traces of old gasket material from the cylinder head and manifold mating surfaces. Clean the surfaces with lacquer thinner or acetone.

18    Install the intake manifold with a new gasket and tighten the bolts finger-tight. Starting at the center and working out in both directions, tighten the bolts in a criss-cross pattern until the torque listed in this Chapter's Specifications is reached.

18    The remainder of the installation procedure is the reverse of removal.

## 8    Exhaust manifold - removal and installation

### Removal

*Refer to illustrations 8.9 and 8.10*

1    Disconnect the negative battery cable from the battery.

2    Drain the cooling system (see Chapter 1).

3    Remove the air cleaner (see Chapter 4).

4    Loosen the power steering pump and remove the belt (see Chapter 1).

5    Raise the front of the vehicle and support it securely on jackstands. Detach the exhaust pipe from the exhaust manifold (see Chapter 4). Apply penetrating oil to the fastener threads if they are difficult to remove.

6    Disconnect the air injection tube assembly from the air pump and move the tube assembly to one side.

7    Remove the power steering pump (if equipped) and set it aside (see Chapter 10).

8    Remove the heat cowl from the exhaust manifold. Be sure to soak the bolts and nuts with penetrating oil before attempting to remove them from the manifold.

9    Remove the carburetor air heater from the exhaust manifold assembly **(see illustration)**.

10    Remove the exhaust manifold nuts **(see illustration)** and detach the exhaust manifold.

11    Separate the front catalytic converter from the exhaust manifold.

**8.9  Remove the carburetor air heater from the exhaust manifold**

**8.10  Remove the exhaust manifold nuts from the exhaust manifold.  Be sure to soak the nuts with penetrating oil before attempting to remove them**

### Installation

12    Discard the old gaskets and use a scraper to clean the gasket mating surfaces on the manifold and head, then clean the surfaces with a rag soaked in lacquer thinner or acetone.

13    Place the exhaust manifold and converter assembly in position on the cylinder head and install the nuts. Starting at the center, tighten the nuts in a criss-cross pattern until the torque listed in this Chapter's Specifications is reached.

14    The remainder of installation is the reverse of removal.

15    Start the engine and check for exhaust leaks between the manifold and the cylinder head and between the manifold and the exhaust pipe.

## 9    Balance shaft chain/sprockets - removal, inspection and installation

### Removal

*Refer to illustrations 9.5a, 9.5b, 9.7 and 9.8*

1    Disconnect the cable from the negative terminal of the battery. Remove the air cleaner assembly.

2    Remove the drivebelts. Remove the alternator, power steering pump and air conditioning compressor, if equipped, and lay them aside. **Warning:** *The air conditioning system is under high pressure - don't disconnect the hoses!*

3    Remove the valve cover (see Section 4). Remove the two front cylinder head-to-timing chain cover bolts. **Caution:** *Do not loosen any other cylinder head bolts.*

**9.5a  Remove the bolts (arrows) and separate the engine mount from the chassis**

4    Raise the vehicle and support it securely on jackstands. Remove the right-side splash guard. Remove the large bolt at the front of the crankshaft and slide the pulley off. **Note:** *To keep the crankshaft from turning while you're removing this bolt, remove the starter (see Chapter 5) and wedge a large screwdriver or prybar into the flywheel/driveplate ring gear. If the pulley does not come off easily, puller sets are available at auto parts stores that will make removal easier.*

5    Position a floor jack with a block of wood on the jack head under the engine. Jack the engine up slightly to relieve the pressure and remove the right-side engine mount **(see illustration).** Remove the engine mounting plate and the timing indicator from the timing cover **(see illustration).**

6    Drain the engine oil and remove the oil pan (see Section 15).

7    Remove the bolts attaching the timing chain cover to the engine block **(see illustration).** Draw a simple diagram showing the location of each bolt so they can be returned to the same holes from which they were removed. Tap the timing chain cover with a soft-faced hammer to break the gasket seal, then remove the cover from the engine block. **Caution:** *Prying between the cover and the engine block can damage the gasket sealing surface.*

8    Remove the chain guides labeled A, B and C **(see illustration).**

**9.5b  Engine mounting plate installation details**

**9.7  Timing chain cover installation details**

**9.8  An exploded view of the balance shaft chain and the timing chain**

2B

**9.16a  Installing the balance shaft chain guide C**

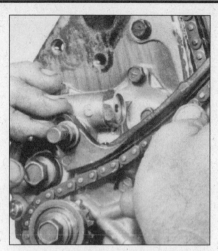

**9.16b  Installing the balance shaft chain guide B**

**9.16c  Push in the direction of arrow F to remove the slack from the balance shaft chain**

Each guide is held in place by two bolts. Again, draw a simple diagram showing the location of each bolt so that it can be returned to the same hole from which it was removed.

9    Reinstall the large bolt in the end of the crankshaft. Hold it in place with a wrench to prevent the crankshaft from turning while loosening the bolt on the end of the rear (firewall side) balance shaft, the bolt attaching the rear balance shaft drive sprocket to the oil pump shaft and the bolt in the end of the front (radiator side) balance shaft.

10    Slide the crankshaft sprocket, the balance shaft sprockets and the chain off the engine as an assembly. Leave the bolt in the end of the crankshaft in place. Do not lose the keys that index the sprockets to the shafts.

### Inspection

11    Check the sprocket teeth for wear and damage. Check the sprocket cushion rings and ring guides (balance shaft sprockets only) for wear and damage. Rotate the cushion rings and check for smooth operation. Inspect the chain for cracked side plates and pitted or worn rollers. Replace any defective or worn parts with new ones.

### Installation

*Refer to illustrations 9.16a, 9.16b and 9.16c*

12    Before installing the balance shaft chain and sprockets, the timing chain must be properly installed and the number one piston must be at TDC on the compression stroke. Both balance shafts and the oil pump must also be in place.

13    Slide the crankshaft sprocket part way onto the front of the crankshaft by lining up the keyway in the sprocket with the key on the shaft.

14    Install the front balance shaft sprocket part way. The dished or recessed side of the front balance shaft sprocket must face out. Install the balance shaft chain onto the crankshaft sprocket and the front balance shaft sprocket. Line up the plated links on the chain with the mating marks stamped into the sprockets **(see illustration 9.16c)**.

15    With the dished or recessed side facing in, slide rear balance shaft sprocket part way onto the lower oil pump gear shaft. Line up the plated link on the chain with the mating mark on the sprocket. Push the balance shaft sprockets all the way onto their respective shafts, lining up the keyways in the sprockets with the keys on the shafts. Simultaneously, push the crankshaft sprocket back until it bottoms on the crankshaft timing chain sprocket. Recheck the position of the mating marks on the chain and sprockets, then install the balance shaft sprocket bolts and tighten them to the torque listed in this Chapter's Specifications.

16    Install the chain guides labeled A, B and C **(see illustrations)** and tighten the mounting bolts for chain guides A and C securely (leave the mounting bolts for chain guide B finger-tight). Note the difference between the upper and lower chain guide B mounting bolts. Make sure they are installed in the proper location.

17    Adjust the chain slack as follows: rotate the rear balance shaft clockwise and the front balance shaft counterclockwise so the chain slack is collected at point F **(see illustration 9.16c)**. Pull the chain with your finger tips in the direction of arrow F, then move the lower end of the chain guide B up or down, as required, until the clearance between the chain and the guide (chain slack) is as specified **(see illustration 9.16c)**. Tighten the chain guide B mounting bolts securely, then recheck the slack to make sure it has not changed. If the chain is not tensioned properly, engine noise will result.

18    Apply a coat of clean moly-based grease to the chain and chain guides.

19    Using a hammer and punch, drive the oil seal out of the timing chain case (see Section 12).

20    Lay a new seal in place - make sure the lip faces inward - and tap around its circumference with a block of wood and a hammer until it is properly seated.

21    Using a new gasket and RTV-type gasket sealant, fit the timing chain cover onto the engine **(see illustration 9.6)**. Install the bolts in a crisscross pattern and tighten them to the torque listed in this Chapter's Specifications. If the gasket protrudes beyond the top or bottom of the case and engine block, trim off the excess with a razor blade.

22    Install the engine mounting plate onto the face of the timing chain cover **(see illustration 9.5)**. Tighten the bolts to the timing chain cover bolt torque listed in this Chapter's Specifications.

23    Apply a thin layer of clean moly-based grease to the seal contact surface of the crankshaft pulley, then slide it onto the crankshaft. Install the bolt and tighten it finger-tight only. **Note:** *The bolt should be tightened to the specified torque only after the cylinder head and camshaft have been installed.*

24    The remainder of installation is the reverse of removal.

### 10    Timing chain/sprockets - removal, inspection and installation

*Refer to illustrations 10.6, 10.7, 10.8, 10.9a and 10.9b*

### Removal

1    The balance shaft chain and sprockets must be removed to gain access to the timing chain assembly (see Section 9).

2    Remove the camshaft sprocket holder and the right and left timing chain guides from the front of the engine block **(see illustration 9.8)**.

10.6  Lubricate the timing chain tensioner plunger and install it in the oil pump bore

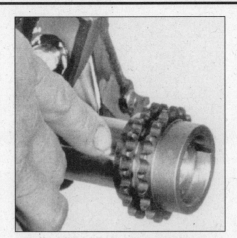

10.7  Install he timing chain sprocket on the end of the crankshaft with the wide shoulder facing out

10.8  Mesh the camshaft sprocket and the timing chain with the mark on the sprocket directly opposite the plated link on the chain

3    Depress the timing chain tensioner plunger on the oil pump and slide the camshaft sprocket, the crankshaft sprocket and the timing chain off the engine as an assembly. Do not lose the key that indexes the crankshaft sprocket in the proper place. Remove the timing chain tensioner plunger and spring from the oil pump.

## Inspection

4    Inspect the sprocket teeth for wear and damage. Check the chain for cracked plates and pitted or worn rollers. Check the chain tensioner rubber shoe for wear and the tensioner spring for cracks and deterioration. Check the chain guides for wear and damage. Replace any defective parts with new ones.

## Installation

5    Install the sprocket holder and the right and left timing chain guides onto the engine block. Tighten the bolts securely. The upper bolt in the left timing chain guide should be installed finger-tight only. Then coat the entire length of the chain contact surfaces of the guides with clean, high-quality moly-based grease.
6    Turn the crankshaft bolt with a large wrench until the number one piston is at Top Dead Center (TDC) (refer to Section 3 for TDC locating). Apply a layer of clean moly-based grease or engine assembly lube to the timing chain tensioner plunger and install the tensioner spring and plunger loosely into the oil pump body (see illustration). Note: *Chrysler Corporation officially recognizes a problem with the timing*

*chain at start-up. Because of insufficient oil pressure, the timing chain will make a knocking noise when the engine is first started. This will not harm the engine, but it is necessary to update the tensioner. Purchase from a dealership parts department, a rubber spacer and insert it into the tensioner spring. This spacer will prevent the oil from flowing out of the tensioner and back into the oil pump.*
7    Position the timing chain sprocket on the end of the crankshaft with the wide shoulder facing out (see illustration). Line up the keyway in the sprocket with the key on the crankshaft.
8    Install the camshaft sprocket onto the chain, lining up the plated link on the chain with the marked tooth on the sprocket (see illustration).
9    Slip the chain over the crankshaft sprocket, lining up the plated link on the chain with the marked tooth on the sprocket (see illustration). Slide the crankshaft sprocket all the way onto the crankshaft while depressing the chain tensioner so the chain fits into place in the guides. Rest the camshaft sprocket on the sprocket holder (see illustration) and make sure the plated links and mating marks are aligned properly. Caution: *Do not rotate the crankshaft for any reason until the cylinder head and camshaft have been properly installed.*
10    The remainder of installation is the reverse of removal.

2B

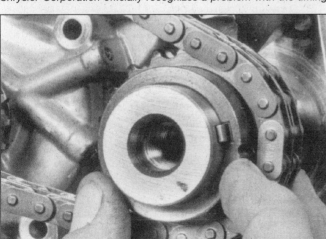

10.9a  Installing the timing chain on the crankshaft sprocket (note that the sprocket mark and the plated link are opposite each other)

10.9b  Correct timing chain and sprocket relationship

**11.2 Use a special tool (C-4847-1) to remove the seal from the cylinder head**

**11.5 Tap the seal in place with a special tool (C-4848)**

**12.3 Crankshaft front oil seal**

## 11 Camshaft (water pump pulley) oil seal - replacement

*Refer to illustrations 11.2 and 11.5*

1   Remove the water pump pulley from the camshaft (see Chapter 3).

2   Use a special tool (C-4847-1) and remove the seal from the cylinder head **(see illustration)**. If the special tool is not available, wrap the tip of a small screwdriver with tape and use it to carefully pry out the seal. Don't nick or scratch the camshaft journal or the new seal will leak.

3   Thoroughly clean and inspect the seal bore and the seal journal on the camshaft. Both must be clean and smooth. Use emery cloth or 400-grit sandpaper to remove small burrs.

4   If a groove has been worn into the journal on the camshaft (from contact with the seal lip), installing a new seal probably won't stop the leak. Such wear normally indicates the camshaft or the bearing surfaces in the caps are worn. It's probably time to overhaul the cylinder head (see Chapter 2, Part E) or replace the head or camshaft.

5   Coat the lip of the new seal with clean engine oil or moly-base grease and carefully tap the seal into place with a special tool (C-4848) **(see illustration)**. If a special tool is not available, use a large socket or piece of pipe and a hammer. If you don't have a socket as large in diameter as the seal, tap around the outer edge of the seal with the large end of a punch.

6   Install the water pump pulley and belt (see Chapter 3).

7   Start the engine and check for oil leaks.

## 12 Crankshaft front oil seal - replacement

*Refer to illustration 12.3*

1   Remove the drivebelts (see Chapter 1).

2   Remove the crankshaft pulley.

3   Carefully pry the seal out of the front cover **(see illustration)** with a seal removal tool or a screwdriver. Don't scratch the seal bore or damage the crankshaft in the process (if the crankshaft is damaged, the new seal will end up leaking).

4   Clean the bore in the timing chain cover and coat the outer edge of the new seal with engine oil or multi-purpose grease. Using a socket with an outside diameter slightly smaller than the outside diameter of the seal, carefully drive the seal into place with a hammer. If a socket is not available, a short section of a large diameter pipe will work. Check the seal after installation to be sure the spring did not pop out.

5   Installation is the reverse of removal.

6   Run the engine and check for leaks.

## 13 Camshaft - removal, inspection and installation

### Removal

*Refer to illustration 13.6*

1   Remove the valve cover (see Section 4).

2   Remove the distributor (see Chapter 5).

3   Remove the rocker arm assembly (see Section 5). If the camshaft bearing caps do not have numbers on them, number them before removal. Be sure to put the marks on the same ends of all the caps to prevent incorrect orientation of the caps during installation.

4   In order to keep the tensioner from collapsing once the sprocket has been removed, install a special retaining tool between the timing chain, near the tensioner **(see illustration 14.7)**. The tool will extend down into the timing chain cover, so be sure the strap or wire hanger on the tool does not fall into the cover or it will be very difficult to remove the tool when the camshaft has been installed.

5   If a tensioner retaining tool is not available, try using a block of wood with some mechanics wire tied through it as an alternative.

6   Remove the camshaft sprocket bolt and distributor drive gear. **Note:** *Lock the camshaft using a large pair of Vise-grips or Channellocks. Fasten the tool onto the camshaft without contacting the camshaft lobes. Position the tool only on the spaces between the lobes that are equipped with a notched relief specifically designed for retaining the camshaft. Remove the timing chain and camshaft sprocket as a single unit from the camshaft* **(see illustration)**. *Suspend the camshaft sprocket, with the chain still attached, out of the way.*

7   Lift out the camshaft, wipe it off with a clean shop towel and set it aside.

### Inspection

*Refer to illustrations 13.8 and 13.11*

8   To check camshaft endplay:

a)   *Install the camshaft and secure it with caps 1 and 5.*

b)   *Mount a dial indicator on the head* **(see illustration)**.

c)   *Using a large screwdriver as a lever at the opposite end, move the camshaft forward-and-backward and note the dial indicator reading.*

d)   *Compare the reading with the endplay listed in this Chapter's Specifications.*

e)   *If the indicated reading is higher, either the camshaft or the head is worn. Replace parts as necessary.*

9   To check camshaft runout:

a)   *Support the camshaft with a pair of V-blocks and attach a dial indicator with the stem resting against the center bearing journal on the camshaft.*

**13.6  An exploded view of the rocker arm assembly and cylinder head**

SEAL

WITHOUT JET VALVE

WITH JET VALVE

VALVE GUIDE

VALVE SEAT

SEMI-CIRCULAR SEAL

b)  *Rotate the camshaft and note the indicated runout.*
c)  *Compare the results to the camshaft runout listed in this Chapter's Specifications.*
d)  *If the indicated runout exceeds the specified runout, replace the camshaft.*

10    Check the camshaft bearing journals and caps for scoring and signs of wear. If they are worn, replace the cylinder head with a new or rebuilt unit. Measure the journals on the camshaft with a micrometer, comparing your readings with this Chapter's Specifications. If the diameter of any of the journals is out of specification, replace the camshaft.

11    Check the cam lobes for wear:
a)  *Check the toe and ramp areas of each cam lobe for score marks and uneven wear. Also check for flaking and pitting.*
b)  *If there's wear on the toe or the ramp, replace the camshaft, but first try to find the cause of the wear. Look for abrasive substances in the oil and inspect the oil pump and oil passages for blockage. Lobe wear is usually caused by inadequate lubrication or dirty oil.*

**13.8  To check the crankshaft endplay, set up a dial indicator like this, with the gauge plunger touching the nose of the camshaft**

**13.11 Measure the height of the camshaft lobes at the wear zone and unworn area, then subtract the wear zone measurement from the unworn area measurement to get the actual wear - compare the wear limit listed in this Chapter's Specifications**

**13.16 Install the camshaft with the dowel pin pointing up**

c)  *Using a micrometer, calculate the lobe wear* **(see illustration)**. *If the lobe wear is greater than listed in this Chapter's Specifications, replace the camshaft.*

12    Inspect the rocker arms for wear, galling and pitting of the contact surfaces.

13    If any of the conditions described above are noted, the cylinder head is probably getting insufficient lubrication or dirty oil, so make sure you track down the cause of this problem (low oil level, low oil pump capacity, clogged oil passage, etc.)  before installing a new head, camshaft or followers.

## *Installation*

*Refer to illustration 13.16*

14    Thoroughly clean the camshaft, the bearing surfaces in the head and caps and the rocker arms. Remove all sludge and dirt. Wipe off all components with a clean, lint-free cloth.

15    Lubricate the contact surfaces on the top of the rocker arms with assembly lube or moly-base grease. Install the rocker arms, making sure you put them in their original locations.

16    Lubricate the camshaft bearing surfaces in the head and the bearing journals and lobes on the camshaft with assembly lube or moly-base grease. Carefully lower the camshaft into position with the dowel pin pointing up **(see illustration)**. **Caution:** *Failure to adequately lubricate the camshaft and related components can cause serious damage to bearing and friction surfaces during the first few seconds after engine start-up, when the oil pressure is low or nonexistent.*

17    Apply a thin coat of assembly lube or moly-base grease to the bearing surfaces of the camshaft bearing caps.

18    Apply anaerobic-type sealant to the cylinder head contact surfaces of bearing caps 1 and 5 and install the rocker arm assembly.

19    Install the bolts for bearing caps 2 and 4. Gradually tighten all four fasteners - 1/4-turn at a time - until the camshaft is drawn down and seated in the bearing saddles. Don't tighten the fasteners completely at this time.

20    Install the bolts into bearing caps 3 and 5 and tighten the fasteners the same way you did for caps 2 and 4.

21    Install a new oil seal on the camshaft, then install bearing cap 1. Don't tighten the fasteners completely at this time.

22    Remove any excess sealant from the two end bearing caps.

23    Working in a criss-cross pattern, tighten the fasteners for bearing caps 2 and 4 to the torque listed in this Chapter's Specifications. Then torque the fasteners for bearing caps 3 and 5 the same way. Finally, tighten the fasteners for bearing cap 1.

24    Install the camshaft sprocket and timing chain and related components (see Section 10). If you suspended the camshaft sprocket out of the way and didn't disturb the timing chain or sprockets, the valve timing should still be correct. Rotate the camshaft as necessary to

reattach the sprocket to the camshaft. If the valve timing was disturbed, align the sprockets and install the chain as described in Section 10.

25    Remove the spark plugs and rotate the crankshaft by hand to make sure the valve timing is correct. After two revolutions, the timing marks on the sprockets should still be aligned. If they're not, reindex the timing chain to the sprockets (see Section 10). **Note:** *If you feel resistance while rotating the crankshaft, stop immediately and check the valve timing by referring to Section 10.*

26    The remainder of installation is the reverse of removal.

## 14    Cylinder head - removal and installation

**Caution:** *Allow the engine to cool completely before beginning this procedure.*

## *Removal*

*Refer to illustrations 14.7 and 14.8*

1    Position the number one piston at Top Dead Center (see Section 3).

2    Disconnect the negative cable from the battery.

3    Drain the cooling system and remove the spark plugs (see Chapter 1).

4    Remove the intake and exhaust manifold (see Sections 7 and 8). **Note:** *If you're only replacing the cylinder head gasket, it isn't necessary to remove the manifolds. If you leave the manifolds attached, you may need an assistant to help lift the head off the engine, since it will be quite heavy.*

5    Remove the valve cover (see Section 4).

**14.7 Before removing the camshaft sprocket, position the tensioner locking tool between the chain, at the tensioner - be sure the tool has long rope or wire attached to the end of it so it can be easily removed after the job - if the tool is not available, a block of wood and a length of mechanic's wire may also work**

**14.8 Loosen the bolts 1/4-turn at a time, in the sequence shown, until they can be removed by hand**

94 N•m (69 FT. LBS.) COLD ENGINE
103 N•m (75 FT. LBS.) HOT ENGINE

18 N•m (156 IN. LBS.)

**14.16 Cylinder head bolt TIGHTENING sequence**

6    Remove the distributor (see Chapter 5), including the cap and wires.

7    Remove the balance shaft chain and sprockets (see Section 9) and the timing chain and sprocket (see Section 10). **Note:** *It is possible to use a tensioner locking tool* **(see illustration)** *to hold the chain and tensioner in place while the cylinder head is off the engine. This will save time you by not having to remove the timing chain and balance shaft chain assemblies. Be sure to install the tool very tight to prevent it from popping out when the engine is shaken or jarred.*

8    Loosen the head bolts in 1/4-turn increments until they can be removed by hand. Follow the recommended sequence to avoid warping the head **(see illustration)**. Note where each bolt goes so it can be returned to the same location on installation.

9    Lift the head off the engine. If resistance is felt, don't pry between the head and block gasket mating surfaces - damage to the mating surfaces will result. Instead, pry against the casting protrusions on the sides of the cylinder head. Set the head on blocks of wood to prevent damage to the gasket sealing surfaces.

10   Cylinder head disassembly and inspection procedures are covered in detail in Chapter 2, Part C. It's a good idea to have the head checked for warpage, even if you're just replacing the gasket.

## Installation

*Refer to illustration 14.16*

11   The mating surfaces of the cylinder head and block must be perfectly clean when the head is installed.

12   Use a gasket scraper to remove all traces of carbon and old gasket material, then clean the mating surfaces with lacquer thinner or acetone. If there's oil on the mating surfaces when the head is installed, the gasket may not seal correctly and leaks may develop. When working on the block, stuff the cylinders with clean shop rags to keep out debris. Use a vacuum cleaner to remove material that falls into the cylinders. Since the head is made of aluminum, aggressive scraping can cause damage. Be extra careful not to nick or gouge the mating surfaces with the scraper.

13   Check the block and head mating surfaces for nicks, deep scratches and other damage. If damage is slight, it can be removed with a file; if it's excessive, machining may be the only alternative.

14   Use a tap of the correct size to chase the threads in the head bolt holes. Mount each head bolt in a vise and run a die down the threads to remove corrosion and restore the threads. Dirt, corrosion, sealant and damaged threads will affect torque readings.

15   Place a new gasket on the block. Check to see if there are any markings (such as "TOP") on the gasket that say how it is to be installed. Set the cylinder head in position.

16   Install the bolts. They must be tightened in a specific sequence **(see illustration)**, in the stages and to the torques listed in this Chapter's Specifications. **Note:** *Use the first and second ("engine cold") steps in the Specifications.*

17   Reinstall the timing chain and balance shaft chain, if removed. If a tensioner locking tool was used, attach the camshaft sprocket and

remove the tool.

18   Reinstall the remaining parts in the reverse order of removal.

19   Be sure to refill the cooling system and check all fluid levels.

20   Rotate the crankshaft clockwise slowly by hand through two complete revolutions. Recheck the camshaft timing marks (see Section 10). **Caution:** *If you feel any resistance while turning the engine over, stop and recheck the camshaft timing. The valves may be hitting the pistons.*

21   Start the engine and check the ignition timing (see Chapter 1).

22   Run the engine until normal operating temperature is reached. Check for leaks and proper operation.

23   Remove the valve cover and re-torque the cylinder head bolts while the engine is hot (use Step 3 in the Specifications), then re-install the valve cover.

## 15   Oil pan - removal and installation

*Refer to illustration 15.4*

**Note:** *The following procedure is based on the assumption that the engine is in the vehicle.*

1    Warm up the engine, then drain the oil and replace the oil filter (see Chapter 1).

2    Detach the cable from the negative battery terminal.

3    Raise the vehicle and support it securely on jackstands.

4    Remove the bolts securing the oil pan to the engine block **(see illustration)**.

5    Tap on the pan with a soft-face hammer to break the gasket seal, then detach the oil pan from the engine. Don't pry between the block and oil pan mating surfaces.

6    Using a gasket scraper, remove all traces of old gasket and/or sealant from the engine block and oil pan. Remove the seals from each

**15.4  Remove the bolts from the oil pan**

**2B**

**16.3  An exploded view of the oil pump assembly and the oil pan**

**16.5  Check oil pump bearing clearance on each gear**

**16.6a  Use a straightedge and a feeler gauge to check the endplay on the driven gear**

end of the engine block or oil pan. Clean the mating surfaces with lacquer thinner or acetone. Make sure the threaded bolt holes in the block are clean.

7     Clean the oil pan with solvent and dry it thoroughly. Check the gasket flanges for distortion, particularly around the bolt holes. If necessary, place the pan on a block of wood and use a hammer to flatten and restore the gasket surfaces.

8     Install the oil pan end seals, then apply a 1/8-inch wide bead of RTV sealant to the oil pan gasket surfaces. Continue the bead across the end seals. Make sure the sealant is applied to the inside edge of the bolt holes.

9     Carefully place the oil pan in position.

10    Install the bolts and tighten them in 1/4-turn increments to the torque listed in this Chapter's Specifications. Start with the bolts closest to the center of the pan and work out in a spiral pattern. Don't overtighten them or leakage may occur.

11    Add oil, run the engine and check for oil leaks.

## 16  Oil pump - removal, inspection and installation

### Removal

*Refer to illustration 16.3*

1     Remove the timing chain (see Section 10).

2     Remove the oil pan (see Section 15).

3     Remove the oil pump mounting bolts (**see illustration**) and remove the oil pump assembly.

### Inspection

*Refer to illustrations 16.5, 16.6a 16.6b, 16.7, 16.8, 16.9 and 16.11*

4     Remove the bolts and lift off the oil pump cover.

5     Check the oil pump bearing clearance on each gear (**see illustration**).

6     Using feeler gauges and a straightedge, check the endplay of the driven gear and the drive gear (**see illustrations**).

7     Check the clearance between the driven gear and the pump housing with feeler gauges (**see illustration**).

8     Check the clearance between the drive gear and the pump housing with feeler gauges (**see illustration**).

9     Extract the spring and oil pump relief valve from the pump housing (**see illustration**). Measure the free length of the oil pressure relief valve spring.

10    Compare the measurements to the oil pump Specifications at the beginning of this Chapter. If any of them are outside the limits, replace the pump.

11    Install the gears with the mating marks aligned together (**see illustration**). Install the oil pressure relief valve and spring assembly. Install the pump cover and tighten the bolts to the torque listed in this Chapter's Specifications.

16.6b  Use a straightedge and a feeler gauge to check the endplay on the drive gear

16.7  Check the driven gear-to-housing clearance

16.8  Check the drive gear-to-housing clearance

16.9  Remove the oil pressure relief valve spring and measure its free length

## Installation

12    Apply a thin coat of RTV sealant to the mating surface of the pump and place the pump in position. Rotate it back-and-forth a little to ensure there's positive contact between the pump and the engine block.

13    Coat the threads of the mounting bolts with RTV sealant and, while holding the pump securely in place, install the bolts. Tighten them to the torque listed in this Chapter's Specifications.

14    Install a new gasket on the oil pick-up tube - if removed - **(see illustration 16.3)** and Install the oil pick-up tube and screen. Tighten the bolts to the torque listed in this Chapter's Specifications.

15    Install the oil pan (see Section 15).

## 17   Flywheel/driveplate - removal and installation

This procedure is essentially the same for all engines. Refer to Part A and follow the procedure outlined there. However, use the bolt torque listed in this Chapter.

16.11  Be sure the mating marks on the oil pump gears are aligned when assembling the oil pump

**18.1  An exploded view of the rear main oil seal assembly**

**★CAUTION: NUT "C" MUST BE TIGHTENED BEFORE BOLT "B"**

**19.1a  An exploded view of the right engine mount on the 2.6L engine**

**19.1b  An exploded view of the front engine mount on the 2.6L engine**

## 18   Rear main oil seal - replacement

*Refer to illustration 18.1*

   This procedure is essentially the same for all engines. Refer to Part A and follow the procedure outlined there. However, use the bolt torque listed in this Chapter's Specifications **(see illustration)**.

## 19   Engine mounts - check, replacement and adjustment

*Refer to illustrations 19.1a and 19.1b*

   This procedure is essentially the same for all engines. Refer to Part A and follow the procedure outlined there **(see illustrations)**. However, use the bolt torque listed in this Chapter's Specifications.

# Chapter 2 Part C
# General engine overhaul procedures

## Contents

**2C**

## Specifications

### 2.2L and 2.5L engines

#### General
| | |
|---|---|
| Displacement | |
|   2.2L | 135 cubic inches |
|   2.5L | 153 cubic inches |
| Cylinder compression pressure | 130 to 150 psi at 250 rpm |
| Oil pressure (at 3000 rpm) | 25 to 80 psi |

#### Engine block
| | |
|---|---|
| Cylinder taper limit | |
|   1984 and earlier | 0.010 inch |
|   1985 on | 0.005 inch |
| Cylinder out-of-round limit | |
|   1984 and earlier | 0.005 inch |
|   1985 on | 0.002 inch |

#### Pistons and rings
| | |
|---|---|
| Piston diameter | |
|   2.2L engine | 3.443 to 3.445 inches |
|   2.5L engine | 3.442 to 3.445 inches |
| Piston-to-bore clearance | 0.001 to 0.003 inch |
| Piston ring side clearance | |
|   Top compression ring | |
|     Standard | 0.0015 to 0.0031 inch |
|     Service limit | 0.004 inch |
|   Second compression ring | |
|     Standard | 0.0015 to 0.0037 inch |
|     Service limit | 0.004 inch |
|   Oil ring | 0.008 inch |
| Piston ring end gap | |
|   Top compression ring | |
|     Standard | 0.010 to 0.020 inch |
|     Service limit | 0.039 inch |

## 2.2L and 2.5L engines (continued)

Piston ring end gap (continued)
  Second compression ring
    Standard ........................................................................ 0.011 to 0.021 inch
    Service limit.................................................................... 0.039 inch
  Oil ring
    Standard ........................................................................ 0.015 to 0.055 inch
    Service limit.................................................................... 0.074 inch

## Crankshaft and connecting rods

Endplay
  Standard ............................................................................ 0.002 to 0.007 inch
  Service limit........................................................................ 0.014 inch
Main bearing journal
  Diameter ............................................................................ 2.362 to 2.363 inches
  Taper limit.......................................................................... 0.0003 inch
  Out-of-round limit.............................................................. 0.0005 inch
Connecting rod journal
  Diameter ............................................................................ 1.968 to 1.969 inches
  Out-of-round/taper limits .................................................. 0.0003 inch
Main bearing oil clearance
  Standard ............................................................................ 0.0004 to 0.0028 inch
  Service limit........................................................................ 0.004 inch
Connecting rod bearing oil clearance
  Standard ............................................................................ 0.0008 to 0.0034 inch
  Service limit........................................................................ 0.004 inch
Connecting rod endplay (side clearance) ................................ 0.005 to 0.013 inch

## Camshaft

Endplay
  Standard ............................................................................ 0.005 to 0.013 inch
  Service limit........................................................................ 0.020 inch

## Cylinder head and valves

Head warpage limit.................................................................. 0.004 inch
Valve seat angle...................................................................... 45-degrees
Valve face angle...................................................................... 45-degrees
Valve margin width
  Intake
    Standard ........................................................................ 1/16 inch
    Service limit.................................................................... 1/32 inch
  Exhaust
    Standard ........................................................................ 1/16 inch
    Service limit.................................................................... 3/64 inch
Valve stem diameter
  Intake .................................................................................. 0.3124 inch
  Exhaust................................................................................ 0.3103 inch
Valve stem-to-guide clearance
  Intake .................................................................................. 0.0009 to 0.0026 inch
  Exhaust................................................................................ 0.003 to 0.0047 inch
Valve spring free length
  1984 and earlier .................................................................. 2.28 inches
  1985 on ............................................................................... 2.39 inches
Valve spring installed height .................................................. 1.62 to 1.68 inches

## Torque specifications*                           **Ft-lbs** (unless otherwise indicated)

Main bearing cap bolts
  Step 1 .................................................................................. 30
  Step 2 .................................................................................. Tighten an additional 1/4-turn
Connecting rod bearing cap nuts
  Step 1 .................................................................................. 40
  Step 2 .................................................................................. Tighten an additional 1/4-turn
Balance shaft assembly (2.5L engine only)
  Carrier-to-block bolts .......................................................... 40
  Double-ended stud and gear cover bolts ........................... 105 in-lbs
  Crankshaft sprocket bolts................................................... 130 in-lbs
  Tensioner bolts.................................................................... 105 in-lbs
  Guide bolts.......................................................................... 105 in-lbs
  Balance shaft gear bolt ...................................................... 21

* **Note:** *Refer to Part A for additional torque specifications.*

## 2.6L engine

### General
Displacement .................................................................. 156 cubic inches
Cylinder compression pressure ................................... 130 to 150 psi at 250 rpm
Oil pressure (at 3000 rpm) .......................................... 25 to 90 psi

### Engine block
Cylinder taper limit ....................................................... 0.0008 inch
Cylinder out-of-round limit .......................................... 0.0008 inch

### Pistons and rings
Piston diameter .............................................................. 3.5866 inches
Piston ring side clearance
  Top compression ring
    Standard ............................................................ 0.0024 to 0.0039 inch
    Service limit ...................................................... 0.006 inch
  Second compression ring
    Standard ............................................................ 0.0008 to 0.0024 inch
    Service limit ...................................................... 0.0039 inch
Piston ring end gap
  Top compression ring
    Standard ............................................................ 0.010 to 0.018 inch
    Service limit ...................................................... 0.039 inch
  Second compression ring
    Standard ............................................................ 0.010 to 0.018 inch
    Service limit ...................................................... 0.039 inch
  Oil ring
    Standard ............................................................ 0.0078 to 0.0350 inch
    Service limit ...................................................... 0.059 inch

### Crankshaft and connecting rods
Endplay ........................................................................... 0.002 to 0.007 inch
Main bearing journal
  Diameter ................................................................. 2.3622 inches
  Taper limit ............................................................... 0.0004 inch
  Out-of-round limit .................................................. 0.0004 inch
Connecting rod journal
  Diameter ................................................................. 2.0866 inches
  Out-of-round/taper limits ..................................... 0.0003 inch
Main bearing oil clearance
  Standard .................................................................. 0.0008 to 0.0028 inch
  Service limit ........................................................... 0.004 inch
Connecting rod bearing oil clearance ....................... 0.0008 to 0.0028 inch
Connecting rod endplay (side clearance) ................. 0.004 to 0.010 inch

### Camshaft
Endplay ........................................................................... 0.004 to 0.008 inch

### Balance shaft
Front bearing journal diameter ................................... 0.906 inch
Front bearing oil clearance ......................................... 0.0008 to 0.0024 inch
Rear bearing journal diameter .................................... 1.693 inch
Rear bearing oil clearance .......................................... 0.0020 to 0.0035 inch

### Cylinder head and valves
Head warpage limit ....................................................... 0.004 inch
Valve seat angle ............................................................ 45-degrees
Valve face angle ............................................................ 45-degrees
Valve margin width
  Intake
    Standard ............................................................ 0.047 inch
    Service limit ...................................................... 0.028 inch
  Exhaust
    Standard ............................................................ 0.079 inch
    Service limit ...................................................... 0.039 inch
Valve stem-to-guide clearance
  Intake
    Standard ............................................................ 0.0012 to 0.0024 inch
    Service limit ...................................................... 0.004 inch

**2C**

## 2.6L engine (continued)

Valve stem-to-guide clearance
  Exhaust
    Standard ................................................................................. 0.0020 to 0.0035 inch
    Service limit ............................................................................ 0.006 inch
Valve spring free length
  Standard .................................................................................... 1.869 inches
  Service limit .............................................................................. 1.479 inches

Valve spring installed height
  Standard .................................................................................... 1.590 inch
  Service limit .............................................................................. 1.629 inch
Jet valve
  Stem diameter .......................................................................... 0.1693 inch
  Seat angle ................................................................................. 45-degrees
  Spring free length ..................................................................... 1.1654 inch

## Torque specifications*                                **Ft-lbs** (unless otherwise indicated)

Main bearing cap bolts ..................................................................... 58
Connecting rod bearing cap nuts ..................................................... 34

**\* Note:** *Refer to Part B for additional torque specifications.*

## 1   General information

Included in this portion of Chapter 2 are the general overhaul procedures for the cylinder head(s) and internal engine components.

The information ranges from advice concerning preparation for an overhaul and the purchase of replacement parts to detailed, step-by-step procedures covering removal and installation of internal engine components and the inspection of parts.

The following Sections have been written based on the assumption the engine has been removed from the vehicle. For information concerning in-vehicle engine repair, as well as removal and installation of the external components necessary for the overhaul, see Part A (2.2L and 2.5L engine) or B (2.6L engine) of this Chapter.

The Specifications included in this Part are only those necessary for the inspection and overhaul procedures which follow. Refer to Parts A or B for additional Specifications.

## 2   Engine overhaul - general information

*Refer to illustrations 2.4a and 2.4b*

It's not always easy to determine when, or if, an engine should be completely overhauled, as a number of factors must be considered.

High mileage isn't necessarily an indication an overhaul is

needed, while low mileage doesn't preclude the need for an overhaul. Frequency of servicing is probably the most important consideration. An engine that's had regular and frequent oil and filter changes, as well as other required maintenance, will most likely give many thousands of miles of reliable service. Conversely, a neglected engine may require an overhaul very early in its life.

Excessive oil consumption is an indication that piston rings, valve seals and/or valve guides are in need of attention. Make sure oil leaks aren't responsible before deciding the rings and/or guides are bad. Perform a cylinder compression check to determine the extent of the work required (see Section 3).

Remove the oil pressure sending unit and check the oil pressure with a gauge installed in its place **(see illustrations)**. Compare the results to this Chapter's Specifications. As a general rule, engines should have ten psi oil pressure for every 1,000 rpm. If the pressure is extremely low, the bearings and/or oil pump are probably worn out.

Loss of power, rough running, knocking or metallic engine noises, excessive valve train noise and high fuel consumption rates may also point to the need for an overhaul, especially if they're all present at the same time. If a complete tune-up doesn't remedy the situation, major mechanical work is the only solution.

An engine overhaul involves restoring the internal parts to the specifications of a new engine. During an overhaul, the piston rings are replaced and the cylinder walls are reconditioned (rebored and/or honed). If a rebore is done by an automotive machine shop, new over-size pistons will also be installed. The main bearings, connecting rod

**2.4a  Remove the oil pressure sending unit and install an oil pressure gauge in it's place (2.5L engine shown)**

**2.4b  Location of the oil pressure sending unit on 2.6L engines**

**3.6 A compression gauge with a threaded fitting for the spark plug hole is preferred over the type that requires hand pressure to maintain the seal**

bearings and camshaft bearings are generally replaced with new ones and, if necessary, the crankshaft may be reground to restore the journals. Generally, the valves are serviced as well, since they're usually in less-than-perfect condition at this point. While the engine is being overhauled, other components, such as the starter and alternator, can be rebuilt as well. The end result should be a like new engine that will give many trouble free miles. **Note:** *Critical cooling system components such as the hoses, drivebelts, thermostat and water pump MUST be replaced with new parts when an engine is overhauled. The radiator should be checked carefully to ensure it isn't clogged or leaking (see Chapter 3). Also, we don't recommend overhauling the oil pump - always install a new one when an engine is rebuilt.*

Before beginning the engine overhaul, read through the entire procedure to familiarize yourself with the scope and requirements of the job. Overhauling an engine isn't particularly difficult, if you follow all of the instructions carefully, have the necessary tools and equipment and pay close attention to all specifications; however, it can be time consuming. Plan on the vehicle being tied up for a minimum of two weeks, especially if parts must be taken to an automotive machine shop for repair or reconditioning. Check on availability of parts and make sure any necessary special tools and equipment are obtained in advance. Most work can be done with typical hand tools, although a number of precision measuring tools are required for inspecting parts to determine if they must be replaced. Often an automotive machine shop will handle the inspection of parts and offer advice concerning reconditioning and replacement. **Note:** *Always wait until the engine has been completely disassembled and all components, especially the engine block, have been inspected before deciding what service and repair operations must be performed by an automotive machine shop. Since the block's condition will be the major factor to consider when determining whether to overhaul the original engine or buy a rebuilt one, never purchase parts or have machine work done on other components until the block has been thoroughly inspected. As a general rule, time is the primary cost of an overhaul, so it doesn't pay to install worn or substandard parts.*

As a final note, to ensure maximum life and minimum trouble from a rebuilt engine, everything must be assembled with care in a spotlessly clean environment.

## 3   Cylinder compression check

*Refer to illustration 3.6*

1    A compression check will tell you what mechanical condition the upper end (pistons, rings, valves, head gaskets) of the engine is in. Specifically, it can tell you if the compression is low due to leakage caused by worn piston rings, defective valves or a blown head gasket. **Note:** *The engine must be at normal operating temperature and the battery must be fully charged for this check.*

2    Begin by cleaning the area around the spark plugs before you remove them. Compressed air should be used, if available, otherwise a small brush or even a bicycle tire pump will work. The idea is to prevent dirt from getting into the cylinders during the compression check.

3    Remove all of the spark plugs from the engine (see Chapter 1).

4    Block the throttle wide open.

5    Disable the fuel and ignition systems by removing the ECM fuse (see Chapter 6).

6    Install the compression gauge in the number one spark plug hole **(see illustration)**.

7    Crank the engine over at least seven compression strokes and watch the gauge. The compression should build up quickly in a healthy engine. Low compression on the first stroke, followed by gradually increasing pressure on successive strokes, indicates worn piston rings. A low compression reading on the first stroke, which doesn't build up during successive strokes, indicates leaking valves or a blown head gasket (a cracked head could also be the cause). Deposits on the undersides of the valve heads can also cause low compression. Record the highest gauge reading obtained.

8    Repeat the procedure for the remaining cylinders and compare the results to this Chapter's Specifications.

9    If the readings are below normal, add some engine oil (about three squirts from a plunger-type oil can) to each cylinder, through the spark plug hole, and repeat the test.

10   If the compression increases after the oil is added, the piston rings are definitely worn. If the compression doesn't increase significantly, the leakage is occurring at the valves or head gasket. Leakage past the valves may be caused by burned valve seats and/or faces or warped, cracked or bent valves.

11   If two adjacent cylinders have equally low compression, there's a strong possibility the head gasket between them is blown. The appearance of coolant in the combustion chambers or the crankcase would verify this condition.

12   If one cylinder is about 20-percent lower than the others, and the engine has a slightly rough idle, a worn exhaust lobe on the camshaft could be the cause.

13   If the compression is unusually high, the combustion chambers are probably coated with carbon deposits. If that's the case, the cylinder head(s) should be removed and decarbonized.

14   If compression in one or more cylinders is zero or varies greatly between cylinders, it would be a good idea to have a leak-down test performed by an automotive repair shop. This test will pinpoint exactly where the leakage is occurring and how severe it is.

## 4   Vacuum gauge diagnostic checks

A vacuum gauge provides valuable information about what is going on in the engine at a low cost. You can check for worn rings or cylinder walls, leaking head or intake manifold gaskets, incorrect fuel mixtures, restricted exhaust, stuck or burned valves, weak valve springs, improper ignition or valve timing and ignition problems.

Unfortunately, vacuum gauge readings are easy to misinterpret, so they should be used in conjunction with other tests to confirm the diagnosis.

Both the gauge readings and the rate of needle movement are important for accurate interpretation. Most gauges measure vacuum in inches of mercury (in-Hg). As vacuum increases (or atmospheric pressure decreases), the reading will increase. Also, for every 1,000-foot increase in elevation above sea level, the gauge readings will decrease about one inch of mercury.

Connect the vacuum gauge directly to intake manifold vacuum. Be sure no hoses are left disconnected during the test or false readings will result.

Before you begin the test, allow the engine to warm up completely. Block the wheels and set the parking brake. With the transmis-

**2C**

sion in Park, start the engine and allow it to run at normal idle speed. **Warning:** *Carefully inspect the fan blades for cracks or damage before starting the engine. Keep your hands and the vacuum tester clear of the fan and do not stand in front of the vehicle or in line with the fan when the engine is running.*

Read the vacuum gauge; an average, healthy engine should normally produce about 17 to 22 inches of vacuum with a fairly steady needle. Refer to the following vacuum gauge readings and what they indicate about the engines condition:

1    A low, steady reading usually indicates a leaking gasket between the intake manifold and throttle body, a leaky vacuum hose, late ignition timing or incorrect camshaft timing. Eliminate all other possible causes, utilizing the tests provided in this Chapter before you remove the timing chain cover to check the timing marks.

2    If the reading is three to eight inches below normal and it fluctuates at that low reading, suspect an intake manifold gasket leak at an intake port.

3    If the needle has regular drops of about two to four inches at a steady rate, the valves are probably leaking. Perform a compression or leak-down test to confirm this.

4    An irregular drop or down-flick of the needle can be caused by a sticking valve or an ignition misfire. Perform a compression or leak-down test and read the spark plugs.

5    A rapid vibration of about four inches-Hg vibration at idle combined with exhaust smoke indicates worn valve guides. Perform a leak-down test to confirm this. If the rapid vibration occurs with an increase in engine speed, check for a leaking intake manifold gasket or head gasket, weak valve springs, burned valves or ignition misfire.

6    A slight fluctuation, say one inch up and down, may mean ignition problems. Check all the usual tune-up items and, if necessary, run the engine on an ignition analyzer.

7    If there is a large fluctuation, perform a compression or leak-down test to look for a weak or dead cylinder or a blown head gasket.

8    If the needle moves slowly through a wide range, check for a clogged PCV system, incorrect idle fuel mixture, throttle body or intake manifold gasket leaks.

9    Check for a slow return after revving the engine by quickly snapping the throttle open until the engine reaches about 2,500 rpm and let it shut. Normally the reading should drop to near zero, rise above normal idle reading (about 5 in-Hg over) and then return to the previous idle reading. If the vacuum returns slowly and doesn't peak when the throttle is snapped shut, the rings may be worn. If there is a long delay, look for a restricted exhaust system (often the muffler or catalytic converter). An easy way to check this is to temporarily disconnect the exhaust ahead of the suspected part and re-test.

## 5    Engine removal - methods and precautions

If you've decided the engine must be removed for overhaul or major repair work, several preliminary steps should be taken.

Locating a suitable place to work is extremely important. Adequate work space, along with storage space for the vehicle, will be needed. If a shop or garage isn't available, at the very least a flat, level, clean work surface made of concrete or asphalt is required.

Cleaning the engine compartment and engine before beginning the removal procedure will help keep tools clean and organized.

An engine hoist or A-frame will also be necessary. Make sure the equipment is rated in excess of the combined weight of the engine and transaxle. Safety is of primary importance, considering the potential hazards involved in lifting the engine out of the vehicle.

If the engine is being removed by a novice, a helper should be available. Advice and aid from someone more experienced would also be helpful. There are many instances when one person cannot simultaneously perform all of the operations required when lifting the engine out of the vehicle.

Plan the operation ahead of time. Arrange for or obtain all of the tools and equipment you'll need prior to beginning the job. Some of the equipment necessary to perform engine removal and installation safely and with relative ease are (in addition to an engine hoist) a heavy duty floor jack, complete sets of wrenches and sockets as described in the front of this manual, wooden blocks and plenty of rags and cleaning solvent for mopping up spilled oil, coolant and gasoline. If the hoist must be rented, be sure to arrange for it in advance and perform all of the operations possible without it beforehand. This will save you money and time.

Plan for the vehicle to be out of use for quite a while. A machine shop will be required to perform some of the work which the do-it-yourselfer can't accomplish without special equipment. These shops often have a busy schedule, so it would be a good idea to consult them before removing the engine in order to accurately estimate the amount of time required to rebuild or repair components that may need work.

Always be extremely careful when removing and installing the engine. Serious injury can result from careless actions. Plan ahead, take your time and a job of this nature, although major, can be accomplished successfully.

## 6    Engine - removal and installation

*Refer to illustrations 6.5 and 6.18*

**Warning:** *Gasoline is extremely flammable, so take extra precautions when disconnecting any part of the fuel system. Don't smoke or allow open flames or bare light bulbs in or near the work area and don't work in a garage where a natural gas appliance (such as a clothes dryer or water heater) is installed. If you spill gasoline on your skin, rinse it off immediately. Have a fire extinguisher rated for gasoline fires handy and know how to use it! Also, the air conditioning system is under high pressure - have a dealer service department or service station discharge the system before disconnecting any of the hoses or fittings.*

**Note:** *Read through the following steps carefully and familiarize yourself with the procedure before beginning work.*

### *Removal*

1    If the vehicle is equipped with air conditioning, have the air conditioning system discharged and the refrigerant recovered by a dealer service department or service station. **Note:** *On most models the air conditioning compressor can be unbolted and repositioned aside without disconnecting the hoses. If you wish to attempt this, and save the cost of recharging the air conditioning system, skip this step.*

2    Refer to Chapter 4 and relieve the fuel system pressure, then disconnect the negative cable from the battery.

3    Cover the fenders and cowl and remove the hood (see Chapter 11). Special pads are available to protect the fenders, but an old bedspread or blanket will also work.

4    Remove the air cleaner assembly (see Chapter 4).

5    Label the vacuum lines, emissions system hoses, wiring connec-

**6.5  Label each wire before unplugging the connector**

tors, ground straps and fuel lines to ensure correct reinstallation, then detach them. Pieces of masking tape with numbers or letters written on them work well **(see illustration)**. If there's any possibility of confusion, make a sketch of the engine compartment and clearly label the lines, hoses and wires.

6    Raise the vehicle and support it securely on jackstands. Drain the cooling system (see Chapter 1).

7    Label and detach all coolant hoses from the engine.

8    Remove the coolant reservoir, cooling fan, shroud and radiator (see Chapter 3).

9    Remove the drivebelt(s) and idler, if equipped (see Chapter 1).

10    Disconnect the fuel lines running from the engine to the chassis (see Chapter 4). Plug or cap all open fittings/lines.

11    Disconnect the throttle linkage (and TV linkage/cruise control cable, if equipped) from the engine (see Chapters 4 and 7).

12    Unbolt the power steering pump and set it aside (see Chapter 10). Leave the lines/hoses attached and make sure the pump is kept in an upright position in the engine compartment.

13    Unbolt the air conditioning compressor (see Chapter 3) and either remove it or secure it aside. **Caution:** *Make sure the system is properly discharged before loosening any refrigerant hoses.*

14    Drain the engine oil and remove the filter (see Chapter 1).

15    Remove the starter and the alternator (see Chapter 5).

16    Check for clearance and remove the brake master cylinder, if necessary, to allow clearance for the transaxle (see Chapter 9).

17    Disconnect the exhaust system from the engine (see Chapter 4).

18    Mark the relationship of the torque converter to the driveplate, then remove the torque converter bolts **(see illustration)**. The bolts are much easier to access at this time before the engine and transaxle are removed. Do not remove any of the transaxle-to-engine mounting bolts.

19    Support the transaxle with a jack. Position a block of wood on the jack head to prevent damage to the transaxle.

20    Attach an engine sling or a length of chain to the lifting brackets on the engine.

21    Roll the hoist into position and connect the sling to it. Take up the slack in the sling or chain, but don't lift the engine. **Warning:** *DO NOT place any part of your body under the engine when it's supported only by a hoist or other lifting device.*

22    Remove the driveaxles (see Chapter 8).

23    Remove the transaxle-to-body mount through-bolt and pry the mount out of the frame bracket. Refer to the appropriate Chapter (2A or 2B) for complete illustrations of the engine mounts.

24    Remove the engine mount-to-chassis bolts/nuts.

25    Recheck to be sure nothing is still connecting the engine to the vehicle (or transaxle, where applicable). Disconnect anything still remaining.

26    Raise the engine (or engine/transaxle assembly) slightly to disen-

gage the mounts. Slowly raise the engine out of the vehicle. Check carefully to make sure nothing is hanging up as the hoist is raised.

27    Once the engine/transaxle assembly is out of the vehicle, lower it to the ground and support it on wood blocks. Remove the transaxle-to-engine block bolts and carefully separate the engine from the transaxle. If you're working on a vehicle with an automatic transaxle, be sure the torque converter stays in place (clamp a pair of vise-grips to the housing to keep the converter from sliding out). If you're working on a vehicle with a manual transaxle, the input shaft must be completely disengaged from the clutch.

28    Remove the clutch and flywheel or driveplate and mount the engine on an engine stand.

## Installation

29    Check the engine and transaxle mounts. If they're worn or damaged, replace them.

30    If you're working on a manual transaxle equipped vehicle, install the clutch and pressure plate (see Chapter 7). Now is a good time to install a new clutch. Apply a dab of high-temperature grease to the input shaft.

31    **Caution:** *DO NOT use the transaxle-to-engine bolts to force the transaxle and engine together. If you're working on an automatic transaxle equipped vehicle, take great care when installing the torque converter, following the procedure outlined in Chapter 7.*

32    Carefully lower the engine/transaxle into the engine compartment - make sure the mounts line up. Reinstall the remaining components in the reverse order of removal. Double-check to make sure everything is hooked up right.

33    Add coolant, oil, power steering and transmission fluid as needed. If the brake master cylinder was removed, bleed the brakes (see Chapter 9). Recheck the fluid level and test the brakes.

34    Run the engine and check for leaks and proper operation of all accessories, then install the hood and test drive the vehicle.

35    If the air conditioning system was discharged, have it evacuated, recharged and leak tested by the shop that discharged it.

---

### 7    Engine rebuilding alternatives

The home mechanic is faced with a number of options when performing an engine overhaul. The decision to replace the engine block, piston/connecting rod assemblies and crankshaft depends on a number of factors, with the number one consideration being the condition of the block. Other considerations are cost, access to machine shop facilities, parts availability, time required to complete the project and the extent of prior mechanical experience.

Some of the rebuilding alternatives include:

**Individual parts** - If the inspection procedures reveal the engine block and most engine components are in reusable condition, purchasing individual parts may be the most economical alternative. The block, crankshaft and piston/connecting rod assemblies should all be inspected carefully. Even if the block shows little wear, the cylinder bores should be surface-honed.

**Short block** - A short block consists of an engine block with a crankshaft and piston/connecting rod assemblies already installed. All new bearings are incorporated and all clearances will be correct. The existing camshaft, valve train components, cylinder head(s) and external parts can be bolted to the short block with little or no machine shop work necessary.

**Long block** - A long block consists of a short block plus an oil pump, oil pan, cylinder head(s), rocker arm cover(s), camshaft and valve train components, timing sprockets and chain and timing chain cover. All components are installed with new bearings, seals and gaskets incorporated throughout. The installation of manifolds and external parts is all that's necessary.

Give careful thought to which alternative is best for you and discuss the situation with local automotive machine shops, auto parts dealers and experienced rebuilders before ordering or purchasing replacement parts.

**6.18  Use a box-end wrench to remove the torque converter bolts**

**2C**

## 8   Engine overhaul - disassembly sequence

*Refer to illustrations 8.5a, 8.5b and 8.5c*

1    It's much easier to disassemble and work on the engine if it's mounted on a portable engine stand. A stand can often be rented quite cheaply from an equipment rental yard. Before it's mounted on a stand, the flywheel/driveplate should be removed from the engine.

2    If a stand isn't available, it's possible to disassemble the engine with it blocked up on the floor. Be extra careful not to tip or drop the engine when working without a stand.

3    If you're going to obtain a rebuilt engine, all external components must come off first, to be transferred to the replacement engine, just as they will if you're doing a complete engine overhaul yourself. These include:

> Alternator and brackets
> Emissions control components
> Distributor, ignition coil, spark plug wires and spark plugs
> Thermostat and housing cover
> Water pump
> Carburetor or EFI components
> Intake/exhaust manifolds
> Oil filter
> Engine mounts
> Clutch and flywheel/driveplate

**Note:** *When removing the external components from the engine, pay close attention to details that may be helpful or important during installation. Note the installed position of gaskets, seals, spacers, pins, brackets, washers, bolts and other small items.*

4    If you're obtaining a short block, which consists of the engine block, crankshaft, pistons and connecting rods all assembled, then the cylinder head, oil pan and oil pump will have to be removed as well. See Engine rebuilding alternatives for additional information regarding the different possibilities to be considered.

5    If you're planning a complete overhaul, the engine must be disassembled and the internal components removed in the following general order **(see illustrations):**

**2.2L and 2.5L engines**

> Valve cover
> Intake/exhaust manifolds
> Rocker arm assembly
> Hydraulic lash adjusters
> Cylinder head
> Timing belt cover
> Timing belt and sprockets
> Camshaft
> Oil pan
> Oil pump
> Piston/connecting rod assemblies
> Crankshaft and main bearings

**8.5a  Exploded view of the engine block and related components - 2.2L engine**

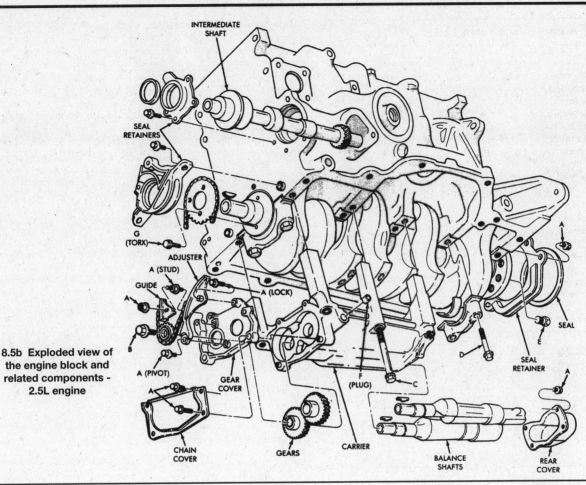

**8.5b  Exploded view of the engine block and related components - 2.5L engine**

2C

## 2.6L engine

*Valve cover*
*Timing chain housing*
*Balance shaft chain and sprockets*
*Timing chain and sprockets*
*Cylinder head and camshaft*
*Oil pan*
*Oil pump*
*Piston/connecting rod assemblies*
*Rear main oil seal housing*
*Crankshaft and main bearings*

6   Before beginning the disassembly and overhaul procedures, make sure the following items are available. Also, refer to Engine overhaul - reassembly sequence for a list of tools and materials needed for engine reassembly.

*Common hand tools*
*Small cardboard boxes or plastic bags for storing parts*
*Gasket scraper*
*Ridge reamer*
*Vibration damper puller*
*Micrometers*
*Telescoping gauges*
*Dial indicator set*
*Valve spring compressor*
*Cylinder-surfacing hone*
*Piston ring groove-cleaning tool*
*Electric drill motor*
*Tap and die set*
*Wire brushes*
*Oil gallery brushes*
*Cleaning solvent*

**8.5c  Exploded view of the engine block and related components - 2.6L engine**

**9.2   A small plastic bag, with an appropriate label, can be use to store the valve train components so the can be kept together and reinstalled in the original location**

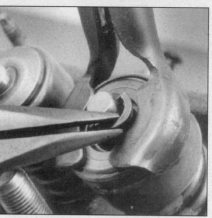

**9.3   Use a valve spring compressor to compress the spring, then remove the keepers from the valve stem**

**9.4   If the valve won't pull through the guide, deburr the edge of the stem end and the area around the top of the keeper groove with a file or whetstone.**

## 9   Cylinder head - disassembly

*Refer to illustrations 9.2, 9.3 and 9.4*

**Note:** *New and rebuilt cylinder heads are commonly available for most engines at dealerships and auto parts stores. Due to the fact that some specialized tools are necessary for the disassembly and inspection procedures, and replacement parts aren't always readily available, it may be more practical and economical for the home mechanic to purchase replacement head(s) rather than taking the time to disassemble, inspect and recondition the original(s).*

1    Cylinder head disassembly involves removal of the intake and exhaust valves and related components. The camshafts and housings must be removed before beginning the cylinder head disassembly procedure (see Part A or B of this Chapter). Label the parts or store them separately so they can be reinstalled in their original locations.

2    Before the valves are removed, arrange to label and store them, along with their related components, so they can be kept separate and reinstalled in their original locations **(see illustration)**.

3    Compress the springs on the first valve with a spring compressor and remove the keepers **(see illustration)**. Carefully release the valve spring compressor and remove the retainer, the spring and the spring seat (if used).

4    Pull the valve out of the head, then remove the oil seal from the guide. If the valve binds in the guide (won't pull through), push it back into the head and deburr the area around the keeper groove with a fine file or whetstone **(see illustration)**.

5    Repeat the procedure for the remaining valves. Remember to keep all the parts for each valve together so they can be reinstalled in the same locations.

6    Once the valves and related components have been removed and stored in an organized manner, the head should be thoroughly cleaned and inspected. If a complete engine overhaul is being done, finish the engine disassembly procedures before beginning the cylinder head cleaning and inspection process.

## 10   Cylinder head - cleaning and inspection

1    Thorough cleaning of the cylinder head(s) and related valve train components, followed by a detailed inspection, will enable you to decide how much valve service work must be done during the engine overhaul. **Note:** *If the engine was severely overheated, the cylinder head is probably warped and will require surfacing to restore flatness.*

### *Cleaning*

2    Scrape all traces of old gasket material and sealant off the head gasket, intake manifold and exhaust manifold mating surfaces. Be very careful not to gouge the cylinder head. Special gasket removal solvents that soften gaskets and make removal much easier are available at auto parts stores.

3    Remove all built up scale from the coolant passages.

4    Run a stiff wire brush through the various holes to remove deposits that may have formed in them.

5    Run an appropriate size tap into each of the threaded holes to remove corrosion and thread sealant that may be present. If compressed air is available, use it to clear the holes of debris produced by this operation. **Warning:** *Wear eye protection when using compressed air!*

6    Clean the rocker arm bolt threads with a wire brush.

7    Clean the cylinder head with solvent and dry it thoroughly. Compressed air will speed the drying process and ensure that all holes and recessed areas are clean. **Note:** *Decarbonizing chemicals are available and may prove very useful when cleaning cylinder heads and valve train components. They're very caustic and should be used with caution. Be sure to follow the instructions on the container.*

8    Clean the rocker arms and shafts with solvent and dry them thoroughly (don't mix them up during the cleaning process). Compressed air will speed the drying process and can be used to clean out the oil passages.

9    Clean all the valve springs, spring seats, keepers and retainers with solvent and dry them thoroughly. Do the components from one valve at a time to avoid mixing up the parts.

10    Scrape off any heavy deposits that may have formed on the valves, then use a motorized wire brush to remove deposits from the valve heads and stems. Again, make sure the valves don't get mixed up.

### *Inspection*

*Refer to illustrations 10.12, 10.14, 10.15, 10.16, 10.17 and 10.18*

**Note:** *Be sure to perform all of the following inspection procedures before concluding machine shop work is required. Make a list of the items that need attention.*

### Cylinder head

11    Inspect the head very carefully for cracks, evidence of coolant leakage and other damage. If cracks are found, check with an automotive machine shop concerning repair. If repair isn't possible, a new cylinder head should be obtained.

12    Using a straightedge and feeler gauge, check the head gasket mating surface for warpage **(see illustration)**. If the warpage exceeds the limit in this Chapter's Specifications, it can be resurfaced at an automotive machine shop.

13    Examine the valve seats in each of the combustion chambers. If

**10.12  Check the cylinder head gasket surface for warpage by trying to slip a feeler gauge under the straightedge (see this Chapter's Specifications for the maximum warpage allowed and use a feeler gauge of that thickness)**

**10.14  A dial indicator can be used to determine the valve stem-to-guide clearance (move the stem as indicated by the arrows)**

they're pitted, cracked or burned, the head will require valve service that's beyond the scope of the home mechanic.

14   Check the valve stem-to-guide clearance by measuring the lateral movement of the valve stem with a dial indicator attached securely to the head **(see illustration)**. The valve must be in the guide and approximately 1/16-inch off the seat. The total valve stem movement indicated by the gauge needle must be divided by two to obtain the actual clearance. After this is done, if there's still some doubt regarding the condition of the valve guides, they should be checked by an automotive machine shop (the cost should be minimal).

## Valves

15   Carefully inspect each valve face for uneven wear, deformation, cracks, pits and burned areas **(see illustration)**. Check the valve stem for scuffing and galling and the neck for cracks. Rotate the valve and check for any obvious indication that it's bent. Look for pits and excessive wear on the end of the stem. The presence of any of these conditions indicates the need for valve service by an automotive machine shop.

16   Measure the margin width on each valve **(see illustration)**. Any valve with a margin narrower than that specified in this Chapter's Specifications will have to be replaced with a new one.

**10.15  Check the valve for wear or damage at the areas shown**

## Valve components

17   Check each valve spring for damage, broken coils, wear (on the ends) and pits. Measure the free length and compare it to this Chapter's Specifications **(see illustration)**. Any springs that are shorter than specified have sagged and shouldn't be reused. The tension of all springs should be checked with a special fixture before deciding

**10.16  The margin width on each valve must be as specified (if no margin exists, the valve cannot be reused)**

**10.17  Measure the free length of each valve spring with a dial or vernier caliper**

**10.18 Check each valve spring for squareness**

**12.4 Make sure the valve stem seals are installed evenly and carefully to avoid damage**

**12.6 Apply a small dab of grease to each keeper as shown here before installation - it'll hold them in place on the valve stem as the spring is released**

they're suitable for use in a rebuilt engine (take the springs to an automotive machine shop for this check).

18    Stand each spring on a flat surface and check it for squareness **(see illustration)**. If any of the springs are distorted or sagged, replace all of them with new parts.

19    Check the spring retainers and keepers for obvious wear and cracks. Any questionable parts should be replaced with new ones, as extensive damage will occur if they fail during engine operation.

20    If the inspection process indicates the valve components are in generally poor condition and worn beyond the limits specified, which is usually the case in an engine that's being overhauled, reassemble the valves in the cylinder head and refer to Section 11 for valve servicing recommendations.

## 11   Valves - servicing

1    Because of the complex nature of the job and the special tools and equipment needed, servicing of the valves, the valve seats and the valve guides, commonly known as a valve job, should be done by a professional.

2    The home mechanic can remove and disassemble the head, do the initial cleaning and inspection, then reassemble and deliver it to a dealer service department or an automotive machine shop for the actual service work. Doing the inspection will enable you to see what condition the head and valvetrain components are in and will ensure that you know what work and new parts are required when dealing with an automotive machine shop.

3    The dealer service department, or automotive machine shop, will remove the valves and springs, recondition or replace the valves and valve seats, recondition the valve guides, check and replace the valve springs, rotators, spring retainers and keepers (as necessary), replace the valve seals with new ones, reassemble the valve components and make sure the installed spring height is correct. The cylinder head gasket surface will also be resurfaced if it's warped.

4    After the valve job has been performed by a professional, the head will be in like new condition. When the head is returned, be sure to clean it again before installation on the engine to remove any metal particles and abrasive grit that may still be present from the valve service or head resurfacing operations. Use compressed air, if available, to blow out all the oil holes and passages.

## 12   Cylinder head - reassembly

*Refer to illustrations 12.4 and 12.6*

1    Regardless of whether or not the head was sent to an automotive repair shop for valve servicing, make sure it's clean before beginning reassembly.

2    If the head was sent out for valve servicing, the valves and related components will already be in place. Begin the reassembly procedure with Step 8.

3    Install the spring seats or valve rotators (if equipped) before the valve seals.

4    Install new seals on each of the valve guides. Using a hammer and a deep socket or seal installation tool, gently tap each seal into place until it's completely seated on the guide **(see illustration)**. Don't twist or cock the seals during installation or they won't seal properly on the valve stems.

5    Beginning at one end of the head, lubricate and install the first valve. Apply clean engine oil to the valve stem.

6    Position the valve springs (and shims, if used) over the valves. Compress the springs with a valve spring compressor and carefully install the keepers in the groove, then slowly release the compressor and make sure the keepers seat properly. Apply a small dab of grease to each keeper to hold it in place if necessary **(see illustration)**.

7    Repeat the procedure for the remaining valves. Be sure to return the components to their original locations - don't mix them up!

8    Check the installed valve spring height with a ruler graduated in 1/32-inch increments or a dial caliper. If the head was sent out for service work, the installed height should be correct (but don't automatically assume it is). The measurement is taken from the top of each spring seat to the bottom of the retainer. If the height is greater than specified in this Chapter, shims can be added under the springs to correct it. **Caution:** *Do not, under any circumstances, shim the springs to the point where the installed height is less than specified.*

9    Apply engine assembly lube to the rocker arm faces and the shaft, then install the rocker arm assembly on the cylinder head.

10    Refer to Part A or B and install the camshafts, hydraulic lash adjusters and rocker arm assemblies onto the head.

## 13   Pistons and connecting rods - removal

*Refer to illustrations 13.1, 13.3 and 13.6*
**Note:** *Prior to removing the piston/connecting rod assemblies, remove the cylinder head(s), the oil pan and the oil pump by referring to the appropriate Sections in Parts A or B of Chapter 2.*

1    Use your fingernail to feel if a ridge has formed at the upper limit of ring travel (about 1/4-inch down from the top of each cylinder). If carbon deposits or cylinder wear have produced ridges, they must be completely removed with a special tool **(see illustration)**. Follow the manufacturer's instructions provided with the tool. Failure to remove the ridges before attempting to remove the piston/connecting rod assemblies may result in piston breakage.

2    After the cylinder ridges have been removed, turn the engine upside-down so the crankshaft is facing up.

**13.1  A ridge reamer is required to remove the ridge from the top of each cylinder - do this before removing the pistons!**

**13.3  Check the connecting rod side clearance with a feeler gauge as shown**

3    Before the connecting rods are removed, check the endplay with feeler gauges. Slide them between the first connecting rod and the crankshaft throw until the play is removed **(see illustration)**. The endplay is equal to the thickness of the feeler gauge(s). If the endplay exceeds the service limit, new connecting rods will be required. If new rods (or a new crankshaft) are installed, the endplay may fall under the minimum specified in this Chapter (if it does, the rods will have to be machined to restore it - consult an automotive machine shop for advice if necessary). Repeat the procedure for the remaining connecting rods.

4    Check the connecting rods and caps for identification marks. If they aren't plainly marked, use a small center punch to make the appropriate number of indentations on each rod and cap (1, 2, 3, etc., depending on the engine type and cylinder they're associated with).

5    Loosen each of the connecting rod cap nuts 1/2-turn at a time until they can be removed by hand. Remove the number one connecting rod cap and bearing insert. Don't drop the bearing insert out of the cap.

6    Slip a short length of plastic or rubber hose over each connecting rod cap bolt to protect the crankshaft journal and cylinder wall as the piston is removed **(see illustration)**.

7    Remove the bearing insert and push the connecting rod/piston assembly out through the top of the engine. Use a wooden or plastic hammer handle to push on the upper bearing surface in the connecting rod. If resistance is felt, double-check to make sure all of the ridge was removed from the cylinder.

8    Repeat the procedure for the remaining cylinders.

9    After removal, reassemble the connecting rod caps and bearing inserts in their respective connecting rods and install the cap nuts fin-

ger tight. Leaving the old bearing inserts in place until reassembly will help prevent the connecting rod bearing surfaces from being accidentally nicked or gouged.

10   Don't separate the pistons from the connecting rods (see Section 19 for additional information).

## 14   Balance shafts (2.5L engine only) - removal and installation

**Note:** *The balance shafts should only be removed after the engine has been removed from the vehicle. It's assumed the flywheel or driveplate, timing belt, oil pan, oil pump and piston/connecting rod assemblies have already been removed.*

### Removal

*Refer to illustrations 14.2, 14.3, 14.4 and 14.5*

1    The balance shafts are installed in a carrier that is mounted to the lower engine block **(see illustration 8.5b)**. The shafts are interconnected through two gears rotating the shafts in opposite directions. These gears are driven by a chain from the crankshaft and they are geared to rotate twice the crankshaft speed. This motion will balance certain reciprocating masses within the engine.

2    Remove the chain cover, guide and tensioner from the engine block **(see illustration)**.

**13.6  To prevent damage to the crankshaft journals and cylinder walls, slip sections of rubber or plastic hose over the rod bolts before removing the pistons**

**14.2  Balance shaft chain cover, guide and tensioner details**

2C

14.3  Balance shaft chain and sprocket details

14.4  Balance shaft drive gear cover and gear details - note the difference between the drive gear and the driven gear (driven gear has longer hub)

14.5  Withdraw the balance shafts from the rear of the carrier

14.8  Balance shaft drive and driven gear details - align the dots together on installation

3    Loosen both balance shaft gear retaining bolts first, then remove the Torx bolts retaining the crankshaft sprocket **(see illustration)**. Remove the chain and sprocket assembly. **Note:** *Further disassembly of the balance shaft assembly is not required, proceed to Step 6 unless inspection is necessary.*

4    Remove the special double-ended stud from the gear cover and remove the gear cover and balance shaft gears **(see illustration)**.

5    Remove the rear cover from the carrier and remove the balance shafts **(see illustration)**. Inspect the balance shaft journals and carrier bearing surfaces for wear or damage. Inspect the gears for worn, broken or chipped teeth.

6    Remove the six bolts that retain the carrier to the crankcase.

## Installation

*Refer to illustrations 14.8, 14.11 and 14.16*

7    Lubricate the balance shaft bearing journals with engine assembly lube and install the balance shafts into the carrier. Install the rear cover. Install the carrier assembly onto the engine block and tighten the six bolts to the torque listed in this Chapter's Specifications.

8    Rotate the balance shafts until both shaft keyways face up. Install the drive gear and the driven gear onto the shafts with the alignment dots aligned **(see illustration)**.

9    Lubricate the gears with clean engine oil, install the gear cover and tighten the double-ended stud to the torque listed in this Chapter's Specifications.

10    Install the crankshaft sprocket and tighten the Torx bolts to the torque listed in this Chapter's Specifications.

11    Turn the crankshaft until the number one cylinder is at Top Dead Center (TDC) (see Chapter 2A). The timing marks on the chain sprocket should line up with the parting line on the left side of number one main bearing cap **(see illustration)**.

12    Place the chain over the crankshaft sprocket so that the nickel plated link of the chain is over the timing mark on the crankshaft sprocket.

13    Install the balance shaft sprocket into the chain so that the timing mark on the sprocket (yellow dot) mates with the yellow painted link on the chain.

14    With the balance shaft keyways pointing up, slide the balance shaft sprocket onto the end of the balance shaft. **Note:** *The timing mark on the sprocket, the painted link and the arrow on the side of the gear cover should line up if the balance shafts are correctly timed.*

15    Install the balance shaft gear bolts and tighten the bolts to the

**14.11 The mark on the crankshaft sprocket, the colored chain links and the mark on the balance shaft sprocket must be aligned for the correct timing**

torque listed in this Chapter's Specifications. **Note:** *Wedge a wood block between the crankcase and the crankshaft to prevent the crankshaft from rotating while tightening the bolts.*

16    Install the chain tensioner loosely. Place a shim (0.039 inch thick and 2.75 inches long) between the tensioner and the chain **(see illustration)** (a special tool, Chrysler tool no. C-4916, is available). Push the tensioner up against the chain. Apply firm pressure (approximately five to seven pounds) directly behind the adjustment slot to take up all the slack.

17    With pressure applied, tighten the top tensioner bolt first, then the bottom pivot bolt to the torque listed in this Chapter's Specifications. Remove the shim stock or tool.

18    Place the chain guide onto the double-ended stud, making sure the tab on the guide fits into the slot on the gear cover. Tighten the nut to the torque listed in this Chapter's Specifications.

19    Install the chain cover and tighten the bolts to the torque listed in this Chapter's Specifications.

**14.16 Apply tension to the chain directly behind the adjustment bolt on the tensioner**

## 15    Crankshaft - removal

*Refer to illustrations 15.1, 15.3, 15.4a and 15.4b*
**Note:** *The crankshaft can be removed only after the engine has been removed from the vehicle. It's assumed the flywheel or driveplate, crankshaft balancer/vibration damper, timing chain or belt, oil pan, oil pump, balance shafts (if equipped) and piston/connecting rod assemblies have already been removed. The rear main oil seal housing must be unbolted and separated from the block before proceeding with crankshaft removal.*

1    Before the crankshaft is removed, check the endplay. Mount a dial indicator with the stem in line with the crankshaft, touching one of the crank throws or on the nose of the crankshaft **(see illustration)**.

2    Push the crankshaft all the way to the rear and zero the dial indicator. Next, pry the crankshaft to the front as far as possible and check the reading on the dial indicator. The distance it moves is the endplay. If it's greater than the value listed in this Chapter's Specifications, check the crankshaft thrust surfaces for wear. If no wear is evident, new main bearings should correct the endplay.

3    If a dial indicator isn't available, feeler gauges can be used. Gently

**15.1 Checking the crankshaft endplay with a dial indicator**

**15.3 Checking the crankshaft endplay with a feeler gauge**

**2C**

**15.4a  Use a center punch or number stamping dies to mark the main bearing cap to ensure installation in the original locations on the block (make the punch marks near one of the head bolts)**

**15.4b  The main bearing caps on the 2.6L engine have arrows that point to the front of the engine**

pry or push the crankshaft all the way to the front of the engine. Slip feeler gauges between the crankshaft and the front face of the thrust main bearing to determine the clearance **(see illustration)**.

4    Check the main bearing caps to see if they're marked to indicate their locations. They should be numbered consecutively from the front of the engine to the rear. If they aren't, mark them with number stamping dies or a center-punch **(see illustration)**. Main bearing caps generally have a cast-in arrow, which points to the front of the engine **(see illustration)**. Loosen the main bearing cap bolts 1/4-turn at a time each, until they can be removed by hand. Note if any stud bolts are used and make sure they're returned to their original locations when the crankshaft is reinstalled.

5    Gently tap the caps with a soft-face hammer, then separate them from the engine block. If necessary, use the bolts as levers to remove the caps. Try not to drop the bearing inserts if they come out with the caps.

6    Carefully lift the crankshaft out of the engine. It may be a good idea to have an assistant available, since the crankshaft is quite heavy. With the bearing inserts in place in the engine block and main bearing caps, return the caps to their respective locations on the engine block and tighten the bolts finger tight.

## 16   Engine block - cleaning

*Refer to illustrations 16.4, 16.8 and 16.10*

1    Remove the main bearing caps and separate the bearing inserts from the caps and the engine block. Tag the bearings, indicating which cylinder they were removed from and whether they were in the cap or the block, then set them aside.

2    Using a gasket scraper, remove all traces of gasket material from the engine block. Be very careful not to nick or gouge the gasket sealing surfaces.

3    Remove all of the covers and threaded oil gallery plugs from the block. The plugs are usually very tight - they may have to be drilled out and the holes retapped. Use new plugs when the engine is reassembled.

4    Remove the freeze plugs from the engine block. To do this, knock one side of the plugs into the block with a hammer and punch, then grasp them with large pliers and pull them back through the holes **(see illustration)**.

5    If the engine is extremely dirty, it should be taken to an automotive machine shop to be steam cleaned or hot tanked.

6    After the block is returned, clean all oil holes and oil galleries one more time. Brushes specifically designed for this purpose are available at most auto parts stores. Flush the passages with warm water until

**16.4 Use a hammer and large punch to knock the core plugs sideways in their bores, then pull them out with pliers**

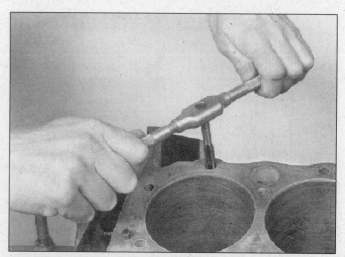

**16.8 All holes in the block - particularly the main bearing cap and head bolt holes - should be cleaned and restored with a tap (be sure to remove debris from the holes after this is done)**

**16.10 A large socket on an extension can be use to drive the new core plugs into the bores**

**17.4a Measure the diameter of each cylinder at a right angle to the engine centerline (A), and parallel to the engine centerline (B) - out-of-round is the difference between A and B; taper is the difference between A and B at the top of the cylinder and A and B at the bottom of the cylinder**

the water runs clear, dry the block thoroughly and wipe all machined surfaces with a light, rust preventive oil. If you have access to compressed air, use it to speed the drying process and blow out all the oil holes and galleries. **Warning:** *Wear eye protection when using compressed air!*

7    If the block isn't extremely dirty or sludged up, you can do an adequate cleaning job with hot soapy water and a stiff brush. Take plenty of time and do a thorough job. Regardless of the cleaning method used, be sure to clean all oil holes and galleries very thoroughly, dry the block completely and coat all machined surfaces with light oil.

8    The threaded holes in the block must be clean to ensure accurate torque readings during reassembly. Run the proper size tap into each of the holes to remove rust, corrosion, thread sealant or sludge and restore damaged threads **(see illustration)**. If possible, use compressed air to clear the holes of debris produced by this operation. Now is a good time to clean the threads on the head bolts and the main bearing cap bolts as well.

9    Reinstall the main bearing caps and tighten the bolts finger tight.

10    After coating the sealing surfaces of the new core plugs with Permatex no. 2 sealant, install them in the engine block **(see illustration)**. Make sure they're driven in straight and seated properly or leakage could result. Special tools are available for this purpose, but a large socket, with an outside diameter that will just slip into the core plug, a 1/2-inch drive extension and a hammer will work just as well.

11    Apply non-hardening sealant (such as Permatex no. 2 or Teflon pipe sealant) to the new oil gallery plugs and thread them into the holes in the block. Make sure they're tightened securely.

12    If the engine isn't going to be reassembled right away, cover it with a large plastic trash bag to keep it clean.

## 17    Engine block - inspection

*Refer to illustrations 17.4a, 17.4b and 17.4c*

1    Before the block is inspected, it should be cleaned as described in Section 16.

2    Visually check the block for cracks, rust and corrosion. Look for stripped threads in the threaded holes. It's also a good idea to have the block checked for hidden cracks by an automotive machine shop that has the special equipment to do this type of work. If defects are found, have the block repaired, if possible, or replaced.

3    Check the cylinder bores for scuffing and scoring.

4    Check the cylinders for taper and out-of-round conditions as follows **(see illustrations)**:

5    Measure the diameter of each cylinder at the top (just under the ridge area), center and bottom of the cylinder bore, parallel to the crankshaft axis.

**2C**

**17.4b The ability to "feel" when the telescoping gauge is at the correct point will be developed over time, so work slowly and repeat the check until you're satisfied the bore measurement is accurate**

**17.4c The gauge is then measured with a micrometer to determine the bore size**

**18.3a A "bottle brush" hone will produce better results if you've never honed cylinders before**

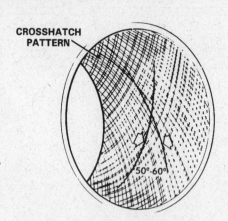

**18.3b The cylinder hone should leave a smooth, crosshatch pattern with the lines intersecting at approximately a 60-degree angle**

**19.4a The piston ring grooves can be cleaned with a special tool, as shown here,. . .**

6    Next, measure each cylinder's diameter at the same three locations perpendicular to the crankshaft axis.

7    The taper of each cylinder is the difference between the bore diameter at the top of the cylinder and the diameter at the bottom. The out-of-round specification of the cylinder bore is the difference between the parallel and perpendicular readings. Compare your results to this Chapter's Specifications.

8    Repeat the procedure for the remaining pistons and cylinders.

9    If the cylinder walls are badly scuffed or scored, or if they're out-of-round or tapered beyond the limits given in this Chapter's Specifications, have the engine block rebored and honed at an automotive machine shop. If a rebore is done, oversize pistons and rings will be required.

10    If the cylinders are in reasonably good condition and not worn to the outside of the limits, and if the piston-to-cylinder clearances can be maintained properly, they don't have to be rebored. Honing is all that's necessary (see Section 18).

## 18    Cylinder honing

*Refer to illustrations 18.3a and 18.3b*

1    Prior to engine reassembly, the cylinder bores must be honed so the new piston rings will seat correctly and provide the best possible combustion chamber seal. **Note:** *If you don't have the tools or don't want to tackle the honing operation, most automotive machine shops will do it for a reasonable fee.*

2    Before honing the cylinders, install the main bearing caps and tighten the bolts to the torque listed in this Chapter's Specifications.

3    Two types of cylinder hones are commonly available - the flex hone or "bottle brush" type and the more traditional surfacing hone with spring-loaded stones. Both will do the job, but for the less experienced mechanic the "bottle brush" hone will probably be easier to use. You'll also need some honing oil (kerosene will work if honing oil isn't available), rags and an electric drill motor. Proceed as follows:

a)  *Mount the hone in the drill motor, compress the stones and slip it into the first cylinder* **(see illustration)**. *Be sure to wear safety goggles or a face shield!*

b)  *Lubricate the cylinder with plenty of honing oil, turn on the drill and move the hone up-and-down in the cylinder at a pace that will produce a fine crosshatch pattern on the cylinder walls. Ideally, the crosshatch lines should intersect at approximately a 60-degree angle* **(see illustration)**. *Be sure to use plenty of lubricant and don't take off any more material than is absolutely necessary to produce the desired finish.* **Note:** *Piston ring manufacturers may specify a smaller crosshatch angle than the traditional 60-*

*degrees - read and follow any instructions included with the new rings.*

c)  *Don't withdraw the hone from the cylinder while it's running. Instead, shut off the drill and continue moving the hone up-and-down in the cylinder until it comes to a complete stop, then compress the stones and withdraw the hone. If you're using a "bottle brush" type hone, stop the drill motor, then turn the chuck in the normal direction of rotation while withdrawing the hone from the cylinder.*

d)  *Wipe the oil out of the cylinder and repeat the procedure for the remaining cylinders.*

4    After the honing job is complete, chamfer the top edges of the cylinder bores with a small file so the rings won't catch when the pistons are installed. Be very careful not to nick the cylinder walls with the end of the file.

5    The entire engine block must be washed again very thoroughly with warm, soapy water to remove all traces of the abrasive grit produced during the honing operation. **Note:** *The bores can be considered clean when a lint-free white cloth - dampened with clean engine oil - used to wipe them out doesn't pick up any more honing residue, which will show up as gray areas on the cloth. Be sure to run a brush through all oil holes and galleries and flush them with running water.*

6    After rinsing, dry the block and apply a coat of light rust-preventive oil to all machined surfaces. Wrap the block in a plastic trash bag to keep it clean and set it aside until reassembly.

## 19    Pistons and connecting rods - inspection

*Refer to illustrations 19.4a, 19.4b, 19.10 and 19.11*

1    Before the inspection process can be carried out, the piston/connecting rod assemblies must be cleaned and the original piston rings removed from the pistons. **Note:** *Always use new piston rings when the engine is reassembled.*

2    Using a piston ring installation tool, carefully remove the rings from the pistons. Be careful not to nick or gouge the pistons in the process.

3    Scrape all traces of carbon from the top of the piston. A hand held wire brush or a piece of fine emery cloth can be used once the majority of the deposits have been scraped away. Do not, under any circumstances, use a wire brush mounted in a drill motor to remove deposits from the pistons. The piston material is soft and may be eroded away by the wire brush.

4    Use a piston ring groove cleaning tool to remove carbon deposits from the ring grooves. If a tool isn't available, a piece broken off the old ring will do the job. Be very careful to remove only the carbon deposits

**19.4b . . . or a section of broken ring**

**19.10  Check the ring side clearance with a feeler gauge at several points around the groove**

**19.11  Measure the piston diameter at a 90-degree angle to the piston pin**

2C

- don't remove any metal and do not nick or scratch the sides of the ring grooves **(see illustrations)**.

5    Once the deposits have been removed, clean the piston/rod assemblies with solvent and dry them with compressed air (if available). **Warning:** *Wear eye protection. Make sure the oil return holes in the back sides of the ring grooves are clear.*

6    If the pistons and cylinder walls aren't damaged or worn excessively, and if the engine block isn't rebored, new pistons won't be necessary. Normal piston wear appears as even vertical wear on the piston thrust surfaces and slight looseness of the top ring in its groove. New piston rings, however, should always be used when an engine is rebuilt.

7    Carefully inspect each piston for cracks around the skirt, at the pin bosses and at the ring lands.

8    Look for scoring and scuffing on the thrust faces of the skirt, holes in the piston crown and burned areas at the edge of the crown. If the skirt is scored or scuffed, the engine may have been suffering from overheating and/or abnormal combustion, which caused excessively high operating temperatures. The cooling and lubrication systems should be checked thoroughly. A hole in the piston crown is an indication that abnormal combustion (preignition) was occurring. Burned areas at the edge of the piston crown are usually evidence of spark knock (detonation). If any of the above problems exist, the causes must be corrected or the damage will occur again. The causes may include intake air leaks, incorrect fuel/air mixture, low octane fuel, ignition timing and EGR system malfunctions.

9    Corrosion of the piston, in the form of small pits, indicates coolant is leaking into the combustion chamber and/or the crankcase. Again, the cause must be corrected or the problem may persist in the rebuilt engine.

10    Measure the piston ring side clearance by laying a new piston ring in each ring groove and slipping a feeler gauge in beside it **(see illustration)**. Check the clearance at three or four locations around each groove. Be sure to use the correct ring for each groove - they are different. If the side clearance is greater than specified in this Chapter, new pistons will have to be used.

11    Check the piston-to-bore clearance by measuring the bore (see Section 17) and the piston diameter. Make sure the pistons and bores are correctly matched. Measure the piston across the skirt, at a 90-degree angle to the piston pin **(see illustration)**. The measurement must be taken at a specific point, depending on the engine type, to be accurate.

   a)  *The piston diameter on 2.2L and 2.5L engines is measured 1.14 inches (28.9 mm) below the top of the piston.*

   b)  *2.6L engine pistons are measured 0.080 inches (2.0 mm) above the bottom of the piston skirt.*

12    Subtract the piston diameter from the bore diameter to obtain the clearance. If it's greater than specified, the block will have to be

rebored and new pistons and rings installed.

13    Check the piston-to-rod clearance by twisting the piston and rod in opposite directions. Any noticeable play indicates excessive wear, which must be corrected. The piston/connecting rod assemblies should be taken to an automotive machine shop to have the pistons and rods resized and new pins installed.

14    If the pistons must be removed from the connecting rods for any reason, they should be taken to an automotive machine shop. While they are there have the connecting rods checked for bend and twist, since automotive machine shops have special equipment for this purpose. **Note:** *Unless new pistons and/or connecting rods must be installed, do not disassemble the pistons and connecting rods.*

15    Check the connecting rods for cracks and other damage. Temporarily remove the rod caps, lift out the old bearing inserts, wipe the rod and cap bearing surfaces clean and inspect them for nicks, gouges and scratches. After checking the rods, replace the old bearings, slip the caps into place and tighten the nuts finger tight. **Note:** *If the engine is being rebuilt because of a connecting rod knock, be sure to install new rods.*

## 20  Crankshaft - inspection

*Refer to illustrations 20.1, 20.2, 20.5 and 20.7*

1    Remove all burrs from the crankshaft oil holes with a stone, file or scraper **(see illustration)**.

**20.1  The oil holes should be chamfered so sharp edges don't gouge or scratch the new bearings**

**20.2  Use a wire or stiff plastic bristle brush to clean the oil passages in the crankshaft**

**20.5  Measure the diameter of each crankshaft journal at several points to detect taper and out-of-round conditions**

2    Clean the crankshaft with solvent and dry it with compressed air (if available). **Warning:** *Wear eye protection when using compressed air.* Be sure to clean the oil holes with a stiff brush **(see illustration)** and flush them with solvent.

3    Check the main and connecting rod bearing journals for uneven wear, scoring, pits and cracks.

4    Check the rest of the crankshaft for cracks and other damage. It should be magnafluxed to reveal hidden cracks - an automotive machine shop will handle the procedure.

5    Using a micrometer, measure the diameter of the main and connecting rod journals and compare the results to this Chapter's Specifications **(see illustration)**. By measuring the diameter at a number of points around each journal's circumference, you'll be able to determine whether or not the journal is out-of-round. Take the measurement at each end of the journal, near the crank throws, to determine if the journal is tapered.

6    If the crankshaft journals are damaged, tapered, out-of-round or worn beyond the limits given in this Chapter's Specifications, have the crankshaft reground by an automotive machine shop. Be sure to use the correct size bearing inserts if the crankshaft is reconditioned.

7    Check the oil seal journals at each end of the crankshaft for wear and damage. If the seal has worn a groove in the journal, or if it's nicked or scratched **(see illustration)**, the new seal may leak when the engine is reassembled. In some cases, an automotive machine shop may be able to repair the journal by pressing on a thin sleeve. If repair isn't feasible, a new or different crankshaft should be installed.

8    Refer to Section 21 and examine the main and rod bearing inserts.

## 21   Main and connecting rod bearings - inspection

*Refer to illustration 21.1*

1    Even though the main and connecting rod bearings should be replaced with new ones during the engine overhaul, the old bearings should be retained for close examination, as they may reveal valuable information about the condition of the engine **(see illustration)**.

2    Bearing failure occurs because of lack of lubrication, the presence of dirt or other foreign particles, overloading the engine and corrosion. Regardless of the cause of bearing failure, it must be corrected before the engine is reassembled to prevent it from happening again.

**20.7  If the seals have worn grooves in the crankshaft journals, or if the seal contact surfaces are nicked or scratched, the new seals will leak**

**21.1  Typical bearing failures**

3    When examining the bearings, remove them from the engine block, the main bearing caps, the connecting rods and the rod caps and lay them out on a clean surface in the same general position as their location in the engine. This will enable you to match any bearing problems with the corresponding crankshaft journal.

4    Dirt and other foreign particles get into the engine in a variety of ways. It may be left in the engine during assembly, or it may pass through filters or the PCV system. It may get into the oil, and from there into the bearings. Metal chips from machining operations and normal engine wear are often present. Abrasives are sometimes left in engine components after reconditioning, especially when parts aren't thoroughly cleaned using the proper cleaning methods. Whatever the source, these foreign objects often end up embedded in the soft bearing material and are easily recognized. Large particles won't embed in the bearing and will score or gouge the bearing and journal. The best prevention for this cause of bearing failure is to clean all parts thoroughly and keep everything spotlessly clean during engine assembly. Frequent and regular engine oil and filter changes are also recommended.

5    Lack of lubrication (or lubrication breakdown) has a number of interrelated causes. Excessive heat (which thins the oil), overloading (which squeezes the oil from the bearing face) and oil leakage or throw off (from excessive bearing clearances, worn oil pump or high engine speeds) all contribute to lubrication breakdown. Blocked oil passages, which usually are the result of misaligned oil holes in a bearing shell, will also oil starve a bearing and destroy it. When lack of lubrication is the cause of bearing failure, the bearing material is wiped or extruded from the steel backing of the bearing. Temperatures may increase to the point where the steel backing turns blue from overheating.

6    Driving habits can have a definite effect on bearing life. Low speed operation in too high a gear (lugging the engine) puts very high loads on bearings, which tends to squeeze out the oil film. These loads cause the bearings to flex, which produces fine cracks in the bearing face (fatigue failure). Eventually the bearing material will loosen in pieces and tear away from the steel backing. Short-trip driving leads to corrosion of bearings because insufficient engine heat is produced to drive off the condensed water and corrosive gases. These products collect in the engine oil, forming acid and sludge. As the oil is carried to the engine bearings, the acid attacks and corrodes the bearing material.

7    Incorrect bearing installation during engine assembly will lead to bearing failure as well. Tight-fitting bearings leave insufficient oil clearance and will result in oil starvation. Dirt or foreign particles trapped behind a bearing insert result in high spots on the bearing which lead to failure.

## 22   Engine overhaul - reassembly sequence

1    Before beginning engine reassembly, make sure you have all the necessary new parts, gaskets and seals as well as the following items on hand:

*Common hand tools*
*Torque wrench (1/2-inch drive)*
*Piston ring installation tool*
*Piston ring compressor*
*Vibration damper installation tool*
*Short lengths of rubber or plastic hose to fit over connecting*
    *rod bolts*
*Plastigage*
*Feeler gauges*
*Fine-tooth file*
*New engine oil*
*Engine assembly lube*
*Gasket sealant*
*Thread locking compound*

2    In order to save time and avoid problems, engine reassembly must be done in the following general order:

### 2.2L and 2.5L engines

*Crankshaft and main bearings*
*Rear main oil seal housing*
*Piston/connecting rod assemblies*
*Balance shafts (if equipped)*
*Oil pump*
*Cylinder head, camshaft and rocker arms*
*Timing belt and sprockets*
*Timing belt cover*
*Oil pan*
*Intake/exhaust manifolds*
*Valve cover*
*Flywheel/driveplate*

### 2.6L engine

*Crankshaft and main bearings*
*Rear main oil seal housing*
*Piston/connecting rod assemblies*
*Oil pump*
*Timing chain and sprockets*
*Balance shaft chain and sprockets*
*Timing chain housing*
*Cylinder head and camshaft*
*Oil pan*
*Intake and exhaust manifolds*
*Valve cover*
*Flywheel/driveplate*

## 23   Piston rings - installation

*Refer to illustrations 23.3, 23.4, 23.5, 23.9a, 23.9b and 23.12*

1    Before installing the new piston rings, the ring end gaps must be checked. It's assumed the piston ring side clearance has been checked and verified correct (see Section 19).

2    Lay out the piston/connecting rod assemblies and the new ring sets so the ring sets will be matched with the same piston and cylinder during the end gap measurement and engine assembly.

3    Insert the top (number one) ring into the first cylinder and square it up with the cylinder walls by pushing it in with the top of the piston **(see illustration)**. The ring should be near the bottom of the cylinder, at the lower limit of ring travel.

4    To measure the end gap, slip feeler gauges between the ends of

**23.3  When checking piston ring end gap, the ring must be square in the cylinder bore (this is done by pushing the ring down with the top of a piston as shown)**

**23.4  With the ring in the cylinder, measure the end gap with a feeler gauge**

**23.5  If the end gap is too small, clamp a file vise and file the ring ends (from the outside in only) to enlarge the gap slightly**

**23.9a  Installing the spacer/expander in the oil control ring groove**

the ring until a gauge equal to the gap width is found **(see illustration)**. The feeler gauge should slide between the ring ends with a slight amount of drag. Compare the measurement to this Chapter's Specifications. If the gap is larger or smaller than specified, double-check to make sure you have the correct rings before proceeding.

5    If the gap is too small, it must be enlarged or the ring ends may come in contact with each other during engine operation, which can cause serious engine damage. The end gap can be increased by filing the ring ends very carefully with a fine file. Mount the file in a vise equipped with soft jaws, slip the ring over the file with the ends contacting the file teeth and slowly move the ring to remove material from the ends. When performing this operation, file only from the outside in **(see illustration)**. **Note:** *When you have the gap correct, deburr the filed ends of the rings with a fine stone.*

6    Excess end gap isn't critical unless it's greater than 0.040-inch. Again, double-check to make sure you have the correct rings for the engine.

7    Repeat the procedure for each ring that will be installed in the first cylinder and for each ring in the remaining cylinders. Remember to keep rings, pistons and cylinders matched up.

8    Once the ring end gaps have been checked/corrected, the rings can be installed on the pistons.

9    The oil control ring (lowest one on the piston) is usually installed first. It's composed of three separate components. Slip the spacer/expander into the groove **(see illustration)**. If an anti-rotation tang is used, make sure it's inserted into the drilled hole in the ring groove. Next, install the lower side rail. Don't use a piston ring installation tool on the oil ring side rails, as they may be damaged. Instead,

place one end of the side rail into the groove between the spacer/expander and the ring land, hold it firmly in place and slide a finger around the piston while pushing the rail into the groove **(see illustration)**. Next, install the upper side rail in the same manner.

10    After the three oil ring components have been installed, check to make sure both the upper and lower side rails can be turned smoothly in the ring groove.

11    The number two (middle) ring is installed next. It's usually stamped with a mark, which must face up, toward the top of the piston. **Note:** *Always follow the instructions printed on the ring package or box - different manufacturers may require different approaches. Don't mix up the top and middle rings, as they have different cross sections.*

12    Use a piston ring installation tool and make sure the identification mark is facing the top of the piston, then slip the ring into the middle groove on the piston **(see illustration)**. Don't expand the ring any more than necessary to slide it over the piston.

13    Install the number one (top) ring in the same manner. Make sure the mark is facing up. Be careful not to confuse the number one and number two rings.

14    Repeat the procedure for the remaining pistons and rings.

## 24  Crankshaft - installation and main bearing oil clearance check

*Refer to illustrations 24.11 and 24.15*

1    Crankshaft installation is the first step in engine reassembly. It's assumed at this point that the engine block and crankshaft have been

**23.9b  DO NOT use a piston ring installation tool when installing the oil ring side rails**

**23.12  Installing the compression rings with a ring expander - the mark (arrow) must face up**

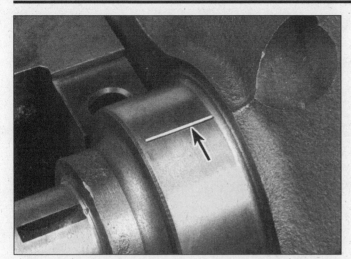

**24.11 Lay the Plastigage strips (arrow) on the main bearing journals, parallel to the crankshaft centerline**

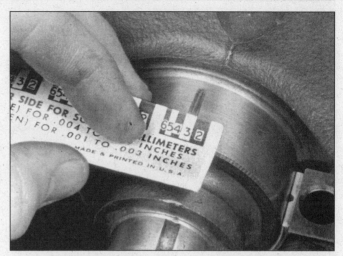

**24.15 Compare the width of the crushed Plastigage to the scale on the envelope to determine the main bearing oil clearance(always take the measurement at the widest point of the Plastigage); be sure to use the correct scale - standard and metric ones are included**

cleaned, inspected and repaired or reconditioned.

2  Position the engine with the bottom facing up.

3  Remove the main bearing cap bolts and lift out the caps. Lay them out in the proper order to ensure correct installation.

4  If they're still in place, remove the original bearing inserts from the block and the main bearing caps. Wipe the bearing surfaces of the block and caps with a clean, lint-free cloth. They must be kept spotlessly clean.

### Main bearing oil clearance check

**Note:** *Don't touch the faces of the new bearing inserts with your fingers. Oil and acids from your skin can etch the bearings.*

5  Clean the back sides of the new main bearing inserts and lay one in each main bearing saddle in the block. If one of the bearing inserts from each set has a large groove in it, make sure the grooved insert is installed in the block. Lay the other bearing from each set in the corresponding main bearing cap. Make sure the tab on the bearing insert fits into the recess in the block or cap. **Caution:** *The oil holes in the block must line up with the oil holes in the bearing inserts. Do not hammer the bearing into place and don't nick or gouge the bearing faces. No lubrication should be used at this time.*

6  The flanged thrust bearing must be installed in the number two cap and saddle (counting from the front of the engine) on 2.6L engines. On the 2.2L and 2.5L, the thrust bearing must be installed in the number three (center) cap and saddle.

7  Clean the faces of the bearings in the block and the crankshaft main bearing journals with a clean, lint-free cloth.

8  Check or clean the oil holes in the crankshaft, as any dirt here can go only one way - straight through the new bearings.

9  Once you're certain the crankshaft is clean, carefully lay it in position in the main bearings.

10  Before the crankshaft can be permanently installed, the main bearing oil clearance must be checked.

11  Cut several pieces of the appropriate-size Plastigage (they should be slightly shorter than the width of the main bearings) and place one piece on each crankshaft main bearing journal, parallel with the journal axis **(see illustration)**.

12  Clean the faces of the bearings in the caps and install the caps in their original locations (don't mix them up) with the arrows pointing toward the front of the engine. Don't disturb the Plastigage.

13  Starting with the center main and working out toward the ends, tighten the main bearing cap bolts, in three steps, to the torque figure listed in this Chapter's Specifications. Don't rotate the crankshaft at any time during this operation.

14  Remove the bolts and carefully lift off the main bearing caps. Keep them in order. Don't disturb the Plastigage or rotate the crankshaft. If any of the main bearing caps are difficult to remove, tap them

gently from side-to-side with a soft-face hammer to loosen them.

15  Compare the width of the crushed Plastigage on each journal to the scale printed on the Plastigage envelope to obtain the main bearing oil clearance **(see illustration)**. Check the Specifications to make sure it's correct.

16  If the clearance is not as specified, the bearing inserts may be the wrong size (which means different ones will be required). Before deciding different inserts are needed, make sure no dirt or oil was between the bearing inserts and the caps or block when the clearance was measured. If the Plastigage was wider at one end than the other, the journal may be tapered (see Section 20).

17  Carefully scrape all traces of the Plastigage material off the main bearing journals and/or the bearing faces. Use your fingernail or the edge of a credit card - don't nick or scratch the bearing faces.

### Final crankshaft installation

18  Carefully lift the crankshaft out of the engine.

19  Clean the bearing faces in the block, then apply a thin, uniform layer of engine assembly lube to each of the bearing surfaces. Be sure to coat the thrust faces as well as the journal face of the thrust bearing.

20  Make sure the crankshaft journals are clean, then lay the crankshaft back in place in the block.

21  Clean the faces of the bearings in the caps, then apply lubricant to them.

22  Install the caps in their original locations with the arrows pointing toward the front of the engine.

23  Install the bolts.

24  Tighten all except the thrust bearing cap bolts to the torque listed in this Chapter's Specifications (work from the center out and approach the final torque in three steps).

25  Tighten the thrust bearing cap bolts to 10-to-12 ft-lbs.

26  Tap the ends of the crankshaft forward and backward with a lead or brass hammer to line up the main bearing and crankshaft thrust surfaces.

27  Retighten all main bearing cap bolts to the torque specified in this Chapter's Specifications, starting with the center main and working out toward the ends.

28  Rotate the crankshaft a number of times by hand to check for any obvious binding.

29  The final step is to check the crankshaft endplay with feeler gauges or a dial indicator as described in Section 15. The endplay should be correct if the crankshaft thrust faces aren't worn or damaged and new bearings have been installed.

30  Refer to Section 25 and install the new rear main oil seal.

**2C**

**25.1  To remove the old crankshaft rear seal, support the housing on a pair of wood blocks and drive out the seal with a punch or screwdriver and hammer - make sure you don't damage the seal bore**

**25.2  To install the new crankshaft rear seal in the housing, simply lay the housing on a clean, flat workbench, lay a block of wood on the seal and carefully tap it into place with a hammer**

**25.3  Apply anaerobic sealant onto the upper portion of the retainer (2.2L and 2.5L engines)**

## 25   Rear main oil seal - installation

*Refer to illustrations 25.1, 25.2 and 25.3*
**Note:** *The crankshaft must be installed and the main bearing caps bolted in place before the new seal and housing assembly can be bolted to the block.*
1    Remove the old seal from the housing with a hammer and punch by driving it out from the back side **(see illustration)**. Be sure to note how far it's recessed into the housing bore before removing it; the new seal will have to be recessed an equal amount. Be very careful not to scratch or otherwise damage the bore in the housing or oil leaks could develop.
2    Make sure the housing is clean, then apply a thin coat of engine oil to the outer edge of the new seal. The seal must be pressed squarely into the housing bore, so hammering it into place isn't recommended. If you don't have access to a press, sandwich the housing and seal between two smooth pieces of wood and press the seal into place with the jaws of a large vise. If you don't have a vise big enough, lay the housing on a workbench and drive the seal into place with a block of wood and hammer **(see illustration)**. The pieces of wood must be thick enough to distribute the force evenly around the entire circumference of the seal. Work slowly and make sure the seal enters the bore squarely.
3    On 2.2L and 2.5L engines, apply anaerobic sealant on the upper portion of the retainer **(see illustration)** before installing the housing. On a 2.6L engine, install the separator with the oil hole located at the bottom of the housing and install a new gasket. Lubricate the seal lips with clean engine oil or multi-purpose grease before you slip the seal/housing over the crankshaft and bolt it to the block.
4    Tighten the housing bolts a little at a time until they're all snug.

## 26   Pistons and connecting rods - installation and rod bearing oil clearance check

*Refer to illustrations 26.4, 26.5, 26.9a, 26.9b, 26.9c, 26.11, 26.13 and 26.17*
1    Before installing the piston/connecting rod assemblies, the cylinder walls must be perfectly clean, the top edge of each cylinder must be chamfered, and the crankshaft must be in place.
2    Remove the cap from the end of the number one connecting rod (check the marks made during removal). Remove the original bearing inserts and wipe the bearing surfaces of the connecting rod and cap with a clean, lint-free cloth. They must be kept spotlessly clean.

**26.4  The tab on the bearing (arrow) must fit into the cap recess so the bearing will seat properly**

**26.5  Position the ring gaps as shown here before installing the piston/connecting rod assemblies in the engine**

VALVE CUT(S) TOWARDS MANIFOLD SIDE

OIL HOLE-ASSEMBLE TOWARD FRONT OF ENGINE

MARK

2.2L

2.5L

DISHED WITH VALVE CUTOUTS

**26.9a  On 2.2L and 2.5L engines, the indent on the piston and oil hole on the rod must face the front of the engine (timing belt end) and the valve cuts must face the manifold side of the engine**

MANIFOLD SIDE

DISTRIBUTOR SIDE

**26.9b  Piston orientation after installation (2.2L engine shown, 2.5L engine similar)**

**26.9c  Piston orientation after installation - 2.6L engine**

2C

## Connecting rod bearing oil clearance check

**Note:** *Don't touch the faces of the new bearing inserts with your fingers. Oil and acids from your skin can etch the bearings.*

3    Clean the back side of the new upper bearing insert, then lay it in place in the connecting rod. Make sure the tab on the bearing fits into the recess in the rod. Don't hammer the bearing insert into place and be very careful not to nick or gouge the bearing face. Don't lubricate the bearing at this time.

4    Clean the back side of the other bearing insert and install it in the rod cap. Again, make sure the tab on the bearing fits into the recess in the cap **(see illustration)**, and don't apply any lubricant. It's critically important that the mating surfaces of the bearing and connecting rod are perfectly clean and oil free when they're assembled.

5    Position the piston ring gaps at 120-degree intervals around the piston **(see illustration)**.

6    Slip a section of plastic or rubber hose over each connecting rod cap bolt.

7    Lubricate the piston and rings with clean engine oil and attach a piston ring compressor to the piston. Leave the skirt protruding about 1/4-inch to guide the piston into the cylinder. The rings must be compressed until they're flush with the piston.

8    Rotate the crankshaft until the number one connecting rod journal is at BDC (bottom dead center) and apply a coat of engine oil to the cylinder walls.

9    With the mark or notch on top of the piston facing the front of the engine **(see illustrations)**, gently insert the piston/connecting rod assembly into the number one cylinder bore and rest the bottom edge of the ring compressor on the engine block. If you're working on a 2.2L or 2.5L engine, make sure the oil hole in the lower end of the connecting rod is facing the front (timing belt) side of the engine.

10   Tap the top edge of the ring compressor to make sure it's contacting the block around its entire circumference.

11   Gently tap on the top of the piston with the end of a wooden or plastic hammer handle **(see illustration)** while guiding the end of the connecting rod into place on the crankshaft journal. The piston rings may try to pop out of the ring compressor just before entering the cylinder bore, so keep some downward pressure on the ring compressor. Work slowly, and if any resistance is felt as the piston enters the cylinder, stop immediately. Find out what's hanging up and fix it before

proceeding. Do not, for any reason, force the piston into the cylinder - you might break a ring and/or the piston.

12   Once the piston/connecting rod assembly is installed, the connecting rod bearing oil clearance must be checked before the rod cap is permanently bolted into place.

13   Cut a piece of the appropriate-size Plastigage slightly shorter than the width of the connecting rod bearing and lay it in place on the

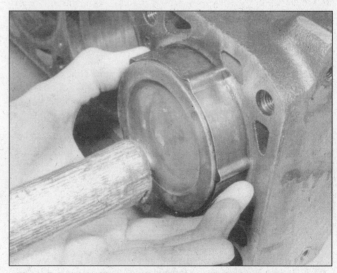

**26.11  Drive the piston gently into the cylinder bore with the end of  wooden or plastic hammer handle**

**26.13  Lay the Plastigage strips on each rod bearing journal, parallel to the crankshaft centerline**

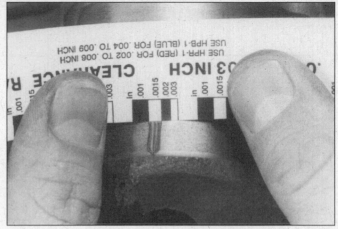

**26.17  Measure the width of the crushed Plastigage to determine the rod bearing oil clearance (be sure to use the correct scale - standard and metric ones are included)**

number one connecting rod journal, parallel with the journal axis **(see illustration)**.

14    Clean the connecting rod cap bearing face, remove the protective hoses from the connecting rod bolts and install the rod cap. Make sure the mating mark on the cap is on the same side as the mark on the connecting rod.

15    Install the nuts and tighten them to the torque listed in this Chapter's Specifications. Work up to it in three steps. **Note:** *Use a thin-wall socket to avoid erroneous torque readings that can result if the socket is wedged between the rod cap and nut. If the socket tends to wedge itself between the nut and the cap, lift up on it slightly until it no longer contacts the cap. Do not rotate the crankshaft at any time during this operation.*

16    Remove the nuts and detach the rod cap, being very careful not to disturb the Plastigage.

17    Compare the width of the crushed Plastigage to the scale printed on the Plastigage envelope to obtain the oil clearance **(see illustration)**. Compare it to this Chapter's Specifications to make sure the clearance is correct.

18    If the clearance is not as specified, the bearing inserts may be the wrong size (which means different ones will be required). Before deciding different inserts are needed, make sure no dirt or oil was between the bearing inserts and the connecting rod or cap when the clearance was measured. Also, recheck the journal diameter. If the Plastigage was wider at one end than the other, the journal may be tapered (refer to Section 20).

### Final connecting rod installation

19    Carefully scrape all traces of the Plastigage material off the rod journal and/or bearing face. Be very careful not to scratch the bearing - use your fingernail or the edge of a credit card.

20    Make sure the bearing faces are perfectly clean, then apply a uniform layer of engine assembly lube to both of them. You'll have to push the piston into the cylinder to expose the face of the bearing insert in the connecting rod - be sure to slip the protective hoses over the rod bolts first.

21    Slide the connecting rod back into place on the journal, remove the protective hoses from the rod cap bolts, install the rod cap and tighten the nuts to the torque listed in this Chapter's Specifications. Again, work up to the torque in three steps.

22    Repeat the entire procedure for the remaining pistons/connecting rods.

23    The important points to remember are:

a)  *Keep the back sides of the bearing inserts and the insides of the connecting rods and caps perfectly clean when assembling them.*

b)  *Make sure you have the correct piston/rod assembly for each cylinder.*

c)  *The arrow or mark on the piston must face the front (timing chain end) of the engine.*

d)  *Lubricate the cylinder walls with clean oil.*

e)  *Lubricate the bearing faces when installing the rod caps after the oil clearance has been checked.*

24    After all the piston/connecting rod assemblies have been properly installed, rotate the crankshaft a number of times by hand to check for any obvious binding.

25    As a final step, the connecting rod endplay must be checked. Refer to Section 13 for this procedure.

26    Compare the measured endplay to this Chapter's Specifications to make sure it's correct. If it was correct before disassembly and the original crankshaft and rods were reinstalled, it should still be right. If new rods or a new crankshaft were installed, the endplay may be inadequate. If so, the rods will have to be removed and taken to an automotive machine shop for resizing.

## 27   Initial start-up and break-in after overhaul

**Warning:** *Have a fire extinguisher handy when starting the engine for the first time.*

1    Once the engine has been installed in the vehicle, double-check the engine oil and coolant levels.

2    With the spark plugs out of the engine and the ignition system disabled (see Section 3), crank the engine until oil pressure registers on the gauge or the light goes out.

3    Install the spark plugs, hook up the plug wires and restore the ignition system functions (see Section 3).

4    Start the engine. It may take a few moments for the fuel system to build up pressure, but the engine should start without a great deal of effort. **Note:** *If backfiring occurs through the carburetor or throttle body, recheck the valve timing and ignition timing.*

5    After the engine starts, it should be allowed to warm up to normal operating temperature. While the engine is warming up, make a thorough check for fuel, oil and coolant leaks.

6    Shut the engine off and recheck the engine oil and coolant levels.

7    Drive the vehicle to an area with no traffic, accelerate sharply from 30 to 50 mph, then allow the vehicle to slow to 30 mph with the throttle closed. Repeat the procedure 10 or 12 times. This will load the piston rings and cause them to seat properly against the cylinder walls. Check again for oil and coolant leaks.

8    Drive the vehicle gently for the first 500 miles (no sustained high speeds) and keep a constant check on the oil level. It isn't unusual for an engine to use oil during the break-in period.

9    At approximately 500 to 600 miles, change the oil and filter.

10    For the next few hundred miles, drive the vehicle normally. Don't pamper it or abuse it.

11    After 2000 miles, change the oil and filter again and consider the engine broken in.

# Chapter 3
# Cooling, heating and air conditioning systems

## Contents

**3**

## Specifications

### General

| | |
|---|---|
| Radiator cap pressure rating ........................................... | 14 to 18 psi |
| Thermostat rating (opening temperature) | |
| 2.2L and 2.5L engines................................................... | 195-degrees F |
| 2.6L engine................................................................... | 180-degrees F |
| Cooling system capacity .................................................. | 8.5 to 9 quarts |
| Refrigerant type ............................................................... | R-12 |
| Refrigerant capacity......................................................... | 33 to 34 ounces |

### Torque specifications

| | Ft-lbs (unless otherwise indicated) |
|---|---|
| Thermostat housing nuts/bolts | |
| 1981 to 1985 ................................................................. | 15 |
| 1986 and later .............................................................. | 20 |
| Water pump pulley bolts.................................................... | 120 in-lbs |
| Water pump mounting bolts | |
| 2.2L and 2.5L engines | |
| Cover-to-housing bolts................................................ | 108 in-lbs |
| Housing-to-block bolts | |
| Upper three bolts..................................................... | 20 |
| Lower bolt................................................................. | 40 |
| 2.6L engine | |
| Pivot bolts and locking bolt ........................................ | 17 |
| Cover-to-housing bolts................................................ | 80 in-lbs |
| Radiator mounting bolts ..................................................... | 108 in-lbs |

## 1   General information

### Engine cooling system

All vehicles covered by this manual employ a pressurized engine cooling system with thermostatically controlled coolant circulation. An impeller-type water pump mounted on the front of the block (on the rear of the block on 2.6L engines) pumps coolant through the engine. The coolant flows around the combustion chambers and toward the rear of the engine. Cast-in coolant passages direct coolant near the intake ports, exhaust ports, and spark plug areas.

A wax pellet type thermostat is located in a housing near the front of the engine. During warm-up, the closed thermostat prevents coolant from circulating through the radiator. As the engine nears normal operating temperature, the thermostat opens and allows hot coolant to travel through the radiator, where it's cooled before returning to the engine.

The cooling system is sealed by a pressure-type radiator cap, which raises the boiling point of the coolant and increases the cooling efficiency of the radiator. If the system pressure exceeds the cap pressure relief value, the excess pressure in the system forces the spring-loaded valve inside the cap off its seat and allows the coolant to escape through the overflow tube into a coolant reservoir. When the system cools the excess coolant is automatically drawn from the reservoir back into the radiator.

The coolant reservoir does double duty as both the point at which coolant is added to the cooling system to maintain the proper fluid level and as a holding tank for overheated coolant.

This type of cooling system is known as a closed design because coolant that escapes past the pressure cap is saved and reused.

### Heating system

The heating system consists of a blower fan and heater core located in the heater box, the hoses connecting the heater core to the engine cooling system and the heater/air conditioning control head on the dashboard. Hot engine coolant is circulated through the heater core. When the heater mode is activated, a flap door opens to expose the heater box to the passenger compartment. A fan switch on the control head activates the blower motor, which forces air through the core, heating the air.

### Air conditioning system

The air conditioning system consists of a condenser mounted in front of the radiator, an evaporator mounted adjacent to the heater core, a compressor mounted on the engine, a filter/drier or receiver/drier (accumulator) which contains a high pressure relief valve and the plumbing connecting all of the above components.

A blower fan forces the warmer air of the passenger compartment through the evaporator core, transferring the heat from the air to the refrigerant (sort of a "radiator in reverse"). The liquid refrigerant boils off into low pressure vapor, taking the heat with it when it leaves the evaporator.

## 2   Antifreeze - general information

**Warning:** *Do not allow antifreeze to come in contact with your skin or painted surfaces of the vehicle. Rinse off spills immediately with plenty of water. Antifreeze is highly toxic if ingested. Never leave antifreeze lying around in an open container or in puddles on the floor; children and pets are attracted by it's sweet smell and may drink it. Check with local authorities about disposing of used antifreeze. Many communities have collection centers which will see that antifreeze is disposed of safely. Never dump used antifreeze on the ground or pour it into drains.*
**Note:** *Non-toxic antifreeze is now manufactured and available at local auto parts stores, but even these types should be disposed of properly.*

The cooling system should be filled with a water/ethylene glycol based antifreeze solution which will prevent freezing down to at least -20-degrees F (even lower in cold climates). It also provides protection against corrosion and increases the coolant boiling point.

**3.8 Loosen the hose clamp and remove the hose from the thermostat cover**

The cooling system should be drained, flushed and refilled at least every other year (see Chapter 1). The use of antifreeze solutions for periods of longer than two years is likely to cause damage and encourage the formation of rust and scale in the system.

Before adding antifreeze to the system, check all hose connections. Antifreeze can leak through very minute openings.

The exact mixture of antifreeze to water which you should use depends on the relative weather conditions. The mixture should contain at least 50-percent antifreeze, but should never contain more than 70-percent antifreeze. Consult the mixture ratio chart on the antifreeze container before adding coolant. Hydrometers (a graduated squeeze-bulb syringe) are available at most auto parts stores to test the coolant. Use antifreeze which meets the vehicle manufacturer's specifications, and look on the antifreeze container for specific mention of ingredients for maximum protection of aluminum cooling system components.

## 3   Thermostat - check and replacement

**Warning:** *Do not remove the radiator cap, drain the coolant or replace the thermostat until the engine has cooled completely.*

### Check

1    Before assuming the thermostat is to blame for a cooling system problem, check the coolant level, drivebelt tension (see Chapter 1) and temperature gauge operation.
2    If the engine seems to be taking a long time to warm up (based on heater output or temperature gauge operation), the thermostat is probably stuck open. Replace the thermostat with a new one.
3    If the engine runs hot, use your hand to check the temperature of the upper radiator hose. If the hose isn't hot, but the engine is, the thermostat is probably stuck closed, preventing the coolant inside the engine from escaping to the radiator. Replace the thermostat. **Caution:** *Don't drive the vehicle without a thermostat. The computer may stay in open loop and emissions and fuel economy will suffer.*
4    If the upper radiator hose is hot, it means that the coolant is flowing and the thermostat is open. Consult the *Troubleshooting* section at the front of this manual for cooling system diagnosis.

### Replacement

*Refer to illustrations 3.8, 3.10a, 3.10b and 3.12*
5    Disconnect the negative battery cable from the battery.
6    Drain the cooling system down to the thermostat level or just below (see Chapter 1). If the coolant is relatively new or is in good condition, save and reuse it (see the **Warning** in Section 2).
7    Follow the upper radiator hose to locate the thermostat housing.
8    Loosen the hose clamp, then detach the hose from the fitting **(see illustration)**. If it's stuck, grasp it near the end with a pair of adjustable

3.10a  Thermostat installation details - 2.2L and 2.5L engines

3.10b  Thermostat installation details - 2.6L engine

3.12  Carefully remove all traces of old gasket material

pliers and twist it to break the seal, then pull it off. If the hose is old or deteriorated, cut it off and install a new one.

9    If the outer surface of the large fitting that mates with the hose is deteriorate (corroded, pitted, etc.) it may be damaged by removing the hose. If it is, the thermostat housing must be replaced.

10    Remove the bolts and detach the housing from the water box **(see illustrations)**. If the housing is stuck, tap it with a soft-face hammer, to jar it loose. Some coolant may spill as the seal is broken.

11    Note how it's installed (which end is facing the water box), then remove the thermostat.

12    Remove all traces of old gasket material and sealant from the water box and thermostat housing with a gasket scraper **(see illustration)**.

13    Apply a thin, uniform coat of RTV sealant to both sides of the new gasket, then place the new gasket on the water box. Install the thermostat over the new gasket on the water box. Make sure the spring end is directed into the water box (or engine).

14    Install the housing and bolts. Tighten the bolts to the torque listed in this Chapter's Specifications.

15    Reattach the upper radiator hose to the housing and tighten the hose clamp securely.

16    Refill the cooling system (see Chapter 1).

17    Start the engine and allow it to reach normal operating temperature, then check for leaks and proper thermostat operation (as described in Steps 3 and 4).

**4    Engine cooling fan and switch - check and replacement**

**Warning:** *To avoid possible injury or damage, DO NOT operate the engine with a damaged fan. Do not attempt to repair fan blades - replace a damaged fan with a new one. Also, be aware that on 2.6L models the cooling fan may operate with the ignition key in the Off position; do not place your hands, hair, clothing, tools or any other objects in the vicinity of the cooling fan blades while checking the system.*

**Check**

*Refer to illustrations 4.1 and 4.2*

1    If the engine is overheating and the cooling fan is not operating, unplug the electrical connector at the fan motor and use jumper wires to connect the fan directly to the battery **(see illustration)**. If the fan still doesn't work, replace the motor.

4.1  Terminal polarity of the cooling fan electrical connector

**4.2  The fan switch is threaded into the bottom of the radiator (arrow) on all models equipped with a 2.6L engine and 1984 and earlier 2.2L models**

**4.8a  Detach the two clips at the top of the fan shroud housing with a screwdriver . . .**

**4.8b  . . . then lift the assembly out of the engine compartment**

**4.9  Remove the fan retaining clip with needle-nose pliers**

**4.10  Remove the fan motor mounting nuts**

**5.4a  Loosen the clamp, slide it back and detach the hose from the radiator by twisting it back and forth**

2    If the fan motor is good but still doesn't come on when the engine gets hot, the fault lies with the fan switch **(see illustration)**, the fan motor relay (if equipped), the coolant temperature sensor, the engine control computer or the wiring which connects the components (on 1885 and later 2.2L/2.5L models, fan operation is controlled by the on-board computer and the coolant temperature sensor). Unplug the electrical connector from the sensor/switch. If the fan operates, the sensor is defective. If the fan still doesn't come on, use a voltmeter or test light to check the fan circuit (wiring diagrams are included at the end of Chapter 12). Carefully check all wiring and connections. If no obvious problems are found, further diagnosis should be done by a dealer service department or repair shop.

3    On computer-controlled models, refer to Chapter 6 for procedures to check the coolant temperature sensor.

4    Check the fuse for the radiator fan circuit, and if that checks OK , check the fan control relay, located on the left shock tower. **Note:** Early models without air conditioning do not use a relay.

5    With the ignition key in the RUN position, remove the relay and check for battery voltage in the circuit from the fuse panel or ignition switch (see the wiring diagrams at the end of Chapter 12). If there is battery voltage present, the circuit is OK. Have your relay checked or substitute a known-good relay. If there was no voltage, check for opens in the circuit back to the fuse panel.

### *Replacement*

*Refer to illustrations 4.8a, 4.8 b, 4.9 and 4.10*

#### Fan

6    Disconnect the negative battery cable.

7    Unplug the fan motor electrical connector.

8    Detach the two clips at the top of the fan shroud with a small screwdriver, then carefully lift it out of the engine compartment **(see illustrations)**.

9    To detach the fan from the motor, remove the clip from the motor shaft **(see illustration)**.

10    To detach the motor from the shroud, remove the nuts and slide the motor out of the shroud **(see illustration)**.

11    Installation is the reverse of removal.

### Coolant temperature sensor/fan switch

12    Drain the cooling system (see the **Warning** in Section 2).

13    Unplug the electrical connector from the sensor/switch.

14    Wrap Teflon tape on the threads of the new sensor/switch to prevent leaks.

15    Unscrew the sensor/switch from the thermostat housing or bottom of the radiator.

16    Install the sensor/switch and plug in the electrical connector.

17    Fill the cooling system (see Chapter 1).

18    Start the engine to check for leaks and for proper operation of the cooling fan.

---

**5    Radiator - removal and installation**

---

**Warning:** *Wait until the engine is cool before beginning this procedure.*

### *Removal*

*Refer to illustrations 5.4a, 5.4b, 5.5, 5.6 and 5.8*

1    Disconnect the negative battery cable.

**5.4b The lower radiator hose is accessible from under the vehicle**

**5.5 Detach the coolant reservoir hose from the fitting**

**5.6 Disconnect the transmission cooler lines (arrows) from the radiator**

**5.8 Remove the radiator mounting bolts (one on each side)**

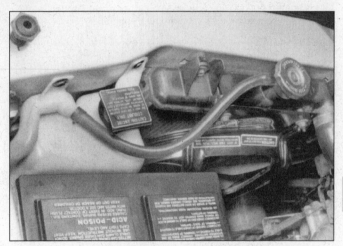

**6.2 Coolant reservoir mounting details (2.6L shown, others similar)**

3

2　Drain the cooling system making sure the heater control is in the maximum heat position (see Chapter 1). If the coolant is relatively new and is in good condition, save and reuse it (see the **Warning** in Section 2).

3　Remove the fan motor and shroud assembly (see Section 4).

4　Loosen the hose clamps, then detach the radiator hoses from the fittings **(see illustrations)**. If they're stuck, grasp each hose near the end with a pair of adjustable pliers and twist it to break the seal, then pull it off. Be careful not to distort the radiator fittings! If the hoses are old or deteriorated, cut them off and install new ones.

5　Remove the coolant reservoir hose **(see illustration)**.

6　If the vehicle is equipped with an automatic transmission, disconnect and plug the cooler lines **(see illustration)**.

7　Unplug the electrical connector from the radiator fan switch, if equipped (see Section 4).

8　Remove the radiator mounting bolts **(see illustration)**.

9　Carefully lift out the radiator. Don't spill coolant on the vehicle or scratch the paint.

10　Check the radiator for leaks and damage. If it needs repair, have a radiator shop or dealer service department perform the work, as special techniques are required.

11　Remove bugs and dirt from the radiator with compressed air and a soft brush taking care not to damage radiator cooling fins or water tubes.

## Installation

12　Inspect the radiator mounts for deterioration and make sure there's no dirt or gravel in them when the radiator is installed.

13　Lower the radiator into place and push down to seat the radiator lower tabs in the mount holes provided.

14　Install the radiator mounting bolts and tighten them securely.

15　Lubricate all of the hose fittings lightly with silicone spray lubricant to ease the installation.

16　Install the radiator, heater and reservoir hoses.

17　Install the transmission cooling lines, if equipped.

18　Install the fan motor and shroud assembly, and connect the electrical connector to the motor. Connect the electrical connector to the fan switch, if equipped.

19　Fill the cooling system with the proper mixture of antifreeze and water (see Chapter 1).

20　Connect the negative battery cable.

21　Start the engine and allow it to reach normal operating temperature (indicated by the upper radiator hose becoming hot) and check for leaks. Recheck the coolant level and add more if needed.

22　If you're working on an automatic transmission equipped vehicle, check and add fluid as needed (see Chapter 1).

## 6　Coolant reservoir - removal and installation

*Refer to illustration 6.2*

1　Detach the overflow hose at the radiator filler neck. Plug the hose so you don't spill any coolant out of the reservoir during removal (see the **Warning** in Section 2).

2　Remove the mounting screws **(see illustration)** and lift the reservoir straight up. On earlier models, it will be necessary to remove the battery.

3　Installation is the reverse of the removal.

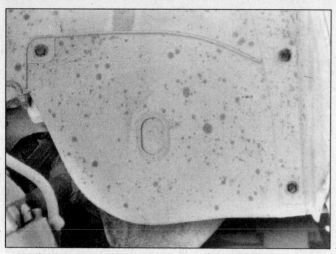

**8.3 Remove the right-side splash shield for access to the water pump - it's retained by three bolts**

**8.6 Water pump mounting bolt locations (2.2L/2.5L engine)**

## 7 Water pump - check

1   A failure in the water pump can cause serious damage due to overheating.

2   There are two ways to check the operation of the water pump while it's installed on the engine. If the pump is defective, it should be replaced with a new or rebuilt unit.

3   Water pumps are equipped with weep or vent holes. If a failure occurs in the pump seal, coolant will leak from the hole. In most cases you'll need a flashlight to find the hole on the water pump from underneath to check for leaks.

4   If the water pump shaft bearings fail there may be a howling sound at the front of the engine while it's running. With the engine off, shaft wear can be felt if the water pump pulley is rocked up-and-down. Don't mistake drivebelt slippage, which causes a squealing sound, for water pump bearing failure.

## 8 Water pump - replacement

*Refer to illustration 8.3*

**Warning:** *Wait until the engine is completely cool before beginning this procedure.*

1   Disconnect the negative battery cable from the battery.

2   Drain the cooling system (see Chapter 1). If the coolant is relatively new or in good condition, save and reuse it (see the **Warning** in Section 2).

3   Remove the splash shield under the right front fender for easy access to the water pump bolts **(see illustration)**. On all models except those equipped with the 2.6L engine, remove the drivebelt(s) (see Chapter 1).

4   Loosen the clamps and disconnect the hoses from the water pump. If they're stuck, grasp each hose near the end with a pair of adjustable pliers and twist it to break the seal, then pull it off. If the hoses are deteriorated, cut them off and install new ones.

## 2.2L and 2.5L engines

*Refer to illustrations 8.6, 8.7a, 8.7b and 8.11*

5   On models equipped with air conditioning, unbolt the compressor (see Section 15 ). Secure the compressor aside - DO NOT disconnect the refrigerant lines. Remove the alternator and set it aside (see Chapter 5).

6   Remove the water pump housing bolts **(see illustration)**, detach the drivebelt and separate the water pump and housing assembly from the engine.

7   Remove the bolts and separate the water pump from the housing

**8.7a Remove the water pump-to-housing bolts**

**(see illustrations).**

8   Discard the gasket and clean the mating surfaces to remove any remaining gasket material. Remove the old O-ring from the housing and carefully clean out the groove.

9   Clean the bolt threads and the threaded holes to remove any cor-

**8.7b You may have to use a hammer and chisel to separate the water pump from the housing, but be extremely careful - don't damage the mating surface of the housing**

**8.11 Apply a continuous bead of RTV sealant between the bolt holes and the inner edge of the housing**

3mm (.12 IN.) DIAMETER BEAD-RTV

**8.15 Water pump mounting details - 2.6L engine**

PULLEY SHIELD
DRIVE PULLEY
HEATER HOSE OUTLET
PIVOT SCREWS
LOCKING SCREW

rosion and sealant.

10    If you're installing a new pump, compare the new pump to the old pump to make sure they're identical.

11    Apply a bead of RTV sealant to the mating surfaces of the housing **(see illustration)**. Install a new O-ring in the housing groove.

12    Attach the new pump to the housing and tighten the bolts to the torque listed in this Chapter's Specifications.

13    Clean the mating surfaces of the water pump housing and the engine block. Using a new gasket, install the pump/housing assembly on the engine and tighten the bolts to the torque listed in this Chapter's Specifications.

14    Proceed to Step 25.

## 2.6L engine

*Refer to illustrations 8.15 and 8.17*

15    Remove the camshaft pulley shield **(see illustration)**.

16    Remove the water pump pivot bolts and locking bolt and separate the water pump/housing assembly from the engine.

17    Remove the four water pump body bolts and separate the water pump cover from the housing **(see illustration)**.

18    Discard the gasket and clean the mating surfaces to remove all

remaining gasket material.

19    Remove the O-ring from the housing and carefully clean out the groove.

20    Clean the bolt threads and threaded holes to remove any corrosion and sealant.

21    If you're installing a new pump, compare the new pump to the old pump to make sure they're identical.

22    Apply a thin film of RTV sealant to the gasket. Set the gasket on the housing and assemble the pump cover to the housing. Install the bolts and tighten them to the torque listed in this Chapter's Specifications. Install a new O-ring in the housing groove.

23    Install the water pump assembly on the engine. Install the pivot bolts and locking bolt finger-tight.

24    Install the drivebelt and cam pulley shield, adjust the belt to the proper tension (see Chapter 1) and tighten the pivot bolts and locking bolt to the torque listed in this Chapter's Specifications.

## All engines

25    Attach the hoses to the water pump and tighten the clamps securely.

26    Reinstall any parts that were removed to gain access to the pump.

27    Install the drivebelt(s) and adjust them to the proper tension (see Chapter 1).

28    Install the splash shield.

29    Refill the cooling system with coolant (see Chapter 1).

29    Reconnect the cable to the negative terminal of the battery.

30    Start the engine and allow it to warm up, then check for leaks.

## 9    Coolant temperature sending unit - check and replacement

## Check

*Refer to illustrations 9.1a and 9.1b*

1    The coolant temperature indicator system is composed of a light or gauge mounted in the instrument panel and a coolant temperature sending unit mounted on the thermostat housing or water box. Some

GASKET
BY-PASS HOSE
"O" RING

**8.17 Exploded view of the water pump - 2.6L engine**

of the engines covered by this manual have more than one sending unit, but only one is used for the temperature indicator system **(see illustrations)**. **Note:** *The coolant sensor used by the computer usually has a two wire connector, while the temperature gage sending unit always uses a single wire terminal.*

2    If an overheating indication occurs, check the coolant level in the system. Be sure the cooling system has cooled enough to remove the radiator cap (about 30-to-45 minutes). During that time you can check the wiring between the light or gauge and the sending unit, to be sure that all wiring circuits are closed and all fuses are intact.

3    With the ignition switch turned to the start position and the starter cranking the engine, the indicator light should be on or the gauge should give an overheat condition.

**9.1a  Location of the coolant temperature sending unit - 2.2L and 2.5L engines**

4    If the light is not on, the bulb may be burned out, the ignition switch may be faulty or the circuit may be open. To test the circuit, disconnect the sending unit connector and using a jumper wire, ground the connector terminal to the engine block. Turn the ignition On (engine not running) and check the indicator light or gauge. If the light comes on, or the gauge moves all the way to Hot (indicating the light or gauge is operating properly), replace the sending unit and reconnect the wiring connector.

5    As soon as the engine starts, the light should go out and remain out unless the engine overheats. Should the light stay on it may be due to a grounded wire between the light and the sending unit, a defective sending unit, or a faulty ignition switch. Check the coolant mixture to make sure it's the proper mix for your vehicle, engine type, and weather conditions.

### Replacement

6    Drain the cooling system down to the level of the sensor (make sure the cooling system is cool before starting work). Unscrew the sensor from the cylinder head, thermostat housing, or water box, and install a new replacement. Use Teflon tape or a small amount of RTV sealant on the threads. There will be some coolant loss as the unit is removed, so be prepared to catch it. After replacement, fill the cooling system to the proper level and check for leaks.

**10   Heater/air conditioning blower motor - circuit check and component replacement**

### Check

*Refer to illustration 10.5*

1    Check the fuse and all connections in the circuit for looseness and corrosion. Make sure the battery is fully charged.

**9.1b  Location of the coolant temperature sending unit (coolant switch) - 2.6L engine**

**10.5  Remove the cowl plenum grille (five screws), then the air intake shield (four screws) for access to the blower resistor**

2    Backprobe the blower motor electrical connector with two small paper clips (straightened out) and connect a voltmeter to the blower motor connector. Then turn the key to ON, but do not start the vehicle.

3    Move the blower switch through each of its positions and note the voltage readings. Changes in voltage indicate that the motor speeds will also vary as the switch is moved to the different positions.

4    If there is voltage present, but the blower motor does not operate, the blower motor is probably faulty. Disconnect the blower motor connector and hook one side to a chassis ground and the other to a fused source of battery voltage. If the blower doesn't operate, it is faulty.

5    If there was no voltage present at the blower motor at one or more speeds, and the motor itself tested OK, check the blower motor resistor, located in most models on the engine compartment side of the firewall, under the cowl plenum grille (see illustration). On some models the resistor block is located under the dash on the heater/air conditioning housing.

6    Disconnect the electrical connector from the blower motor resistor. With the ignition on, check for voltage at each of the terminals in the connector as the switch is moved to the different positions. If the voltmeter responds correctly to the switch then the resistor is probably faulty. If there is no voltage present from the switch then the switch, control panel or related wiring is probably faulty.

7    Using a continuity tester on the blower motor resistor, check between each input terminal (from the blower speed switch side) to the output terminal (to the blower). There should be continuity. If not, replace the resistor.

## Replacement

*Refer to illustration 10.11*

8    Disconnect the negative battery cable from the battery.

WATER VALVE    BRAKE BOOSTER
HEATER HOSES
EXPANSION VALVE
RADIATOR
DISCHARGE LINE
SECTION LINE
FILTER DRIER
COMPRESSOR ASSEMBLY
CONDENSER ASSEMBLY

**11.3  Heater and air conditioning component locations (typical)**

**10.11  To detach the fan from the motor shaft, remove the retainer with pliers**

9    Working under the dash on the passenger side, disconnect the electrical connector from the blower motor.

10    Remove the attaching screws and lower the blower motor and fan assembly from the heater/air conditioning assembly.

11    To detach the fan, remove the retainer and slide it off the motor shaft (see illustration).

12    Installation is the reverse of removal.

## 11  Heater core - replacement

*Refer to illustrations 11.3, 11.4, 11.8, 11.11, 11.18 and 11.19*

**Warning:** *The air conditioning system is under high pressure. DO NOT loosen any fittings or remove any components until after the system has been discharged. Air conditioning refrigerant should be properly discharged into an EPA-approved container at a dealer service department or an automotive air conditioning repair facility. Always wear eye protection when disconnecting air conditioning system fittings.*

1    Have the air conditioning system discharged and the refrigerant recovered by a dealer service department or automotive air conditioning repair facility.

2    Drain the cooling system (see Chapter 1). Disconnect the negative cable from the battery.

3    Disconnect the heater hoses from the heater core tubes at the firewall (see illustration) and plug the tubes to prevent coolant from spilling out during removal.

4    Remove the 8mm bolt from the center of the evaporator sealing plate (see illustration).

5    Remove the two Torx bolts and carefully detach the H valve.

"H" VALVE
EVAPORATOR SEALING PLATE
CONTROL HEAD
LOW PRESSURE CUT-OFF SWITCH
"H" VALVE
ALUMINUM "N" GASKET
DASH PANEL
PLUMBING SEALING PLATE
CYCLING CLUTCH SWITCH
LOW PRESSURE CUT-OFF SWITCH

**11.4  "H" valve mounting details**

3

**11.8 Remove the condensate drain tube**

6    Carefully move the refrigerant lines to the front of the vehicle (do not scratch the valve sealing surfaces).

7    Plug the refrigerant lines to prevent contamination to the air conditioning system.

8    Remove the condensate drain tube **(see illustration)**.

9    Remove the steering column-to-dash bolts and lower the column to the drivers seat.

10   Remove the lower instrument panel and the forward console (see Chapter 11).

11   Remove the four nuts that retain the assembly to the firewall **(see illustration)**.

12   Pull the right side of the instrument panel back until it reaches the passenger seat.

13   Disconnect the electrical connectors to the resistor, blower motor and the temperature control cable.

14   Disconnect the hanger strap from the heater/air conditioning assembly and bend it out of the way.

15   Pull the heater/air conditioning assembly out from under the dash

**11.18 Remove the screws and lift the top off the heater/air conditioning assembly to expose the heater core (and the evaporator)**

**11.19 Remove the screws and lift the heater core straight up**

**11.11 Heater/air conditioning assembly mounting nut locations (arrows)**

panel and remove it from the vehicle.

16   Place the heater core/evaporator assembly on a workbench.

17   Remove the screw holding the vacuum harness and feed the harness through the hole.

18   Remove the clips and screws and lift the cover off **(see illustration)**.

19   Remove the screw from the heater core tube retaining bracket and lift the heater core out **(see illustration)**.

20   Installation is the reverse of removal.

## 12   Heater/air conditioning control assembly - removal and installation

*Refer to illustrations 12.3, 12.4 and 12.6*

1    Disconnect the negative battery cable.

2    Remove the control assembly cover plate (see Chapter 11).

3    Remove the two control assembly mounting screws **(see illustration)**.

4    Pull the heater/air conditioning control assembly out and disconnect the electrical connectors from the backside of the control assembly **(see illustration)**.

5    Disconnect the temperature control cable.

6    Release the locking tab with pliers and, using a screwdriver, pry the temperature control cable out of the control assembly **(see illustration)**.

7    Disconnect the vacuum harness and remove the assembly from the dash.

8    Installation is the reverse of removal.

**12.3 The heater/air conditioning control assembly is retained by two screws**

**12.4  With the controls pulled away from the dash, unplug the electrical connectors from the control assembly**

**12.6  Detach the temperature control cable from the lever by prying the wire loop off, then depress the locking tab with pliers and pry the tab up and out of the receiver**

## 13  Air conditioning and heating system - check and maintenance

**Warning:** *The air conditioning system is under high pressure. DO NOT loosen any fittings or remove any components until after the system has been discharged. Air conditioning refrigerant should be properly discharged into an EPA-approved container at a dealer service department or an automotive air conditioning repair facility. Always wear eye protection when disconnecting air conditioning system fittings.*

### Check

*Refer to illustration 13.1*

1　The following maintenance checks should be performed on a regular basis to ensure the air conditioning continues to operate at peak efficiency.

  a) *Check the compressor drivebelt. If it's deteriorated or worn, replace it (see Chapter 1).*

  b) *Check the drivebelt tension and if necessary adjust it (see Chapter 1).*

  c) *Check the system hoses. Look for cracks, bubbles, hard spots and deterioration. Inspect the hoses and all fittings for oil bubbles and seepage* **(see illustration)**. *If there's any evidence of wear, damage or leaks, replace the hose(s).*

  d) *Inspect the condenser fins for leaves, bugs and other debris. Use a "fin comb" or compressed air to clean the condenser.*

  e) *Make sure the system has the correct refrigerant charge.*

2　It's a good idea to operate the system for about 10 minutes at least once a month, particularly during the winter. Long non-use can cause hardening and subsequent failure of the seals.

3　Because of the complexity of the air conditioning system and the special equipment necessary to service it, in-depth troubleshooting and repairs are not included in this manual (refer to the *Haynes Automotive Heating and Air Conditioning Repair Manual*). However, simple checks and component replacement procedures are provided in this Chapter.

### Checking the refrigerant charge

*Refer to illustration 13.7*

4　The most common cause of poor cooling is simply a low system refrigerant charge. If a noticeable drop in cool air output occurs, the following quick check will help you determine if the refrigerant is low.

5　Warm the engine up to normal operating temperature.

6　Place the air conditioning temperature selector at the coldest setting and put the blower at the highest setting. Open the doors (to make sure the air conditioning system doesn't cycle off as soon as it cools the passenger compartment).

7　With the compressor engaged - the clutch will make an audible click and the center of the clutch will rotate - inspect the sight glass **(see illustration)**. If the refrigerant looks foamy, it's low. Have the system charged by a dealer service department or other qualified shop.

**13.1  Inspect your air conditioning system for leaks at these locations**

*\*POSSIBLE LEAK LOCATIONS*

**13.7  The sight glass on top of the filter-drier (or receiver-drier) assembly enables you to view the condition of the refrigerant in the air conditioning system while the system is operating - if the refrigerant looks foamy, the charge is low**

3

**14.5 Typical filter-drier installation details - if you plan to reinstall the same unit, be sure to plug the openings immediately after detaching the refrigerant lines**

**15.5 Each refrigerant line is held to the compressor with two bolts (arrows)**

8    The earliest warning that a system is low on refrigerant is the air coming out of the ducts inside the vehicle. Insert a thermometer in the center duct while operating the air conditioning system - the output should be 35 to 40-degrees F below the ambient air temperature (down to approximately 40-degrees F). If the air isn't as cold as it used to be, and the compressor is engaged, the system probably needs a charge. Further inspection or testing of the system is beyond the scope of the home mechanic and should be left to a professional. Since the federal restrictions by the EPA on the sale of R-12 refrigerant to the public, you can no longer charge your own R-12 system at home.

## Heating systems

9    If the carpet under the heater core is damp, or if antifreeze vapor or steam is coming through the vents, the heater core is leaking. Remove it (see Section 11) and install a new unit (most radiator shops will no longer repair a leaking heater core).

10    If the air coming out of the heater vents isn't hot, the problem could stem from any of the following causes:

a) *The thermostat is stuck open, preventing the engine coolant from warming up enough to carry heat to the heater core. Replace the thermostat (see Section 3).*

b) *A heater hose is blocked, preventing the flow of coolant through the heater core. Feel both heater hoses at the firewall. They should be hot. If one of them is cold, there is an obstruction in one of the hoses or in the heater core. Detach the hoses and back flush the heater core with a water hose. If the heater core is clear but circulation is impeded, remove the two hoses and flush them out with a water hose.*

c) *If flushing fails to remove the blockage from the heater core, the core must be replaced (see Section 11).*

11    It is also possible that the water pump could be bad, failing to circulate enough hot water to the heater core. Refer to Sections 7 and 8.

## 14    Air conditioning filter-drier - removal and installation

*Refer to illustration 14.5*

**Warning:** *The air conditioning system is under high pressure. DO NOT loosen any fittings or remove any components until after the system*

has been discharged. Air conditioning refrigerant should be properly discharged into an EPA-approved container at a dealer service department or an automotive air conditioning repair facility. Always wear eye protection when disconnecting air conditioning system fittings.

**Caution:** *Replacement filter-drier units are so effective at absorbing moisture that they can quickly saturate upon exposure to the atmosphere. When installing a new unit, have all tools and supplies ready for quick reassembly to avoid having the system open any longer than necessary.*

1    The filter-drier acts as a reservoir for the system refrigerant. It's located near the condenser.

2    Have the air conditioning system discharged and the refrigerant recovered by a dealer service department or automotive air conditioning repair facility.

3    Disconnect the negative battery cable from the battery.

4    Unplug any electrical connectors from the filter-drier.

5    Disconnect the refrigerant lines from the filter-drier **(see illustration)**.

6    Plug the open fittings to prevent entry of dirt and moisture.

7    Loosen the mounting bracket bolts and lift the filter-drier out.

8    Installation is the reverse of the removal.

9    Take the vehicle back to the shop that discharged it. Have the system evacuated, recharged and leak tested.

## 15    Air conditioning compressor - removal and installation

*Refer to illustrations 15.5 and 15.6*

**Warning:** *The air conditioning system is under high pressure. DO NOT loosen any fittings or remove any components until after the system has been discharged. Air conditioning refrigerant should be properly discharged into an EPA-approved container at a dealer service department or an automotive air conditioning repair facility. Always wear eye protection when disconnecting air conditioning system fittings.*

**Note:** *The filter-drier (see Section 14) should be replaced whenever the compressor is replaced.*

1    Have the air conditioning system discharged and the refrigerant recovered by a dealer service department or automotive air conditioning repair facility.

2    Disconnect the negative cable from the battery.

3    Unplug the electrical connector from the compressor clutch.

4    Remove the drivebelt (see Chapter 1).

5    Disconnect the refrigerant lines from the rear of the compressor **(see illustration)**. Plug the open fittings to prevent entry of dirt and moisture.

6    Unbolt the compressor from the mounting bracket **(see illustration)** and lift it from the vehicle.

**15.6 Typical air conditioning compressor mounting details**

**16.4 Condenser installation details**

7    If a new compressor is being installed, follow the directions with the compressor regarding the draining of excess oil prior to installation. **Note:** *Before installing the new compressor, it may be a good idea to hold the compressor nose down while rotating the hub. The unit may have been sitting in a warehouse for some time, and this procedure will help lubricate the front seal in the compressor and prevent a vacuum leak during recharging.*

8    The clutch may have to be transferred from the original to the new compressor.

9    Installation is the reverse of the removal. Replace all O-rings with new ones specifically made for air conditioning system use, and lubricate them with clean refrigerant oil.

10   Have the system evacuated, recharged and leak tested by the shop that discharged it.

## 16   Air conditioning condenser - removal and installation

*Refer to illustration 16.4*

**Warning:** *The air conditioning system is under high pressure. DO NOT loosen any fittings or remove any components until after the system has been discharged. Air conditioning refrigerant should be properly discharged into an EPA-approved container at a dealer service department or an automotive air conditioning repair facility. Always wear eye protection when disconnecting air conditioning system fittings.*

**Note:** *The filter-drier should be replaced whenever the condenser is replaced (see Section 14).*

1    Have the air conditioning system discharged and the refrigerant recovered by a dealer service department or automotive air conditioning repair facility.

2    Disconnect the negative cable from the battery.

3    Remove the grille (see Chapter 11).

4    Disconnect the refrigerant lines from the condenser **(see illustration)**.

5    Plug all refrigerant lines to prevent dirt and moisture from contaminating the system.

6    Remove the two mounting bolts from the condenser **(see illustration 16.4)**.

7    Lift the condenser out of the vehicle.

8    If the original condenser will be reinstalled, store it with the line fittings on top to prevent the oil from draining out.

9    If a new condenser is being installed, pour one ounce of clean refrigerant oil into it prior to installation.

**17.3 Lift the evaporator from the heater/evaporator case**

10   Installation is the reverse of removal. Be sure the rubber pads are in place under the condenser.

11   Have the system evacuated, recharged and leak-tested by the shop that discharged it.

## 17   Air conditioning evaporator - removal and installation

*Refer to illustration 17.3*

**Warning:** *The air conditioning system is under high pressure. DO NOT loosen any fittings or remove any components until after the system has been discharged. Air conditioning refrigerant should be properly discharged into an EPA-approved container at a dealer service department or an automotive air conditioning repair facility. Always wear eye protection when disconnecting air conditioning system fittings.*

1    Have the air conditioning system discharged and the refrigerant recovered by a dealer service department or automotive air conditioning repair facility.

2    Remove the heater/air conditioning unit (see Section 11).

3    Lift the evaporator straight up and out of the heater/air conditioning unit **(see illustration)**.

4    Installation is the reverse of removal. Have the system evacuated, recharged and leak tested by the shop that discharged it.

**3**

# Notes

# Chapter 4
# Fuel and exhaust systems

## Contents

## Specifications

### Fuel pressure

| | |
|---|---|
| Carbureted models | 4.5 to 6 psi |
| Fuel injected models (engine idling) | 14.5 psi |

### Carburetor adjustments

| | |
|---|---|
| Curb idle speed | See the *Emissions Control Information label* in the engine compartment |
| Fast idle speed | See the *Emissions Control Information label* in the engine compartment |

2.2L engine choke vacuum kick adjustment
  Carburetor number
    1981

| | |
|---|---|
| R9060A(1) | 0.030 inch |
| R9061A(2) | |
| R9125A(1) | |
| R9126A(2) | |
| R9602A(1) | 0.065 inch |
| R9603A(2) | |
| R9604A(1) | |
| R9605A(2) | |
| R9064A(1) | 0.070 inch |
| R9065A(2) | |
| R9684A(1) | 0.060 inch |
| R9685A(2) | |

## Carburetor adjustments (continued)

1982
   R9503A(1) ............................................................... 0.085 inch
   R9504A(2)
   R9750A(1)
   R9751A(2)
   R9507A(1)
   R9508A(2)
   R9509A(1)
   R9510A(2)
   R9505A(1) ............................................................... 0.100 inch
   R9506A(2)
   R9752A(1)
   R9753A(2)
   R9511A(1) ............................................................... 0.120 inch
   R9512A(2)
   R9512A(1) ............................................................... 0.130 inch
   R9513A(2) ............................................................... 0.120 inch
   R9582A(1) ............................................................... 0.060 inch
   R9583A(2)
   R9584A(1)
   R9585A(2)

1983
   R40003A ............................................................... 0.070 inch
   R40007A
   R40008A
   R40012A
   R40004A ............................................................... 0.080 inch
   R40005A
   R40006A
   R40010A
   R40014A
   R40080A ............................................................... 0.045 inch
   R40081A

1984
   R40060-1A ............................................................... 0.055 inch
   R40107-1A
   R40085-1A ............................................................... 0.040 inch
   R40170A ............................................................... 0.060 inch
   R40171A
   R40067A ............................................................... 0.070 inch
   R40068-1A
   R40058-1A
   R40064-1A ............................................................... 0.080 inch
   R40081-1A
   R40082-1A
   R40071A
   R40122A

1985
   R40060A ............................................................... 0.055 inch
   R40058A ............................................................... 0.070 inch
   R40134A ............................................................... 0.075 inch
   R40135A
   R40138A
   R40139A
   R40116A ............................................................... 0.095 inch
   R40117A

1986
   R40116A ............................................................... 0.095 inch
   R40117A
   R40134A ............................................................... 0.075 inch
   R40135-1A
   R40138-1A
   R40139-1A
   R40138A

1987
   R40295A ............................................................... 0.075 inch
   R40296A
2.2L engine float drop ............................................................... 1-7/8 inch

## Carburetor adjustments (continued)

Dry float level
    2.2L engine............................................................ 31/64 inch
    2.6L engine............................................................ 25/32 inch
2.6L engine choke breaker opening ................................ 5/64 inch or less at 50-degrees F
2.6L engine choke unloader opening ............................. 3/64 inch or more at 32-degrees F

## Torque specifications                                     **Ft-lbs** (unless otherwise indicated)

Carburetor mounting nuts
    2.2L engine............................................................ 17
    2.6L engine............................................................ 12.5
Fuel pressure regulator screws (EFI) ............................. 48 in-lbs
Throttle body mounting bolts/nuts ................................. 17

---

## 1  General information

### Fuel system

The fuel system consists of the fuel tank, a mechanical or electric fuel pump, an air cleaner, either a carburetor or a fuel injection system and the hoses and lines which connect these components.

Earlier models are carbureted. A Holley carburetor (5220 or 6520) is used on models with the 2.2L engine. A Mikuni carburetor is used on models with the 2.6L engine. Both models have a mechanical fuel pump mounted on the engine block. The pump is driven by an eccentric cam off the intermediate shaft (2.2L) or camshaft (2.6L).

Later models are fuel-injected. A single-point (one injector) Electronic Fuel Injection (EFI) system is used on these engines. This system is also referred to as a Throttle Body Injection (TBI) system.

### Exhaust system

The exhaust system consists of the exhaust manifold, exhaust pipes, catalytic converter and muffler. For information regarding the removal and installation of the exhaust manifold, refer to Chapter 2, Part A. For information regarding exhaust system and catalytic converter servicing, refer to the last Section in this Chapter. For further information regarding the catalytic converter, refer to Chapter 6.

## 2  Fuel pressure relief procedure (fuel-injected models only)

*Refer to illustration 2.4*

**Warning:** *Gasoline is extremely flammable, so take extra precautions when you work on any part of the fuel system. Don't smoke or allow open flames or bare light bulbs near the work area, and don't work in a garage where a natural gas-type appliance (such as a water heater or a clothes dryer) with a pilot light is present. Since gasoline is carcinogenic, wear latex gloves when there's a possibility of being exposed to fuel, and, if you spill any fuel on your skin, rinse it off immediately with soap and water. Mop up any spills immediately and do not store fuel-soaked rags where they could ignite. The fuel system on fuel-injected models is under constant pressure, so, if any fuel lines are to be disconnected, the fuel pressure in the system must be relieved first. When you perform any kind of work on the fuel system, wear safety glasses*

**2.4  You can easily ground an injector terminal in the connector right at the throttle body to bleed the fuel pressure - but don't activate it for more than five seconds**

*and have a Class B type fire extinguisher on hand.*

1    The fuel system operates under pressure and may be under residual pressure even when the engine is off. Consequently, any time the fuel system is worked on (such as when the fuel filter is replaced) the system must be depressurized to avoid the spraying of fuel when a component is disconnected.

2    Loosen the fuel tank cap to release any pressure in the tank.

3    Unplug the electrical connector from the fuel injector located on the throttle body.

4    Ground the terminal directly on the injector that corresponds to the number 1 terminal with a jumper wire and also using another jumper wire, apply battery voltage from the positive (+) post of the battery to the terminal that corresponds to the number 2 terminal on the injector, which will open the injector and depressurize the fuel system **(see illustration)**.

**Caution:** *Do not energize the injector for more than five seconds. It's recommended that the pressure be bled in several spurts of one to two seconds to make sure the injector isn't damaged. The fuel pressure can be heard escaping into the throttle body or combustion chamber. When the sound is no longer heard, the system is depressurized.*

**3.1 Attach the T-fitting as close to the carburetor as possible and use a six-inch (maximum) length of hose when hooking up the pressure gauge to check the fuel pump pressure**

## 3   Fuel pump/fuel pressure - check

**Warning:** *Gasoline is extremely flammable, so take extra precautions when you work on any part of the fuel system. Don't smoke or allow open flames or bare light bulbs near the work area, and don't work in a garage where a natural gas-type appliance (such as a water heater or a clothes dryer) with a pilot light is present. Since gasoline is carcinogenic, wear latex gloves when there's a possibility of being exposed to fuel, and, if you spill any fuel on your skin, rinse it off immediately with soap and water. Mop up any spills immediately and do not store fuel-soaked rags where they could ignite. The fuel system on fuel-injected models is under constant pressure, so, if any fuel lines are to be disconnected, the fuel pressure in the system must be relieved first. When you perform any kind of work on the fuel system, wear safety glasses and have a Class B type fire extinguisher on hand.*

### Mechanical pump

*Refer to illustration 3.1*

1   Disconnect the fuel line from the carburetor and install a T-fitting **(see illustration)**. Connect a fuel pressure gauge to the T-fitting with a section of fuel hose that's no longer than six inches.

2   Disconnect the gauge from the end of the fuel hose and direct the end of the hose into an approved gasoline container. Operate the starter for a few seconds, until fuel spurts out of the hose, to vent the pump (this eliminates any air in the fuel chamber, which could affect the pressure reading). Reattach the gauge to the fuel hose.

3   Start the engine and allow it to idle. The pressure on the gauge should be about 4.5 to 6 psi, remain constant and return to zero slowly when the engine is shut off.

**3.12 Be sure the fuel gauge is connected to the inlet line (1) and not the return line (2) (TBI system)**

**3.8 The electrical connectors for the fuel pump (1) and the fuel gauge sending unit (2) are easily accessible at the fuel tank**

4   An instant pressure drop indicates a faulty outlet valve. If this occurs, or if the pressure is too high or low, replace the fuel pump with a new one. **Note:** *If the pressure is too high, check the air vent to see if it's plugged before replacing the pump.*

### Electric (in-tank) pump

#### Voltage check

*Refer to illustration 3.8*

5   Remove the fuel tank cap and place your ear close to the filler neck. Have an assistant turn the ignition key to On while you listen for the sound of the in-tank pump. It should make a whirring sound. If you don't hear the pump, make the following quick checks.

6   Relieve the fuel system pressure (see Section 2).

7   Raise the rear of the vehicle and place it securely on jackstands.

8   Lower the fuel tank slightly (see Section 5) and locate the wire harness to the fuel pump **(see illustration)**.

9   Using a voltmeter, verify that there's voltage to the pump when the key is turned to On and Start.

a) *If there is voltage to the pump, replace it.*

b) *If there is no voltage to the pump, locate the fuel pump relay or fuse, check it and replace as necessary. Trace the wires for a open or short circuit condition.*

10   If the pump still doesn't work, have it checked by a dealer service department or a repair shop. Further testing requires special equipment.

**3.14 Attach the fuel pressure gauge between the fuel tank and the fuel filter**

**3.16 Disconnect the return line and attach a length of fuel hose, directing the free end of the hose into a container - if the fuel pressure is within specifications when the assistant cranks the engine (with the ignition system disabled), check for a plugged return line**

### Fuel pressure check

*Refer to illustrations 3.12, 3.14 and 3.16*

11  Relieve the fuel pressure (see Section 2).

12  Disconnect the 5/16-inch fuel line from the throttle body and install a T-fitting and a fuel pressure gauge between the fuel inlet hose and the throttle body **(see illustration)**.

13  Start the engine and allow the engine to idle. Record the fuel pressure, comparing your findings with the values listed in this Chapter's Specifications. Raise the engine rpm and observe the fuel pressure. Pressure should increase slightly as engine speed increases.

14  If the fuel pressure is BELOW specifications, install the pressure gauge between the fuel filter and the fuel tank **(see illustration)**.

15  If the fuel pressure increases, the fuel filter or line (between the filter and throttle body) is plugged or restricted. If the fuel pressure is still low, pinch the return line with a pair of pliers (wrap a rag around the hose first to prevent damage). If the pressure now goes up, replace the fuel pressure regulator. If no change in the fuel pressure is observed, check for a plugged fuel pump sock filter (screen) or a defective fuel pump.

16  If the fuel pressure is ABOVE specifications, disconnect the primary wires from the ignition coil, remove the return hose from the throttle body and connect a short section of hose to it. Direct the end of the hose into a suitable container and have an assistant crank the engine **(see illustration)**.

17  If the pressure is now correct, the problem is a restricted return line.

### 4    Fuel lines and fittings - replacement

*Refer to illustration 4.4*

**Warning:** *Gasoline is extremely flammable, so take extra precautions when you work on any part of the fuel system. Don't smoke or allow open flames or bare light bulbs near the work area, and don't work in a garage where a natural gas-type appliance (such as a water heater or a clothes dryer) with a pilot light is present. Since gasoline is carcinogenic, wear latex gloves when there's a possibility of being exposed to fuel, and, if you spill any fuel on your skin, rinse it off immediately with soap and water. Mop up any spills immediately and do not store fuel-soaked rags where they could ignite. The fuel system on fuel-injected models is under constant pressure, so, if any fuel lines are to be disconnected, the fuel pressure in the system must be relieved first. When you perform any kind of work on the fuel system, wear safety glasses*

**4.4 You'll see two fuel lines between the fuel tank and the carburetor or fuel injection system:  A supply (larger diameter) line and a return (smaller diameter) line - drain or siphon the fuel tank through the supply hose or line**

*and have a Class B type fire extinguisher on hand.*

**Note:** *Since the EFI system is under considerable pressure, always replace all clamps released or removed with new ones.*

1    Remove the air cleaner assembly.

2    Relieve the fuel system pressure (see Section 2).

3    Disconnect the negative cable from the battery.

4    On carbureted engines and fuel-injected engines with conventional fuel hose clamps **(see illustration)**, loosen the hose clamps, wrap a cloth around each end of the hose to catch the residual fuel and twist and pull to remove the hose.

5    When replacing hoses on fuel-injected models which use conventional hose clamps, always use hoses marked EFI/EFM and use new original equipment-type hose clamps.

6    Connect the negative battery cable, start the engine and check for leaks.

7    Install the air cleaner assembly.

### 5    Fuel tank - removal and installation

**Warning:** *Gasoline is extremely flammable, so take extra precautions when you work on any part of the fuel system. Don't smoke or allow open flames or bare light bulbs near the work area, and don't work in a garage where a natural gas-type appliance (such as a water heater or a clothes dryer) with a pilot light is present. Since gasoline is carcinogenic, wear latex gloves when there's a possibility of being exposed to fuel, and, if you spill any fuel on your skin, rinse it off immediately with soap and water. Mop up any spills immediately and do not store fuel-soaked rags where they could ignite. The fuel system on fuel-injected models is under constant pressure, so, if any fuel lines are to be disconnected, the fuel pressure in the system must be relieved first. When you perform any kind of work on the fuel system, wear safety glasses and have a Class B type fire extinguisher on hand.*

### Removal

*Refer to illustrations 5.7a and 5.7b*

1    Disconnect the negative battery cable from the battery.

2    Raise the rear of the vehicle and support it securely on jackstands.

3    Remove the fuel tank filler cap.

4    Disconnect the fuel tank line (the large diameter supply line) located adjacent to the right front shock tower in the engine compartment **(see illustration 4.4)**, connect a hose and drain or siphon the tank into an approved fuel container. **Warning:** *Do not use your mouth to start the siphoning action - use a siphoning kit, which can be purchased at most auto parts stores.*

5    Remove the screws retaining the filler tube to the body.

6    Disconnect all wires and hoses from the tank (label them first to avoid problems during installation).

**4**

**5.7a Typical fuel tank installation and fuel line routing details**

7   Remove the mounting bolts or nuts **(see illustrations)**, lower the tank slightly and remove the filler tube.

8   Lower the tank further and support it while disconnecting the rollover/vapor separator valve hose.

9   Remove the tank and insulator pad.

## Installation

*Refer to illustrations 5.12a and 5.12b*

10   To install the tank, raise it into position with a jack, connect the rollover/vapor separator valve hose and place the insulator pad on the top. Connect the filler tube. **Caution:** *Be sure the vapor vent hose is not pinched between the tank and floor pan.*

11   Raise the tank with the jack, connect the retaining strap and install the retaining nuts. Tighten them securely.

12   Connect the fuel lines **(see illustrations)** and wiring and install the filler tube retaining screws.

13   Fill the fuel tank, install the cap, connect the negative battery cable and check for leaks.

**5.7b Location of the fuel tank mounting straps and nuts**

**5.12a Fuel tank connections on a carbureted model**

**5.12b Fuel tank connections on a fuel-injected model**

**6.1  Fuel pump assembly and fuel line mounting details on the 2.2L engine**

## 6   Fuel pump - removal and installation

**Warning:** *Gasoline is extremely flammable, so take extra precautions when you work on any part of the fuel system. Don't smoke or allow open flames or bare light bulbs near the work area, and don't work in a garage where a natural gas-type appliance (such as a water heater or a clothes dryer) with a pilot light is present. Since gasoline is carcinogenic, wear latex gloves when there's a possibility of being exposed to fuel, and, if you spill any fuel on your skin, rinse it off immediately with soap and water. Mop up any spills immediately and do not store fuel-soaked rags where they could ignite. The fuel system on fuel-injected models is under constant pressure, so, if any fuel lines are to be disconnected, the fuel pressure in the system must be relieved first. When you perform any kind of work on the fuel system, wear safety glasses and have a Class B type fire extinguisher on hand.*

### *Mechanical pump*

**2.2L engine**

*Refer to illustration 6.1*

1    The fuel pump is bolted to the engine block adjacent to the oil filter **(see illustration)**.
2    Disconnect the cable from the negative terminal of the battery. Place clean rags or newspaper under the fuel pump to catch any gasoline that may spill during removal.
3    Carefully unscrew the fuel line fittings and detach the lines from

**6.19  When installing the fuel pump on a 2.6L engine, be sure to place a gasket on each side of the spacer block**

**6.8  Fuel pump location (arrow) on the 2.6L engine**

the pump. A flare-nut wrench should be used to prevent damage to the line fittings.
4    Unbolt and remove the fuel pump.
5    Before installation, coat both sides of the spacer block with RTV sealant, position the fuel pump and spacer in place and install the bolts.
6    Attach the lines to the pump and tighten the fittings securely (use a flare-nut wrench, if one is available, to prevent damage to the fittings).
7    Reconnect the cable to the battery, run the engine and check for leaks.

**2.6L engine**

*Refer to illustrations 6.8 and 6.19*

8    The fuel pump is mounted on the cylinder head, adjacent to the carburetor **(see illustration)**. It is held in place with two nuts.
9    Disconnect the cable from the negative terminal of the battery, Carefully number each spark plug wire to help during reinstallation, then remove the spark plugs.
10    Place your thumb over the number one cylinder spark plug hole and rotate the crankshaft in a clockwise direction (with a wrench on the large bolt attaching the pulley to the front of the crankshaft) until you can feel the compression pressure rising in the number one cylinder.
11    Continue rotating the crankshaft until the notch on the crankshaft pulley lines up with the T or zero on the timing mark tab on the timing chain case. At this point, the lift of the fuel pump drive cam is reduced to a minimum, which will make the pump easier to remove (and install).
12    Install the spark plugs and hook up the wires.
13    Remove the air intake housing and carburetor-to-valve cover bracket, then remove the fuel filter mounting bolt. Loosen the hose clamps and remove the fuel hoses from the pump fittings. Plug the ends of the hoses.
14    Remove the fuel pump mounting nuts and pull the pump off the engine. You may have to tap the pump body with a soft-faced hammer to break the gasket seal.
15    If the pump is difficult to remove, take off the valve cover and guide the pump rocker arm out of the head from the inside.
16    Remove the spacer block and scrape off all traces of the old gaskets and sealant.
17    Before installing the new pump, make sure that the rocker arm moves up and down without binding or sticking.
18    Coat both sides of the new gaskets with RTV-type gasket sealant before installation.
19    Slip the first gasket, the spacer block and the second gasket (in that order) onto the fuel pump mounting studs **(see illustration)**.
20    Install the fuel pump. It may be necessary to guide the rocker arm into place from inside the head. Work slowly; there is not much clearance between the rocker arm and the valve gear.
21    Once the fuel pump is properly seated, install the mounting nuts and tighten them evenly. Do not overtighten them or the spacer block may crack.

**4**

22   Install the valve cover if it was removed.
23   Install the hoses (after inspecting them for cracks) and new hose clamps.
24   Install the filter mounting bolt, the bracket and the air intake housing.
25   Reconnect the cable to the battery, start the engine and check for fuel leaks at the hose fittings. Check for oil leaks where the fuel pump mounts on the cylinder head.

### Electric in-tank pump

*Refer to illustration 6.27*

26   Remove the fuel tank (see Section 5).
27   Use a hammer and a brass punch (a steel punch may cause a spark, which could be extremely dangerous when working on the fuel tank!) to remove the fuel pump lock ring. Drive it in a counterclockwise direction until it can be removed **(see illustration)**.
28   Lift the fuel pump and O-ring out of the fuel tank. Discard the old O-ring.
29   Clean the sealing area of the fuel tank and install a new O-ring on the fuel pump.
30   Inspect the fuel inlet sock filter (strainer) on the fuel pump suction tube for damage and contamination. Replace it if it's damaged.
31   Insert the fuel pump into the tank, reattach the reservoir fuel return hose (if equipped) to the pump assembly, place the pump in its installed position, set the lock ring in place and lock the pump into place with a hammer and a brass punch (drive the lock ring in a clockwise direction).
32   Install the fuel tank (see Section 5).

### 7   Fuel tank cleaning and repair - general information

1   All repairs to the fuel tank or filler neck should be carried out by a professional who has experience in this critical and potentially dangerous work. Even after cleaning and flushing of the fuel system, explosive fumes can remain and ignite during repair of the tank.
2   If the fuel tank is removed from the vehicle, it shouldn't be placed in an area where sparks or open flames could ignite the fumes coming out of the tank. Be especially careful inside garages where a natural gas-type appliance is located, because the pilot light could cause an explosion.

### 8   Fuel level sending unit - check and replacement

### Check

1   Remove the fuel tank (see Section 5).
2   Remove the fuel level sending unit assembly (see Steps 7 through 10).
3   Position the probes of an ohmmeter onto the fuel level sending unit electrical connector terminals and check for resistance.
4   First, check the resistance of the sending unit with the fuel tank completely full. Move the float to the up position. The resistance of the sending unit should vary considerably.
5   Position the float in the down (empty) direction. Measure the resistance.
6   If the readings do not vary or there is very little change in resistance as the float travels from full to empty, replace the fuel level sending unit assembly.

### Replacement

*Refer to illustration 8.9*

7   Use a hammer and brass punch and tap on the lock ring in a counterclockwise direction.
8   When the tabs align properly, lift the fuel level sending unit assembly.
9   On fuel-injected models, remove the internal return line from the sending unit assembly before attempting to remove the sending unit **(see illustration)**.
10   Installation is the reverse of removal.

**6.27  To remove the lock ring from an electric fuel pump assembly, rotate it counterclockwise with a hammer and brass punch**

### 9   Air cleaner housing - removal and installation

1   Remove the air filter element (see Chapter 1).
2   Loosen the hose clamps that attach the fresh air inlet tube to the air cleaner housing. On carbureted (2.2L and 2.6L) engines, also loosen the hose clamp for the heated inlet air pipe at the air cleaner housing. Detach all hoses and tubes from the air cleaner housing. Label any small hoses to assure proper reassembly.
3   Remove the fastener(s) from all air cleaner mounting brackets.
4   Remove the air cleaner housing assembly.
5   While the air cleaner housing is removed, inspect the fresh air inlet tube and the heated inlet air stove pipe for cracks or other damage. If either tube is damaged, replace it.
6   Installation is the reverse of removal.

### 10   Accelerator cable - removal and installation

### Carbureted engines

*Refer to illustrations 10.1, 10.2a and 10.2b*

1   Working inside the vehicle, remove the retaining plug and detach the cable end from the accelerator pedal shaft **(see illustration)**.
2   Working in the engine compartment, remove the clip and separate the cable from the pin or stud on the throttle lever, then detach the cable from the mounting bracket **(see illustrations)**. Compress the cable-to-bracket fitting with wide-jaw pliers.
3   Pull the cable assembly into the engine compartment and remove it from the vehicle.
4   Installation is the reverse of removal.

**8.9  Remove the fuel return line clamp and remove the fuel line before attempting to remove the sending unit from the fuel tank**

**10.1 Typical accelerator pedal and cable details**

**10.2a Accelerator cable details - 2.2L engine**

## Fuel-injected engines

*Refer to illustrations 10.6a and 10.6b*

5    Working inside the vehicle, remove the retainer or plug and detach the cable end from the accelerator pedal shaft **(see illustration 10.1)**. Remove the retainer clip from the cable assembly housing at the grommet and pull the cable through the firewall.

6    Working in the engine compartment, remove the retainer clip and separate the cable from the pin or stud, then detach the cable from the mounting bracket **(see illustration)**. Compress the cable-to-bracket fitting with a pair of pliers **(see illustration)**, then pull the cable through the bracket. **Note:** *If the vehicle is equipped with cruise control, mark the position of the retaining clip on the throttle lever with paint before disconnecting it.*

7    Remove the cable from the engine compartment.

8    Installation is the reverse of removal.

## 11  Carburetor - description and service information

## *Description*

### 2.2L engine

*Refer to illustrations 11.1a and 11.1b*

1    Holley models 5220 and 6520 are staged dual venturi carburetors **(see illustrations)**. The primary bore is smaller than the secondary bore.

2    The secondary stage is mechanically operated by a linkage connecting the primary and secondary throttle levers.

**10.2b Accelerator cable details - 2.6L engine**

3    The primary stage includes a curb idle and transfer system, diaphragm type accelerator pump system, main metering system and power enrichment system. On model 6520 carburetors, there's also an oxygen feedback solenoid that responds to input from the oxygen sensor.

4    The secondary stage includes a main metering system and power system. Both the primary and secondary venturi draw fuel from a common float bowl.

5    The electric automatic choke has a bi-metal two-stage heating element.

6    In normal service, the idle mixture shouldn't require adjustment. The idle speed can be checked without removing the tamper resistant plug.

### 2.6L engine

*Refer to illustrations 11.7a and 11.7b*

7    The Mikuni carburetor used on these models is a downdraft two-barrel carburetor **(see illustrations)**.

**4**

**10.6a  Use a small pair of needle-nose pliers to remove the retaining clip from the throttle lever**

**10.6b  Squeeze the grommet with a pair of pliers to allow the tabs to clear the brackets**

11.1a  Holley Model 5220 carburetor

11.1b  Holley Model 6520 carburetor

COASTING AIR VALVE

FUEL INLET

BOWL VENT VALVE

TO CANISTER

JET AIR CONTROL VALVE

TO CANISTER

THROTTLE CABLE BRACKET

THROTTLE OPENER

FRONT OF VEHICLE

**11.7a  Mikuni carburetor (California and high-altitude models)**

JET AIR CONTROL VALVE

SUB EGR VALVE

FRONT OF VEHICLE

THROTTLE OPENER

TAMPER PROOF CHOKE COVER

CHOKE HEATER HOSE

SECONDARY VACUUM CONTROL DIAPHRAGM

CHOKE WATER OUTLET

FUEL INLET

THROTTLE OPENER

CHOKE HEATER HOSE

SUB EGR VALVE

CONCEALED IDLE MIXTURE SCREW

FUEL CUT-OFF SOLENOID

TO CANISTER

FUEL INLET

BOWL VENT VALVE

SECONDARY VACUUM CONTROL DIAPHRAGM

TAMPER PROOF CHOKE COVER

THROTTLE OPENER

CHOKE HEATER HOSE

CHOKE WATER OUTLET

SECONDARY VACUUM CONTROL DIAPHRAGM

THROTTLE CABLE BRACKET

FUEL INLET

**11.7b  Mikuni carburetor (Federal and Canadian models)**

TO CANISTER

BOWL VENT SOLENOID

AIR CONDITIONING SWITCH

FUEL INLET

AIR SWITCHING VALVE

THROTTLE OPENER

CHOKE HEATER HOSE

CONCEALED IDLE MIXTURE SCREW

FUEL CUTOFF SOLENOID

**4**

8    The basic components of the fuel inlet system are the fuel filter, the float needle valve and the float assembly.

9    The idle and primary metering system consists of the primary main jet, the primary pilot jet, the idle mixture adjusting screw and the primary main nozzle.

10   A fuel cut-off solenoid prevents dieseling.

11   The secondary metering system consists of the secondary main jet, secondary pilot jet, secondary main nozzle and a vacuum-controlled diaphragm.

12   The enrichment system consists of a spring-loaded, vacuum actuated diaphragm connected to an enrichment valve.

13   A mechanical accelerator pump consists of a flexible diaphragm, a diaphragm spring, a lever, a link rod and a follow-up spring.

14   A thermo-wax type automatic choke is controlled by engine coolant temperature.

## Service information

15   A thorough road test and check of carburetor adjustments should be done before any major carburetor service. Specifications for some adjustments are listed on the *Vehicle Emission Control Information* label found in the engine compartment.

16   Some performance complaints directed at the carburetor are actually a result of loose, misadjusted or malfunctioning engine or electrical components. Others develop when vacuum hoses leak, are disconnected or are incorrectly routed. The proper approach to analyzing carburetor problems should include a routine check of the following areas:

17   Inspect all vacuum hoses and actuators for leaks and proper installation.

18   Tighten the intake manifold nuts and carburetor mounting nuts evenly and securely.

19   Perform a cylinder compression test.

20   Clean or replace the spark plugs as necessary.

21   Check the resistance of the spark plug wires (see Chapter 5).

22   Inspect the ignition primary wires and check the vacuum advance operation. Replace any defective parts.

23   Check the ignition timing (see Chapter 1).

24   Inspect the heat control valve in the air cleaner for proper operation (see Chapters 1 and 6).

25   Remove the carburetor air filter element and blow out any dirt with compressed air. If the filter is extremely dirty, replace it with a new one.

26   Inspect the crankcase ventilation system (see Chapters 1 and 6).

27   Carburetor problems usually show up as flooding, hard starting, stalling, severe backfiring and poor acceleration. A carburetor that is leaking fuel and/or covered with wet-looking deposits definitely needs attention.

28   Diagnosing carburetor problems may require that the engine be started and run with the air cleaner removed. While running the engine without the air cleaner it is possible that it could backfire. A backfiring situation is likely to occur if the carburetor is malfunctioning, but removal of the air cleaner alone can lean the air/fuel mixture enough to produce an engine backfire. **Warning:** *Do not position your face directly over the carburetor opening in case of engine backfire.*

29   Once it is determined that the carburetor is indeed at fault, it should be replaced with a new or rebuilt unit, or disassembled, cleaned and reassembled using new parts where necessary. Before dismantling the carburetor, make sure you have a carburetor rebuild kit, which will include all necessary gaskets and internal parts, carburetor cleaning solvent and some means of blowing out all the internal passages of the carburetor. To do the job properly, you will also need a clean place to work and plenty of time and patience.

## 12   Carburetor - removal and installation

**Warning:** *Gasoline is extremely flammable, so take extra precautions when you work on any part of the fuel system. Don't smoke or allow open flames or bare light bulbs near the work area, and don't work in a garage where a natural gas-type appliance (such as a water heater or a clothes dryer) with a pilot light is present. Since gasoline is carcinogenic, wear latex gloves when there's a possibility of being exposed to fuel, and, if you spill any fuel on your skin, rinse it off immediately with soap and water. Mop up any spills immediately and do not store fuel-soaked rags where they could ignite. When you perform any kind of work on the fuel system, wear safety glasses and have a Class B type fire extinguisher on hand.*

## 2.2L engine
### Removal

1    Disconnect the negative battery cable from the battery.

2    Remove the air cleaner assembly.

3    Remove the fuel tank filler cap as the tank could be under some pressure.

4    Place a metal container under the fuel inlet fitting and disconnect the fitting.

5    Disconnect the wiring harness from the carburetor.

6    Disconnect the throttle linkage.

7    Tag and remove all hoses from the carburetor.

8    Remove the mounting nuts and carefully detach the carburetor from the manifold, taking care to hold it level. Do not remove the isolator mounting screws unless the isolator must be replaced with a new one.

### Installation

9    Inspect the mating surfaces of the carburetor and the isolator for nicks, burrs and debris that could cause air leaks.

10   Place the carburetor in position and install the mounting nuts, taking care not to damage the fast idle lever.

11   Tighten the nuts to the torque listed in this Chapter's Specifications, following a criss-cross pattern.

12   Check all of the vacuum hoses and connections for damage, replacing them with new parts if necessary, and install them.

13   Connect the throttle linkage and the fuel line.

14   Check the operation of the throttle linkage and the choke plate.

15   Connect the wiring harness and install the air cleaner.

16   Connect the negative battery cable.

17   Start the engine and check for fuel leaks.

18   Check the engine idle speed.

## 2.6L engine
### Removal

19   Disconnect the negative battery cable from the battery.

20   Remove the intake housing from the carburetor air horn.

21   Release any pressure which may exist in the fuel tank by removing the filler cap.

22   Drain the cooling system (see Chapter 1).

23   Remove the carburetor protector, tag the locations of the vacuum and coolant hoses and detach them from the carburetor.

24   Unplug the carburetor wiring harness connectors.

25   Place a metal container under the carburetor fuel inlet to catch any residual fuel and disconnect the fuel hose from the inlet fitting.

26   Disconnect the throttle linkage.

27   Remove the mounting bolt and nuts and carefully detach the carburetor from the manifold. Keep the carburetor level to avoid spilling fuel.

### Installation

28   Check the mating surfaces of the carburetor and intake manifold for nicks, burrs and old gasket material which could cause air leaks.

29   Using a new gasket, place the carburetor in position and install the mounting nuts and bolt. Tighten them to the torque listed in this Chapter's Specifications, following a criss-cross pattern.

30   Connect the throttle linkage and the fuel hose.

31   Connect the coolant and vacuum hoses and install the carburetor protector.

32   Refill the radiator with the specified coolant (see Chapter 1).

33   Check the operation of the throttle linkage and choke plate.

34   Install the air intake housing and the fuel tank cap.

35   Connect the negative battery cable.

36   Start the engine and check for fuel leaks.

37   Check the engine idle speed (see Section 16).

13.1a  Remove the fuel inlet fitting (2.2L engine)

13.1b  Disconnect the choke rod (2.2L engine)

13.1c  Remove the feedback solenoid mounting screws . . .

13.1d  . . . and detach the solenoid from the air horn (2.2L engine)

13.1e  Disconnect the air conditioner/idle speed solenoid anti-rattle spring (2.2L engine)

13.1f  The solenoid is held in place with two bolts (2.2L engine)

4

## 13  Carburetor (2.2L engine) - overhaul

**Warning:** *Gasoline is extremely flammable, so take extra precautions when you work on any part of the fuel system. Don't smoke or allow open flames or bare light bulbs near the work area, and don't work in a garage where a natural gas-type appliance (such as a water heater or a clothes dryer) with a pilot light is present. Since gasoline is carcinogenic, wear latex gloves when there's a possibility of being exposed to fuel, and, if you spill any fuel on your skin, rinse it off immediately with soap and water. Mop up any spills immediately and do not store fuel-soaked rags where they could ignite. When you perform any kind of work on the fuel system, wear safety glasses and have a Class B type fire extinguisher on hand.*

### *Disassembly*

*Refer to illustrations 13.1a through 13.1w*

1    With the carburetor removed from the engine and a rebuild kit in hand, disassembly can begin. Carburetor disassembly is illustrated in a step-by-step fashion with photos. Follow the photos in the proper sequence and read the caption under each photo **(see illustrations).**

2    Have a large, clean work area to lay out the parts as they are removed from the carburetor. Many of the parts are very small and can be lost easily if the area is cluttered.

3    Take your time during disassembly. Sketch the relationship of the various components of any assembly which appears complicated or tag the various parts to avoid confusion during reassembly. Care taken during disassembly will pay off during reassembly. Begin disassembly starting with illustration 13.1a.

13.1g  The secondary throttle valves on 1985 and 1986 models are operated by a vacuum diaphragm which is held in place by three screws - remove the E-clip from the link post and disconnect the control rod (2.2L engine)

### *Cleaning and inspection*

4    After disassembly, clean the carburetor components with a commercial carburetor solvent. Make sure you keep track of primary and secondary main metering jet and bleed assemblies as they must be reinstalled in their original locations.

5    The choke, vacuum diaphragms, O-rings, feedback solenoid,

**13.1h**   Remove the Wide Open Throttle cut-out switch (2.2L engine)

**13.1i**   Loosen the air horn screws in a criss-cross pattern to avoid warping it (2.2L engine)

**13.1j**   Carefully pry up on the air horn to release it from the main body (2.2L engine)

**13.1k**   Be careful not to bend the float as the air horn is removed (2.2L engine)

**13.1l**   Withdraw the pivot pin and remove the float (2.2L engine)

**13.1m**   Loosen and remove the fuel inlet needle and seat (2.2L engine)

**13.1n**   Remove the primary and secondary main metering jets (note the numbers on them to ensure reinstallation in the correct positions) (2.2L engine)

**13.1o**   Remove the primary and secondary air bleeds and main well tubes (note the sizes to ensure correct reinstallation) (2.2L engine)

**13.1p**   Remove the accelerator pump discharge assembly (2.2L engine)

floats and seals should not be placed in the solvent as they could be damaged.

6    Clean the external surfaces of the carburetor with a soft brush and soak all of the parts in the solvent. If the instructions on the solvent or cleaner recommend the use of water for rinsing, hot water will produce the best results. After rinsing, all traces of water must be blown from the passages with compressed air. **Caution:** *Never clean jets with a wire, drill bit or other metal objects. The orifices could become*

*enlarged, making the mixture too rich for proper performance.*

7    When checking parts removed from the carburetor, it is often difficult to be sure if they are serviceable. It is therefore recommended that new parts be installed, if available, when the carburetor is reassembled. The required parts should be included in the rebuild kit.

8    After the parts have been cleaned and dried, check the throttle shaft for excessive wear.

9    Check the jets for damage and restrictions. Replace them if

**13.1q Invert the carburetor and catch the accelerator pump discharge weight and check balls (2.2L engine)**

**13.1r Remove the accelerator pump cover (2.2L engine)**

**13.1s Remove the pump diaphragm and spring (be careful not to damage the diaphragm) (2.2L engine)**

**13.1t File the head off the choke diaphragm cover rivet (if equipped) (2.2L engine)**

**13.1u Remove the screws and detach the cover (2.2L engine)**

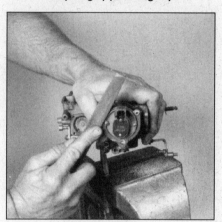

**13.1v File the heads off the choke retainer ring rivets and remove the ring (2.2L engine)**

**4**

**13.1w Detach the choke housing (2.2L engine)**

**13.12 Rotate the choke diaphragm clockwise when installing it**

**13.13 Install the breakaway screw (if equipped) in the bottom hole (2.2L engine)**

damage is evident.

10　Check for freedom of movement of the choke mechanism in the air horn. It should move freely for proper operation.

11　Replace any worn or damaged components with new ones.

## Reassembly

*Refer to illustrations 13.12, 13.13, 13.15, 13.16, 13.25, 13.26, 13.27, 13.28, 13.30, 13.31, 13.36, 13.37, 13.40a, 13.40b, 13.41 and 13.42*

12　Press down on the choke lever, insert the choke diaphragm and

rotate it into position **(see illustration)**.

13　Position the spring and fit the cover in place. Install the two top screws snugly, followed by the breakaway screw in the bottom hole **(see illustration)**.

14　Tighten the breakaway screw until the head breaks off. Tighten the top screws evenly and securely.

15　Install the accelerator pump, spring (small end first), cover and screws **(see illustration)**.

16　Fill the float bowl with fuel to a depth of one inch and drop the

13.15 Insert the screws through the cover holes before installing the screw (2.2L engine)

13.16 Accelerator pump discharge passage (2.2L engine)

13.25 Measuring the distance between the bottom of the float and the air horn to determine dry float level (2.2L engine)

13.26 Measuring the distance from the air horn surface to the top of the float to determine float drop (2.2L engine)

13.27 Carefully bend the tang up or down to change the dry float level (2.2L engine)

13.28 Be sure to support the pivot when bending the float drop adjusting tang (2.2L engine)

13.30 Be very careful not to bend the float tangs when installing the air horn (2.2L engine)

13.31 Tighten the air horn screws in a criss-cross pattern (2.2L engine)

13.36 Install a new O-ring in the solenoid groove (2.2L engine)

check ball into the accelerator pump discharge passage **(see illustration)**.

17   Use a small brass dowel to hold the check ball in place and push the throttle lever to make sure there is resistance felt and consequently no leakage. If there is leakage, drain the fuel and stake the ball in place with one or two taps of the dowel. Remove the old ball and install the new one from the rebuild kit. Install the weight and repeat the test.

18   Install the accelerator pump discharge nozzle assembly.

19   Install the primary main well tube and high speed bleed.

20   Install the secondary main well tube and high speed bleed.

21   Install the primary main metering jet. On these carburetors the primary main metering jet will have a smaller number stamped on it than the secondary main metering jet.

22   Install the secondary main metering jet.

23   Install the fuel inlet needle and seat assembly.

24   Hook the new needle onto the float tang and lower the assembly

**13.37 Rock the solenoid gently from side-to-side to seat the O-ring**

**13.40a Installing the choke lever bushing (2.2L engine)**

**13.40b Rotate the housing approximately 1/8-turn clockwise to align the holes (2.2L engine)**

**13.41 Install pop rivets to hold the retainer ring in place (2.2L engine)**

**13.42 Be sure to install a new air intake housing gasket (2.2L engine)**

**14.8 Idle speed adjusting screw location (2.2L engine)**

**4**

into place. Install the float pivot pin.

25    Measure the dry float level **(see illustration)**.

26    Invert the air horn and measure the float drop **(see illustration)**.

27    Adjust the dry float level by carefully bending the inner adjustment tang until the level is within the range listed in this Chapter's Specifications **(see illustration)**.

28    Bend the outer adjustment tang to bring the float drop within the range listed in this Chapter's Specifications **(see illustration)**.

29    Install the choke seal and link and squeeze the link retainer bushing into place.

30    Position the gasket, engage the choke link and lower the air horn assembly into place **(see illustration)**.

31    Install the air horn screws and tighten them securely **(see illustration)**.

32    Install the wide open throttle cutout switch. Move the switch until the circuit is open with the throttle valve 10-degrees before the wide open position.

33    Adjust the solenoid switch by loosening the retaining screw and using a screwdriver to rotate the switch until a click is felt.

34    Tighten the bolt and screws and install the anti-rattle spring.

35    Install the idle speed solenoid.

36    Lubricate the feedback solenoid tip lightly with petroleum jelly and install a new O-ring **(see illustration)**.

37    Install a new gasket and insert the solenoid into position **(see illustration)**.

38    Install the solenoid screws and tighten them evenly and securely.

39    Wrap a piece of Teflon tape around the threads and install the fuel inlet fitting.

40    Install the choke inner housing lever bushing, followed by the spacer and outer housing with the spring end loop over the lever **(see**

illustrations)**.

41    Install the choke housing rivets **(see illustration)**. The shorter rivet goes in the bottom hole.

42    Install the intake housing gasket **(see illustration)**.

---

## 14 Carburetor (2.2L engine) - adjustments

### Idle speed adjustment

*Refer to illustration 14.8*

1    Start the engine and run it until normal operating temperature is reached.

2    Check the ignition timing and adjust as necessary (see Chapter 1), then shut off the engine.

3    On 1984 and 1985 models, disconnect and plug the vacuum connector at the CVSCC (see Chapter 6 if necessary). On 1986 models, disconnect the wires from the kicker solenoid on the left inner fender panel. On all models, disconnect the oxygen feedback system test connector located on the left inner fender panel (6520 carbureted models only).

4    Unplug the fan electrical connector and install a jumper wire so the fan will run continuously.

5    Remove the PCV valve from the vent module so the valve will draw air from the engine compartment.

6    Leave the air cleaner in place and connect a tachometer. Ground the carburetor switch with a jumper wire.

7    Start the engine.

8    Check the idle speed reading on the tachometer and compare it to the Emissions Control Information label. Turn the idle speed screw **(see illustration)** as necessary to achieve the specified idle speed.

**14.17  Fast idle speed adjustment details (2.2L engine)**

**14.25  Choke vacuum kick adjustment details (2.2L engine)**

9    Shut off the engine and remove the tachometer.
10    Remove the carburetor switch jumper wire, plug in the fan connector, install the PCV valve and reinstall any vacuum hoses and wires which were disconnected.

### Air conditioning idle speed adjustment

11    Air-conditioned models are equipped with a system which boosts idle speed when the air conditioning compressor engages, to compensate for the greater load placed on the engine. Prior to checking the air conditioning idle speed, check the curb idle and timing (see Chapter 1) to make sure they are correct. The checks should be made with the engine at normal operating temperature.
12    When the air conditioner is engaged, the idle speed is increased by a vacuum or solenoid-type kicker.
13    Kicker operation can be checked by running the engine (at normal operating temperature), moving the temperature control to the coldest setting and then turning the air conditioning on. The kicker plunger should move in and out as the compressor clutch engages and disengages. Remove the air cleaner for better visual access to the kicker, if necessary **(see illustration 14.8)**.
14    If the idle speed doesn't change as the air conditioner cycles on and off, check the system hoses and diaphragm for leaks and make sure the vacuum solenoid (which directs vacuum to the kicker) is operating. If no defective parts are found, replace the kicker with a new one and repeat the check.

### Fast idle adjustment

*Refer to illustration 14.17*
15    Perform Steps 1 through 6.
16    On 1986 models, disconnect the vacuum hoses from the CVSCC and plug both hoses.
17    Start the engine, open the throttle slightly and set the fast idle screw on the slowest step of the fast idle cam **(see illustration)**.
18    With the choke valve fully open, adjust the fast idle speed to the specification on the Emissions Control Information label by turning the adjustment screw.
19    Return the engine to idle, then reposition the fast idle screw on the slowest step of the fast idle cam to verify the fast idle speed. Adjust as necessary.
20    Turn off the engine, remove the tachometer and reconnect all components removed for the adjustment procedure.

### Choke vacuum kick adjustment

*Refer to illustration 14.25*
21    Remove the air cleaner.
22    Open the throttle, close the choke and then close the throttle so the fast idle system is trapped at the closed choke position.

23    Disconnect the carburetor vacuum hose, connect a vacuum pump and apply 15-inches of vacuum.
24    Push the choke closed so the plates are at their smallest opening (use very light pressure and do not distort the linkage). The choke system internal spring will now be compressed.
25    Insert the appropriate size drill bit or gauge (see this Chapter's Specifications) between the plate and the air horn wall at the primary throttle end of the carburetor. Check the clearance against the Specifications and adjust as necessary by turning an Allen wrench inserted into the diaphragm **(see illustration)**.
26    After adjustment, replace the vacuum hose and the air cleaner assembly.

### Anti-diesel adjustment

*Refer to illustration 14.30*
27    Warm up the engine to operating temperature, check the ignition timing (see Chapter 1), then shut it off. Connect a tachometer.
28    Remove the red wire from the 6-way connector on the carburetor side of the connector.
29    With the transaxle in Neutral, the parking brake set securely and the wheels blocked to prevent any movement, ground the carburetor idle stop switch with a jumper wire and turn the headlights off. Start the engine.
30    Adjust the throttle stop speed screw **(see illustration)** to achieve an idle speed of 700 rpm.
31    Shut off the engine, remove the tachometer, remove the jumper wire and connect the carburetor idle stop switch wire.

**14.30  Anti-diesel adjustment details (2.2L engine)**

15.3a  Choke cover screw locations (2.6L engine)

15.3b The remaining choke cover screws must be unscrewed with a hammer and punch (2.6L engine)

15.4 Removing the throttle assembly (2.6L engine)

## 15  Carburetor (2.6L engine) - overhaul

**Warning:** *Gasoline is extremely flammable, so take extra precautions when you work on any part of the fuel system. Don't smoke or allow open flames or bare light bulbs near the work area, and don't work in a garage where a natural gas-type appliance (such as a water heater or a clothes dryer) with a pilot light is present. Since gasoline is carcinogenic, wear latex gloves when there's a possibility of being exposed to fuel, and, if you spill any fuel on your skin, rinse it off immediately with soap and water. Mop up any spills immediately and do not store fuel-soaked rags where they could ignite. When you perform any kind of work on the fuel system, wear safety glasses and have a Class B type fire extinguisher on hand.*

### Disassembly

*Refer to illustrations 15.3a, 15.3b, 15.4, 15.5, 15.7 and 15.10 through 15.26*

1    With the carburetor removed from the vehicle (see Section 12) and a rebuild kit on hand, disassembly can begin. Have a large, clean work area to lay out parts as they are removed. Many of the parts are very small and can be lost easily if the work area is cluttered. Take your time during disassembly and sketch the relationship of the various parts to simplify reassembly.

2    Remove the coolant hoses from the choke and throttle valve assemblies.

3    Remove the choke cover by grinding or filing off the heads of the screws **(see illustration)**. Use a small hammer and pointed punch to tap the edge of the remaining screw until it is loose **(see illustration)**. Note the relationship between the punched mark and scribed lines on the choke pinion plate. During reassembly the marks must be realigned.

4    Remove the throttle opener link E-clip, followed by the two mounting screws. Lift the opener assembly off **(see illustration)**.

5    Disconnect the ground wire, remove the mounting screw and detach the fuel cut-off solenoid **(see illustration)**.

6    Remove the throttle return spring and damper spring.

7    Remove the choke unloader clips and link, followed by the vacuum chamber (two screws) **(see illustration)**.

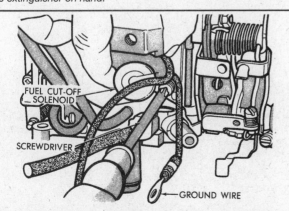

15.5 Removing the fuel cut-off solenoid (2.6L engine)

15.7 Removing the choke link and vacuum chamber (2.6L engine)

**4**

**15.10  Air horn mounting screw locations (2.6L engine)**

**15.11  Removing the float and inlet needle (2.6L engine)**

**15.12  Removing the retainer and needle seat assembly (note the O-ring and the filter screen) (2.6L engine)**

**15.13  Removing the venturis (2.6L engine)**

8    Disconnect the accelerator pump link from the throttle lever.
9    Remove the vacuum hose connector and hoses from the air horn (two screws).
10   Remove the six screws and detach the air horn from the carburetor body **(see illustration)**.
11   Slide the pivot pin out and remove the float and needle assembly **(see illustration)**. Discard the air horn gasket.
12   Unscrew the retainer and remove the needle seat and screen assembly, taking care not to lose the shim located under the seat **(see**

illustration).
13   Remove the venturis and retainers, discarding the O-rings. Mark the primary and secondary venturis so they can be reinstalled in the same positions. The primary venturis are the larger of the two **(see illustration)**.
14   Unscrew the primary and secondary main jets with a screwdriver

**15.14  Removing the main jets (2.6L engine)**

**15.15  Removing the main jet pedestals (2.6L engine)**

15.16  An exploded view of the bowl vent assembly components

15.17  An exploded view of the CAV assembly components
(2.6L engine)

15.18  An exploded view of the enrichment valve components
(2.6L engine)

15.19  An exploded view of the Air Switching Valve (ASV)
components (2.6L engine)

**4**

(see illustration). Be sure to note the numbers on the jets to simplify reassembly.

15    Remove the retaining screws and the primary and secondary jet pedestals (see illustration). Discard the gaskets.

16    Remove the bowl vent valve solenoid and spring (three screws), followed by the remaining screw and the bowl vent assembly (see illustration). Discard the O-ring.

17    Remove the Coasting Air Valve (CAV) assembly (three screws) (see illustration).

18    Remove the enrichment valve assembly and jet (see illustration).

19    Remove the Air Switching Valve (ASV) assembly (see illustration).

20    Remove the screw, lock and primary pilot jet set (see illustration).

21    Remove the screw, lock and secondary pilot jet set (see illustration).

15.20  Primary pilot jet set mounting details (2.6L engine)

15.21  Secondary pilot jet set mounting details (2.6L engine)

**15.22  Air bleed jet locations (2.6L engine)**

22   Remove the primary and secondary air bleed jets from the top of the air horn **(see illustration)**. Be sure to note their sizes as they must be reinstalled in the same locations.
23   Turn the carburetor body over carefully and catch the weight, check ball and hex nut **(see illustration)**.
24   Remove the accelerator pump assembly **(see illustration)**.
25   Remove the Jet Air Control Valve (JACV) assembly **(see illustration)**.
26   Remove the E-clip and carefully slide the sub EGR valve pin from the lever, taking care not to lose the steel ball and spring which maintain tension on the lever. Remove the sub EGR valve assembly **(see illustration)**.

## Cleaning and inspection

27   Once the carburetor has been completely disassembled, clean the parts with a commercial carburetor solvent.
28   The choke, vacuum diaphragms, O-ring;, electric solenoids, floats and seals should not be placed in the solvent as they could be damaged.
29   Clean the external surfaces of the carburetor with a soft brush and soak all of the parts in the solvent. If the instructions on the solvent or cleaner recommend the use of water for rinsing, hot water will produce the best results. After rinsing, all traces of water must be blown from the passages with compressed air. **Caution:** *Never clean jets with a wire, drill bit or other metal objects. The orifices may be enlarged, making the mixture too rich for proper performance.*
30   When checking parts removed from the carburetor, it is often difficult to be sure if they are serviceable. It is therefore recommended

**15.23  The weight, check ball and hex nut must be reinstalled in their original locations (2.6L engine)**

**15.24  An exploded view of the accelerator pump components (2.6L engine)**

that new parts be installed, if available, when the carburetor is reassembled. The required parts should be included in the carburetor rebuild kit.
31   After the parts have been cleaned and dried, check the throttle valve shaft for proper operation. If sticking or binding occurs, clean the shafts with solvent and lubricate them with engine oil.
32   Check the jets for damage and restrictions. Replace them if damage is evident.

**15.25  An exploded view of the Jet Air Control Valve (JACV) components (2.6L engine)**

**15.26  An exploded view of the sub-EGR valve assembly components (2.6L engine)**

**15.50 Checking the dry float level (2.6L engine)**

SCALE

GASKET SURFACE

33    Check the strainer screen for restrictions and damage.

34    Check the vacuum chamber. Push the chamber rod in, seal off the nipple and release the rod. If the rod does not return, the vacuum chamber is most likely in good condition. If the rod returns when released, the diaphragm is defective. The vacuum chamber should be replaced with a new one if this condition exists.

35    To check the fuel cut-off solenoid, connect a jumper wire to the positive (+) terminal of a 12-volt battery and the wire from the solenoid. Connect a second jumper wire to the negative (-) terminal of the battery and the solenoid ground wire. The needle should move in (toward the solenoid) when the battery is connected and out when the battery is disconnected.

### Reassembly

*Refer to illustrations 15.50, 15.58a and 15.58b*

36    Install the sub EGR valve components **(see illustration 15.26)**, attach the assembly to the carburetor body and secure it with the E-clip.

37    Attach the JACV components to the throttle body **(see illustration 15.25)**.

38    Install the accelerator pump assembly components **(see illustration 15.24)**.

39    Install the primary and secondary air jet bleeds in the air horn, noting that the secondary bleed has the highest number.

40    Install a new O-ring on the secondary pilot jet set, insert the assembly and install the retaining screw.

41    Install a new O-ring on the primary pilot jet set and install the assembly.

42    Attach the ASV components to the carburetor **(see illustration 15.19)**.

43    Install the jet, followed by the rest of the enrichment valve components **(see illustration 15.18)**.

44    Assemble the CAV components **(see illustration 15.17)**, attach the assembly to the air horn and retain it with the three mounting screws.

45    Assemble the bowl vent valve **(see illustration 15.16)**, install the valve and solenoid and tighten the mounting screws.

46    Using new gaskets, install the primary and secondary pedestals and mounting screws, followed by the main primary and secondary jets. Remember that the secondary jet has the largest number.

47    Attach new O-rings to the primary and secondary venturis and install the venturis and retainers.

48    Install a new O-ring and screen on the needle seat and install the shim in the air horn. Install the needle seat retainer and screw and tighten it securely.

49    Place the needle and float assembly in position and retain it in the air horn with the pivot pin.

50    Invert the air horn and measure the distance from the gasket surface (gasket removed) to the bottom surface of the float **(see illustration)** to determine the dry float level. Compare it to this Chapter's Specifications.

51    If the dry float level is more or less than it was during disassembly, remove the float, unscrew the inlet needle seat and add or remove shims (as necessary) to change the float height. Repeat the procedure as required until the distance is as specified.

52    Using a new gasket, attach the main body to the throttle body and install the nut, check ball and weight.

53    Attach the air horn, using a new gasket, to the main body and secure it with the six mounting screws.

54    Attach the two vacuum hoses and the wiring connector to the throttle body and engage the accelerator rod link in the throttle lever.

55    Place the vacuum chamber in position on the bracket, install the retaining screws and connect the vacuum hose and link to the secondary throttle lever. Connect the choke unloader link and retain it with the E-clips.

56    Install a new O-ring on the fuel cut-off solenoid, place the solenoid on the mixing body and install the retaining screw. Place the ground wire in position and retain it with the screw.

57    Install the throttle opener on the air horn and connect the link with the E-clip.

58    Install the choke cover, using the special breakaway screws. Make sure the punch and scribe marks and the cam lever are correctly aligned **(see illustrations)**.

59    Attach the coolant hose to the carburetor and tighten the clamps.

**4**

CAM LEVER

PAINTED PUNCH MARK

SCRIBED LINES

PINION PLATE

**15.58a  When installing the choke, make sure the punch mark and scribed lines are correctly aligned . . .**

CAM LEVER

PUNCH MARK

PAINT MARK ON GEAR

PINION PLATE

**15.58b  . . . and index the painted gear tooth with the punch mark on the cam lever before tightening the screws**

**16.4  Idle speed adjusting screw location (2.6L engine)**

## 16  Carburetor (2.6L engine) - idle speed adjustment

*Refer to illustrations 16.4 and 16.5*

1    With the transaxle in Neutral, the parking brake set and the wheels blocked to prevent any movement, turn off the lights and all accessories. Connect a tachometer to the engine, start the engine and allow it to warm up to normal operating temperature so the choke is fully open. Check the ignition timing (see Chapter 1).

2    Disconnect the cooling fan wire, then open the throttle and run the engine at 2,500 rpm for 10 seconds. Return the engine to idle and wait two minutes.

3    After waiting two minutes with the curb idle stabilized, check the rpm indicated on the tachometer and make sure it is the same as specified on the Emissions Control Information label.

4    If it isn't, turn the idle speed screw to bring the rpm to the proper curb idle setting **(see illustration)**.

5    On air-conditioned models, turn on the air conditioner and, with the compressor running, adjust the idle speed to the specified rpm by turning the idle-up adjustment screw **(see illustration)**.

6    Shut off the engine, reconnect the cooling fan and remove the tachometer.

## 17  Fuel injection system - general information

The fuel injection system on models so equipped is of the single-point, Throttle Body Injection (TBI) type. This system is an electronically controlled fuel injection system which combines electronic fuel injection and electronic spark advance. The main sub-systems include

**16.5  Air conditioner idle-up adjustment screw location (2.6L engine)**

the air induction, fuel delivery, fuel control, emission control and the Single Module Engine Controller (SMEC) (1987 through 1989 models). **Note:** *1985 and 1986 models are equipped with the Logic Module that flashes a POWER LOSS light on the dash for diagnosis.*

### Air induction system

The air induction system includes the air cleaner, throttle body, Throttle Position Sensor (TPS) and Automatic Idle Speed (AIS) motor.

### Fuel delivery system

The fuel delivery system provides fuel from the fuel tank into the fuel control system. It also returns any excess fuel back into the fuel tank. The system includes an in-tank electric fuel pump, fuel filter, check valves and return line. Power is supplied to the fuel pump through the power module via the Automatic Shutdown (ASD) relay. The ASD relay also controls the ignition coil, the fuel injector and parts of the power module.

### Fuel control system

The components of the fuel control system are the fuel pressure regulator, the fuel injector and the throttle body **(see illustration 19.4)**.

### Fuel injector

On this system, the conventional carburetor is replaced by a throttle body and injector (single-point). The fuel is mixed with air in the throttle body and sprayed into the intake manifold, which directs it to the intake ports and cylinders.

Because of the complexity of the EFI system - and the special equipment required to troubleshoot it - the home mechanic can do little diagnosis. But checking electrical and vacuum connections to make sure they're clean, tight and undamaged can often eliminate a potential or current problem. Because the Logic Module/SMEC is dependent on the data provided by information sensors and transmitted through electrical and vacuum connections, a thorough visual check and repair of any damaged or loose connections, wires or vacuum hoses can save diagnostic time and unnecessary trips to the dealer or repair shop.

## 18  Fuel injection system - check

**Note:** *The following procedure is based on the assumption that the fuel pressure is adequate (see Section 3).*

1    Check the ground wire connections on the intake manifold for tightness. Check all wiring harness connectors that are related to the system. Loose connectors and poor grounds can cause many problems that resemble more serious malfunctions.

2    Check to see that the battery is fully charged, as the control unit and sensors depend on an accurate supply voltage in order to properly meter the fuel.

3    Check the air filter element - a dirty or partially blocked filter will severely impede performance and economy (see Chapter 1).

4    If a blown fuse is found, replace it and see if it blows again. If it does, search for a grounded wire in the harness to the fuel pump.

5    Check the air intake duct to the intake manifold for leaks, which will result in an excessively lean mixture. Also check the condition of all vacuum hoses connected to the intake manifold.

6    With the engine running, you should see a symetrical cone of fuel being sprayed from the injector onto the throttle plate.

7    The remainder of the system checks can be found in the following Sections.

## 19  Fuel injection system - component check and replacement

**Warning:** *Gasoline is extremely flammable, so take extra precautions when you work on any part of the fuel system. Don't smoke or allow open flames or bare light bulbs near the work area, and don't work in a*

**19.4  Throttle body details (1987 through 1989 2.5L engine)**

*garage where a natural gas-type appliance (such as a water heater or a clothes dryer) with a pilot light is present. Since gasoline is carcinogenic, wear latex gloves when there's a possibility of being exposed to fuel, and, if you spill any fuel on your skin, rinse it off immediately with soap and water. Mop up any spills immediately and do not store fuel-soaked rags where they could ignite. The fuel system is under constant pressure, so, if any fuel lines are to be disconnected, the fuel pressure in the system must be relieved first. When you perform any kind of work on the fuel system, wear safety glasses and have a Class B type fire extinguisher on hand.*

## *Throttle body*

### Removal

*Refer to illustrations 19.4 and 19.8*

1    Remove the air cleaner assembly (see Section 9).

2    Relieve the fuel system pressure (see Section 2).

3    Disconnect the negative cable from the battery.

4    Disconnect the vacuum hoses and electrical connectors **(see illustration)**.

5    Disconnect the accelerator cable (see Section 10), and (if equipped) the cruise control and transaxle kickdown cable (see Chapter 7).

6    Remove the throttle return spring.

7    Place rags or newspapers under the fuel hoses to catch the residual fuel. Loosen the clamps, wrap a cloth around each fuel hose and

**19.8  Remove the two long bolts and the two short bolts (arrows) from the throttle body (the shorter rear bolt is hidden from view)**

pull them off. Remove the copper washers from the hoses, noting their locations.

8    Remove the mounting bolts or nuts **(see illustration)** and lift the throttle body off the manifold.

**19.24  Use a Torx drive socket (no. 25) and remove the three bolts from the regulator**

## Installation

9    Inspect the mating surfaces of the throttle body and the manifold for nicks, burrs and debris that could cause air leaks.

10    Using a new gasket, place the throttle body in position and install the mounting bolts or nuts.

11    Tighten the bolts or nuts to the torque listed in this Chapter's Specifications, following a criss-cross pattern. Work up to the final torque in three or four steps.

12    Check all of the vacuum hoses and electrical connectors for damage, replacing them with new parts if necessary, then connect them.

13    Connect the accelerator cable and (if equipped) cruise control and kickdown cable.

14    Connect the throttle return spring.

15    Using new clamps and washers, install the fuel hoses.

16    Check the operation of the throttle linkage.

17    Install the air cleaner assembly.

18    Connect the negative battery cable.

19    Start the engine and check for fuel leaks.

## *Fuel pressure regulator*

### Check

20    Follow the fuel pressure checking procedure in Section 3 for diagnosis of the fuel pressure regulator.

### Removal

*Refer to illustrations 19.24 and 19.26*

21    Remove the air cleaner assembly (see Section 9).

22    Relieve the fuel system pressure (see Section 2).

23    Disconnect the negative cable from the battery.

24    Remove the three screws (this will require a no. 25 Torx drive socket) from the regulator **(see illustration)**.

INJECTOR CAP

USE 2 SCREWDRIVERS IN CAP SLOTS
TO REMOVE INJECTOR CAP

**19.38  Use two small screwdrivers to pry the injector cap off**

**19.26  If the regulator is still fastened to the throttle body after the bolts have been removed, wiggle the regulator to free-up the rubber seal**

25    Wrap a cloth around the fuel inlet chamber to catch any residual fuel, which is under pressure.

26    Withdraw the pressure regulator from the throttle body **(see illustration)**.

27    Carefully remove the O-ring from the pressure regulator, followed by the gasket.

### Installation

28    Place a new gasket in position on the pressure regulator and carefully install a new O-ring.

29    Place the pressure regulator in position on the throttle body, press it into position and install the three mounting screws. Tighten the screws securely.

30    Connect the negative battery cable. Check carefully for any fuel leaks.

31    Install the air cleaner assembly (see Section 9).

## *Fuel injector*

### Check

32    With the engine running, or cranking, listen to the sound from the injector with an automotive stethoscope and verify that the injector sounds as if it's operating normally. If you don't have a stethoscope, touch the area of the throttle body immediately above the fuel injector with your finger and try to determine whether the injector feels like it's operating smoothly. It should sound/feel smooth and uniform and its sound/feel should rise and fall with engine rpm. If the injector isn't operating, or sounds/feels erratic, check the injector electrical connector. If the connector is snug, check for voltage to the injector using a special injector harness test light (available at most auto parts stores). If there's voltage to the injector and it isn't operating, or if it's operating erratically, replace it.

FUEL INJECTOR          SCREWDRIVER

**19.39  Remove the fuel injector by inserting a small screwdriver into the slot on the injector and gently prying it up**

FUEL INJECTOR
ELECTRICAL
TERMINALS

FUEL
INJECTOR
POD

UPPER
O-RING

LOWER
O-RING

**19.40  Fuel injector details**

LOCATING
LOBE

LOCATING
NOTCH

O-RING

**19.43a  Alignment details of the cap and injector (1987 models)**

## Removal

*Refer to illustrations 19.38, 19.39 and 19.40*

33   Remove the air cleaner assembly (see Section 9).

34   Relieve the fuel system pressure (see Section 2).

35   Disconnect the negative cable from the battery.

36   On 1987 models, remove the fuel pressure regulator.

37   Remove the Torx screw that holds the injector cap.

38   Use two small screwdrivers and carefully pry the cap off the injector using the appropriate slots **(see illustration)**.

39   Place a small screwdriver into the hole in the injector and gently pry the injector from the throttle body unit **(see illustration)**.

40   Peel the upper and lower O-rings off the fuel injector **(see illustration)**. If the lower O-ring isn't on the injector, be sure to retrieve it from the throttle body.

## Installation

*Refer to illustrations 19.43a, 19.43b and 19.44*

41   Install new O-rings on the injector and a new O-ring on the injector cap. **Note:** *New injectors come equipped with a new upper O-ring. Coat the O-rings with engine oil to help injector installation.*

42   Insert the injector into the throttle body.

43   Place the injector cap onto the injector. The injector and cap are keyed and must be aligned properly **(see illustrations)**.

44   Rotate the cap and injector to line up the attachment hole **(see illustration)**. Tighten the screws securely.

45   Connect the negative battery cable, start the engine and check for leaks.

46   Turn off the engine and install the air cleaner assembly.

## 20   Exhaust system servicing - general information

*Refer to illustration 20.1*

**Warning:** *Inspection and repair of exhaust system components should*

FUEL PRESSURE
REGULATOR

O-RING

ALIGN WIRING
TERMINALS
WITH HOLE

LOCATING
NOTCH

LOCATING LOBE

**19.43b  Alignment details of the cap and injector
(1988 and 1989 models)**

*be done only with the engine and exhaust components completely cool. Also, when working under the vehicle, make sure it's securely supported on jackstands.*

1   The exhaust system **(see illustration)** consists of the exhaust manifold(s), the catalytic converter, the muffler, the tailpipe and all connecting pipes, brackets, hangers and clamps. The exhaust system is attached to the body with mounting brackets and rubber hangers. If

**4**

SEAT INJECTOR CAP
THEN
ROTATE CAP SO FASTENER
CAN BE INSTALLED

**19.44  Rotate the cap
so the screw aligns
with the slot in the cap**

AIR LINE

FRONT CATALYTIC CONVERTER
WITH AIR INJECTION

RESONATOR

HEAT
SHIELD

UNDERFLOOR
CATALYST

MUFFLER

**20.1  Exhaust system components**

any of the parts are improperly installed, excessive noise and vibration will be transmitted to the body.

2    Conduct regular inspections of the exhaust system to keep it safe and quiet. Look for any damaged or bent parts, open seams, holes, loose connections, excessive corrosion or other defects which could allow exhaust fumes to enter the vehicle. Deteriorated exhaust system components shouldn't be repaired; they should be replaced with new parts.

3    If the exhaust system components are extremely corroded or rusted together, welding equipment will probably be required to remove them. The convenient way to accomplish this is to have a muffler repair shop remove the corroded sections with a cutting torch. If, however, you want to save money by doing it yourself (and you don't have a welding outfit with a cutting torch), simply cut off the old components with a hacksaw. If you have compressed air, special pneumatic cutting chisels can also be used. If you do decide to tackle the job at home, be sure to wear safety goggles to protect your eyes from metal chips and work gloves to protect your hands.

4    Here are some simple guidelines to follow when repairing the exhaust system:

a)  *Work from the back to the front when removing exhaust system components.*

b)  *Apply penetrating oil to the component fasteners to make them easier to remove.*

c)  *Use new gaskets, hangers and clamps when installing exhaust system components.*

d)  *Apply anti-seize compound to the threads of all exhaust system fasteners during reassembly.*

e)  *Be sure to allow sufficient clearance between newly installed parts and all points on the underbody to avoid overheating the floor pan and possibly damaging the interior carpet and insulation. Pay particularly close attention to the catalytic converter and heat shields.*

# Chapter 5
# Engine electrical systems

## Contents

**5**

## Specifications

### Ignition coil resistance (by coil manufacturer)

Mitsubishi
    1981 through 1985
        Primary .................................................................................. 0.7 to 0.85 ohms
        Secondary ............................................................................ 9 to 11 k-ohms
Essex
    1981 through 1985
        Primary .................................................................................. 1.41 to 1.62 ohms
        Secondary ............................................................................ 9 to 12.2 k-ohms
    1986 through 1989
        Primary .................................................................................. 1.34 to 1.55 ohms
        Secondary ............................................................................ 9 to 12.2 k-ohms
Prestolite
    1981 through 1985
        Primary .................................................................................. 1.60 to 1.79 ohms
        Secondary ............................................................................ 9.4 to 11.7 k-ohms
    1986 through 1989
        Primary .................................................................................. 1.34 to 1.55 ohms
        Secondary ............................................................................ 9.4 to 11.7 k-ohms
Diamond
    1988 and 1989
        Primary .................................................................................. 1.34 to 1.55 ohms
        Secondary ............................................................................ 15 to 19 k-ohms

## 1   General information

The engine electrical systems include all ignition, charging and starting components. Because of their engine-related functions, these components are discussed separately from chassis electrical devices such as the lights, the instruments, etc. (which are included in Chapter 12). Always observe the following precautions when working on the electrical systems:

a) *Be extremely careful when servicing engine electrical components. They are easily damaged if checked, connected or handled improperly.*
b) *Never leave the ignition switch on for long periods of time with the engine off.*
c) *Don't disconnect the battery cables while the engine is running.*
d) *Maintain correct polarity when connecting a battery cable from another vehicle during jump starting.*
e) *Always disconnect the negative cable first and hook it up last or the battery may be shorted by the tool being used to loosen the cable clamps. It's also a good idea to review the safety-related information regarding the engine electrical systems located in the Safety First Section near the front of this manual before beginning any operation included in this Chapter.*

## 2   Battery - emergency jump starting

Refer to the *Booster battery (jump) starting* procedure at the front of this manual.

## 3   Battery - removal and installation

*Refer to illustration 3.2*
1   Disconnect both cables from the battery terminals (negative cable first, positive cable last).
2   Remove the battery hold-down clamp **(see illustration)**.
3   Lift out the battery. Be careful - it's heavy.
4   While the battery is out, inspect the carrier (tray) for corrosion (see Chapter 1).
5   If you're replacing the battery, make sure you purchase one that's identical, with the same dimensions, amperage rating, cold cranking rating, etc.
6   Installation is the reverse of removal. When installing the cables, connect the positive cable first, followed by the negative cable.

## 4   Battery cables - check and replacement

1   Periodically inspect the entire length of each battery cable for damage, cracked or burned insulation and corrosion. Poor battery cable connections can cause starting problems and decreased engine performance.
2   Check the cable-to-terminal connections at the ends of the cables for cracks, loose wire strands and corrosion. The presence of white, fluffy deposits under the insulation at the cable terminal connection is a sign that the cable is corroded and should be replaced. Check the terminals for distortion, missing mounting bolts and corrosion.
3   When removing the cables, always disconnect the negative cable first and hook it up last or the battery may be shorted by the tool used to loosen the cable clamps. Even if only the positive cable is being replaced, be sure to disconnect the negative cable from the battery first (see Chapter 1 for further information regarding battery cable removal).
4   Disconnect the old cables from the battery, then trace each of them to their opposite ends and detach them from the starter solenoid and ground terminals. Note the routing of each cable to ensure correct installation.
5   If you're replacing either or both of the old cables, take them with you when buying new cables. It's very important to replace the cables with identical parts. Cables have characteristics that make them easy

**3.2  To remove the battery, unscrew the hold-down bolt (arrow) and remove the hold-down clamp**

to identify: Positive cables are usually red, larger in cross-section and have a larger diameter battery post clamp; ground cables are usually black, smaller in cross-section and have a slightly smaller diameter clamp for the negative post.
6   Clean the threads of the solenoid or ground connection with a wire brush to remove rust and corrosion. Apply a light coat of battery terminal corrosion inhibitor, or petroleum jelly, to the threads to prevent future corrosion.
7   Attach the cable to the solenoid or ground connection and tighten the mounting nut/bolt securely.
8   Before connecting a new cable to the battery, make sure it reaches the battery post without having to be stretched.
9   Connect the positive cable first, followed by the negative cable.

## 5   Ignition system - general information

The ignition system includes the ignition switch, the battery, the coil, the primary (low voltage) and secondary (high voltage) wiring circuits, the distributor and the spark plugs.

On 1981 through 1987 models with the 2.2L engine, the ignition system is controlled by the Spark Control Computer (SCC). On 1988 and 1989 models, it's controlled by a computer known as the Single Module Engine Controller (SMEC). The SMEC monitors coolant temperature, engine rpm and available intake manifold vacuum to ensure a perfectly timed spark under all driving conditions. For more information regarding the SMEC, refer to Chapter 6.

## 6   Ignition system - check

**Warning:** *The secondary ignition system voltage is very high (over 30,000 volts). Use extreme care when performing the following checks so you don't get shocked.*

### 2.2L engine
*Refer to illustrations 6.2a, 6.2b, 6.4, 6.8, 6.11, 6.13, 6.14, 6.16, 6.17, 6.18, 6.19, 6.21 and 6.22*
1   Prior to testing the spark control computer (SCC), check the coil and battery to make sure they are in good operating condition. Inspect the electrical harness and wires for shorts, cracked and worn insulation and all connectors for security. Check the vacuum hose for kinks, damage and secure connection.
2   Connect the special test tool **(see illustration)** to the negative terminal of the coil and ground the other end. Pull the coil wire from the distributor and place it 1/4-inch from a good ground **(see illustration)**. With the ignition switch on, momentarily touch the remaining test lead to the negative coil terminal. A spark should jump from the coil wire to the ground.
3   If there is a spark, proceed to Step 8.

**6.2a When checking the SCC, a special test tool can be fabricated from a 0.33 mfd capacitor, some wire and alligator clips**

**6.2b The spark at the coil wire must be bright blue and well defined**

**6.4 Disconnect the ten-wire harness connector from the SCC (2.2L engine)**

**6.8 Use a thin piece of cardboard to hold the carburetor switch open and measure the voltage at the switch wire terminal (2.2L engine)**

4    If there is no spark, turn off the ignition switch, disconnect the ten wire electrical connector at the SCC **(see illustration)** and repeat the test. If a spark is now produced, the computer output is shorted and the spark control computer must be replaced with a new one.

5    If there was no spark, check the voltage at the coil positive terminal to make sure it is within one volt of battery voltage.

6    If there was no voltage reading, check the wiring between the battery and the positive terminal of the coil.

7    If there was a proper voltage reading, check the voltage at the coil negative terminal. This reading should also be within one volt of battery voltage. If there is no voltage or there is voltage but no spark was produced when performing the test in Step 2, replace the coil with a new one.

8    If there is a voltage reading but the engine will not start, use a thin piece of cardboard to hold the carburetor switch open **(see illustration)** and measure the voltage at the switch. The reading should be at least five volts.

9    If the voltage reading is correct, go on to Step 16.

10   If there is no voltage, turn off the ignition switch and unplug the SCC ten wire connector.

11   Turn the switch on and check the voltage at cavity 2 of the connector **(see illustration)**. It should be within one volt of battery voltage.

12   If there is no voltage reading, check for continuity between cavity 2 and the battery. Repair the circuit and repeat the test in Step 11.

13   If there is voltage present, turn off the ignition switch and check for continuity between cavity 7 and the carburetor switch **(see illustration)**. If no continuity is present, check for an open wire between cavity 7 and the carburetor switch and repair the circuit.

**6.11 Check the voltage at the ten-wire connector cavity (2.2L engine)**

**6.13 Check for continuity between cavity 7 and the carburetor switch (2.2L engine)**

**6.14  Check for continuity between cavity 10 and a good ground (2.2L engine)**

**6.17  Rotor shutter blade and ground strap locations**

**6.16  The jumper wire must be connected between cavities 2 and 3 in the distributor wiring harness connector (2.2L engine)**

**6.18  Checking for voltage between the distributor harness connector cavity 1 and a good ground**

14   If there is continuity present, check for continuity between cavity 10 and a good ground **(see illustration)**. If there is continuity, it will be necessary to replace the computer with a new one as power is going into it but not out. Repeat the test in Step 8.

15   If continuity is not present, check for an open wire.

16   If the wiring is alright and the engine will not start, plug the ten wire connector into the computer and unplug the distributor wire harness connector. Connect a jumper wire between cavities 2 and 3 of the connector **(see illustration)**. Hold the coil wire near a good ground, turn the ignition switch on and break the circuit at cavity 2 or 3 several times. A bright blue spark should occur at the coil wire.

17   If sparks are produced but the engine still does not start, replace the distributor pick-up assembly (also called a Hall effect switch) (see Section 10), making sure the shutter blades are grounded **(see illustration)**. With the ignition switched off, check for a good ground on the distributor shaft with an ohmmeter. It may be necessary to seat the rotor securely on the shaft to obtain a good ground. Connect one lead of the ohmmeter to the shutter blade and the other to a good ground and make sure there is continuity. If there is none, push the rotor down on the shaft until continuity is indicated.

18   Repeat the test in Step 16 and if there is no spark present, measure the voltage at cavity 1 of the distributor connector **(see illustration)**. It should be within one volt of battery voltage.

19   If the voltage is correct, turn off the ignition, unplug the ten wire connector from the computer and check for continuity between cavity 2 of the distributor harness and cavity 9 of the computer connector. Follow this by checking between cavity 3 of the distributor harness and cavity 5 of the computer connector **(see illustration)**. If there is no continuity, find and repair the fault in the harness. If there is continuity, replace the computer with a new one as power is going into it but not coming out.

20   Repeat the test in Step 16.

21   If no voltage is present when making the check in Step 18, turn off the ignition, unplug the computer ten wire connector and check for

**6.19  Checking for continuity between the distributor and the SCC connector cavities (2.2L engine)**

**6.21  Checking for continuity between the distributor harness connector cavity 1 and the SCC connector cavity 3 (2.2L engine)**

6.22  Checking for voltage between SCC connector cavities 10 and 2 (2.2L engine)

6.28  Check the coil for spark (2.5L engine)

TERMINAL SIDE

6.33  Terminal guide for the SMEC 14-way electrical connector (1987 through 1989 2.5L engine)

continuity between cavity 1 of the distributor harness connector and cavity 3 of the computer connector (see illustration). If there is no continuity, repair the wire and repeat the test in Step 16.

22   If there is continuity, turn on the ignition switch and check for voltage between cavities 2 and 10 of the computer connector (see illustration). If there is voltage, the computer is faulty and must be replaced with a new one. Repeat the test in Step 16. If there is no voltage, check and repair the ground wire, as the computer is not grounded. Repeat the Step 16 test.

### 2.6L engine

23   Remove the coil wire from the distributor cap and, using and insulated tool, hold the end about 1/4-inch from a good engine ground. Operate the starter and look for a series of bright blue sparks at the coil wire.

24   If sparks occur, and they are bright blue and well defined, continue to operate the starter while slowly moving the coil wire away from the ground. As this is done, look for arcing and sparking at the coil tower. If it occurs, replace the coil with a new one. If arcing does not

6.39  To use a calibrated tester (available at most auto parts stores), simply disconnect a spark plug wire, attach the wire to the tester and clip the tester to a good ground - if there is enough power to fire the plug, sparks will be clearly visible between the electrode tip and the tester body as the engine is turned over

occur at the coil tower, the ignition system is producing the necessary high secondary voltage. However, make sure the voltage is getting to the spark plugs by checking the rotor, distributor cap, spark plug wires and spark plugs as described in Chapter 1. If the results are positive, the ignition system is not the reason the engine will not start.

25   If no sparks occurred, or if they were weak or intermittent, measure the voltage at the ignition coil negative terminal with the ignition switch on. It should be the same as battery voltage. If it is three volts or less, the igniter is defective. If no voltage was present, check the coil and wires for an open circuit.

26   Refer to Step 2 and perform the check described there.

27   If no spark was produced, check for voltage at the positive coil terminal with the ignition switch on. Battery voltage should be indicated. If it is, the coil is defective. If no voltage is present, check the associated wires and connections.

### 1987 through 1989 SMEC systems

*Refer to illustrations 6.28 and 6.33*

28   Remove the coil wire from the distributor cap. Using and insulated tool, hold the end of the wire about 1/4-inch from a good engine ground and crank the engine. Check for a consistent spark as the engine is cranked (see illustration).

29   If the spark is not constant or there is no spark, connect a voltmeter to the coil positive terminal and crank the engine for five seconds. If the voltage is near zero during this test refer to the Trouble Codes in Chapter 6.

30   If the voltage is at near battery voltage (approximately 12.4 volts) at the start of the test but drops to zero after one to two seconds of cranking, refer to the Trouble Codes in Chapter 6.

31   If the voltage remains at near battery voltage for the five seconds, turn off the ignition key, remove the 14-way connector from the SMEC and check for any spread terminals.

32   Remove the coil positive terminal lead and connect a jumper wire between the battery positive terminal and the coil positive terminal.

33   Momentarily ground terminal No. 12 of the 14-way connector (see illustration) with a jumper wire.

34   If a spark is generated, replace the SMEC.

35   If no spark is generated, connect a special jumper wire (see illustration 6.2a) to ground the coil negative terminal.

36   If a spark is now produced, check the wiring harness for an open condition.

37   If no spark is produced, replace the coil.

### Quick test for any engine

*Refer to illustration 6.39*

38   If the engine turns over but won't start, disconnect the spark plug wire from any spark plug and attach it to a calibrated ignition tester (available at most auto parts stores).

39   Connect the clip on the tester to a bolt or metal bracket on the engine (see illustration). If you're unable to obtain a calibrated ignition tester, remove the wire from one of the spark plugs and, using an insulated tool, hold the end of the wire about 1/4-inch from a good ground.

5

**7.2 To remove the coil from the right inner fenderwall, disconnect the primary wires and the high-tension cable (1), then remove the mounting bracket bolt - if the coil is bad, loosen the clamp pinch screw (2) and transfer the clamp/mounting bracket to the new coil**

**7.4 To check the coil primary resistance, touch the leads of an ohmmeter to the positive and negative primary terminals (arrows) and compare your reading with the coil primary resistance listed in this Chapter's Specifications**

**7.5 To check the coil secondary resistance, touch one lead of the ohmmeter to one of the primary terminals and the other lead to the high-tension terminal (arrows), then compare your reading to the coil secondary resistance listed in this Chapter's Specifications**

40    Crank the engine and watch the end of the tester or spark plug wire to see if bright blue, well-defined sparks occur. If you're not using a calibrated tester, have an assistant crank the engine for you. **Warning:** *Keep clear of drivebelts and other moving engine components that could injure you.*

41    If sparks occur, sufficient voltage is reaching the plug to fire it (repeat the check at the remaining plug wires to verify the wires, distributor cap and rotor are OK). However, the plugs themselves may be fouled, so remove them and check them as described in Chapter 1.

42    If no sparks or intermittent sparks occur, remove the distributor cap and check the cap and rotor as described in Chapter 1. If moisture is present, dry out the cap and rotor, then reinstall the cap.

43    If there's still no spark, detach the coil secondary wire from the distributor cap and hook it up to the tester (reattach the plug wire to the spark plug), then repeat the spark check. Again, if you don't have a tester, hold the end of the wire about 1/4-inch from a good ground. If sparks occur now, the distributor cap, rotor or plug wire(s) may be defective.

44    If no sparks occur, check the wire connections at the coil to make sure they're clean and tight. Check for voltage to the coil. Make any necessary repairs, then repeat the check again.

45    If there's still no spark, the coil-to-cap wire may be bad (check the resistance with an ohmmeter - it should be 7,000 ohms per foot or less). If a known good wire doesn't make any difference in the test results, check the coil (see Section 7). If it's OK, the pick-up assembly (see Section 10) or ignition module may be defective.

## 7    Ignition coil - check and replacement

*Refer to illustrations 7.2, 7.4 and 7.5*

1    Detach the cable from the negative battery terminal.

2    Mark the wires and terminals with pieces of numbered tape, then remove the primary wires and the high-tension lead from the coil **(see illustration)**. Disconnect the coil mounting bracket, remove the coil/bracket assembly, clean the outer case and check it for cracks and other damage.

3    Clean the coil primary terminals and check the coil tower terminal for corrosion. Clean it with a wire brush if any corrosion is found.

4    Check the coil primary resistance by attaching the leads of an ohmmeter to the positive and negative terminals **(see illustration)**. Compare your readings to the primary resistance listed in this Chapter's Specifications.

5    Check the coil secondary resistance by hooking one of the ohmmeter leads to one of the primary terminals and the other ohmmeter lead to the large center terminal **(see illustration)**. Compare your readings to the secondary resistance listed in this Chapter's Specifications.

6    If the measured resistances are not as specified, the coil is probably defective and should be replaced with a new one.

7    For proper ignition system operation, all coil terminals and wire leads must be kept clean and dry.

8    Install the coil in the vehicle and hook up the wires.

9    Attach the cable to the negative battery terminal.

## 8    Distributor - removal and installation

### *Removal*

*Refer to illustrations 8.3, 8.4, 8.7 and 8.8*

1    Disconnect the cable from the negative terminal of the battery.

2    Detach the primary lead from the coil.

3    Unplug the electrical connector for the Hall Effect pick-up (2.2L engines) **(see illustration)** or the pick-up coil (2.6L engine). Follow the wires as they exit the distributor to find the connector.

4    Remove the distributor splash shield, if equipped **(see illustration)**.

5    Look for a raised "1" on the distributor cap. This marks the location for the number one cylinder spark plug wire terminal. If the cap doesn't have a mark for the number one terminal, locate the number one spark plug and trace the wire back to the terminal on the cap.

6    Remove the distributor cap (see Chapter 1) and turn the engine over until the rotor is pointing toward the number one spark plug wire

8.3  Before you remove the distributor from a 2.2L engine, trace the electrical lead for the Hall Effect pick-up from the distributor to it's connector (arrow) at the engine wire harness and unplug it (2.2L shown)

8.4  Remove these two screws (arrows) and remove the distributor splash shield (if equipped)

8.7  Mark the position of the rotor tip on the distributor base and mark the relationship of the base to the block (arrows)

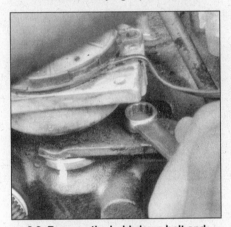

8.8  Remove the hold-down bolt and clamp, then pull the distributor straight up

8.10a  When you install the distributor on a 2.2L or 2.5L engine, be sure to align the tangs (arrows) on the end of the distributor shaft . . .

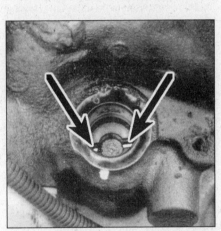

8.10b  . . . with the slots (arrows) in the top of the oil pump driveshaft

**5**

terminal (see the locating TDC procedure in Chapter 2, if necessary).

7    Make a mark on the edge of the distributor base directly below the rotor tip and in line with it. Also, mark the distributor base and the engine block to ensure that the distributor will be reinstalled correctly **(see illustration)**.

8    Remove the distributor hold-down bolt and clamp **(see illustration)**, then pull the distributor straight up to remove it. **Caution:** *DO NOT turn the crankshaft while the distributor is out of the engine, or the alignment marks will be useless.*

## Installation

*Refer to illustrations 8.10a and 8.10b*

**Note:** *If the crankshaft has been moved while the distributor is out, the number one piston must be repositioned at TDC. This can be done by feeling for compression pressure at the number one plug hole as the crankshaft is turned. Once compression is felt, align the ignition timing zero mark with the pointer.*

9    Insert the distributor into the engine in exactly the same relationship to the block that it was in when removed.

10   On 2.2L and 2.5L engines, make sure the lugs on the lower end of the distributor shaft fit into the slot in the upper end of the oil pump shaft **(see illustrations)**. If they don't, the distributor won't seat completely. On all distributors, recheck the alignment marks between the distributor base and block to verify the distributor is in the same position it was in before removal. Also check the rotor to see if it's aligned with the mark you made on the edge of the distributor base.

11   Place the hold-down clamp (if equipped) in position and loosely install the hold-down bolt.

12   Install the distributor cap.

13   Plug in the electrical connector for the Hall Effect pick-up (2.2L and 2.5L engines) or the pick-up coil (2.6L engine).

14   Reattach the spark plug wires to the plugs (if removed).

15   Connect the cable to the negative terminal of the battery.

16   Check the ignition timing (see Chapter 1) and tighten the distributor hold-down bolt securely.

## 9    Governor (centrifugal advance) unit (2.6L engine) - check and replacement

### Check

1    Connect a timing light to the engine in accordance with the manufacturer's instructions (see the ignition timing procedure in Chapter 1). Start the engine and allow it to warm up. With the engine idling, detach the vacuum line (the one without stripes) from the vacuum chamber. Slowly accelerate the engine and see if the ignition timing advances evenly, proportionate to engine speed.

2    If the advance is excessive, the governor spring is weakened; if the advance is abrupt, the spring is broken. If the advance is insufficient, a governor weight or a cam is defective. In either case, replace the governor assembly.

**9.5  Use a socket or box-end wrench to remove the governor assembly retaining bolt (2.6L engine)**

**9.6  Remove the governor assembly (2.6L engine)**

## Replacement

*Refer to illustrations 9.5 and 9.6*

3    Remove the distributor (see Section 8). **Note:** *The governor unit can be removed with the distributor installed on the engine, but it's easier with the distributor removed.*

4    Remove the rotor (see Chapter 1).

5    Remove the governor assembly retaining bolt **(see illustration)**. **Note:** *This bolt is torqued very tightly - use a box-end wrench or socket - not an open-end wrench - to loosen it.*

6    Remove the governor assembly **(see illustration)**. **Note:** *We recommend replacing the entire governor assembly as a single unit. But the individual springs and weights are also available separately. If you decide to replace an individual spring or weight, make sure you note which spring is attached to each weight prior to disassembly. The tension of each spring is calibrated to match its respective weight, so it must be reinstalled in its original position. The easiest way to identify a spring is to note the number of its coils: The stronger spring has more coils, the weaker spring, less.*

7    Reassembly is the reverse of disassembly.

8    Install the rotor (see Chapter 1) and the distributor, if removed (see Section 8).

---

## 10   Pick-up assembly - replacement

1    Disconnect the cable from the negative terminal of the battery.

### Hall effect pick-up assembly (2.2L and 2.5L engines)

*Refer to illustration 10.4*

**Note:** *The Hall Effect pick-up assembly inside the distributor supplies the basic ignition timing signal to the computer. The check for the Hall Effect pick-up is part of the ignition system check in Section 6.*

2    Remove the distributor splash shield and cap and disconnect the Hall Effect electrical connector (see Section 8).

3    Remove the distributor cap and rotor (see Chapter 1).

4    Lift the pick-up assembly off the distributor shaft **(see illustration)**.

5    Installation is the reverse of removal. Check that the shutter blades are grounded (see Section 6, Step 17).

### Pick-up coil/IC igniter assembly (2.6L engine)

*Refer to illustrations 10.9, 10.10a and 10.10b*

6    Remove the distributor (see Section 8). **Note:** *The pick-up coil/IC igniter assembly can be removed with the distributor installed on the engine, but it's easier with the distributor removed.*

7    Remove the rotor (see Chapter 1).

8    Remove the governor assembly (see Section 9).

**10.4  To replace the Hall Effect pick-up assembly on the distributor used on 2.2L engines, simply remove the rotor and lift the pick-up unit off the distributor housing (distributor assembly removed for clarity**

9    Remove the screw from the clamp which secures the lead for the pick-up coil to the distributor housing **(see illustration)**.

10    Remove the two retaining screws from the pick-up coil/IC igniter assembly **(see illustration)** and remove the assembly **(see illustration)**.

11    Reassembly is the reverse of disassembly.

12    Install the governor assembly (see Section 9), the distributor, if removed (see Section 8), and the rotor and cap (see Chapter 1).

**10.9  Before removing the pick-up assembly from the distributor used on the 2.6L engine, remove the screw (arrow) to detach the clamp that secures the electrical lead to distributor housing**

10.10a Remove these two screws from the pick-up coil/IC igniter unit (2.6L engine)

10.10b Remove the pick-up coil/IC igniter unit from the distributor housing (2.6L engine)

11.8 Remove the two vacuum governor screws (arrows) (2.6L engine)

11.9 Remove the vacuum governor assembly (2.6L engine)

## 11 Vacuum advance unit (2.6L engine) - check and replacement

**Note:** *The vacuum advance unit is also referred to as a vacuum chamber and a vacuum governor assembly.*

### Check

1    Here's a little test for quickly checking the vacuum advance unit: Start the engine and warm it up, hook up a tachometer in accordance with the manufacturer's instructions, bring the engine speed up to 2,500 rpm and see if the engine speed is affected as you disconnect, then reconnect, the vacuum line. If there's no change in engine speed, the vacuum advance unit is faulty.

2    Here's a more precise way to check the vacuum advance unit: Disconnect the vacuum line from the distributor and connect a vacuum pump in its place. Hook up a timing light in accordance with the manufacturer's instructions (see the ignition timing procedure in Chapter 1). Run the engine at idle and slowly apply vacuum - the timing should advance evenly, proportionate to the amount of vacuum applied.

3    If the advance is excessive, the vacuum controller spring is worn or sagging; if the advance is abrupt, the spring is broken. If the advance is insufficient - or there's no advance at all - the breaker plate is faulty or the diaphragm is broken. In either case, replace the vacuum advance unit.

### Replacement

*Refer to illustrations 11.8 and 11.9*

4    Remove the distributor (see Section 8). **Note:** *The vacuum advance unit can be removed with the distributor installed on the engine, but it's much easier to replace with the distributor removed.*

5    Remove the rotor (see Chapter 1).

6    Remove the governor assembly (see Section 9).

7    Remove the pick-up coil and IC igniter assembly (see Section 10).

8    Remove the two retaining screws from the vacuum governor assembly **(see illustration)**.

9    Remove the vacuum governor assembly **(see illustration)**.

10    Reassembly is the reverse of disassembly.

11    Install the distributor (see Section 8).

## 12 Charging system - general information and precautions

The charging system includes the alternator, an internal or external voltage regulator or a regulator within the logic module (computer), a charge indicator, the battery, a fusible link and the wiring between all the components. The charging system supplies electrical power for the ignition system, the lights, the radio, etc. The alternator is driven by a drivebelt at the front of the engine.

The purpose of the voltage regulator is to limit the alternator's voltage to a preset value. This prevents power surges, circuit overloads, etc., during peak voltage output.

5

The fusible link is a short length of insulated wire integral with the engine compartment wiring harness. The link is several wire gauges smaller in diameter than the circuit it protects. Production fusible links and their identification flags are identified by the flag color. See Chapter 12 for additional information regarding fusible links.

The charging system doesn't ordinarily require periodic maintenance. However, the drivebelt, battery and wires and connections should be inspected at the intervals outlined in Chapter 1.

The dashboard warning light should come on when the ignition key is turned to Start, then go off immediately. If it remains on, there is a malfunction in the charging system (see Section 13). Some vehicles are also equipped with a voltmeter. If the voltmeter indicates abnormally high or low voltage, check the charging system (see Section 13). Be very careful when making electrical circuit connections to a vehicle equipped with an alternator and note the following:

a) *When reconnecting wires to the alternator from the battery, be sure to note the polarity.*

b) *Before using arc welding equipment to repair any part of the vehicle, disconnect the wires from the alternator and the battery terminals.*

c) *Never start the engine with a battery charger connected.*

d) *Always disconnect both battery leads before using a battery charger.*

e) *The alternator is turned by an engine drivebelt which could cause serious injury if your hands, hair or clothes become entangled in it with the engine running.*

f) *Because the alternator is connected directly to the battery, it could arc or cause a fire if overloaded or shorted out.*

g) *Wrap a plastic bag over the alternator and secure it with rubber bands before steam cleaning the engine.*

## 13   Charging system - check

1    If a malfunction occurs in the charging circuit, don't automatically assume the alternator is causing the problem. First check the following items:

a) *Check the drivebelt tension and condition (Chapter 1). Replace it if it's worn or deteriorated.*

b) *Make sure the alternator mounting and adjustment bolts are tight.*

c) *Inspect the alternator wiring harness and the connectors at the alternator and voltage regulator. They must be in good condition and tight.*

d) *Check the fusible link (if equipped) located between the starter solenoid and the alternator. If it's burned, determine the cause, repair the circuit and replace the link (the vehicle won't start and/or the accessories won't work if the fusible link blows). Sometimes a fusible link may look good, but still be bad. If in doubt, remove it and check it for continuity.*

e) *Start the engine and check the alternator for abnormal noises (a shrieking or squealing sound indicates a bad bearing).*

f) *Check the specific gravity of the battery electrolyte. If it's low, charge the battery (doesn't apply to maintenance free batteries).*

g) *Make sure the battery is fully charged (one bad cell in a battery can cause overcharging by the alternator).*

h) *Disconnect the battery cables (negative first, then positive). Inspect the battery posts and the cable clamps for corrosion. Clean them thoroughly if necessary (see Chapter 1). Reconnect the cable to the positive terminal.*

i) *With the key off, connect a test light between the negative battery post and the disconnected negative cable clamp.*

   1) *If the test light does not come on, reattach the clamp and proceed to the next Step.*

   2) *If the test light comes on, there is a short (drain) in the electrical system of the vehicle. The short must be repaired before the charging system can be checked.*

   3) *Disconnect the alternator wiring harness.*

    (a) *If the light goes out, the alternator is bad.*

    (b) *If the light stays on, pull each fuse until the light goes out (this will tell you which component is shorted).*

**14.2  Typical alternator electrical connections**

2    Using a voltmeter, check the battery voltage with the engine off. If should be approximately 12-volts.

3    Start the engine and check the battery voltage again. It should now be approximately 14 to 15 volts.

4    Turn on the headlights. The voltage should drop, and then come back up, if the charging system is working properly.

5    If the voltage reading is more than the specified charging voltage, replace the voltage regulator. On later models, the regulator is inside the computer and can't be replaced; on these vehicles, you'll have to replace the computer (see Chapter 6).

6    If the voltage reading is less than the specified voltage, the alternator diode(s), stator or rectifier may be bad or the voltage regulator may be malfunctioning.

## 14   Alternator - removal and installation

*Refer to illustrations 14.2, 14.3a and 14.3b*

1    Detach the cable from the negative terminal of the battery.

2    Detach the electrical connector(s) from the alternator **(see illustration)**. **Note:** *On most models, the alternator is located in front of the engine block.*

3    Loosen the alternator adjustment and pivot bolts and detach the drivebelt **(see illustrations)**.

4    Remove the adjustment and pivot bolts and separate the alternator from the engine.

5    If you're replacing the alternator, take the old one with you when purchasing a replacement unit. Make sure the new/rebuilt unit looks identical to the old alternator. Look at the terminals - they should be the same in number, size and location as the terminals on the old alternator. Finally, look at the identification numbers - they will be stamped into the housing or printed on a tag attached to the housing. Make sure the numbers are the same on both alternators.

6    Many new/rebuilt alternators DO NOT have a pulley installed, so you may have to switch the pulley from the old unit to the new/rebuilt one. When buying an alternator, find out the shop's policy regarding pulleys - some shops will perform this service free of charge.

7    Installation is the reverse of removal.

8    After the alternator is installed, adjust the drivebelt tension (see Chapter 1).

9    Check the charging voltage to verify proper operation of the alternator (see Section 13).

## 15   Alternator brushes - replacement

**Note:** *If the brushes on alternators used on 1990 and later models are worn, the alternator must be exchanged for a rebuilt unit.*

1    Disconnect the negative cable at the battery. Label the wires and detach them from the alternator terminals.

**14.3a  An exploded view of the mounting hardware for a typical earlier Chrysler alternator installation**

**14.3b  An exploded view of a typical later Chrysler alternator installation**

**15.2  On Bosch alternators, loosen the brush holder mounting screws (arrows) in small increments, moving from screw to screw, so the holder won't be warped . . .**

**15.3  . . . and remove the brush holder assembly**

**15.5  Using an ohmmeter, check for continuity between each brush and the appropriate field terminal (if there's no continuity, switch one of the leads to the other field terminal or brush)**

**5**

## Bosch alternator

*Refer to illustrations 15.2, 15.3 and 15.5*

2    Loosen the brush holder mounting screws a little at a time to prevent distortion of the holder, then remove them **(see illustration)**.

3    Remove the brush holder from the alternator **(see illustration)**.

4    If the brushes appear to be significantly worn, or if they don't move smoothly in the brush holder, replace the brush holder assembly.

5    Before installing the brush holder assembly, check for continuity between each brush and the appropriate field terminal **(see illustration)**.

6    Install the brush holder. Make sure the brushes seat correctly.

7    Hold the brush holder securely in place and install the screws. Tighten them evenly, a little at a time, so the holder isn't distorted. Once the screws are snug, tighten them securely.

8    Reconnect the negative battery cable.

## Chrysler 60, 65 and 78-amp alternators

*Refer to illustration 15.11*

9    Remove the alternator (see Section 14).

10    The brushes are mounted in plastic holders which locate them in the proper position.

**15.11  On Chrysler 60, 65 and 78-amp alternators, the brushes are held in the holders with screws - when installing the brushes, the insulating washers must be in place**

11    Remove the brush mounting screws and insulating washers and separate the brush assemblies from the rectifier end shield **(see illustration)**.

**15.16  On Chrysler 40 and 90-amp alternators, remove the nut and detach the dust cover**

**15.17a  To replace the brushes on Chrysler 40 and 90-amp alternators, remove the brush holder mounting screws . . .**

**15.17b  . . . and detach the brush holder**

**15.18  Before installing the brush holder assembly on 40 and 90-amp Chrysler alternators, use an ohmmeter to verify continuity between each brush and the appropriate field terminal (if there's no continuity, switch one of the leads to the other field terminal or brush)**

12    If the brushes appear to be significantly worn or are oil soaked or damaged, replace them with new ones.

13    Make sure the brushes move smoothly in the holders.

14    Insert the brush assemblies into the rectifier end shield and install the screws and washers. Tighten the screws securely. Make sure the brushes aren't grounded.

15    Install the alternator.

### Chrysler 40 and 90-amp alternators

*Refer to illustrations 15.16, 15.17a, 15.17b and 15.18*

16    Remove the nut and detach the dust cover from the rear of the alternator **(see illustration)**.

17    Remove the brush holder mounting screws and separate the brush holder from the end shield **(see illustrations)**.

18    Before installing the new brush holder assembly, check for continuity between each brush and the appropriate field terminal **(see illustration)**.

19    Installation is the reverse of removal. Be careful when sliding the brushes over the slip rings and don't overtighten the brush holder screws.

### Nippondenso alternators

*Refer to illustrations 15.20, 15.21, 15.22a, 15.22b and 15.24*

20    With the alternator removed from the vehicle (see the previous Section), remove the B+ insulator nut and insulator **(see illustration)**.

21    Remove the rear cover attaching nuts and remove the rear cover **(see illustration)**.

22    Remove the brush holder attaching screws and lift the brush holder from the alternator **(see illustrations)**.

23    Before installing the new brush holder assembly, check for continuity between each brush and the appropriate field terminal

(see illustrations 15.5 and 15.18).

24    To install the brush holder assembly, use your finger to depress the brushes **(see illustration)**, then slide the holder over the commutator slip rings and screw it into place.

25    Installation is otherwise the reverse of removal. When installing the B+ insulator, be sure to align the guide tang with the hole in the rear cover.

**15.20  To replace the brushes on Nippondenso alternators, remove the B+ terminal insulator nut, washer and insulator**

**15.21  remove the rear cover attaching nuts (arrows) and remove the rear cover (Nippondenso alternators)**

**15.22a  Remove the brush holder attaching screws (arrows) . . .**

**15.22b  . . . and remove the brush holder assembly (Nippondenso alternators)**

## 16   Voltage regulator - description

*Refer to illustration 16.2*

1   The voltage regulator is a device that regulates vehicle electrical system voltage by limiting output voltage generated by the alternator. It accomplishes this task by limiting the amount of current passing through the alternator field windings. The regulators used on some models covered by this manual are electronic - there are no moving parts and they're not adjustable like older mechanical regulators.

2   On pre-1987 models, the voltage regulator used with Chrysler alternators is an external solid-state device **(see illustration)** located in the engine compartment. If this type of regulator goes bad, replacement is straightforward. The regulator used with Mitsubishi alternators (2.6L engines) is an internal component located inside the alternator. If a Mitsubishi regulator is bad, exchange the alternator for a rebuilt unit; replacement of the voltage regulator - which involves considerable disassembly of the alternator and some soldering - is impractical.

3   On some 1987 and all later models, the voltage regulator is integrated into the logic module or the Single Module Engine Controller (SMEC) of the fuel injection system. Special diagnostic tools are needed to check the regulator. Only a dealer service department and some repair shops have these tools. If the regulator is faulty, the computer must be replaced. Computer replacement is covered by a Federally mandated extended warranty (see your owner's manual or consult your dealer for details). If the computer is out of warranty and you want to replace it yourself, see Chapter 6.

## 17   Starting system - general information and precautions

The sole function of the starting system is to rotate the engine quickly enough to allow it to start.

The starting system consists of the battery, the starter motor, the starter solenoid, the switch and the wires connecting them. The solenoid is mounted directly on the starter motor.

The solenoid/starter motor assembly is installed on the lower part of the engine, next to the transaxle bellhousing.

When the ignition key is turned to the Start position, the starter solenoid is actuated through the starter control circuit. The starter solenoid then connects the battery to the starter. The battery supplies the electrical energy to the starter motor, which does the actual work of cranking the engine.

The starter on a vehicle equipped with an automatic transmission can only be operated when the transmission selector lever is in Park or Neutral.

Always observe the following precautions when working on the starting system:

a) *Excessive cranking of the starter motor can overheat it and cause serious damage. Never operate the starter motor for more than 15 seconds at a time without pausing to allow it to cool for at least two minutes.*

b) *The starter is connected directly to the battery and could arc or cause a fire if mishandled, overloaded or shorted out.*

c) *Always detach the cable from the negative terminal of the battery before working on the starting system.*

**15.24  Depress the brushes with your index finger as you slide the brush holder into place**

**16.2  A typical Chrysler external electronic voltage regulator**

5

**19.3  Label the wire (arrows) before disconnecting them from the starter assembly**

**19.4a  On 2.2L and 2.5L engines, remove this starter motor mounting bolt (arrow) from underneath the vehicle . . .**

## 18   Starter motor - in-vehicle check

**Note:** *Before diagnosing starter problems, make sure the battery is fully charged.*

1    If the starter motor doesn't turn at all when the switch is operated, make sure the shift lever is in Neutral or Park (automatic transmission).

2    Make sure the battery is charged and all cables, both at the battery and starter solenoid terminals, are clean and secure.

3    If the starter motor spins but the engine isn't cranking, the overrunning clutch in the starter motor is slipping and the starter motor must be replaced.

4    If, when the switch is actuated, the starter motor doesn't operate at all but the solenoid clicks, then the problem lies with either the battery, the main solenoid contacts or the starter motor itself (or the engine is seized).

5    If the solenoid plunger can't be heard when the switch is actuated, the battery is bad, the fusible link is burned (the circuit is open) or the solenoid itself is defective.

6    To check the solenoid, connect a jumper lead between the battery (+) and the ignition switch wire terminal (the small terminal) on the solenoid. If the starter motor now operates, the solenoid is OK and the problem is in the ignition switch, neutral start switch or the wiring.

7    If the starter motor still doesn't operate, remove the starter/solenoid assembly for disassembly, testing and repair.

8    If the starter motor cranks the engine at an abnormally slow speed, first make sure the battery is fully charged and all terminal connections are tight. If the engine is partially seized, or has the wrong viscosity oil in it, it will crank slowly.

9    Run the engine until normal operating temperature is reached, then disconnect the coil wire from the distributor cap and ground it on

the engine.

10    Connect a voltmeter positive lead to the positive battery post and connect the negative lead to the negative post.

11    Crank the engine and take the voltmeter readings as soon as a steady figure is indicated. Don't allow the starter motor to turn for more than 15 seconds at a time. A reading of 9 volts or more, with the starter motor turning at normal cranking speed, is normal. If the reading is 9 volts or more but the cranking speed is slow, the motor is faulty. If the reading is less than 9 volts and the cranking speed is slow, the solenoid contacts are probably burned, the starter motor is bad, the battery is discharged or there's a bad connection.

## 19   Starter motor assembly - removal and installation

*Refer to illustrations 19.3, 19.4a, 19.4b and 19.4c*

1    Detach the cable from the negative terminal of the battery.

2    Raise the vehicle and support it securely on jackstands.

3    Clearly label, then disconnect the wires from the terminals on the starter motor and solenoid **(see illustration)**.

4    Remove the mounting bolts **(see illustrations)** and detach the starter.

5    Installation is the reverse of removal.

## 20   Starter motor/solenoid/gear reduction assembly - replacement

1    Disconnect the cable from the negative terminal of the battery.

2    Remove the starter motor (see Section 19).

**19.4b  . . . and remove the other mounting bolt and nut (arrows) from above, then remove the starter**

**19.4c  On 2.6L engines, remove these two starter mounting bolts (arrows) and remove the starter**

20.3a  Before disconnecting the solenoid from a Bosch starter motor, remove the field terminal nut, . . .

20.3b  . . . disconnect the field terminal . . .

20.3c  . . . and remove the washer

20.4  To detach the solenoid from a Bosch starter motor, remove these three screws (arrows)

## Bosch

*Refer to illustrations 20.3a, 20.3b, 20.3c, 20.4 and 20.5*

3    Remove the field terminal nut, disconnect the field terminal and remove the washer **(see illustrations)**.
4    Remove the three solenoid mounting screws **(see illustration)**.
5    Work the solenoid off the shift fork and detach it from the drive end housing **(see illustration)**.
6    Installation is the reverse of removal.

## Nippondenso

*Refer to illustrations 20.7, 20.8a, 20.8b, 20.9a and 20.9b*

7    If you're replacing the starter motor or solenoid, disconnect the field coil strap from the solenoid terminal **(see illustration)**; if you're replacing the gear reduction assembly, skip this step and proceed to the next step.

20.5  On a Bosch starter motor, work the solenoid off the shift fork and detach it from the drive end housing

20.7  If you're replacing the starter motor or solenoid on a Nippondenso starter motor, disconnect the field coil strap from the solenoid terminal (if you're replacing the gear reduction assembly, you can leave the solenoid and starter wired together and simply disconnect both of them as a single unit from the gear reduction housing)

5

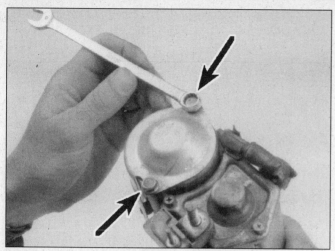

**20.8a** To detach a Nippodenso starter motor from the gear reduction assembly, remove these two long through-bolts (arrows) . . .

**20.8b** . . . and separate the starter motor from the gear reduction housing

**20.9a** To detach a Nippondenso solenoid from the gear reduction assembly, remove the starter, remove these two Phillips screws (arrows) . . .

**20.9b** . . . and separate the solenoid from the gear reduction housing

8   To detach the starter motor from the gear reduction assembly, simply remove the two long through-bolts and pull off the starter **(see illustrations)**.

9   To detach the solenoid from the gear reduction assembly, remove the starter, then remove the two Phillips screws from the gear reduction assembly and pull off the solenoid **(see illustrations)**.

10   Installation is the reverse of removal.

# Chapter 6
# Emissions and engine control systems

## Contents

## Specifications

### General

| | |
|---|---|
| Charcoal canister delay valve test vacuum | 10 in-Hg |
| EGR valve test vacuum | 10 in-Hg |
| EGR valve travel | 1/8 inch |

### Torque specifications

| | Ft-lbs (unless otherwise indicated) |
|---|---|
| EGR valve (all engines) | |
| EGR valve mounting bolts | 200 in-lbs |
| EGR tube bolts | 200 in-lbs |
| EGR tube-to-valve screws | 95 in-lbs |
| Automatic idle speed (AIS) motor screws | 20 in-lbs |

## 1  General information

*Refer to illustrations 1.10a through 1.10n and 1.13*

To prevent pollution of the atmosphere from incompletely burned and evaporating gases, and to maintain good driveability and fuel economy, a number of emission control systems are incorporated. The principal systems are . . .

*Air aspirator system (2.6L Federal and Canadian models)*
*Air injection system (2.2L engine)*
*Automatic choke system (2.2L and 2.6L engines)*
*Catalytic converter (all engines)*
*Electronic feedback carburetor system (2.2L engine)*
*Evaporative emissions control system (all engines)*
*Exhaust Gas Recirculation (EGR) system (all engines)*
*Heated inlet air system (2.2L and 2.5L engines)*
*High altitude compensation system (2.6L engine)*
*Jet Air Control Valve (JACV) (2.6L engine)*
*Oxygen sensor (all engines)*
*Mikuni carburetor system (2.6L engine)*
*Positive Crankcase Ventilation (PCV) system (all engines)*

*Pulse Air Feeder (PAF) system (2.6L engine)*
*Single Module Engine Controller (SMEC) (1988 and 1989) and self-diagnosis system*
*Logic Module Engine Controller (1985 through 1987) and self-diagnosis system*
*Throttle opener (idle-up) system (2.6L engine)*

Since these vehicles are equipped with either a 2.2L, 2.5L or 2.6L engine, many emission control devices are used. Some of these devices or systems are exclusive to a particular engine, while others are applicable to all models. All systems will be described in this Chapter so that all models will be covered.

All engines are equipped with a Fuel Evaporative Emissions Control (EVAP) system, an Exhaust Gas Recirculation (EGR) system, a Positive Crankcase Ventilation (PCV) system, a heated inlet air system and a catalytic converter. Carbureted engines also use an automatic choke and various other emissions systems to improve cold starting and/or enhance driveability while the engine is still cold or is being driven at high altitude.

The 2.2L engine has an air injection system and an electronic feedback carburetor system. The electronic feedback carburetor works in conjunction with an oxygen sensor located in the exhaust

1.10a  Vacuum hose routing for 1984 and 1985 2.2L TBI models

system and a spark control computer. The three work together to constantly monitor exhaust gas oxygen content and vary the spark timing and fuel mixture so that emissions are always within limits.

The 2.6L engine features a Pulse Air Feeder (PAF) air injection system which injects air into the exhaust system between the front and rear catalytic converter to reduce emissions. Also, a Jet Air Control Valve (JACV) system is used to inject a very lean fuel mixture into the combustion chamber and improve efficiency and thus emissions.

The 2.5L engine is equipped with a computer-controlled, "single-point" (one injector in the throttle body) electronic fuel injection (EFI) system; EFI systems deliver a precise air/fuel mixture ratio under all driving conditions. At their heart is a computer known as a Single Module Engine Controller (SMEC).

1.10b  Vacuum hose routing for 1984 through 1986 2.2L carbureted Federal models

The SMEC regulates ignition timing, the air/fuel ratio, various emission control devices, the cooling fan, the charging system, the idle speed. Various sensors provide the necessary inputs for the SMEC to regulate the flow of fuel to the injector. These include the Manifold Absolute Pressure (MAP) sensor, the Throttle Position Sensor (TPS), the oxygen sensor, the coolant temperature sensor, the throttle body temperature sensor and the vehicle distance sensor.

Besides these sensors, various switches and relays also provide information to the SMEC. These include the neutral safety switch and air conditioning clutch switch (or cut-out relay), the auto shutdown relay and the brake switch. All inputs to the SMEC are converted into digital signals which are "read" by the SMEC and converted into changes in either the fuel flow, the ignition timing, or both. The SMEC constantly monitors

1.10c  Vacuum hose routing for 1984 through 1986 2.2L carbureted California models

1.10d  Vacuum hose routing for 1984 through 1986 2.2L Canadian models

**1.10e  Vacuum hose routing for 1984 through 1986 2.2L High Altitude carbureted models**

**1.10f  Vacuum hose routing for 1984 and 1985 2.6L Federal models**

many of its own input and output circuits. If a fault is found in a system, the information is stored in the SMEC's memory. You can output this information and display it on the CHECK ENGINE light on the dash.

The Sections in this Chapter include general descriptions, checking procedures within the scope of the home mechanic and component replacement procedures (when possible) for each of the systems listed above.

Before assuming an emissions control system is malfunctioning, check the fuel and ignition systems carefully. The diagnosis of some emission control devices requires specialized tools, equipment and training. If checking and servicing become too difficult or if a procedure is beyond your ability, consult a dealer service department.

Remember, the most frequent cause of emissions problems is simply a loose or broken vacuum hose or wire, so always check the hose and wiring connections first **(see illustrations)**.

This doesn't mean, however, that emission control systems are particularly difficult to maintain and repair. You can quickly and easily perform many checks and do most of the regular maintenance at home with common tune-up and hand tools. **Note:** *Because of a Federally mandated extended warranty which covers the emission control system components, check with your dealer about warranty coverage before working on any emissions-related systems. Once the warranty has expired, you may wish to perform some of the component checks and/or replacement procedures in this Chapter to save money.*

**1.10g  Vacuum hose routing for 1984 and 1985 2.6L Canadian models**

**1.10h  Vacuum hose routing for 1984 and 1985 2.6L California models**

1.10i  Vacuum hose routing for 1986 2.2L and 2.5L TBI models

1.10j  Vacuum hose routing for 1987 2.2L California
and Canadian models

Pay close attention to any special precautions outlined in this Chapter. It should be noted that the illustrations of the various systems may not exactly match the system installed on your vehicle because of changes made by the manufacturer during production or from year-to-year.

A Vehicle Emissions Control Information (VECI) label (earlier models) or an Emissions, Adjustment and Routing (EAR) label is located in the engine compartment **(see illustration)**. This label contains important emissions specifications and adjustment information. When servicing the engine or emissions systems, the VECI label in your particular vehicle should always be checked for up-to-date information.

## 2   Electronic feedback carburetor system

**Note:** *This Section applies only to earlier models with the 2.2L engine.*

### General description

1    The electronic feedback carburetor emission system relies on an electronic signal, which is generated by an exhaust gas sensor, to control a variety of devices and keep emissions within limits. The system works in conjunction with a three-way catalyst to control the levels of carbon monoxide, hydrocarbons and oxides of nitrogen.

1.10k  Vacuum hose routing for 1987 through 1989 2.2L
Federal models

1.10l  Vacuum hose routing for 1988 and 1989 Canadian and
Federal High Altitude TBI models

1.10m  Vacuum hose routing for 1988 California TBI models

1.10n  Vacuum hose routing for 1989 California TBI models

1.13  Typical Vehicle Emission Control Information (VECI) label

2    The system operates in two modes: open loop and closed loop. When the engine is cold, the air/fuel mixture is controlled by the computer in accordance with a program designed in at the time of production. The air/fuel mixture during this time will be richer to allow for proper engine warm-up. When the engine is at operating temperature, the system operates at closed loop and the air/fuel mixture is varied depending on the information supplied by the exhaust gas sensor.

3    The system consists of the carburetor, computer, air switching valve, coolant control engine vacuum switch, catalytic converters and oxygen sensor.

2.7  Check the vacuum switch for continuity (2.2L engine)

## Check

4    Prior to checking the system, check the computer for proper operation. Also, make sure that all vacuum hoses and electrical wires are properly routed and securely connected.

5    Apply 16 in-Hg of vacuum to the computer with a vacuum pump. Disconnect the hose from the air switching valve and connect a vacuum gauge to the hose (see Step 6 below). Start the engine and allow it to warm up to operating temperature. Run the engine at approximately 2,000 rpm for two minutes and make sure the carburetor switch is not grounded.

### Air switching system

*Refer to illustration 2.7*

6    Right after starting the engine, there should be a vacuum reading which will slowly drop to zero as the engine warms up.

7    If there is no vacuum, check the Coolant Controlled Engine Vacuum Switch (CCEVS) for continuity. If there is no continuity, correct the fault or replace the switch **(see illustration)**.

8    With the engine at operating temperature, shut it off, remove the vacuum hose from the valve and then connect a hand vacuum pump to the valve. Start the engine and make sure air blows out of the side port. Apply vacuum to the valve. Air should now blow out of the bottom port of the valve.

9    Before proceeding, check the engine temperature sensor.

### Carburetor regulator

*Refer to illustration 2.11*

10    Remove the computer vacuum hose and plug it. Connect a vacuum pump to the carburetor and apply 14 in-Hg of vacuum. With

**2.11  Ground pin 15 of the six-pin connector (2.2L engine)**

**2.14  Ground the oxygen sensor wire to the negative battery post (2.2L engine)**

the engine at 2,000 rpm, disconnect the regulator solenoid connector at the solenoid. On non-air conditioned models, only the green wire should be disconnected. The engine speed should increase at least 50 rpm. Reconnect the solenoid wire(s) and make sure that the engine speed slowly returns to normal.

11    Unplug the six pin connector from the combustion control computer and momentarily connect a ground to connector pin 15 **(see illustration)**.

12    Engine speed should decrease at least 50 rpm. If it does not, check the carburetor for air leaks.

### Electronic fuel control computer

*Refer to illustration 2.14*

13    With the engine at normal operating temperature and the carburetor switch not grounded, connect a tachometer.

14    Start the engine and maintain an idle of 2,000 rpm. Connect a voltmeter to the green solenoid output wire which leads to the carburetor. Disconnect the electrical connector at the oxygen sensor and connect a jumper wire between the harness connector and the negative battery terminal **(see illustration)**.

15    The engine speed should increase at least 50 rpm and the voltmeter should read at least nine volts. With the wire held in one hand, touch the battery positive terminal with your other hand. The engine speed should drop by a least 50 rpm and the voltmeter reading should be three volts or less. Replace the computer with a new one if it fails both tests.

### Oxygen sensor

*Refer to illustration 2.16*

16    Connect the voltmeter to the solenoid output wire, reconnect the oxygen sensor and make sure the carburetor switch is not grounded. Start the engine, run it at 2,000 rpm and hold the choke plates closed **(see illustration)**. This simulates a full rich condition and within ten seconds the voltage should drop to three volts or less. If it does not, disconnect the PCV hose. This simulates a full lean condition and the voltage should increase to nine volts or more. Do not take more than 90 seconds to complete these tests. If the sensor fails both tests, replace it with a new one.

## *Component replacement*

*Refer to illustration 2.20*

17    To replace the Spark Control Computer, remove the battery, disconnect the vacuum hose and electrical connectors, remove the three retaining screws and lift the assembly from the engine compartment.

18    Mark the hose locations on the air switching valve, remove the hoses and disconnect the valve.

19    The CCEVS is replaced by removing the vacuum hoses and unscrewing the valve. Coat the threads of the new valve with gasket sealant prior to installation.

20    To replace the carburetor solenoid, unplug the electrical connector and remove the two retaining screws. Detach the solenoid from the carburetor **(see illustration)**.

21    Disconnect the oxygen sensor wire and use a wrench to unscrew the sensor. Use a tap to clean the threads in the exhaust manifold. If the sensor is to be reinstalled, apply anti-seize compound to the threads. New sensors already have the anti-seize compound on their threads.

**2.16  Hold the choke closed while testing the oxygen sensor (2.2L engine)**

**2.20  The carburetor solenoid is attached to the top of the carburetor with two screws (2.2L engine)**

3.5  Jet Air Control Valve (JACV) system (2.6L engine)

## 3   Mikuni carburetor system

**Note:** *This Section applies only to models with the 2.6L engine.*

### General description

*Refer to illustration 3.5*

1    The Mikuni carburetor on 2.6L engines is equipped with a variety of devices which reduce emissions while maintaining driveability.

2    The system consists of a Coasting Air Valve (CAV), Air Switching Valve (ASV), Deceleration Spark Advance System (DSAS), High Altitude Compensation (HAC) (on some models), Jet Air Control Valve (JACV) and a throttle opener.

3    The CAV, ASV and DSAS reduce hydrocarbon emissions while maintaining driveability and fuel economy by shutting off fuel flow and advancing the spark during deceleration.

4    The HAC maintains the proper fuel/air mixture during high altitude driving by means of an atmospheric pressure sensitive bellows.

5    The JACV helps decrease HC and CO emissions, while the choke is operating, by opening to allow additional jet air flow and eliminating an over-rich condition **(see illustration)**.

6    The throttle opener controls the engine idle speed during operation of the air conditioner.

### Check

#### ASV and CAV

*Refer to illustrations 3.7a and 3.7b*

7    With the engine at idle, unplug the solenoid valve electrical connector. If the idle speed drops or the engine stalls, the ASV and CAV are operating properly. With the engine again at idle, check the solenoid connector with a voltmeter. If no voltage is present, the wiring or speed sensor is faulty. Check the solenoid connector with the engine at 2,500 rpm to make sure there is voltage. If there is no voltage, there is a fault in the speed sensor and it must be replaced with a new one **(see illustrations)**.

3.7a  Air Switching Valve (ASV) system (2.6L engine)

3.7b  Coasting Air Valve (CAV) system (2.6L engine)

### DSAS

*Refer to illustration 3.8*

8    Connect a timing light and allow the engine to run at idle. With the timing light on the timing marks, disconnect the electrical connector from the solenoid valve. If the timing does not advance, the solenoid valve and/or advance mechanism are faulty **(see illustration)**.

### HAC

*Refer to illustration 3.9*

9    Since special equipment is required to test the HAC, checking is confined to making sure associated hoses and connections are secure **(see illustration)**.

3.9  High Altitude Compensation (HAC) system (2.6L engine)

3.8  Deceleration Spark Advance System (DSAS) (2.6L engine)

**4.3 An exploded view of the electric choke components on a 2.2L engine**

**4.4 Details of the choke components on a 2.6L engine**

### Throttle opener

10   With the engine idling, turn on the air conditioner. If the idle speed does not increase, there is a fault in the solenoid kicker, engine speed sensor or wiring.

### Component replacement

11   Locate the solenoid valve or speed sensor by tracing the wires or hoses from the component which they control. Disconnect the wires and/or hoses and install a new unit.

### 4   Automatic choke system

**Note:** *This Section applies only to carbureted models.*

### *General description*

*Refer to illustrations 4.3 and 4.4*

1   The automatic choke system temporarily supplies a rich fuel/air mixture to the engine by closing the choke plate(s) during cold engine starting.
2   On 2.2L engines, the choke is electrically operated, while 2.6L engines use sealed wax pellet-type choke systems.
3   On 2.2L engines, an electric signal from the oil pressure switch operates the choke control switch and activates the choke heater so that it slowly opens the choke plates as the engine warms up **(see illustration)**. This progressively leans out the mixture until the engine is warmed up.
4   On 2.6L engines, the wax pellet thermo sensing unit opens the

**5.1 Typical altitude compensation system (2.2L engine)**

choke as the coolant temperature increases. When started from cold, the choke valve is partially opened by a vacuum kicker actuated by manifold vacuum. This prevents an overly rich air/fuel mixture and the resultant increased emissions. The fast idle cam on the choke set lever controls the rate of throttle valve opening. If the vehicle is driven with a wide open throttle setting when cold, the choke is opened by the choke unloader so the mixture will not be overly rich **(see illustration)**.

### *Check*

5   Refer to Chapter 1 for the automatic choke checking procedure.

### *Component replacement*

6   Choke component replacement is covered in Chapter 4.

### 5   High altitude compensation system

*Refer to illustrations 5.1 and 5.2*
**Note:** *This Section applies only to models with a 2.2L or 2.6L engine.*
1   Some 2.2L models are equipped with an altitude compensation system **(see illustration)** which compensates for thinner air by using various air bleeds which act in parallel with the normal fixed air bleeds in the carburetor idle, primary and secondary circuits at higher altitudes. These air bleeds consist of tapered needles which are moved in orifices by an aneroid bellows housed inside an altitude compensation module mounted in the engine compartment. Outside air passes through an air filter, through the compensation module and into the carburetor. The system is designed so no air can flow through until atmospheric pressure is below a predetermined level. Air flow gradually increases as atmospheric pressure increases.
2   Some 2.6L models are also equipped with an altitude compensation system **(see illustration)**. A small cylindrical bellows chamber, located in the engine compartment, is connected to the carburetor via a pair of air bleed hoses. The bellows is vented to the atmosphere at the top of the carburetor. Atmospheric pressure expands or contracts the bellows. When the vehicle is operated at a higher altitude, i.e. thinner air, the bellows begins to expand. A small brass tapered-seat valve is raised off its seat by the bellows, allowing extra air to enter the main air bleeds. How much the calibrated bellows opens is proportional to the altitude. When the vehicle leaves the higher altitude, i.e. the air gets thicker, the bellows gradually contracts and the extra air bleeds are closed off.
3   Neither of these systems is likely to malfunction. If the engine starts running too rich (mileage goes down suddenly, engine is hard to start, plugs fouled, etc.), check all the hoses in the system. Make sure all connections are tight and there are no tears in the hoses. If the problem persists, take the vehicle to a dealer service department or other repair shop and have the system checked.

### 6   Throttle opener (idle-up) system

**Note:** *This Section applies only to models with a 2.6L engine.*
     The throttle opener (or idle-up) system raises the engine idle speed when the air conditioning compressor is operating. The system

consists of the throttle opener assembly, a solenoid valve, an engine speed sensor and a compressor switch for the air conditioning unit. When the switch is turned on - and the engine speed sensor detects the engine speed at or below the specified value - the solenoid valve opens, transmitting intake manifold vacuum to the throttle opener. The throttle opener opens the throttle valve slightly via the throttle opener lever, increasing engine idle speed to compensate for the extra load imposed by the compressor. When the compressor switch is turned off, the throttle opener system stops working and the engine returns to its normal idle speed. The engine speed sensor in the air switching valve system is used to monitor the engine speed. When engine speed is at or below the specified value, the air switching valve system doesn't operate; when engine speed is above this value, the switching valve system works as designed.

If the throttle opener system fails to operate as described above when the air conditioning system is operating, check the wiring. Make sure all connections are clean and tight. If the throttle opener still doesn't work properly, take the vehicle to a dealer and have it checked.

## 7  Jet Air Control Valve (JACV) system

**Note:** *This Section applies only to models with the 2.6L engine.*
1    The jet air system utilizes an additional intake valve (jet valve) which provides for air, or a super lean mixture, to be drawn from the air intake into the cylinder. The jet valve is operated by the same cam as the intake valve. They use a common rocker arm so the jet valve and the intake valve open and close simultaneously.
2    On the intake stroke of the engine, fuel/air mixture flows through the intake ports into the combustion chamber. At the same time, jet air is forced into the combustion chamber because of the pressure difference between the jet intake in the throttle bore and the jet valve in the cylinder as the piston moves down. At small throttle openings, there is a large pressure difference, giving the jet air a high velocity. This scavenges the residual gases around the spark plug and creates good ignition conditions. It also produces a strong swirl in the combustion chamber, which lasts throughout the compression stroke and improves flame propagation after ignition, assuring high combustion efficiency and lowering exhaust emissions. As the throttle opening is increased, less jet air is forced in and jet swirl diminishes, but the increased flow through the intake valve ensures satisfactory combustion.
3    A thermo valve which works in conjunction with the EGR system controls the air flow to the jet valve.

4    Maintenance consists of adjusting the jet valve clearances at the same time the intake and exhaust valves are adjusted, as described in Chapter 1.

## 8  Air Injection (AI) system

**Note:** *This Section applies only to models with the 2.2L engine.*

### *General description*

*Refer to illustration 8.2*
1    This system supplies air under pressure to the exhaust ports to promote the combustion of unburned hydrocarbons and carbon monoxide before they are allowed to exit the exhaust.
2    The AI system consists of an air pump driven by a belt from the rear of the camshaft, a relief valve and associated hoses and check valves, which protect the system from hot exhaust gases **(see illustration)**.

**5.2  Typical altitude compensation system (2.6L engine)**

**6**

**8.2  An exploded view of the air injection system components (2.2L California model shown, others similar)**

**8.9 Remove the air pump drivebelt shield mounting bolts**

**8.10 Loosen the air pump pivot bolt**

**8.16 Use a breaker bar to apply leverage to the air pump bracket as the bolts are tightened**

## Check

### General

3   Visually check the hoses, tubes and connections for cracks, loose fittings and separated parts. Use soapy water to isolate a suspected leak.
4   Check the drivebelt condition and tension.

### Air pump

5   The air pump can only be checked using special equipment. Noise from the pump can be due to improper drivebelt tension, faulty relief or check valves, loose mounting bolts and leaking hoses or connections. If these conditions have been corrected and the pump still makes excessive noise, there is a good chance that it is faulty.

### Relief valve

6   If air can be heard escaping from the relief valve with the engine at idle, the valve is faulty and must be replaced with a new one.

### Check valve

7   Remove the hose from the inlet tube. If exhaust gas escapes past the inlet tube, the check valve is faulty and must be replaced.

## Component replacement

### Air pump

*Refer to illustrations 8.9, 8.10 and 8.16*

8   Remove the air hoses from the air pump and the relief valve.
9   Remove the air pump drivebelt pulley shield **(see illustration)**.
10   Loosen the pump pivot and adjustment bolts and remove the drivebelt **(see illustration)**.
11   Remove the bolts and detach the pump from the engine.
12   Remove the relief valve from the pump and clean all gasket material from the valve mating surface.
13   Attach the relief valve to the new air pump, using a new gasket. Transfer the pulley from the old pump to the new one.
14   With the drivebelt over the air pump pulley, place the pump in position and loosely install the bolts.
15   Loosen the rear air pump bracket-to-transaxle housing bolts.
16   Place the drivebelt on the camshaft pulley, use a breaker bar to exert pressure on the bracket (not the pump housing) and adjust the belt until the tension is correct (see Chapter 1). Tighten the locking bolt, followed by the pivot bolt **(see illustration)**.
17   Tighten the air pump bracket bolt securely, install the pulley shield and reconnect the hoses to the pump and relief valve.

### Relief valve

18   Disconnect the hoses from the relief valve, remove the two bolts

and detach the valve from the pump. Carefully remove any gasket material from the valve and pump mating surfaces.
19   Place a new gasket in position and install the valve, tightening the bolts securely. Reconnect the hoses.

### Check valve

20   Disconnect the hose from the valve inlet and remove the nut securing the tube to the exhaust manifold or converter. Loosen the starter motor bolt and remove the check valve from the engine.
21   Attach the new valve to the exhaust manifold or converter, tighten the starter motor bolt and connect the air hose.

## 9   Pulse Air Feeder (PAF) system

**Note:** *This Section applies only to models with a 2.6L engine.*

### General description

*Refer to illustration 9.2*
1   The PAF system injects air into the exhaust system between the front and rear catalytic converters, using the engine power pulsations. This injected air increases the efficiency of the rear converter and reduces emissions.
2   The system consists of a main reed valve, sub reed valve and associated hoses. Air is drawn from the air cleaner into the main reed valve which is actuated by the pressure pulsations from within the crankcase. The air passes to the sub reed valve, which is actuated by the exhaust system pulsations, to the exhaust system and then the rear converter **(see illustration)**.

### Check

3   Disconnect the hose from the air cleaner and, with the engine running, place your hand over the end. If no vacuum is felt, check the hoses for leaks. If the hoses are alright, replace the PAF assembly with a new one.

### Component replacement

4   Remove the air deflector duct from the right side of the radiator. Remove the carburetor shield, the oil dipstick and the dipstick tube. Remove the PAF mounting bolts.
5   Raise the vehicle and support it securely.
6   Disconnect the hoses and remove the PAF assembly from the vehicle.
7   Place the new pulse air feeder assembly in position and connect the hoses.
8   Lower the vehicle and install the mounting bolts. Check the dipstick O-ring to make sure it is in good condition and install the dipstick and tube. Install the carburetor shield and radiator air deflector.

9.2 Pulse Air Feeder (PAF) system (2.6L engine)

## 10  Air aspirator system

**Note:** *This Section applies only to models with the 2.6L engine.*

### General description

1    The aspirator system uses exhaust pulsations to draw fresh air from the air cleaner into the exhaust system. This reduces carbon monoxide (CO) and, to a lesser degree, hydrocarbon (HC) emissions.
2    The system is composed of aspirator valves and tubes, a Y connector and various hoses.
3    The aspirator valves work most efficiently at idle and slightly off idle, where the negative exhaust pulses are strongest. The valves remain closed at higher engine speeds.

### Check

*Refer to illustration 10.5*
4    Aspirator valve failure results in excessive exhaust system noise from under the hood and hardening of the rubber hose from the valve to the air cleaner.
5    If exhaust noise is excessive, check the valve-to-exhaust manifold joint and the valve and air cleaner hose connections for leaks **(see illustration)**. If the manifold joint is leaking, retighten the tube fitting securely. If the hose connections are leaking, install new hose clamps (if the hose has not hardened).

6    To determine if the valve has failed, disconnect the hose from the inlet. With the engine idling (transmission in Neutral), the exhaust pulses should be felt at the inlet. If a steady stream of exhaust gases is escaping from the inlet, the valve is defective and should be replaced with a new one.

### Component replacement

7    The valves can be replaced by removing the hose clamp, detaching the hose and unscrewing the tube fitting.
8    The aspirator tubes can be replaced by unscrewing the fittings at the valve and manifold and removing the bracket bolt.

## 11  Logic Module and Power Module (1984 through 1987 EFI models) - description and replacement

### Description

*Refer to illustrations 11.1 and 11.2*
1    The logic module, located in the passenger compartment behind the right kick panel, is a digital computer containing a microprocessor. The power module is located in the left front corner of the engine compartment and works in conjunction with the logic module, handling the heavier electric currents, including the ground for the ignition coil and

6

10.5  Air aspirator system (2.6L engine)

VIEW IN DIRECTION OF ARROW Z

**11.1  Diagram of a typical Logic module/Power module EFI system**

**11.2  On 1985 through 1987 models, the MAP sensor is located on
the logic module**

power for the fuel injection. It directs the voltage to the logic module and the Hall Effect pick-up assembly in the distributor (which then directs voltage to the spark plugs) and the automatic shutdown relay which energizes the fuel tank mounted electric fuel pump. The logic module receives the input signals from all of the sensors and switches which monitor the engine and then determines the fuel injector operation as well as the spark advance, ignition coil dwell, idle speed, canister purge solenoid, cooling fan operation and alternator charge rate **(see illustration)**. The electric fuel pump, which delivers fuel to the injectors and maintains pressure in the system, is located in the fuel tank (Chapter 4).

2    There are four components providing the basic information enabling the logic module to operate the EFI system. They are: the Manifold Absolute Pressure (MAP) sensor, Throttle Position Sensor (TPS), oxygen sensor and the coolant temperature sensor. The MAP sensor, located on or adjacent to the logic module **(see illustration)**, is connected to the throttle body by a vacuum line and monitors the manifold vacuum. The TPS is located in the throttle body and monitors the actual position of the throttle lever which is connected to the throttle pedal. The oxygen sensor (located in the exhaust manifold) provides information on the exhaust gas makeup and the temperature sensor (threaded into the water box) monitors engine operating temperature.

3    Because the EFI system is controlled by the logic module and power module in combination with a variety of sensors and switches, the home mechanic can do very little in the way of diagnosis without a factory Diagnostic Read-Out Tool (Chrysler tool no. C-4805) or its equivalent. Consequently, diagnosis should be confined to inspection and checking of all electrical and vacuum connections to make sure they are secure and not obviously damaged.

4    The logic module is self-testing and a problem in the system will be indicated by the POWER LOSS/LIMITED light on the dash. The POWER LOSS/LIMITED light will come on when there is electrical system voltage fluctuation or a fault in the MAP, throttle position or coolant temperature sensor circuits. If the fault is severe enough to affect driveability, the logic module will go into a "limp-home" mode so

the vehicle can still be driven.

5    The logic module stores trouble codes which can be checked using the POWER LOSS/LIMITED light. Refer to Section 13 for more information.

## Replacement

*Refer to illustration 11.8*

6    Disconnect the negative cable at the battery.

7    Remove the passenger's side cowl trim panel.

8    Remove the nuts, lift the logic module off the studs, unplug the connectors and remove the module from the vehicle (see illustration).

9    Installation is the reverse of removal.

---

## 12   Single Module Engine Controller (SMEC) and information sensors (1988 and later models) - description

## SMEC

*Refer to illustration 12.2*

1    The electronic fuel injection (EFI) system provides the correct air-fuel ratio under all driving conditions. 2.2L/2.5L engines are equipped with a computer-controlled, "single-point" (one injector in the throttle body) electronic fuel injection (EFI) system.

2    The "brain" of the EFI system is a computer known as the Single Module Engine Controller (SMEC) (see illustration). The computer is located at the front left corner of the engine compartment, between the battery and the left inner fender panel.

3    The computer receives variable voltage inputs from a variety of sensors, switches and relays. All inputs are converted into digital signals which are "read" by the computer, which constantly fine-tunes

**11.8 Typical Logic module installation details**

such variables as ignition timing, spark advance, ignition coil dwell, fuel injector pulse width and idle speed to minimize exhaust emissions and enhance driveability. It also controls the operation of the radiator cooling fan, the alternator charging rate and such emissions-related components as the EGR solenoids and the purge solenoid for the EVAP canister. The computer even updates and revises its own programming in response to changing operating conditions.

4    The computer also constantly monitors many of its own input and

**12.2  Single-point EFI system used in the 2.2L/2.5L engines (1988 and later)**

12.6 Typical array of engine compartment relays

12.8 Typical coolant temperature sensor

output circuits. If a fault is found in the EFI system, the information is stored in the computer's memory. You really can't check or test the components of the EFI system without an expensive factory tool, the Diagnostic Readout Box DRB II (Chrysler tool no. C-4805) or its equivalent, but you can often determine where a problem is coming from, or at least which circuit it's in. This process always begins with reading any stored fault codes to identify the general location of a problem, followed by a thorough visual inspection of the system components to ensure that everything is properly connected and/or plugged in. The most common cause of a problem in any EFI system is a loose or corroded electrical connector or a loose vacuum line. To learn how to output this information and display it on the CHECK ENGINE light on the dash, refer to Section 12.

## Information sensors

5   Various components provide basic information to the SMEC; they include:

   *Air conditioning cut-out relay*
   *Auto shutdown relay*
   *Charge temperature sensor*
   *Coolant temperature sensor*
   *Manifold Absolute Pressure (MAP) sensor*
   *Neutral safety switch*
   *Oxygen sensor*
   *Speed control switch*
   *Throttle body temperature sensor*
   *Throttle Position Sensor (TPS)*
   *Transmission neutral-safety switch*
   *Vehicle distance sensor*

### Air conditioning cut-out relay

*Refer to illustration 12.6*

6   The air conditioning cut-out relay **(see illustration)** is connected in series electrically with the air conditioner damped pressure switch, the air conditioner switch and the radiator/condenser fan relay. The cut-out relay is energized (in its closed position) when the engine is operating. When the computer senses a low idle speed, or the throttle position sensor indicates a wide open throttle condition, the cut-out relay is de-energized, its contacts open and the air conditioner clutch is prevented from engaging. The cut-out relay is located on the left inner fender panel, next to the battery and right above the computer.

### Auto shutdown relay

7   If there's no ignition (distributor) signal present when the ignition key is turned to the Run position, the auto shutdown relay interrupts power to the electric fuel pump, the fuel injector, the ignition coil and

12.9 Manifold Absolute Pressure (MAP) sensor used on fuel-injected engines

the heated oxygen sensor. The cut-out relay is located on the left inner fender panel, next to the battery and right above the computer.

### Coolant temperature sensor

*Refer to illustration 12.8*

8   The coolant temperature sensor **(see illustration)**, which is threaded into the thermostat housing, monitors coolant temperature and sends this information to the computer. This data, along with the information from the charge temperature sensor, is used by the computer to determine the correct air/fuel mixture and idle speed while the engine is warming up. The sensor is also used to turn on the radiator fan.

### Manifold Absolute Pressure (MAP) sensor

*Refer to illustration 12.9*

9   The MAP sensor **(see illustration)** is located on the firewall. It monitors intake manifold vacuum through a vacuum line to the throttle body. The MAP sensor transmits this data, along with data on barometric pressure, in the form of a variable voltage output to the computer. When combined with data from other sensors, this information help the computer determine the correct air-fuel mixture ratio.

### Miscellaneous switches

10   Various switches (such as the transmission neutral safety switch,

**12.11  Typical heated oxygen sensor used on all engines**

**12.14  Location of the vehicle distance sensor**

**12.12  Location of the throttle body temperature sensor**

## Vehicle distance (speed) sensor

*Refer to illustration 12.14*

14   The vehicle distance (speed) sensor **(see illustration)**, which is located in the transaxle extension housing, senses vehicle motion. It generates eight pulses for every revolution of the driveaxle and transmits them as voltage signals to the computer. These signals are compared by the computer with a closed throttle signal from the throttle position sensor so it can distinguish between a closed throttle deceleration and a normal idle (vehicle stopped) condition. Under decel conditions, the computer controls the AIS motor to maintain the desired MAP value; under idle conditions, the computer adjusts the AIS motor to maintain the desired engine speed.

## 13   On Board Diagnosis (OBD) system and computer trouble codes

**Note 1:** *Before outputting the trouble codes, thoroughly inspect ALL electrical connectors and hoses. Make sure all electrical connections are tight, clean and free of corrosion; make sure all hoses are properly connected, fit tightly and are in good condition (no cracks or tears).*
**Note 2:** *On the models covered by this manual, the CHECK ENGINE light (1988 and 1989) or POWER LOSS (1987 and earlier), located in the instrument panel, flashes on for three seconds as a bulb test when the engine is started. The light comes on and stays on when there's a problem in the EFI system and can also be used to diagnose problems in the EFI system.*

1   The self-diagnosis information contained in the computer can be accessed either by the ignition key or by using a special tool called the Diagnostic Readout Box (DRB II). This tool is attached to the diagnostic connector in the engine compartment and reads the codes and parameters on the digital display screen. The tool is expensive and most home mechanics prefer to use the alternate method. The drawback with the ignition key method is that it does not access all the available codes for display. If you're still unable to determine the cause of a problem after extracting any stored codes, have the vehicle's self-diagnosis system analyzed by a dealer service department or other properly-equipped repair shop.

2   To obtain the codes using the ignition key method, first set the parking brake and put the transaxle in Park (automatic) or Neutral (manual). Raise the engine speed to approximately 2,500 rpm and slowly let the speed down to idle. Also cycle the air conditioning system (on briefly, then off). Next, if the vehicle is equipped with an automatic transmission, with your foot on the brake, select each position on the transmission (Reverse, Drive, Low etc.) and bring the shifter

the air conditioning switch, the speed control switch and the brake light switch) provide information to the computer, which adjusts engine operation in accordance with what switch states are present at these inputs. The state of these switch inputs (high/low) is difficult to determine without the DRB II diagnostic meter or an equivalent scan tool.

## Oxygen sensor

*Refer to illustration 12.11*

11   The oxygen sensor **(see illustration)**, which is mounted in the exhaust manifold, produces a voltage signal when exposed to the oxygen present in the exhaust gases. The sensor is electrically heated internally for faster switching when the engine is running. When there's a lot of oxygen present (lean mixture), the sensor produces a low voltage signal; when there's little oxygen present (rich mixture), it produces a signal of higher voltage. By monitoring the oxygen content and converting it to electrical voltage, the sensor acts as a lean-rich switch. The voltage signal to the computer alters the pulse width of the injector.

## Throttle body temperature sensor

*Refer to illustration 12.12*

12   The throttle body temperature sensor, which is mounted in the throttle body, monitors the temperature of the throttle body (fuel temperature). When transmitted to the computer, this data helps determine the correct air/fuel mixture during a hot restart condition.

## Throttle Position Sensor (TPS)

13   The TPS, which is located on the throttle body **(see illustration 12.12)**, monitors the angle of the throttle plate. The voltage produced increases or decreases in accordance with the opening angle of the throttle plate. This data, when relayed along with data from several other sensors, enables the computer to adjust the air/fuel ratio in accordance with the operating conditions, such as acceleration, deceleration, idle and wide open throttle.

**6**

back to Park. This will allow the computer to obtain any fault codes that might be linked to any of the sensors controlled by the transmission, engine speed or air conditioning system.

3    To display the codes on the dashboard (CHECK ENGINE light), turn the ignition key ON, OFF, ON, OFF and finally ON. The codes will begin to flash. The light will blink the number of the first digit then pause and blink the number of the second digit. For example: Code 23, throttle body temperature sensor circuit, would be indicated by two flashes, then a pause followed by three flashes. **Note:** *On 1988 and 1989 models, the light on the dash will flash the words CHECK ENGINE. On 1985 through 1987 models, the light on the dash flashes the words POWER LOSS.*

4    Certain criteria must be met for a fault code to be entered into the engine controller memory. The criteria may be a specific range of engine rpm, engine temperature or input voltage to the engine controller. It is possible that a fault code for a particular monitored circuit may not be entered into the memory despite a malfunction. This may happen because one of the fault code criteria has not been met. For

example, the engine must be operating between 750 and 2,000 rpm in order to monitor the Map sensor circuit correctly. If the engine speed is raised above 2,400 rpm, the MAP sensor output circuit shorts to ground and will not allow a fault code to be entered into the memory. Then again, the exact opposite could occur: A code is entered into the memory that suggests a malfunction within another component that is not monitored by the computer. For example, a fuel pressure problem cannot register a fault directly but will instead cause a rich/lean fuel mixture problem. Consequently, this will cause an oxygen sensor malfunction, resulting in a stored code in the computer for the oxygen sensor. In other words, the sensors and circuits are highly interrelated with each other and with the fuel injection system.

5    The following table is a list of the trouble codes, the circuit or system which is causing the code and a brief description of the nature of the problem. From the descriptions provided, you should be able to troubleshoot the faulty circuit or component. If you can't, take the vehicle to a dealer service department or other qualified repair shop.

| Fault code | Circuit | Description of fault condition |
|---|---|---|
| Code 88 | N/A | Start of test |
| Code 11 | No ignition reference signal | No distributor reference signal detected during engine cranking |
| Code 12 | Number of key-ons since last fault or since faults were erased | Direct battery input to controller disconnected within last 50 to 100 ignition key-ons. |
| Code 13* ** | Slow change in MAP idle signal or No change in MAP from Start to Run | No variation in MAP sensor signal is detected. No difference is recognized between the engine MAP reading and the stored barometric pressure reading. |
| Code 14* ** | MAP voltage too low or MAP voltage too high | MAP sensor input below minimum acceptable voltage. MAP sensor input above maximum acceptable level. |
| Code 15** | No vehicle speed signal | No distance sensor signal detected during road load conditions. |
| Code 16* ** | Battery input sense | Battery voltage sense input not detected during engine running. |
| Code 17 | Engine runs cold too long | Engine coolant temperature remains below normal operating temperatures during vehicle travel (thermostat problem). |
| Code 21** | Oxygen sensor signal stays at center or Oxygen sensor shorted to voltage | Neither rich nor lean signal is detected from oxygen sensor input. Oxygen sensor input voltage maintained above normal range (1990 and later models). |
| Code 22* ** | Coolant sensor voltage too low or Coolant sensor voltage too high | Coolant temperature sensor input below minimum acceptable voltage. Coolant temperature sensor input above maximum acceptable voltage. |
| Code 23 | Throttle body temperature voltage low or Throttle body temperature voltage high | Throttle body temperature sensor input below minimum acceptable voltage Throttle body temperature sensor input above maximum acceptable voltage |
| Code 24* ** | Throttle Position Sensor voltage low or Throttle Position Sensor voltage high | Throttle position sensor input below minimum acceptable voltage. Throttle position sensor input above maximum acceptable voltage. |
| Code 25** | Automatic Idle Speed motor circuits | Shorted condition detected in one or more of AIS control circuits. |
| Code 26* ** | Injector 1 peak current | High resistance condition detected in injector output circuit. |
| Code 27* ** | Injector 1 control circuit | Injector output driver doesn't respond properly to the control. |
| Code 31** | Purge solenoid circuit | An open or shorted condition detected in purge solenoid circuit. |
| Code 32** | EGR solenoid circuit | An open or shorted condition detected in the EGR solenoid circuit (some California models). |
|  | EGR system failure | Required change in air/fuel ratio not detected during diagnostic test (some California models). |
| Code 33 | Air conditioning clutch relay circuit | An open or shorted condition detected in the air conditioning clutch relay circuit. |
| Code 34 | Speed control solenoid circuits | An open or shorted condition detected in the speed control vacuum or vent solenoid circuits. |
| Code 35 | Radiator fan relay circuit | An open or shorted condition detected in the radiator fan relay circuit. |
| Code 41 | Alternator field not switching properly | An open or shorted condition detected in the alternator field control circuit. |
| Code 42 | Auto shutdown relay control circuit | An open or shorted condition detected in the auto shutdown relay circuit. |
| Code 43 | Ignition control circuit | Output driver stage for ignition coil doesn't respond properly to the dwell control signal. |
| Code 44 | Voltage sense | No voltage present at logic board during controller operation. |
| Code 46** | Charging system voltage too high | Battery voltage sense input above target charging voltage during engine operation. |

| Fault code | Circuit | Description of fault condition |
|---|---|---|
| Code 47 | Charging system voltage too low | Battery voltage sense input below target charging voltage during engine operation, and no significant change in voltage detected during active test of alternator output. |
| Code 51** | Oxygen sensor signal stays below center | Oxygen sensor signal input indicates lean fuel/air ratio condition during engine operation. |
| Code 52** | Oxygen sensor signal stays above center | Oxygen sensor signal input indicates rich fuel/air ratio condition during engine operation. Adaptive fuel value leaned excessively due to a sustained rich condition. |
| Code 53 | Internal controller failure | Internal engine controller fault condition detected. |
| Code 55 | N/A | Completion of fault code display on the Check Engine light. |
| Code 62 | Controller failure (EMR miles not stored) | Unsuccessful attempt to update EMR mileage in the controller EPROM. |
| Code 63 | Controller failure (EEPROM write denied) | Unsuccessful attempt to write to an EEPROM location by the controller. |

*These codes light up the Check Engine light on the instrument panel*
**These codes light up the Check Engine light on the instrument panel on vehicles with special California emissions controls*

## 14 Information sensors - replacement

### Coolant temperature sensor

*Refer to illustration 14.1*

**Warning:** *Wait until the engine is completely cool before replacing the coolant temperature sensor.*

1    The coolant temperature sensor is mounted in the thermostat housing **(see illustration)**.

2    Open the radiator cap to release any residual pressure. Squeeze the upper radiator hose and reinstall the cap (this will create a slight vacuum in the cooling system, which will minimize coolant loss).

3    Unplug the electrical connector from the coolant temperature sensor, unscrew the sensor and remove it.

4    Coat the threads of the new sensor (or the old one, if you're reinstalling it) with teflon tape or a non-hardening thread sealant, screw it in, tighten securely and reattach the electrical connector.

5    Check the coolant level and add coolant if necessary.

### Distance (speed) sensor

*Refer to illustration 14.6*

6    The distance (speed) sensor is located in the transaxle extension housing **(see illustration)**.

7    Unplug the electrical connector.

8    Remove the retaining bolt and lift the sensor from the transaxle.

9    Installation is the reverse of removal.

### Manifold Absolute Pressure (MAP) sensor

10    Detach the vacuum hose from the sensor **(see illustration 12.9)**.

11    Unplug the electrical connector from the sensor.

12    Remove the sensor mounting bolts and remove the sensor.

13    Installation is the reverse of removal.

**14.1 Coolant temperature sensor location**

### Oxygen sensor

*Refer to illustration 14.14*

14    Unplug the oxygen sensor electrical connector **(see illustration)**.

15    The sensor is threaded into the exhaust manifold. To locate it, simply trace the electrical lead. On some models it may be easier to remove if you raise the front of the vehicle (support it securely on jack-

**6**

**14.6 Typical distance (speed) sensor**

**14.14 Oxygen sensor details**

**14.25  Apply heat transfer compound (included with the new sensor) to the tip of the throttle body temperature sensor**

**14.30  Removing the Throttle Position Sensor (TPS) from the throttle body**

**15.8  Measure the length of the pintle - if it protrudes more than one inch, take it to a dealer service department or other repair shop equipped with the necessary tool to have it retracted**

stands) for access to the underside of the engine compartment.

16   Unscrew the sensor. Chrysler recommends using special tool C-4907 for heated sensors (more important if, for example, you're simply removing a good sensor from a bad manifold and planning to reinstall it in another manifold).

17   Use a tap to clean the threads in the exhaust manifold.

18   If you're reinstalling the same sensor, apply a film of anti-seize compound to the threads. A new sensor should already have the anti-seize compound on the threads; if it doesn't, put some on.

19   Install the sensor, tighten it securely and plug in the electrical connector.

## Throttle body temperature sensor

*Refer to illustration 14.25*

20   Remove the air cleaner (see Chapter 4).

21   Disconnect the throttle cables from the throttle lever (see Chapter 4).

22   Remove the screws from the throttle cable bracket and remove the bracket.

23   Pulling down, unplug the electrical connector from the sensor.

24   Remove the sensor.

25   Apply heat transfer compound (included with sensor) to the sensor tip **(see illustration)**.

26   Install the sensor and tighten it securely.

27   The remainder of installation is the reverse of removal.

## Throttle Position Sensor (TPS)

*Refer to illustrations 14.30*

28   Remove the air cleaner assembly (see Chapter 4).

29   Unplug the electrical connector from the TPS (three-wire connector).

30   Remove the two screws retaining the TPS to the throttle body, pull the TPS off the throttle shaft and remove the TPS **(see illustration)**.

31   Installation is the reverse of removal. Make sure the flat tip of the throttle shaft seats properly into the slot in the TPS. Tighten the retaining screws securely.

## 15   Automatic Idle Speed (AIS) motor - check and replacement

### Check

1   The Automatic Idle Speed (AIS) motor is monitored by the Logic Module or the SMEC (computer). If the AIS malfunctions, a trouble code is stored in the computer's memory. To get the module to display any stored trouble codes, refer to Section 12. If a Code 25 is displayed, check the AIS motor circuit for problems. If necessary, replace the AIS motor.

### Removal

2   Disconnect the negative cable from the battery.

3   Remove the air cleaner assembly (see Section 9).

4   Unplug the electrical connector on the AIS motor.

5   Remove the throttle body temperature sensor (see Chapter 6).

6   Remove the two retaining screws (no. 25 Torx) from the AIS motor.

7   Pull the AIS from the throttle body. Make sure the O-ring doesn't fall into the throttle body opening.

### Installation

*Refer to illustration 15.8*

8   Prior to installation, make sure the pintle is in the retracted position. If the retracted pintle measurement is more than one inch, the AIS motor must be taken to a dealer service department or other repair shop to be retracted **(see illustration)**.

9   Install a new O-ring and insert the AIS motor into the housing, making sure the O-ring isn't dislodged.

10   Install the two retaining screws. Tighten the screws securely.

11   Plug in the electrical connector.

12   Install the throttle body temperature sensor (see Chapter 6).

13   Install the air cleaner assembly and connect the negative battery cable.

16.1a  Positive Crankcase Ventilation (PCV) system
(2.2L/2.5L engine)

16.1b  Positive Crankcase Ventilation (PCV) system (2.6L engine)

## 16  Positive Crankcase Ventilation (PCV) system

### General description

*Refer to illustrations 16.1a and 16.1b*

1    The Positive Crankcase Ventilation (PCV) system **(see illustrations)** is designed to reduce hydrocarbon emissions (HC) by routing blow-by gases (fuel/air mixture that escapes from the combustion chamber past the piston rings into the crankcase) from the crankcase to the intake manifold and combustion chambers, where they are burned during engine operation.

2    The system is very simple and consists of rubber hoses and a small, replaceable metering valve (PCV valve).

### Check and component replacement

*Refer to illustration 16.3*

3    With the engine running at idle, pull the PCV valve out of the mount and place your finger over the valve inlet **(see illustration)**. A strong vacuum will be felt and a hissing noise will be heard if the valve is operating properly. Replace the valve with a new one, as described in Chapter 1, if it is not functioning as described. Do not attempt to clean the old valve.

## 17  Evaporative emissions control (EVAP) system

### General description

1    This system is designed to trap and store fuel that evaporates from the carburetor and fuel tank and would normally enter the atmosphere in the form of hydrocarbon (HC) emissions.

2    The system used on carbureted engines consists of a charcoal-filled canister, a damping canister, a combination rollover/separator valve, a bowl vent valve and connecting lines and hoses. Later carbureted models also have a Vacuum-Controlled Orificed Tank Vapor Valve (VCOTVV). The system used on fuel-injected engines is similar.

3    When the engine is off and a high pressure begins to build up in the fuel tank (caused by fuel evaporation), the charcoal in the canister absorbs the fuel vapor. On some models, vapor from the carburetor float bowl also enters the canister. When the engine is started (cold), the charcoal continues to absorb and store fuel vapor. As the engine warms up, the stored fuel vapors are routed to the intake manifold or

16.3  To check the PCV valve, detach it with the engine running -
you should hear a hissing sound coming from the valve and you
should feel a strong vacuum when you place your finger
over the end of the valve

air cleaner and combustion chambers where they are burned during normal engine operation.

4    The canister is purged using air from the air injection pump delay or purge valve.

5    On 2.6L engines a damping canister serves as a purge control device. The fuel vapors released from the main canister pass through the damping canister and are momentarily held before passing to the intake manifold. When the engine is shut off, a bowl vent valve opens so that the carburetor is vented directly to the main canister.

6    Fuel-injected engines have a device known as a purge solenoid which prevents canister purging during engine warm-up, for a certain time period after hot starts and during certain idle conditions. Under these conditions, the SMEC grounds the purge control solenoid, which energizes it, preventing vacuum from reaching the canister valve. When the engine reaches a specified operating temperature and the specified time delay interval has elapsed, the solenoid is ungrounded, and de-energized. Vacuum can again flow to the canister purge valve and purge fuel vapors through the throttle body.

7    The relief valve, which is mounted in the fuel tank filler cap, is cali-

**17.10 To check the canister delay valve, apply vacuum with a hand pump**

brated to open when the fuel tank vacuum or pressure reaches a certain level. This vents the fuel tank and relieves the high vacuum or pressure.

## Check

### Canister, lines, hoses, fuel filler cap end relief valve

8    Check the canister and lines for cracks and other damage.

9    To check the filler cap and relief valve, remove the cap and detach the valve by unscrewing it. Look for a damaged or deformed gasket and make sure the relief valve is not stuck open. If the valve or gasket is not in good condition, replace the filler cap with a new one.

### Canister vacuum delay valve

*Refer to illustration 17.10*

10    A symptom of a failed delay valve is difficulty in starting the engine when it is hot. Disconnect the top vacuum hose **(see illustration)** and connect a vacuum pump to it. If the valve cannot hold the amount of vacuum listed in this Chapter's Specifications, replace the canister with a new one.

### Canister purge solenoid

11    The canister purge solenoid is controlled by the Logic Module/SMEC. A Code 31 on the CHECK ENGINE light indicates a malfunction somewhere in the circuit for this device, but determining whether the circuit or the solenoid is the problem is part of a larger diagnostic test that - unless you've got a DRB II (Chrysler tool no. C-4805 or equivalent) - can only be conducted by a dealer service department or other repair shop equipped with this tool.

**17.16a Typical canister purge solenoid location on Federal models**

## Component replacement

### Canister

12    The canister is located in the corner of the engine compartment, below the headlight.

13    Disconnect the vacuum hoses.

14    Remove the mounting bolts and lower the canister, removing it from beneath the vehicle.

15    Installation is the reverse of removal.

### Canister purge solenoid

*Refer to illustrations 17.16a and 17.16b*

16    The canister purge solenoid is located on the right inner fender well, right behind the headlight **(see illustrations)**. To replace it, unplug the electrical connector, remove the bracket mounting bolt and detach the solenoid from the bracket. Installation is the reverse of removal.

## 18    Heated inlet air system

## General description

*Refer to illustrations 18.2, 18.3, 18.4 and 18.6*

1    The heated inlet air system is designed to improve driveability, reduce emissions and prevent carburetor/throttle body icing in cold weather by directing hot air from around the exhaust manifold to the air

**17.16b Typical canister purge solenoid location on California models**

**18.2 Heated inlet air system (2.2L carbureted engine)**

18.3  Heated inlet air system (2.6L engine)

18.4  Heated inlet air system on fuel-injected engines

cleaner intake.

2    On carbureted 2.2L engines the system is made up of two circuits **(see illustration)**. When the outside air temperature is below 10-degrees F, the carburetor intake air flows through the flexible connector, up through the air cleaner and into the carburetor. When the air temperature is above 15-degrees F, air enters the air cleaner through the outside air duct.

3    On 2.6L engines, the door in the air cleaner assembly is controlled by a vacuum motor which is actuated by a bi-metal temperature sensor **(see illustration)**. The sensor reacts to both intake manifold vacuum and the air temperature inside the air cleaner itself. When the air temperature inside the air horn is 85-degrees F or below, the air bleed valve in the sensor remains closed and intake manifold vacuum opens the air control door to direct heated air to the carburetor. When the air temperature inside the air cleaner is 113-degrees F or above, the sensor air bleed valve opens the air duct door, allowing outside air directly into the carburetor. At temperatures between the two extremes, the sensor provides a blend of outside and heated air to the carburetor.

4    On fuel injection systems, the temperature of the incoming air is controlled by intake manifold vacuum, a temperature sensor and a vacuum diaphragm which operates the heat control door in the snorkel **(see illustration)**.

5    When ambient air temperature is 15 or more degrees F above the control temperature, incoming air flows through the snorkel (the outside air inlet).

6    When the ambient air temperature is below the control temperature during start-up, air flows through both the snorkel and the stove

(the inlet heated by the exhaust manifold). The colder the ambient air, the greater the flow of air through the stove; the warmer the air, the greater the flow of air through the snorkel. The amount of air flowing through each inlet is regulated by a heat control door in the snorkel to maintain a predetermined temperature at the temperature sensor mounted inside the air cleaner housing **(see illustration)**.

## *Check*
### General

7    Refer to Chapter 1 for the general checking procedure. If the system is not operating properly, check the individual components as follows.

8    Check all vacuum hoses for cracks, kinks, proper routing and broken sections. Make sure the shrouds and ducts are in good condition as well.

### 2.2L carbureted engine
*Refer to illustration 18.11*

9    Remove the air cleaner assembly from the engine and allow it to cool to 65-degrees F. Apply 20 in-Hg of vacuum to the sensor, using a hand vacuum pump.

10    The duct door should be in the up (heat on) position with the vacuum applied. If it is not, check the vacuum diaphragm.

11    To check the diaphragm, slowly apply vacuum with the hand pump while observing the door **(see illustration)**.

18.6  Temperature sensor for the heated inlet air system

18.11  Check the vacuum diaphragm with a vacuum pump
(2.2L carbureted engine)

**18.26  Remove the rivet to replace the vacuum diaphragm on a 2.2L engine**

**18.31  Pry off the temperature sensor retaining clips with a screwdriver**

12   The duct door should not begin to open at less than 2 in-Hg and should be fully open at 4 in-Hg or less. With 20 in-Hg applied, the diaphragm should not bleed down more than 10 in-Hg in five minutes.
13   Replace the sensor and/or vacuum diaphragm with new units if they fail any of the tests. Test the new unit(s) as described before reinstalling the air cleaner assembly.

### 2.6L engine

14   With the engine cold and the air temperature less than 85-degrees F, see if the air control valve is in the up (heat on) position.
15   Warm up the engine to operating temperature. With the air temperature at the entrance to the snorkel at 113-degrees F, the door should be in the down (heat off) position.
16   Remove the air cleaner assembly from the engine and allow it to cool to 85-degrees F. Connect a hand vacuum pump to the sensor.
17   Apply 15 in-Hg of vacuum to the sensor and see if the door is now in the up (heat on) position. If it is not, check the vacuum motor.
18   Apply 10 in-Hg vacuum to the motor with the vacuum pump and see if the valve is in the up position. If it is not, replace the motor with a new one. On these vehicles the vacuum motor is an integral part of the air cleaner body and the entire assembly must be replaced.

### Fuel-injected engines

19   Make sure all vacuum hoses and the flexible connector tube between the stove and the air cleaner are properly connected and free of tears.
20   With a cold engine and ambient temperature below 115-degrees F,

**18.32 . . . then pull it straight out**

the heat control door in the snorkel should be in the up (heat on) position.
21   With the engine warmed up and running, check the air temperature entering the snorkel or at the sensor. When the air temperature entering the outer end of the snorkel is 140 or more degrees F, the door should be in the down or (heat off) position.
22   Remove the air cleaner from the engine and allow it to cool down to 115-degrees F. Apply 20 in-Hg of vacuum to the temperature sensor - the door should be in the up (heat on) position. If the door doesn't rise to the heat on position, check the vacuum diaphragm for proper operation.
23   To test the diaphragm, apply 20 in-Hg of vacuum with a vacuum pump. The diaphragm shouldn't bleed down more than 10 in-Hg of vacuum in five minutes. And the door shouldn't lift off the bottom of the snorkel at less than 2 in-Hg of vacuum, but it should be in the full up position with no more than 4 in-Hg of vacuum.
24   If the vacuum diaphragm doesn't perform as described above, replace the heated air assembly.
25   If the vacuum diaphragm does perform satisfactorily - but the temperature being maintained is still incorrect - replace the temperature sensor and repeat Steps 20 and 21.

## Component replacement

### 2.2L carbureted engine

**Vacuum diaphragm**

*Refer to illustration 18.26*

26   With the air cleaner removed, disconnect the vacuum hose and drill out the retaining rivet **(see illustration)**.
27   Disengage the diaphragm by tipping it forward slightly while turning it slightly counterclockwise. Once disengaged, the unit can be removed by moving it to one side, disconnecting the rod from the control door and detaching it from the air cleaner assembly.
28   Check the control door for free travel by raising it to the full up position and allowing it to fall closed. If it does not close easily, free it up. Check the hinge pin for free movement also, using compressed air or spray cleaner to remove any foreign matter.
29   To install the diaphragm, insert the rod end into the control door and position the diaphragm tangs in the slot, turning the diaphragm clockwise until it engages. Rivet the tab in place.
30   Connect the vacuum hose.

**Sensor**

*Refer to illustrations 18.31 and 18.32*

31   Disconnect the vacuum hoses and use a screwdriver to pry off the retaining clips **(see illustration)**.
32   Detach the sensor from the housing **(see illustration)**.
33   Place the gasket on the new sensor, insert the sensor into the housing, hold it in place so the gasket is compressed to form a good seal and install the new retainer clips.
34   Connect the vacuum hoses.

18.37  Pry off the temperature sensor retaining clip(s)
with a screwdriver

18.39  Install the temperature sensor and gasket
into the air cleaner

### Fuel-injected engine

#### Sensor

*Refer to illustrations 18.37 and 18.39*

35   Remove the air cleaner housing (see Chapter 4).

36   Detach the vacuum hoses from the sensor.

37   Remove the retainer clip(s) with a screwdriver **(see illustration)**. Discard the old clip(s). New clips are supplied with the new sensor.

38   Remove the sensor and gasket. Discard the old gasket. A new one is included with the new sensor.

39   Put the new gasket on the new sensor and install them **(see illustration)**. Pressing against the outer diameter of the sensor to compress the gasket and form an airtight seal, install the retaining clip(s).

40   Reattach the vacuum hoses and install the air cleaner housing.

### 19   Exhaust Gas Recirculation (EGR) system

## General description

1   The Exhaust Gas Recirculation (EGR) system reduces oxides of nitrogen (NOx) in the exhaust emissions and helps prevent spark knock by recirculating some of the exhaust gases back through the intake to dilute the air/fuel mixture, which in turn reduces the peak flame temperature during combustion (a high combustion temperature is the primary cause of NOx). The main component in all EGR systems is the EGR valve.

### Carbureted engines

2   On 2.2L carbureted engines, the EGR valve operates in conjunc-tion with the Coolant Vacuum Switch Cold Closed (CVSCC) valve. This coolant valve and the EGR valve remain shut at low engine temperatures. At higher temperatures, the coolant valve opens, allowing vacuum to be applied to the EGR valve, and exhaust gas to recirculate. On 2.6L engines, a sub-EGR valve is operated directly by the throttle linkage, while a dual EGR valve is controlled by carburetor vacuum. The primary valve of the dual EGR valve operates during small openings of the throttle and the secondary valve takes over when the opening is larger. The vacuum which operates the dual EGR valve is supplied by a coolant temperature actuated thermo valve so that EGR function doesn't affect driveability.

### Fuel-injected engines

*Refer to illustration 19.3*

3   On fuel-injected engines, a backpressure-type EGR valve is ported to the throttle body. A backpressure transducer measures the amount of exhaust gas backpressure on the exhaust side of the EGR valve and varies the strength of the vacuum signal applied to the EGR valve **(see illustration)**. The transducer uses this backpressure signal to provide the correct amount of recirculated gases under any condition. All California models with this system have on-board diagnostic capabilities (see Section 12).

## Check

### 2.2L carbureted engine

*Refer to illustration 19.4*

4   Check all hoses for cracks, kinks, broken sections and proper connection **(see illustration)**. Inspect all connections for damage, cracks and leaks.

**6**

19.3  EGR and backpressure transducer assembly

19.4  An exploded view of the EGR system components
(2.2L carbureted engine)

**19.11 Schematic of the EGR system (2.6L engine)**

5    To check the EGR valve operation, bring the engine up to operating temperature and, with the transmission in Neutral (tires blocked to prevent movement), allow it to idle for 70 seconds. Open the throttle abruptly so that the engine speed is between 2,000 and 3,000 rpm and then allow it to close. The EGR valve stem should move if the control system is working properly. The test should be repeated several times. Movement of the stem indicates that the control system is functioning correctly.

6    If the EGR valve stem does not move, check all of the hose connections to make sure they are not leaking or clogged. Disconnect the vacuum hose and apply the amount of vacuum listed in this Chapter's Specifications with a hand pump. If the stem still does not move, replace the EGR valve with a new one. If the valve does open, measure the valve travel to make sure it is within the specified limit.

7    Apply vacuum with the pump and then clamp the hose shut. The valve should stay open for 30 seconds or longer. If it does not, the diaphragm is leaking and the valve should be replaced with a new one.

8    To check the coolant valve (CVSCC) located in the thermostat housing, bypass it with a length of 3/16-inch tubing. If the EGR valve did not operate under the conditions described in Step 6, but does operate properly with the CVSCC bypassed, the CVSCC is defective and should be replaced.

9    If the EGR valve does not operate with the CVSCC bypassed, the carburetor must be removed to check and clean the slot-type port in the throttle bore and the vacuum passages and orifices in the throttle body. Use solvent to remove deposits and check for flow with light air pressure.

10    Remove the EGR valve and inspect the poppet and seat area for deposits. If the deposits are more than a thin film of carbon, the valve should be cleaned. To clean the valve, apply solvent and allow it to penetrate and soften the deposits, making sure that none gets on the valve diaphragm, as it could be damaged. Use a vacuum pump to hold the valve open and carefully scrape the deposits from the seat and poppet area with a tool. Inspect the poppet and stem for wear and replace the valve with a new one if wear is found.

## 2.6L engine

*Refer to illustration 19.11*

11    Check all hoses and connections for cracks, kinks, damage and correct installation **(see illustration)**.

12    With the engine cold, start and run it at idle. Block the tires to prevent any movement of the vehicle during testing.

13    Increase the speed to 2,500 rpm and check the secondary EGR valve to make sure that it does not operate when the engine is cold. If it does, the thermo valve is faulty and must be replaced with a new one.

14    Allow the engine to warm up and observe the secondary EGR valve to see that it opens as the temperature rises and the idle speed increases. If it does not open, the secondary EGR valve itself or the thermo valve is faulty.

15    To check the secondary EGR valve and the thermo valve, disconnect the green striped vacuum hose from the carburetor and connect a vacuum pump to the hose. Apply six inches of vacuum with the pump as you open the sub EGR valve.

16    If the engine idle becomes unstable, the secondary valve of the dual EGR is operating properly. If the idle speed is unchanged, the secondary valve or the thermo valve is faulty and must be replaced with a new one.

17    Reconnect the green striped hose and disconnect the yellow striped hose at the carburetor.

18    Connect the hand vacuum pump to the hose and, while opening the sub EGR valve, apply six in-Hg of vacuum.

19    If the idle becomes unstable, the EGR primary valve is operating properly. If the idle is unchanged, the EGR primary valve or the thermo valve is not operating and should be replaced with a new one.

## Fuel-injected engines

*Refer to illustration 19.20*

20    Inspect all hoses between the throttle body, intake manifold and EGR control valve for leaks. Make sure all hoses are snug and in good condition **(see illustration)**. Replace any hoses that are hardened, cracked or melted, and replace any faulty connectors.

**19.20  EGR mounting details on a fuel-injected engine**

**19.39  Sub-EGR valve layout (2.6L engine)**

21    Warm up the engine, allow it to idle for 70 seconds with the throttle closed, then abruptly accelerate the engine to about 2,000 (but not over 3,000) rpm. The EGR valve stem should visibly move during this procedure. You can tell if the stem moves by noting any change in the relative position of the groove in the stem. Repeat this operation several times to verify the stem is really moving. Stem movement indicates that the control system is operating correctly. If the stem isn't moving, go to Step 23.

22    To determine whether EGR gas is flowing through the system, hook up a hand-operated vacuum pump to the EGR valve vacuum motor. With the engine running at idle speed, slowly apply vacuum. Engine speed should begin to drop when the applied vacuum reaches 2 to 3.5 in-Hg. Engine speed should drop quickly, and the engine may even stall. This indicates that EGR gas is flowing through the system.

23    The most likely cause of a non-operable EGR valve stem is the hoses. Verify that all hose connections are good. Make sure there are no leaks anywhere in the system and all hoses are open. Replace any defective hoses.

24    Disconnect the hose harness from the EGR vacuum transducer and hook up an auxiliary vacuum supply. Raise the engine rpm to 2,000 rpm and apply 10 in-Hg of vacuum while observing valve stem movement.

25    If the stem still doesn't move, replace the valve/transducer assembly.

26    If the valve stem now moves (about 1/8-inch of travel), hold the vacuum supply to check for a leaking diaphragm. The valve should remain open for 30 seconds or longer.

27    If the diaphragm is leaking, replace the valve/transducer assembly.

28    If the EGR valve stem and diaphragm are operating satisfactorily when an external vacuum source is applied (but didn't work correctly when the system was tested) the control system is probably defective, a passage is plugged or - on California models with EET and on-board diagnostics - a solenoid or the solenoid control circuit in the control system is bad. Go to the next Step.

29    Remove the throttle body (see Chapter 4) and inspect the port in the throttle bore and the associated passages in the throttle body. Remove any deposits with a suitable solvent and check for air flow through these passages with light air pressure. Install the throttle body and re-check the EGR system. Cleaning these passages usually restores normal operation of the EGR system.

30    To verify a defective solenoid or solenoid control circuit on a California model with EET and on-board diagnostics, output any stored trouble codes (see Section 13). The CHECK ENGINE light should display a Code 32. Any further diagnosis of this problem should be referred to a dealer service department.

31    What if the engine won't idle, dies when returning to idle or has a very rough or slow idle? Either the EGR valve is leaking in its closed position, or the EGR tube to the intake manifold is leaking.

32    To determine whether the EGR valve is leaking in its closed position, detach the vacuum hose from the EGR valve with the engine idling. The idle should pick-up immediately and smooth out.

33    If it doesn't, turn off the engine and remove the air cleaner to expose the throttle body inlet. Disconnect the backpressure hose from the EGR valve. Using a nozzle with a rubber tip, force compressed air (about 50 to 60 psi) through the steel backpressure tube on the EGR valve while opening and closing the throttle plate. If the sound from the compressed air changes distinctly, the poppet is leaking and air is entering the intake manifold. Replace the EGR valve.

34    To determine whether the EGR tube to the intake manifold is leaking, loosen the tube and retighten it to the torque listed in this Chapter's Specifications, then recheck the system for leaks.

35    If an EGR leak persists, replace the EGR tube and gaskets.

### Component replacement

#### 2.2L carbureted engine

36    The CVSCC can be replaced by removing the vacuum hoses and unscrewing the valve.

37    To replace the EGR valve, remove the air cleaner, air injection pump and shield. Disconnect the metal tube and vacuum hose, remove the two retaining nuts and detach the valve.

#### 2.6L engine

*Refer to illustration 19.39*

38    The dual EGR valve is located on the lower part of the intake manifold. It is replaced by removing the vacuum hoses and unbolting it. It may be necessary to tap the valve gently with a soft-faced hammer to break the gasket seal so it can be removed. Use a new gasket when installing the valve and check the vacuum hoses for proper routing.

39    The sub EGR valve is located on the base of the carburetor and is connected by a linkage **(see illustration)**. Pry off the spring clip and remove the pin attaching the plunger to the linkage. Hold the end of the linkage up and remove the spring and the steel ball from the end of the plunger.

40    Slip the rubber boot off and slide the plunger out of the carburetor throttle body. Before installing the plunger, lubricate it with a small amount of light oil. Install the steel ball and spring, hold the linkage in place and insert the pin. Carefully slide the spring clip into place, then check for smooth operation of the valve plunger.

41    The thermal valves are threaded into the intake manifold. Drain some coolant (see Chapter 1), then pull off the vacuum hose and unscrew the valve from the housing.

#### Fuel-injected engines

42    To remove the EGR valve, disconnect the vacuum line from the EGR valve (inspect and replace it if damaged), remove the mounting bolts from the valve **(see illustration 19.20)** and remove the valve. Discard the old gasket.

**6**

43   Clean the gasket surface and inspect it for any signs of exhaust gas leaks and cracks.
44   Installation is the reverse of removal. Use a new gasket and tighten the EGR valve to the torque listed in this Chapter's Specifications.
45   To remove the EGR tube, remove the four attaching bolts **(see illustration 19.20)**, remove the tube and discard the gaskets.
46   Clean the gasket mounting surfaces of the intake and exhaust manifold and the EGR tube flanges. Look for evidence of exhaust gas leaks and cracks.
47   Installation is the reverse of removal. Using new gaskets, loosely tighten all four bolts, then tighten them to the torque listed in this Chapter's Specifications.

## 20   Catalytic converter

### General description

1   The catalytic converter is designed to reduce hydrocarbon (HC) and carbon monoxide (CO) pollutants in the exhaust gases. The converter oxidizes these components and converts them to water and carbon dioxide.
2   The system on these vehicles consists of a mini-oxidizer converter and a main under floor converter. The mini-oxidizer converter begins the exhaust gas oxidization, which is then completed by the main converter.
3   If large amounts of unburned gasoline enter the catalyst, it may overheat and cause a fire. Always observe the following precautions:

*Use only unleaded gasoline*
*Avoid prolonged idling*
*Do not run the engine with a nearly empty fuel tank*
*Do not prolong engine compression checks*
*Avoid coasting with the ignition turned Off*
*Do not dispose of a used catalytic converter along with oily or gasoline soaked parts*

### Check

4   The catalytic converter requires little if any maintenance and servicing at regular intervals. However, the system should be inspected whenever the vehicle is raised on a lift or if the exhaust system is checked or serviced.
5   Check all connections in the exhaust pipe assembly for looseness and damage. Also check all the clamps for damage, cracks and missing fasteners. Check the rubber hangers for cracks.
6   The converter itself should be checked for damage and dents (maximum 3/4-inch deep) which could affect its performance and/or be hazardous to your health. At the same time the converter is inspected, check the heat shields under it, as well as the heat insulator above it, for damage and loose fasteners.

### Component replacement

7   Do not attempt to remove the catalytic converter until the complete exhaust system is cool. Raise the vehicle and support it securely on jackstands. Apply some penetrating oil to the clamp bolts and allow it to soak in. Disconnect the oxygen sensor (if equipped) from the converter.
8   Remove the bolts and the rubber hangers, then separate the converter from the exhaust pipe. Remove the old gaskets if they are stuck to the pipes.
9   Installation of the converter is the reverse of removal. Use new exhaust pipe gaskets and tighten the clamp nuts to the specified torque. Replace the oxygen sensor wires (if equipped), start the engine and check carefully for exhaust leaks.

# Chapter 7 Part A
# Manual transaxle

## Contents

## Specifications

**Lubricant type and capacity** ............................................... See Chapter 1

**Torque specifications**  **Ft-lbs** (unless otherwise indicated)

| | |
|---|---|
| Gearshift rod connector clamp bolt | 14 |
| Shift linkage lock pin | 108 in-lbs |
| Shift cable adjusting screws | 70 in-lbs |
| Speedometer drive pinion bolt | 60 in-lbs |
| Transaxle-to-engine block bolts | 70 |

## 1   General information

The vehicles covered by this manual are equipped with either a four- or five-speed manual transaxle or a three-speed automatic transaxle. Information on the manual transaxle is included in this Part of Chapter 7. Service procedures for the automatic transaxle are contained in Chapter 7, Part B.

The manual transaxle is a compact, two-piece, lightweight aluminum alloy housing containing both the transmission and differential assemblies.

These models are equipped with two types of shift linkage: four-speed models use rod-type, while five-speed have shift cables.

Because of the complexity, unavailability of replacement parts and special tools required, internal repair of the manual transaxle by the home mechanic is not recommended. The bulk of information in this Chapter is devoted to removal and installation procedures.

## 2   Shift linkage - check and adjustment

*Refer to illustration 2.3*

1    In the event of hard shifting, disconnect the rod or cables at the transaxle and then operate the shifter from the driver's seat. If the shift lever moves smoothly through all positions with the rod or cables disconnected, then the rod or cable assembly itself should be adjusted as described below.

2    Raise the hood and place a pad or blanket over the left fender to protect it.

3    Remove the lock pin from the transaxle selector shaft housing. Reverse the lock pin so the longer end is down, reinstall it in the hole and move the selector shaft in. When the lock pin aligns with the hole in the selector shaft, thread it into place so the shaft is locked in Neutral **(see illustration)**.

### *Rod-type linkage*

*Refer to illustration 2.6*

4    Raise the vehicle and support it securely on jackstands.

5    Working under the vehicle, loosen the gearshift connector clamp bolt. Make sure connector moves freely within the gearshift tube.

6    Place the shifter mechanism in position with the isolator contact-

**2.3  Use the lock pin to secure the transaxle selector in Neutral prior to cable adjustment**

**2.6  Make sure the ridge on the isolator is centered in the hole in the block-out bracket before tightening the clamp (rod-type shift linkage)**

**2.7  Shift lever and boot details**

**2.9  Fabricate the cable adjusting pins, loosen the adjusting screws and install the pins as shown here**

**2.10a  Adjust the selector cable by tightening the adjusting screw**

**2.10b  Crossover cable adjustment details**

ing the upright flange and the isolator rib aligned with the hole in the blockout bracket. With no pressure applied to the linkage, tighten the clamp bolt securely **(see illustration)**.

## Cable-type linkage

*Refer to illustrations 2.7, 2.9, 2.10a and 2.10.b*

7    Remove the shift knob and boot **(see illustration)**.
8    Remove the center console (see Chapter 11).
9    Fabricate two 5-inch long adjusting pins from 5/16-inch wire. Bend one end of each pin at right angles so they will be easy to grasp. Loosen the adjusting screws on the gearshift mechanism and insert one adjusting pin into the crossover cable hole of the shift mechanism and the other into the selector cable hole **(see illustration)**.
10   Use an inch-pound torque wrench to tighten the crossover cable and selector cable adjusting screws to the torque listed in this Chapter's Specifications **(see Illustrations)**. Remove the adjusting pins.

## All models

11   Lower the vehicle (rod-type) or install the console, boot and shift knob (cable-type).
12   Remove the lock pin, reverse it so the longer end is upright, screw it into place and then tighten it to the torque listed in this Chapter's Specifications.
13   Check the shifter operation in First and Reverse and make sure the reverse lockout mechanism works properly.

**3.2  Speedometer drive pinion installation details**

## 3 Speedometer drive pinion - removal and installation

*Refer to illustration 3.2*

1   The speedometer drive pinion is located in the transaxle differential extension housing. The drive pinion must be removed for certain operations, such as to allow right side driveaxle removal and installation. The manufacturer recommends that the oil seal be replaced before reinstalling the pinion.
2   Remove the retaining bolt and carefully work the speedometer drive assembly up and out of the transaxle extension housing **(see illustration)**.
3   Inspect the pinion for signs that lubricant has leaked past the adapter into the cable.
4   If there is leakage, pry off the retainer, detach the adapter from the pinion gear and replace the O-ring.
5   Connect the adapter to the pinion, making sure the retainer is secure.
6   Make sure the mating surfaces of the adapter and extension housing are clean because any debris could cause misalignment of the gear.
7   Insert the assembly into the transaxle, install the bolt and tighten it securely.

## 4 Oil seal replacement

1   Oil leaks frequently occur due to wear of the driveaxle oil seals and/or the speedometer pinion drive gear O-ring. Replacement of the seals is relatively easy, since the repairs can usually be performed without removing the transaxle from the vehicle.
2   The driveaxle oil seals are located at the sides of the transaxle, where the driveaxles are attached. If leakage at the seal is suspected, raise the vehicle and support it securely on jackstands. If the seal is leaking, lubricant will be found on the sides of the transaxle.
3   Refer to Chapter 8 and remove the driveaxle(s).
4   Using a screwdriver or prybar, carefully pry the oil seal out of the transaxle bore.
5   If the oil seal can't be removed with a screwdriver or prybar, a special oil seal removal tool (available at auto parts stores) will be required.
6   Using a large section of pipe or a large deep socket as a drift, install the new oil seal. Drive it into the bore squarely and make sure it's completely seated. Apply multi-purpose grease to the seal lip before installing the driveaxle.
7   Install the driveaxle(s). Be careful not to damage the lip of the new seal.
8   The speedometer cable and extension housing is located on the transaxle housing. Look for lubricant around the cable housing to determine if the O-ring is leaking.
9   Remove the speedometer drive pinion and replace the O-ring (see Section 3).

## 5 Transaxle mount - check and replacement

1   Insert a large screwdriver or prybar between the mount and the transaxle bracket and pry back and forth.
2   The transaxle bracket should not move away from the mount. If it does, replace the mount.
3   To replace the mount, support the transaxle with a jack, remove the nut and through bolt and the bracket-to-transaxle bolts, then detach the mount. It may be necessary to raise or lower the transaxle slightly to provide enough clearance to remove the mount.
4   Installation is the reverse of removal.

## 6 Manual transaxle - removal and installation

*Refer to illustrations 6.4 and 6.16*

### Removal

1   Disconnect the negative cable from the battery.
2   Raise the vehicle and support it securely on jackstands.
3   Drain the transaxle lubricant (see Chapter 1).
4   Disconnect the shift and clutch linkage from the transaxle **(see illustration)**.

7A

**6.4 Manual transaxle shift mechanism details (typical)**

5    Detach the speedometer cable and wire harness connectors from the transaxle.

6    Remove the exhaust system components as necessary for clearance.

7    Support the engine. This can be done from above with an engine hoist or special fixture or by placing a jack (with a block of wood as an insulator) under the engine oil pan. The engine must remain supported at all times while the transaxle is out of the vehicle!

8    Remove any chassis or suspension components that will interfere with transaxle removal (see Chapter 10).

9    Disconnect the driveaxles from the transaxle (see Chapter 8).

10    Support the transaxle with a jack, then remove the bolts securing the transaxle to the engine.

11    Remove the transaxle mount nuts and bolts.

12    Make a final check that all wires and hoses have been disconnected from the transaxle, then carefully pull the transaxle and jack away from the engine.

13    Once the input shaft is clear, lower the transaxle and remove it from under the vehicle. **Caution:** *Do not depress the clutch pedal while the transaxle is out of the vehicle.*

14    With the transaxle removed, the clutch components are now accessible and can be inspected. In most cases, new clutch components should be routinely installed when the transaxle is removed.

## *Installation*

15    If removed, install the clutch components (see Chapter 8).

16    To make installation of the transaxle easier, it's a good idea to install guide pins in place of the two upper bolts **(see illustration)**. To make guide pins, cut the heads off a pair of extra bolts, taper the cut ends with a grinder, and cut screwdriver slots in the cut ends with a hacksaw.

17    With the transaxle secured to the jack with a chain, raise it into position behind the engine, then carefully slide it forward, engaging the input shaft with the clutch plate hub splines. Do not use excessive force to install the transaxle - if the input shaft does not slide into place, readjust the angle of the transaxle so it is level and/or turn the input shaft so the splines engage properly with the clutch plate hub.

18    Install the transaxle-to-engine bolts. Tighten the bolts securely.

19    Install the transaxle mount nuts or bolts.

20    Install the chassis and suspension components which were removed. Tighten all nuts and bolts securely.

21    Remove the jacks supporting the transaxle and engine.

22    Install the various items removed previously, referring to Chapter 8 for installation of the driveaxles and Chapter 4 for information regarding the exhaust system components.

23    Make a final check that all wires, hoses, linkages and the speedometer cable have been connected and that the transaxle has been filled with lubricant to the proper level (see Chapter 1).

24    Connect the negative battery cable. Road test the vehicle for proper operation and check for leaks.

**6.16  Transaxle installation will be easier if you replace these two bolts temporarily with guide pins made from a pair of extra bolts**

## 7    Manual transaxle overhaul - general Information

Overhauling a manual transaxle is a difficult job for the do-it-yourselfer. It involves the disassembly and reassembly of many small parts. Numerous clearances must be precisely measured and, if necessary, changed with select-fit spacers and snap-rings. As a result, if transaxle problems arise, it can be removed and installed by a competent do-it-yourselfer, but overhaul should be left to a transmission repair shop. Rebuilt transaxles may be available - check with your dealer parts department and auto parts stores. At any rate, the time and money involved in an overhaul is almost sure to exceed the cost of a rebuilt unit.

Nevertheless, it's not impossible for an inexperienced mechanic to rebuild a transaxle if the special tools are available and the job is done in a deliberate step-by-step manner so nothing is overlooked.

The tools necessary for an overhaul include internal and external snap-ring pliers, a bearing puller, a slide hammer, a set of pin punches, a dial indicator and possibly a hydraulic press. In addition, a large, sturdy workbench and a vise or transaxle stand will be required.

During disassembly of the transaxle, make careful notes of how each piece comes off, where it fits in relation to other pieces and what holds it in place.

Before taking the transaxle apart for repair, it will help if you have some idea what area of the transaxle is malfunctioning. Certain problems can be closely tied to specific areas in the transaxle, which can make component examination and replacement easier. Refer to the *Troubleshooting* section at the front of this manual for information regarding possible sources of trouble.

# Chapter 7 Part B
# Automatic transaxle

## Contents

## Specifications

### Fluid type and capacity ............................................................. See Chapter 1

### Torque specifications

| | **Ft-lbs** (unless otherwise indicated) |
|---|---|
| Neutral start and back-up light switch | 25 |
| Shift cable adjustment bolt | 105 in-lbs |
| Throttle pressure cable adjustment bracket lock bolt/screw | 9 |
| Transaxle case-to-engine bolts | 70 |
| Torque converter-to-driveplate bolts | 55 |
| Transaxle mount through-bolts | 40 |
| Transaxle mount attaching bolts | 40 |

## 1   General Information

All vehicles covered in this manual come equipped with either a four- or speed five-speed manual transaxle or a three-speed automatic transaxle. All information on the automatic transaxle is included in this Part of Chapter 7. Information on the manual transaxle can be found in Part A of this Chapter.

Due to the complexity of the automatic transaxle and the need for special equipment and expertise to perform most service operations, this Chapter contains only general diagnosis, seal replacement, adjustments and removal and installation procedures.

If the transaxle requires major repair work, it should be left to a dealer service department or an automotive or transmission repair shop. You can, however, remove and install the transaxle yourself and save the expense, even if the repair work is done by a transmission shop.

## 2   Diagnosis - general

**Note:** *Automatic transaxle malfunctions may be caused by four general conditions: Poor engine performance, improper adjustments, hydraulic malfunctions or mechanical malfunctions. Diagnosis of these problems should always begin with a check of the easily repaired items: Fluid level and condition (see Chapter 1), shift linkage adjustment and throttle linkage adjustment. Next, perform a road test to determine if the problem has been corrected or if more diagnosis is necessary. If the problem persists after the preliminary tests and corrections are completed, additional diagnosis should be done by a dealer service department or transmission repair shop. Refer to the Troubleshooting section at the front of this manual for transaxle problem diagnosis.*

## Preliminary checks

1   Drive the vehicle to warm the transaxle to normal operating temperature.
2   Check the fluid level as described in Chapter 1:

a)  *If the fluid level is unusually low, add enough fluid to bring the level within the designated area on the dipstick, then check for external leaks.*

b)  *If the fluid level is abnormally high, drain off the excess, then check the drained fluid for contamination by coolant. The presence of engine coolant in the automatic transmission fluid indicates that a failure has occurred in the internal radiator walls that separate the coolant from the transmission fluid (see Chapter 3).*

c)  *If the fluid is foaming, drain it and refill the transaxle, then check for coolant in the fluid or a high fluid level.*

3   Check the engine idle speed. **Note:** *If the engine is malfunctioning, don't proceed with the preliminary checks until it has been repaired and runs normally.*

4   Check the throttle pressure cable for freedom of movement. Adjust it if necessary (see Section 4). **Note:** *The throttle pressure cable may function properly when the engine is shut off and cold, but it may malfunction once the engine is hot. Check it cold and at normal engine operating temperature.*

5   Inspect the shift cable (see Section 3). Make sure it's properly adjusted and operates smoothly.

## Fluid leak diagnosis

6   Most fluid leaks are easy to locate visually. Repair usually consists of replacing a seal or gasket. If a leak is difficult to find, the following procedure may help.

7   Identify the fluid. Make sure it's transmission fluid and not engine oil or brake fluid (automatic transmission fluid is a deep red color).

8   Try to pinpoint the source of the leak. Drive the vehicle several

miles, then park it over a large sheet of cardboard. After a minute or two, you should be able to locate the leak by determining the source of the fluid dripping onto the cardboard.

9    Make a careful visual inspection of the suspected component and the area immediately around it. Pay particular attention to gasket mating surfaces. A mirror is often helpful for finding leaks in areas that are hard to see.

10   If the leak still can't be found, clean the suspected area thoroughly with a degreaser or solvent, then dry it.

11   Drive the vehicle for several miles at normal operating temperature and varying speeds. After driving the vehicle, visually inspect the suspected component again.

12   Once the leak has been located, the cause must be determined before it can be properly repaired. If a gasket is replaced but the sealing flange is bent, the new gasket won't stop the leak. The bent flange must be straightened.

13   Before attempting to repair a leak, check to make sure the following conditions are corrected or they may cause another leak. **Note:** *Some of the following conditions can't be fixed without highly specialized tools and expertise. Such problems must be referred to a transmission shop or a dealer service department*

### Gasket leaks

14   Check the pan periodically. Make sure the bolts are all in place (none missing) and tight, the gasket is in good condition and the pan is flat (dents in the pan may indicate damage to the valve body inside).

15   If the pan gasket is leaking, the fluid level or the fluid pressure may be too high, the vent may be plugged, the pan bolts may be too tight, the pan sealing flange may be warped, the sealing surface of the transaxle housing maybe damaged, the gasket may be damaged or the transaxle casting may be cracked or porous. If sealant is used in place of a gasket, it may be the wrong sealant.

### Seal leaks

16   If a transaxle seal is leaking, the fluid level or pressure may be too high, the vent may be plugged (these models are vented through the hollow dipstick), the seal bore may be damaged, the seal itself may be damaged or improperly installed, the surface of the shaft protruding through the seal may be damaged or a loose bearing may be causing excessive shaft movement.

17   Make sure the dip stick tube seal is in good condition and the tube is properly seated. Periodically check the area around the speedometer gear or sensor for leakage. If transmission fluid is evident, check the 0-ring for damage. Also inspect the side gear shaft oil seals for leakage.

### Case leaks

18   If the case itself appears to be leaking, the casting is porous and will have to be repaired or replaced.

19   Make sure the oil cooler hose fittings are tight and in good condition.

### Fluid comes out the filler opening

20   If this condition occurs, the transaxle is overfilled, there is coolant in the fluid, the dipstick is incorrect, the vent is plugged or the drain back holes are plugged.

---

## 3    Shift cable - check and adjustment

### *Check*

1    Check the operation of the transaxle in each shift lever position (try to start the engine in each position - the starter should operate in the Park and Neutral positions only).

### *Adjustment*

2    Place the shift lever in Park.

3    Working in the engine compartment, loosen the shift cable clamp bolt on the transaxle bracket.

4    Pull the shift lever all the way to the front detent (Park position) by hand.

5    Keep pressure on the shift lever and tighten the cable clamp bolt.

6    Check the shift lever in the Neutral and Drive positions to make sure it's within the confines of the lever stops. The engine should start only when the lever is in the Park or Neutral position.

---

## 4    Throttle pressure cable - adjustment

*Refer to illustrations 4.3 and 4.6*

1    The throttle pressure cable controls a valve in the transaxle which governs shift quality and speed. If shifting is harsh or erratic, the throttle pressure cable should be adjusted.

2    The adjustment must be made with the engine at normal operating temperature.

### *1985 and earlier models*

3    Loosen the adjustment bracket lock screw **(see illustration)**.

4    To ensure proper adjustment, the bracket must be free to slide back-and-forth. If necessary, remove it and clean and lubricate the slot, sliding surfaces and screw.

5    Slide the bracket to the left (towards the engine) to the limit of its travel. Release the bracket and move the throttle lever all the way to the right, against the internal stop, then tighten the lock screw to the torque listed in this Chapter's Specifications.

### *1986 and later models*

6    Loosen the cable mounting bracket lock screw and position the bracket so the alignment tabs are in contact with the transaxle casting **(see illustration)**. Tighten the lock screw to the torque listed in this Chapter's Specifications.

7    Release the cross-lock on the cable assembly by pulling up on it. To ensure proper adjustment, the cable must be free to slide all the way toward the engine, against the stop, after the cross-lock is released.

8    Move the transaxle throttle control lever clockwise as far as possible (against the internal stop) and press the cross-lock down into the locked position.

9    Check the cable action. Move the transaxle throttle cable all the way forward, release it slowly and make sure it returns completely.

4.3  1985 and earlier throttle pressure cable details

**4.6 Throttle pressure cable details (1986 and later models)**

## 5 Neutral start and back-up light switch - check and replacement

*Refer to illustration 5.7*

1    The Neutral start and back-up light switch is located at the lower front edge of the transaxle. The switch controls the back-up lights and the center terminal of the switch grounds the starter solenoid circuit when the transaxle is in Park or Neutral, allowing the engine to start.

2    Prior to checking the switch, make sure the shift cable is properly adjusted (see Section 3).

3    Unplug the connector and use an ohmmeter to check for continuity between the center terminal and the case. Continuity should exist only when the transaxle is in Park or Neutral.

4    Check for continuity between the two outer terminals. Continuity should exist only when the transaxle is in Reverse. No continuity should exist between either outer terminal and the case.

5    If the switch fails any of the tests, replace it with a new one.

6    Position a drain pan under the switch to catch the fluid released when the switch is removed.

7    Unscrew the switch from the transaxle, using a box-end wrench to avoid damage to the switch housing **(see illustration)**.

8    Move the shift lever from Park to Neutral and check to see if the switch operating fingers are centered in the opening.

9    Wrap the threads of the new switch with Teflon tape, install it in the case and tighten it to the torque listed in this Chapter's Specifications. Plug in the connector and repeat the checks on the new switch.

10    Check the fluid level and add fluid as required (see Chapter 1).

**5.7 Neutral start and back-up light switch details**

## 6 Automatic transaxle - removal and installation

### *Removal*

*Refer to illustrations 6.6, 6.16, 6.18, 6.19, 6.20a, and 6.20b*

1    Disconnect the negative cable from the battery.

2    Raise the vehicle and support it securely on jackstands. Remove the front wheels.

3    Drain the transaxle fluid (see Chapter 1).

4    Remove the torque converter cover and the left splash shield.

5    Remove the driveaxles from the transaxle (see Chapter 8).

6    Mark the torque converter and driveplate so they can be reinstalled in the same position **(see illustration)**.

7    Remove the torque converter-to-driveplate bolts. Turn the crankshaft to bring each bolt into view. The crank shaft bolt can be reached through an access cover in the passenger side splash shield.

8    Remove the starter motor (see Chapter 5).

9    Disconnect the speedometer cable (see Chapter 7A).

10    Unplug the electrical connector from the Neutral start/back-up light switch. On models equipped with a lockup torque converter, disconnect the converter electrical connector near the dipstick.

11    On models so equipped, disconnect the vacuum hose(s).

12    Remove any exhaust components that will interfere with transaxle removal (see Chapter 4).

13    Disconnect the throttle pressure cable or rod.

14    Disconnect the shift cable.

15    Support the engine with a hoist from above or a jack from below (position a block of wood between the jack and oil pan to spread the load).

16    Support the transaxle with a jack - preferably a special jack made for this purpose **(see illustration)**. Safety chains will help steady the transaxle on the jack.

**7B**

**6.6 Mark across the torque converter and driveplate so they can be reassembled in the same position**

**6.16 Support the transaxle with a transmission jack and use a safety chain to prevent the transaxle from falling off the jack head**

**6.18  Remove the front engine mounting bracket**

**6.19  Remove the front mounting insulator through-bolt and unbolt the insulator from the transaxle**

17   Remove any chassis or suspension components that will interfere with transaxle removal.

18   Remove the engine mount bracket from the front crossmember **(see illustration)**.

19   Remove the front mounting insulator through-bolt and unbolt the insulator from the torque converter housing **(see Illustration)**.

20   Remove the left engine mount attaching bolts and through-bolt **(see Illustrations)**.

21   Remove the bolts securing the transaxle to the engine.

22   Lower the transaxle slightly and disconnect and plug the transaxle cooler lines.

23   Move the transaxle back to disengage it from the engine block dowel pins and make sure the torque converter is detached from the driveplate. Attach a small C-clamp to the transaxle case to prevent the torque converter from falling out during removal. Lower the transaxle from the vehicle.

## Installation

24   Prior to installation, make sure the torque converter hub is securely engaged in the pump.

25   With the transaxle secured to the jack, raise it into position. Be sure to keep it level so the torque converter doesn't slide out. Connect the fluid cooler lines.

26   Rotate the torque converter to align the bolts with the holes in the driveplate. The marks on the torque converter and driveplate must align.

27   Move the transaxle forward carefully until the dowel pins and transaxle housing are engaged.

28   Install the transaxle housing-to-engine bolts. Tighten them securely.

29   Install the torque converter-to-driveplate bolts. Tighten the bolts to the torque listed in this Chapter's Specifications.

30   Install the engine mounts and any suspension and chassis components that were removed. Tighten the bolts and nuts to the torque listed in this Chapter's Specifications.

31   Remove the jacks supporting the transaxle and engine.

32   Install the starter motor (see Chapter 5).

33   Connect the vacuum hose(s) (if equipped).

34   Connect the shift linkage and throttle pressure cable.

35   Attach the electrical connectors to the Neutral start/back-up light switch.

36   Install the torque converter cover and left splash shield.

37   Connect the driveaxles (see Chapter 8).

38   Connect the speedometer cable.

39   Adjust the shift cable (see Section 3).

40   Install any exhaust system components that were removed or disconnected.

41   Lower the vehicle.

42   Fill the transaxle (see Chapter I), run the vehicle and check for fluid leaks.

**6.20a  Remove the left engine mount attaching bolts . . .**

**6.20b  . . . and this long through-bolt**

# Chapter 8
# Clutch and driveaxles

## Contents

## Specifications

### Driveaxle installed length

**1981 to 1983 models** ... Inches: No specifications available

**1984 to 1986 models**

GKN driveaxle (2.2L)
Right (blue tape) ... 19.9 to 20.3
Left (blue tape) ... 10.2 to 10.9

GKN driveaxle (2.6L)
Right (silver tape) ... 19.7 to 20.1
Left (silver tape) ... 10.0 to 10.6

ACI driveaxle
Right (green tape) ... 18.8 to 19.1
Left (green tape) ... 9.0 to 9.6

GKN/ACI driveaxle
Right (orange tape) ... 19.4 to 19.7
Left (orange tape) ... 9.6 to 10.2

Citroen driveaxle
Right (white tape on 2.2L/2.5L, yellow on 2.6L) ... 18.9 to 19.4
Left (white tape on 2.2L/2.5L, yellow on 2.6L) ... 9.4 to 10.0

**1987 models**

2.2L/2.5L engines
GKN driveaxle
Right ... 19.9 to 20.3
Left ... 8.9 to 9.6

ACI driveaxle
Right ... 18.8 to 19.1
Left ... 7.8 to 8.3

GKN/ACI driveaxle
Right ... 19.4 to 19.7
Left ... 8.3 to 8.9

Citroen driveaxle
Right ... 18.9 to 19.4
Left ... 8.1 to 8.8

SSG driveaxle
Right ... 17.9 to 18.5
Left ... 7.2 to 7.9

**8**

## 1987 models (continued)

2.6L engine
    GKN driveaxle
        Right.................................................................... 19.7 to 20.1
        Left...................................................................... 8.7 to 9.3
    Citroen driveaxle
        Right.................................................................... 18.9 to 19.4
        Left...................................................................... 8.1 to 8.8

## 1988 models

2.2L/2.5L engines
    GKN driveaxle (69-92)
        Right.................................................................... 19.9 to 20.3
        Left...................................................................... 8.9 to 9.6
    GKN driveaxle (82-98)
        Right.................................................................... 19.3 to 19.6
        Left...................................................................... 8.9 to 9.2
    ACI driveaxle
        Right.................................................................... 18.8 to 19.1
        Left...................................................................... 7.8 to 8.3
    SSG driveaxle
        Right.................................................................... 18.0 to 18.5
        Left...................................................................... 7.2 to 7.9

## 1989 models

2.2L engine
    ACI driveaxle
        Right.................................................................... 18.8 to 19.1
        Left...................................................................... 7.8 to 8.3
    SSG driveaxle
        Right.................................................................... 18.0 to 18.5
        Left...................................................................... 7.2 to 7.9
    GKN driveaxle (82-98)
        Right.................................................................... 18.9 to 19.2
        Left...................................................................... 8.5 to 8.8
2.5L engine
    SSG driveaxle
        Right.................................................................... 18.0 to 18.5
        Left...................................................................... 7.7 to 7.9
    GKN driveaxle (82-98)
        Right.................................................................... 18.9 to 19.2
        Left...................................................................... 8.5 to 8.8

## Torque specifications                                    Ft-lbs

Pressure plate-to-flywheel bolts........................................ 21
Driveaxle nut............................................................... 180

## 1   General information

The information in this Chapter deals with the components from the engine to the front (drive) wheels (except for the transaxle, which is covered in the previous Chapter). In this Chapter, the components are grouped into two categories: clutch and driveaxles. Separate Sections within this Chapter offer general information, checks and repair procedures for components in each of the two groups. **Warning:** *Since nearly all the procedures included in this Chapter involve working under the vehicle, make sure it's securely supported on sturdy jackstands or on a hoist where it can be easily raised and lowered.*

## 2   Clutch - description and check

1    All vehicles with a manual transaxle have a single dry plate, diaphragm spring-type clutch. The clutch disc has a splined hub which allows it to slide along the splines of the transaxle input shaft or mainshaft. The clutch disc is held in place against the flywheel by the pressure plate springs. During disengagement (when shifting gears for

example), the clutch pedal is depressed, which operates a cable, actuating the release lever so the release bearing or plate pushes on the pressure plate springs, disengaging the clutch.
2    The release mechanism incorporates a self-adjusting device which compensates for clutch disc wear **(see illustration 3.2)**. A spring in the clutch pedal arm maintains tension on the cable and the adjuster pivot grabs the positioner adjuster when the pedal is depressed and the clutch is released. Consequently, the slack is always taken up in the cable, making adjustment unnecessary.
3    When pressure is applied to the pedal to release the clutch, the cable pulls against the end of the release lever, which turns a shaft connected to the clutch release fork. As the fork pivots, the release bearing pushes against the fingers of the diaphragm springs in the pressure plate assembly, which in turn disengages the clutch plate.
4    Terminology can be a problem when discussing the clutch components because common names are in some cases different from those used by the manufacturer. For example, the clutch disc is also called the clutch plate or driven plate, the clutch release bearing is sometimes called a throwout bearing and the release fork is sometimes called the release lever.
5    Other than to replace components with obvious damage, some

**3.2 Clutch pedal and release mechanism details**

preliminary checks should be performed to diagnose clutch problems.

a) *The first check should be of the clutch cable. If there's too much slack in the cable, the clutch won't release completely, making gear engagement difficult or impossible.*

b) *To check clutch "spin-down time," run the engine at normal idle speed with the transaxle in Neutral (clutch pedal up engaged). Disengage the clutch (pedal down), wait several seconds and shift the transaxle into Reverse. No grinding noise should be heard. A grinding noise would most likely indicate a problem in the pressure plate or the clutch disc.*

c) *To check for complete clutch release, run the engine (with the parking brake applied to prevent vehicle movement) and hold the clutch pedal approximately 1/2-inch from the floor. Shift the transaxle between First and Reverse gear several times. If the shift is rough, component failure is indicated, or as stated above, the cable is out of adjustment.*

d) *Visually inspect the pivot bushing at the top of the clutch pedal to make sure there's no binding or excessive play.*

e) *A clutch pedal that's difficult to operate is most likely caused by a faulty clutch cable. Check the cable where it enters the housing for frayed wires, rust and other signs of corrosion. If it looks good, lubricate the cable with penetrating oil. If pedal operation improves, the cable is worn out and should be replaced.*

## 3    Clutch cable - removal and installation

*Refer to illustration 3.2*

1    Raise the front of the vehicle and support it securely on jackstands. Apply the parking brake and block the rear wheels so the vehicle can't roll off the stands.

2    On 1989 models, remove the clip and disengage the cable housing from the retainer bracket on the strut tower **(see illustration)**.

3    Remove the clutch cable retainer and disengage the cable end from the clutch release lever on the transmission **(see illustration 3.2)**.

4    Pull the lower end of the cable out of the grommet in the transmission mount.

5    Working inside the vehicle, disengage the cable end from the clutch pedal.

6    Pull the cable through the firewall to remove it.

7    When installing the new cable, hook the ends to the pedal and transmission lever first, then pull on the housing and engage the cable in the retainer bracket. On 1989 models, don't forget to install the clip.

8    Operate the pedal several times to allow the self-adjuster mechanism to take up slack in the cable.

## 4    Clutch release bearing and release fork - removal and installation

*Refer to illustrations 4.2, 4.4a, 4.4b and 4.4c*

**Warning:** *Dust produced by clutch wear and deposited on clutch components may contain asbestos, which is a health hazard. DO NOT blow it out with compressed air or inhale any of it. DO NOT use gasoline or petroleum-based solvents to clean off the dust. Brake system cleaner should be used to flush the dust into a drain pan. After the clutch components are wiped clean with rags, dispose of the contaminated rags and cleaner in a sealed, marked container.*

1    Remove the transaxle (see Chapter 7, Part A).

2    Disengage the ends of the wire retainer and detach the release bearing from the fork **(see illustration)**.

**8**

**4.2  Before you remove the release bearing, note how it's retained by the spring clip, then slide it off the input shaft**

**4.4a  To remove the release shaft and fork, pry off this E-clip . . .**

**4.4b  . . . slide the shaft out far enough to pull out the housing . . .**

3    Hold the center of the bearing and turn the outer portion while applying pressure. If it doesn't turn smoothly or if it's noisy, install a new one. It's a good idea to replace it anyway, when you consider the time and effort spent on removing the transaxle. However, if you elect to reinstall the old bearing, wipe it off with a clean rag. Don't immerse the bearing in solvent - it's sealed for life and would be ruined by the solvent.

4    Check the release fork ends for excessive wear. If the fork must be replaced, remove the E-clip from the clutch release shaft, slide the shaft out of the clutch housing and remove the fork **(see illustrations)**.

5    If the shaft bushings are worn, replace them.

6    Lubricate the release shaft bushings with high-temperature grease, slide the shaft part way into the housing and hold the fork in position. Continue to slide the shaft into place, through the fork, until it seats in the inner bushing.

7    Install the E-clip in the shaft groove. Make sure it's seated correctly.

8    Lubricate the release fork ends with a small amount of high-temperature grease (don't overdo it). Lubricate the release bearing bore with the same grease.

9    Install the release bearing on the fork. Make sure the wire retainer is properly engaged.

10    Install the transaxle.

## 5    Clutch components - removal, inspection and installation

**Warning:** *Dust produced by clutch wear and deposited on clutch components may contain asbestos, which is a health hazard. DO NOT blow it out with compressed air or inhale any of it. DO NOT use gasoline or petroleum-based solvents to clean off the dust. Brake system cleaner should be used to flush the dust into a drain pan. After the clutch components are wiped clean with rags, dispose of the contaminated rags and cleaner in a sealed, marked container.*

### Removal

*Refer to illustration 5.6*

1    Access to the clutch components is normally accomplished by removing the transaxle, leaving the engine in the vehicle. Of course, if the engine is being removed for major overhaul, then check the clutch for wear and replace worn components as necessary. However, the relatively low cost of the clutch components, compared to the time and trouble spent gaining access to them, warrants their replacement anytime the engine or transaxle is removed (unless they're new or in near perfect condition). The following procedures are based on the assumption the engine will stay in place.

2    Referring to Chapter 7, Part A, remove the transaxle from the vehicle. Support the engine while the transaxle is out. Preferably, an engine hoist should be used to support it from above. However, if a jack is used underneath the engine, make sure a piece of wood is

**4.4c  . . . slide off the fork and remove the shaft**

positioned between the jack and oil pan to spread the load. **Caution:** *The pick-up for the oil pump is very close to the bottom of the oil pan. If the pan is bent or distorted in any way, engine oil starvation could occur.*

3    The clutch release fork and release bearing can remain attached to the transaxle housing (see Section 4 for the procedures to follow when checking and replacing the release bearing and related components).

4    To support the clutch disc during removal, install a clutch alignment tool through the clutch disc hub.

5    Carefully inspect the flywheel and pressure plate for indexing marks. The marks are usually an X, an O or a white letter. If they can't be found, scribe marks yourself so the pressure plate and flywheel will be in the same alignment during installation.

6    Loosen the pressure plate-to-flywheel bolts a little at a time, following a criss-cross pattern, until all spring pressure is relieved. Hold the pressure plate in place and remove the bolts, then detach the pressure plate and clutch disc **(see illustration)**.

### Inspection

*Refer to illustrations 5.9 and 5.11*

7    Ordinarily, when a problem occurs in the clutch, it can be attributed to wear of the clutch disc. However, all components should be inspected at this time. **Note:** *If the clutch components are contaminated with oil, there will be shiny, black, glazed spots on the clutch disc lining, which will cause the clutch to slip. Replacing clutch components won't completely solve the problem - be sure to check the crankshaft rear oil seal and the transaxle input shaft/mainshaft seal for leaks. If it looks like a seal is leaking, be sure to install a new one to avoid the same problem with a new clutch.*

8    Inspect the flywheel for cracks, heat checking, grooves and other obvious defects. If the imperfections are slight, a machine shop can machine the surface flat and smooth, which is highly recommended

**5.6 An exploded view of the clutch components**

UPPER COVER

FLYWHEEL ASSEMBLY

COVER DOWEL (3)

CRANKSHAFT BOLT (6)

BOLT

ENGINE

DOWEL (2)

SCREW AND WASHER ASSEMBLY

CLUTCH DISC

CLUTCH COVER AND PRESSURE PLATE ASSEMBLY

regardless of the surface appearance. Refer to Chapter 2, Part A, for the Flywheel removal and installation procedure.

9    Inspect the lining on the clutch disc. There should be at least 1/32-inch of lining above the rivet heads. Check for loose rivets, distortion, cracks, broken springs and other obvious damage **(see illustration)**. As mentioned above, ordinarily the clutch disc is routinely replaced, so if in doubt about its condition, replace it with a new one.

10    The release bearing should also be replaced along with the clutch disc (see Section 4).

11    Check the machined surface and the diaphragm spring fingers of the pressure plate **(see illustration)**. If the surface is scored or otherwise damaged, replace the pressure plate. Also check for obvious damage, distortion, cracks, etc. Light glazing can be removed with emery cloth. If the pressure plate must be replaced, new and factory-rebuilt units are available.

**5.9 The clutch disc**

1    *Lining* - will wear down in use
2    *Rivets* - secure the lining and will damage the pressure plate or flywheel surface if allowed to contact it
3    *Marks* - "flywheel side" or something similar

## Installation

*Refer to illustration 5.13*

12    Before installation, clean the flywheel and pressure plate machined surfaces with lacquer thinner, acetone or brake system cleaner. It's important to keep these surfaces, and the clutch disc lining, clean and free of oil or grease. Handle the parts only with clean hands.

13    Position the clutch disc and pressure plate against the flywheel with the clutch held in place with an alignment tool **(see illustration)**.

NORMAL FINGER WEAR

EXCESSIVE WEAR

EXCESSIVE FINGER WEAR

EXCESSIVE WEAR

EXCESSIVE FINGER WEAR

BROKEN OR BENT FINGERS

EXCESSIVE SCORING

CLUTCH CHATTER

**5.11 Replace the pressure plate if excessive wear or damage is noted**

PRESSURE PLATE

DOWELS (3)

CLUTCH DISC ALIGNMENT TOOL C-4676

FLYWHEEL

**5.13 Use an alignment tool to center the clutch disc, then tighten the pressure plate bolts**

**8**

**WELDED CONSTRUCTION**  **CITROEN**  **INNER BOOT**
1 2 3 4

**ANGLE**  **OUTER BOOT**
1 2 3 4

**EXPOSED BOOT RETENTION COLLAR**

**ONE PIECE "TRIPLE RAIL" EXTRUSION**  **A.C.I.**  **INNER BOOT**
1 2 3 4

**ANGLE**  **OUTER BOOT**  **RADIUS**
1 2 3 4

**THREE PIECE CONSTRUCTION (OPEN TULIP)**  **G.K.N. OPEN TULIP 69/92**
1 2 3 4

**6.4 Use this chart to identify the driveaxles**
1 2 3

**ONE PIECE ROUND EXTRUSION (CLOSED TULIP)**  **G.K.N. CLOSED TULIP 82/98**  **INNER BOOT**
1 2 3 4

**OUTER BOOT**  **RADIUS**
1 2 3

**ONE PIECE ROUND EXTRUSION (CLOSED TULIP)**  **S.S.G.**
1 2 3 4 5

**OUTER BOOT**  **ANGLE**
1 2 3 4 5 6

Make sure it's installed properly (most replacement clutch plates will be marked "flywheel side" or something similar - if it's not marked, install the clutch disc with the damper springs toward the transaxle).

14   Tighten the pressure plate-to-flywheel bolts only finger tight, working around the pressure plate.

15   Center the clutch disc by ensuring the alignment tool extends through the splined hub and into the pocket in the crankshaft. Wiggle the tool up, down or side-to-side as needed to center the disc. Tighten the pressure plate-to-flywheel bolts a little at a time, working in a criss-cross pattern to prevent cover distortion. After all the bolts are snug, tighten them to the torque listed in this Chapter's Specifications. Remove the alignment tool.

16   Using high-temperature grease, lubricate the release bearing (see Section 4). Also apply a light coat of grease on the release lever

contact areas and the transaxle input shaft.

17   Install the clutch release bearing as described in Section 4.

18   Install the transaxle and all components removed previously. Tighten all fasteners to the proper torque specifications.

## 6   Driveaxles - general information and inspection

### General information

*Refer to illustration 6.4*

Power from the engine passes through the clutch and transaxle to the front wheels via two driveaxles. Models covered by this manual are equipped with unequal-length driveaxles.

**7.1 Have an assistant apply the brakes while you loosen the hub nut (but if you're alone, use a large screwdriver or pry bar to immobilize the hub)**

**7.2a  The driveaxle retaining circlips (arrows) are difficult to see and may be hard to reach with a pair of pliers**

**7.2b  Compress the circlip tangs while pushing the shaft into the differential side gear**

**7.7  Swing the steering knuckle away from the transaxle and pull out the driveaxle**

Each driveaxle assembly consists of three parts: A "tripod" type inner CV joint, an "Rzeppa" type outer CV joint and an axleshaft which connects the two. Outer CV joint housings have a splined stub axle which engages with the front hub and is retained by a large nut. Inner CV joint housings have a short, splined stub axle which engages with the differential side gear. The inner splined end of the CV joint housing is held in place by a spring inside the CV joint housing which pushes the housing toward the transaxle, keeping the stub axle fully seated in the differential side gears.

As the driveaxles move through their range of travel, ball bearings inside the CV joint housings allow them to operate at various lengths and angles. These bearings must be lubricated with special grease and protected by rubber boots. You should periodically inspect these boots for tears and/or grease leaking out. Torn boots allow dirt and moisture to enter the CV joints; if not fixed, a simple tear accelerates bearing wear and eventually causes premature failure.

The vehicles covered by this manual can be equipped with driveaxles manufactured by ACI, Citroen, GKN, or SSG **(see illustration)**. If, after referring to the illustration, you're still unable to determine the manufacturer, take the driveaxle assembly with you when buying boots or CV joint parts. Don't try to substitute one brand of driveaxle for another or swap parts from one brand to another.

## Inspection

Periodically, inspect the boots for leaks, damage and deterioration (see Chapter 1). Replace damaged CV joint boots immediately or the CV joints may be damaged. You must remove the driveaxle (see Section 7) to replace the boots. Some auto parts stores carry a convenient alternative: "Split-type" replacement boots can be installed without removing

the driveaxle from the vehicle. This design is handy for emergency repairs when you're traveling, but it's not a substitute for one-piece boots. When a boot is torn, you must remove the driveaxle and disassemble, clean and inspect the CV joint to make sure no moisture and dirt - which greatly accelerate bearing wear - have already caused damage.

The most common symptom of worn or damaged CV joints, besides lubricant leaks, is a clicking noise in turns, a clunk when accelerating from a coasting condition or vibration at highway speeds. To check for wear in the CV joints and driveaxle shafts, grasp each axle (one at a time) and rotate it in both directions while holding the CV joint housings. Watch for movement, indicating worn splines or sloppy CV joints. Also, check the driveaxle shafts for cracks and distortion.

## 7  Driveaxles - removal and installation

### Removal

*Refer to illustrations 7.1, 7.2a, 7.2b, 7.7 and 7.8*

1    Remove the wheel cover (or hub cover). Remove the front hub nut cotter pin, nut lock and wave washer, if equipped. With the weight of the vehicle on the wheels, loosen the hub nut. Loosen the wheel lug nuts, raise the front of the vehicle and support it securely on jackstands (apply the parking brake and block the rear wheels). Remove the lug nuts, the front wheel, the hub nut and the big washer. **Note:** *On some vehicles the socket for the hub nut won't fit through the wheel's center hole, and the hub nut must be removed with the vehicle on jackstands and the front wheels off* **(see illustration)**.

2    On 1982 and earlier models with an automatic transaxle, the inner ends of the driveaxle are retained by circlips which must be released before the driveaxle can be removed. Drain the differential (see Chapter 1), remove the differential cover and rotate the driveaxle to expose the circlip tangs **(see illustration)**. Compress the circlip tangs with a pair of needle-nose pliers and use a screwdriver to push the axleshaft into the splined cavity of the side gear **(see illustration)**. Pull the axle out slightly.

3    If you're removing the right driveaxle, remove the speedometer drive gear (see Chapter 7) prior to removing the right axle.

4    Remove the steering knuckle-to-balljoint clamp bolt (see Chapter 10).

5    Disconnect the stabilizer bar from the suspension arm to allow enough movement to separate the balljoint (see Chapter 10).

6    Pry the lower balljoint stud out of the steering knuckle (see Chapter 10).

7    Grasp the outer CV joint and the steering knuckle and pull the steering knuckle out to separate the driveaxle from the hub **(see illustration)**. Be careful not to damage the CV joint boot. **Caution:** *Don't pry on or damage the wear sleeve on the CV joint when separating it from the hub.*

**8**

**7.8 Pry the inner end of the CV joint out of the differential side gears with a large screwdriver or prybar**

8   Pry the inner end of the CV joint out of the differential (or intermediate shaft) with a large screwdriver or prybar **(see illustration)**.

9   The driveaxles, when in place, secure the hub bearing assemblies. If the vehicle must be supported or moved on the front wheels while the driveaxles are out, install bolts through the hubs and thread nuts onto them to keep the bearings from loosening.

## Installation

10   Prior to installation, clean the wear sleeve on the driveaxle outer CV joint and the seal in the hub. Lubricate the entire circumference of the seal lip and fill the seal cavity with grease. Apply a 1/4-inch bead of grease to the wear sleeve seal contact area as well.

11   Apply a small amount of multi-purpose grease to the splines at each end of the driveaxle. Place the driveaxle in position and carefully insert the inner end of the shaft into the transaxle.

**7.21 Measure the distance between arrows to verify that the driveaxle is the correct length when installed**

12   Push the steering knuckle out and insert the outer splined shaft of the CV joint into the hub.

13   Insert the balljoint stud into the steering knuckle, install the clamp bolt and tighten it to the torque listed in the Chapter 10 Specifications. **Caution:** *This is a self-locking bolt. If it's worn, replace it with an equivalent new bolt. Don't use an ordinary bolt.*

14   Reattach the stabilizer bar (see Chapter 10).

15   Install the speedometer drive gear (see Chapter 7).

16   Install the wheels and hand tighten the wheel lug nuts. Install the spacer washer and hub nut and tighten the nut securely (don't try to tighten it to the specified torque yet).

17   Lower the vehicle and tighten the wheel lug nuts to the torque listed in the Chapter 1 Specifications.

18   Tighten the driveaxle hub nut to the torque listed in this Chapter's Specifications, then install the wave washer, nut lock and a new cotter pin.

## Driveaxle position check

*Refer to illustration 7.21*

19   All models have engine mounts with slotted holes that allow for side-to-side positioning of the engine. If the vertical bolts on the right or left upper engine mounts have been loosened for any reason, or if the vehicle has been damaged structurally at the front end, driveaxle length must be checked/corrected. A driveaxle that's shorter than required will result in objectionable noise, while a driveaxle that's longer than necessary may result in damage.

**8.3 An exploded view of a typical driveaxle assembly**

**8.4  Carefully pry up on the retainer ring at each bearing roller to disassemble a Citroen driveaxle inner CV joint**

20    The vehicle must be completely assembled, the front wheels must be properly aligned and pointing straight ahead and the weight of the vehicle must be on all four wheels.

21    Using a tape measure, check the distance from the inner edge on the outside of the boot to the inner edge of inside the boot on both driveaxles. Take the measurement at the lower edge of the driveaxles (six o'clock position) **(see illustration)**. Compare the measurement with the length listed in this Chapter's Specifications. Note that the required dimension varies with transaxle type and driveaxle manufacturer **(see illustration 6.4** to identify the driveaxle type).

22    If the dimensions aren't as specified, the mount bolts can be loosened and the engine repositioned to obtain the specified driveaxle lengths. If the engine can't be moved enough within the range of the slotted engine mounts, check for damaged or distorted support brackets and side rails.

23    If the engine is moved, see Chapter 7 and adjust the shift linkage.

## 8    Constant velocity (CV) joints - disassembly, inspection and reassembly

1    Loosen the hub nut and the wheel lug nuts, then raise the vehicle and support it securely on jackstands. Remove the driveaxles (see Section 7) and identify which types of CV joints are installed (see Section 6).

2    Place one of the driveaxles in a vise, using wood blocks to protect it from the vise jaws. If the CV joint has been operating properly with no noise or vibration, replace the boot as described in Section 9. If the CV

**8.5  To separate the tripod from the housing on a GKN inner CV joint, bend up the retaining tabs with a pair of pliers**

joint is badly worn or has run for some time with no lubricant due to a damaged boot, it should be disassembled and inspected.

### Inner CV joint
*Refer to illustrations 8.3 through 8.6, 8.7a, 8.7b, 8.9, 8.10a, 8.10b, 8.11, 8.14, 8.16, 8.17, 8.18, 8.22, 8.24a, 8.24b, 8.24c, 8.25a and 8.25b*

3    Remove the clamps and slide the boot back to gain access to the tripod **(see illustration)**. Depending on the type of CV joint involved, separate the tripod from the housing as follows.

4    Citroen driveaxles utilize a tripod retainer ring which is rolled into a groove in the housing. Slightly deform the retainer ring at each roller with a screwdriver **(see illustration)**. The retention spring will push the housing from the tripod. The retainer can also be cut carefully from the housing. New rings are included in the rebuild kit and can be installed by rolling the edge into the machined groove in the housing with a hammer and punch.

5    On GKN driveaxles, the retaining tabs are an integral part of the housing cover. Hold the housing and lightly compress the retention spring while bending the tabs back with a pair of pliers **(see illustration)**. Support the housing as the retention spring pushes it off the tripod. This will prevent the housing from reaching an unacceptable angle and keep the tripod rollers from being pulled from the tripod studs.

6    On SSG driveaxles, the tripod is retained in the housing with a wire ring which expands into a groove around the top of the housing. Using a screwdriver, pry this ring out of the groove **(see illustration)** and slide the tripod from the housing.

7    On ACI driveaxles, the tripod retaining tabs are part of the boot retaining collar, which is staked in place. On 1984 models, place the housing in position so that the three rollers are flush with the retaining tabs **(see illustration)**. Pull the housing while angling the joint slightly so that the rollers can be snapped through the tabs, one at a time. Be careful not to angle the joint too far as this could cause the tripod rollers to be pulled from the studs. On 1985 and later models, compress the retaining spring lightly while bending the tabs back with a

**8**

**8.6  To separate the tripod from the housing on an SSG inner CV joint, pry out this expander ring with a screwdriver**

**8.7a  On 1984 ACI driveaxles, align the rollers with the tabs and snap them out, one at a time**

pair of pliers **(see illustration)**. Be sure to support the housing as the spring pushes it off the tripod.

8    When removing the housing from the tripod, hold the rollers in place on the studs to prevent the rollers and needle bearings from falling. After the tripod is out of the housing, secure the rollers in place with tape.

9    On all except later GKN axles, remove the snap-ring **(see illustration)**.

10    On later GKN axles, expand the stop ring, slide it away from the tripod and pry off the circlip **(see illustrations)**.

11    Use a brass punch to drive the bearing and tripod assembly off the splined shaft **(see illustration)**. Loosen the boot clamp and remove the boot from the axle.

12    Clean the grease from the tripod assembly. Check for score marks, wear, corrosion and excessive play. Replace any damaged or worn components. Inspect the inner splined area of the bearing tripod for wear and damage. Replace parts as necessary.

13    Remove all old grease from the housing. Inspect the housing splines, ball races, spring, spring cup and the spherical end of the shaft for wear, damage, nicks and corrosion. Replace parts as necessary.

14    On some driveaxles, such as the Citroen assembly, place the housing in a vise and remove the retainer ring with a pair of pliers **(see illustration)**.

15    Install the new boot on the axle.

16    On ACI and early GKN driveaxles, slide the tripod onto the shaft with the non-chamfered end facing out (next to the snap-ring groove)

**8.7b  To separate the tripod from the housing on a later ACI inner CV joint, compress the spring and bend back each tab with pliers**

**(see illustration)**.

17    On later GKN driveaxles, slide the stop ring into its groove on the driveaxle. Install the tripod with its internally chamfered side toward the stop ring **(see illustration)**, then install the circlip. Try to pull the tripod off the shaft by hand; if it comes off, the circlip isn't properly seated.

18    Citroen and SSG driveaxles are equipped with tripods that can be installed with either end out (both sides are the same). Be sure to install the wire ring tripod retainer on the driveaxle shaft before sliding the tri-

**8.9  The tripod, on all except later GKN driveaxles, is held on the axleshaft by a snap-ring - remove it with a pair of snap-ring pliers**

**8.10a  On later GKN driveaxles, expand the snap-ring that secures the inner end of the tripod and move it back along the axleshaft . . .**

**8.10b  . . . then pry off the circlip with a screwdriver**

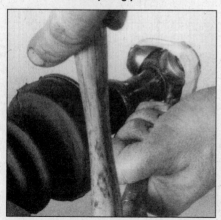

**8.11  Secure the bearings with tape and drive the tripod off the shaft with a brass punch and hammer**

**8.14  Detach the Citroen driveaxle retainer ring with a pair of pliers**

**8.16  On ACI and early GKN CV joints, the non-chamfered end of the tripod must face out when installed on the driveaxle splines**

CHAMFERED SIDE

TRIPOD ASSEMBLY

**8.17  The chamfer must face in on later GKN driveaxles**

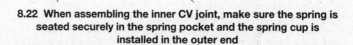

**8.18  Citroen and SSG driveaxles are equipped with tripods that can be installed either way - make sure you tape the bearings as shown to prevent them from falling off during reassembly**

pod onto the shaft **(see illustration)**.

19   If necessary, use a section of pipe or a socket and hammer to carefully tap the tripod onto the shaft until it just clears the snap-ring groove.

20   Install a new snap-ring or circlip and make sure it's seated in the groove.

21   On ACI driveaxles, distribute one of the two supplied packets of grease in the boot and the remaining packet in the housing. On Citroen driveaxles, distribute two-thirds of the grease in the packet on the boot and the remaining amount in the housing. On early GKN driveaxles, distribute two of the three or four packets of grease supplied with the kit in the boot and the remaining packet(s) in the housing. On later GKN and all SSG driveaxles, distribute half the supplied grease in the boot and the other half in the housing. Make sure the grease is applied to the bearing grooves in the housing.

22   Position the spring in the housing spring pocket with the cup attached to the exposed end of the spring **(see illustration)**. Apply a small amount of grease to the concave surface of the spring cup.

23   On early GKN driveaxles, slip the tripod into the housing and bend the retaining ring tabs down to their original positions. Make sure the tabs retain the tripod in the housing. On later GKN driveaxles, secure the shaft in a vise and position the housing over the rollers. Hold the housing at an angle and push it down over each of the tripod rollers in turn so the rollers lock into the housing. Make sure the rollers

SPRING CUP

SPRING POCKET

SPRING

**8.22  When assembling the inner CV joint, make sure the spring is seated securely in the spring pocket and the spring cup is installed in the outer end**

are locked into the housing.

24   On Citroen driveaxles, slide the housing over the tripod until it bottoms **(see illustration)**. Install a new retainer ring by rolling the edge into the machined groove in the housing with a hammer and punch **(see illustration)**. If the retainer ring won't stay in place during this step, hold it with two C-clamps **(see illustration)**. Check the ability of the retainer ring to hold the tripod in the housing.

**8.24a  Make sure the bearing grooves in the housing have been greased, then slide the housing over the tripod until it bottoms**

**8.24b  The new retainer ring should be staked in place with a hammer and punch**

HAMMER

DULL PUNCH

RETENTION GROOVE

CITROEN

**8.24c  If the retainer ring is difficult to hold in place while staking it into the groove, use C-clamps to steady it**

8

**8.25a  On 1984 model ACI driveaxles, snap each roller into place, one at a time**

**8.25b  On 1985 and later ACI driveaxles, press the housing onto the tripod - but don't try to bend the retaining tabs back to their original positions**

25    On 1984 model ACI driveaxles, align the tripod rollers with the retaining tabs and housing tracks and snap one roller at a time through the retaining tabs **(see illustration)**. Make sure the retaining tab holds the tripod securely in the housing. On 1985 and later ACI driveaxles, slip the tripod into the housing but don't bend the retaining tabs **(see illustration)** back to their original positions. Reattach the boot instead, which will hold the housing on the shaft. When the driveaxle is reinstalled on the vehicle, make sure the tripod is re-engaged in the housing.

26    On SSG driveaxles, install the tripod in the housing and secure it with the wire retainer. Try to pull the housing off; the retainer should hold it on.

27    Make sure the retention spring is centered in the housing spring pocket when the tripod is installed and seated in the spring cup.

28    Install the boot and retaining clamp (see Section 9).

## Outer CV joint

*Refer to illustrations 8.30a, 8.30b, 8.30c, 8.34, 8.35, 8.36, 8.37, 8.40, 8.42, 8.43, 8.44a, 8.44b, 8.44c, 8.44d and 8.48*

29    Remove the boot clamps and push the boot back.

30    Wipe the grease out of the joint. Use a soft-face hammer to drive the housing off the axle **(see illustrations)**. Support the CV joint as this is done and rap the housing sharply on the outer edge to dislodge it from the internal circlip installed on the shaft. On SSG driveaxles (axle-shaft equipped with a damper weight), a single circlip located in a groove on the cross locks it to the axleshaft **(see illustration)**. To remove this type, mark the position of the damper weight, loosen the damper weight bolts, slide the weight and the boot toward the inner joint, remove the circlip with snap-ring pliers and slide the inner joint off the axle.

31    Slide the boot off the driveaxle. If the CV joint was operating

**8.30a  On ACI and GKN driveaxles, give the outer CV joint housing a sharp tap with a soft-face hammer to disengage it from the internal circlip installed in a groove on the outer end of the axleshaft**

properly and the grease doesn't appear to be contaminated, just replace the boot (see Section 9). Skip the following disassembly procedure. If the CV joint was noisy or the grease was contaminated, proceed with the disassembly procedure to determine if it should be replaced with a new one.

32    Remove the circlip from the driveaxle groove and discard it (the rebuild kit will include a new circlip). GKN and ACI driveaxles are

**8.30b  Remove the outer CV joint from the housing**

**8.30c  On SSG driveaxles, a single circlip located in a groove in the cross, locks it to the axleshaft**

**8.34  After removing the grease, mark the bearing cage, cross and housing to ensure that they're reinstalled in the same relationship to one another**

**8.35  With the cage and cross tilted like this, remove the ball bearings one at a time**

**8.36  Tilt the cross and cage 90-degrees, then align the windows in the cage with the lands and rotate the cross up and out of the housing**

CAGE WINDOW

BALL RACE

35   Grip the housing shaft securely in the wood blocks in the vise. Push down one side of the cage and remove the ball bearing from the opposite side. Repeat the procedure in a criss-cross pattern until all of the balls are removed **(see illustration)**. If the joint is tight, tap on the cross (not the cage) with a hammer and brass punch.

36   Remove the bearing cage assembly from the housing by tilting it vertically and aligning two opposing elongated cage windows in the area between the ball grooves **(see illustration)**.

37   Turn the cross 90-degrees to the cage and align one of the spherical lands with an elongated cage window. Raise the land into the window and swivel the cross out of the cage **(see illustration)**.

38   Clean all of the parts with solvent and dry them with compressed air (if available).

39   Inspect the housing, splines, balls and races for damage, corrosion, wear and cracks. Check the cross for wear and scoring in the races. If any of the components are not serviceable, the entire CV joint assembly must be replaced with a new one.

40   Check the outer housing wear sleeve for damage and distortion. If it's damaged or worn, pry the sleeve off the housing **(see illustration)** and replace it with a new one. A special tool is available for installing the new sleeve, but a large section of pipe slightly smaller in diameter than the outer edge of the sleeve will work if care is exercised (don't nick or gouge the seal mating surface).

41   Apply a thin coat of oil to all CV joint components before beginning reassembly.

42   Align the marks and install the cross in the cage so one of the lands fits into the elongated window **(see illustration)**.

43   Rotate the cross into position in the cage and install the assembly in the CV joint housing, again using the elongated window for clearance **(see illustration)**.

**8.37  Turn the cross 90-degrees, align the race lands with the cage windows and rotate the race out of the cage**

equipped with a large spacer ring, which must not be removed unless the driveaxle is being replaced with a new one.

33   Clean the axle spline area and check the splines for wear, damage and corrosion.

34   Clean the outer CV joint bearing assembly with a clean cloth to remove excess grease. Mark the relative position of the bearing cage, cross and housing **(see illustration)**.

**8.40  If the wear sleeve (on models so equipped) requires replacement, pry it off the housing with a large screwdriver**

**8.42  The bearing cross will slide into the cage by aligning one of the lands with the elongated window in the cage**

**8.43  Lower the cage and cross assembly into the housing with the elongated window aligned with the race**

8

**8.44a   On GKN and ACI CV joints, make sure the large counterbore faces out when the joint is reassembled**

**8.44b   On Citroen driveaxles, make sure the cross and cage chamfers face OUT when the CV joint is reassembled**

44   Rotate the cage into position in the housing. On GKN and ACI driveaxles, the large counterbore of the cross must face out **(see illustration)**. On Citroen driveaxles, the cage and cross chamfers must face out **(see illustration)**. On SSG driveaxles, the internal circlip in the cross will be facing out from the housing **(see illustration)**. On all driveaxles, make sure the marks made during disassembly face out and are aligned **(see illustration)**.

45   Pack the lubricant from the kit into the ball races and grooves.

46   Install the balls into the elongated holes, one at a time, until they're all in position.

47   Place the driveaxle in the vise and slide the boot over it. On all except SSG driveaxles, install a new circlip in the axle groove, taking care not to twist it. SSG driveaxles have a reusable retainer integral with the driver assembly.

48   Place the CV joint housing in position on the axle, align the splines and rap it sharply with a soft-face hammer **(see illustration)**. Make sure it's seated on the circlip by attempting to pull it off the shaft.

49   Install the boot (see Section 9).

50   Install the driveaxle (see Section 7).

**8.44c   On SSG driveaxles, make sure the internal circlip in the cross is facing out from the housing**

## 9   Constant velocity (CV) joint boots - replacement

**Note:** *If the instructions supplied with the replacement boot kit differ from the instructions here, follow the ones with the new boots. A special tool, available at most auto parts stores, is required to install the factory-supplied boot clamps. Do-it-yourself kits which offer greatly simplified*

**8.44d   Make sure the marks are aligned properly and that the bearing cross is installed with the correct side out (see text for details)**

**8.48   Strike the end of the housing shaft with a soft-face hammer to engage it with the shaft circlip**

9.9  CV joint boot installation details (GKN and ACI)

*installation may be available for your vehicle. Consult an auto parts store or dealer parts department for more information on these kits.*

1    If the boot is cut, torn or leaking, it must be replaced and the CV joint inspected as soon as possible. Even a small amount of dirt in the joint can cause premature wear and failure. Obtain a replacement boot kit before beginning this procedure. There are several different types of boots, each with its own replacement procedure. Compare the boots on your vehicle to the following illustrations to determine which procedure to follow.

2    Remove the driveaxle (see Section 7).

3    Disassemble the CV joint and remove the boot as described in Section 8.

4    Inspect the CV joint to determine if it's been damaged by contamination or running with too little lubricant. If you have any doubts about the condition of the joint components, perform the inspection procedures described in Section 8.

5    Clean the old grease out of the CV joint and repack it with the grease supplied with the kit.

6    Pack the interior of the new boot with the remaining grease.

7    Install the boot and clamps as follows.

## Soft rubber boots

### Earlier boots (except Citroen)

*Refer to illustrations 9.9, 9.11 and 9.12*

8    Earlier boots are usually equipped with metal ladder-type clamps. Two other types of clamps (a small rubber clamp at the axleshaft end of the inner CV joint or a large spring-type clamp) are also used on some models.

9    Slide the small rubber clamp over the shaft. Slide the small end of the boot over the shaft and position it as follows: On right inner joints, the small end of the boot lip must be aligned with the mark on the shaft. On left inner and all outer joints, position the small end of the boot in the groove in the shaft (see illustration).

9.11  Installing a ladder-type boot clamp by hand (GKN driveaxles) - note the rubber clamp installed the small end of the boot

10    Place the rubber clamp in the boot groove (if so equipped) or install the metal clamp.

11    Make sure the boot is properly located on the shaft, then locate the metal clamp tangs in the slots, making the clamp as tight as possible by hand (see illustration).

12    Squeeze the clamp bridge with a special clamp tool (Chrysler tool no. C-4124 or equivalent) to complete the tightening procedure (see illustration). Do not cut through the clamp bridge or damage the rubber boot.

13    Reassemble the CV joints and driveaxle components (see Section 8).

14    Locate the large end of the boot over the shoulder or in the groove in the housing (make sure the boot isn't twisted).

15    Install the spring-type clamp or ladder-type clamp. If a ladder-type clamp is used, repeat the tightening procedure described above in Steps 11 and 12.

### Citroen and later GKN, SSG and ACI driveaxles (except SSG right inner joint)

*Refer to illustrations 9.18, 9.19, 9.21a, 9.21b, 9.22, 9.23a and 9.23b*

16    Slide the small end of the boot over the shaft and align it with the locating mark or groove (see illustration 9.9).

17    Place the large diameter of the boot in the groove (see illustration 9.9). Note: *Clamping procedures are identical for attaching the boot to the shaft and the CV joint housing.*

18    Wrap the clamping strap around the boot twice, plus 2-1/2 inches, and cut it off (see illustration).

9.12  Squeeze the ladder-type boot clamp bridge with the special tool as shown

9.18  Wrap the clamp around the boot twice, leaving about 2-1/2 inches of extra material, then cut off the excess

8

**9.19  Pass the strap around the buckle and fold it back about 1-1/8 inch on the inside of the buckle**

**9.21b  Attach the special boot clamp tool about 1/2-inch from the buckle . . .**

**9.21a  Install the strap on the boot and bend it back so it can't unwind**

**9.22  . . . then push the tool forward and up to engage the tool hook in the buckle eye**

19    Pass the end of the strap through the buckle opening and fold it back about 1-1/8 inch on the inside of the buckle **(see illustration)**.

20    Position the clamping strap around the boot, on the clamping surface, with the eye of the buckle facing you. Wrap the strap around the boot once and pass it through the buckle, then wrap it around a second time and pass it through the buckle again.

21    Fold the strap back slightly to prevent it from unwinding itself **(see illustration)**. Then using a special boot clamp tool (Chrysler tool no.C-4653 or equivalent), place the strap in the narrow slot about 1/2-inch from the buckle **(see illustration)**.

22    Hold the strap with one hand and push the tool forward and up slightly, then fit the tool hook into the buckle eye **(see illustration)**.

23    Tighten the strap by closing the tool handles, then rotate the tool down slowly while releasing the pressure on the handles **(see illustra-**

tions). Allow the handles to open progressively, then open the tool all the way and slide it sideways off the strap. **Caution:** *Never fold the strap back or rotate the tool down while squeezing the handles together (if this is done, the strap will break).*

24    If the strap isn't tight enough, repeat the procedure. Always engage the tool about 1/2-inch from the buckle. Make sure the strap moves smoothly as tightening force is applied and don't allow the buckle to fold over as the strap passes through it.

25    When the strap is tight, cut it off 1/8-inch above the buckle and fold it back neatly. It must not overlap the edge of the buckle.

26    Repeat the procedure for the remaining boot clamps.

### SSG right inner CV joint only

*Refer to illustrations 9.28, 9.31a and 9.31b*

27    Slip the clamp for the small end of the boot onto the driveaxle shaft.

28    Slip the boot onto the shaft and position it on the flat between the

**9.23a  Close the tool handles slowly to tighten the clamp strap . . .**

**9.23b  . . . then rotate the tool down while releasing the pressure on the handles (allow the handles to open)**

9.28  Position the edge of the boot on the flat between the locating shoulders, then secure it with the clamp

9.31b . . . then place the prongs of the special tool in the holes in the clamp and compress the tool until the two ends meet

9.31a  Install the large clamp as shown . . .

9.33  Position the lip of the boot in the third groove on the axleshaft

9.35  Because the clamps used with hard plastic boots must generate approximately 100 times the clamping force of those used with rubber boots, this special tool is necessary to crimp the clamps securely

locating shoulders **(see illustration)**.

29   Slip the small clamp over the boot and crimp it with a special boot clamp tool (Chrysler tool no. C-4124 or equivalent).

30   Install the CV joint (see Section 8).

31   Install the large end of the boot and position its clamp around the boot. Tighten the clamp with a special boot clamp tool (Chrysler tool no. C4124 [automatic transaxle], YA-3050 [manual transaxle] or equivalent) **(see illustrations)**.

## Hard plastic boots (SSG left inner and both outer CV joints)

*Refer to illustrations 9.33 and 9.35*

32   Slip the clamp for the small end of the boot onto the driveaxle shaft.

33   Slip the boot onto the shaft and position its lip in the third locating groove, nearest the center of the driveaxle shaft **(see illustration)**.

34   Center the clamp over the end of the boot **(see illustration 9.33)**.

35   Install a special boot clamp crimping tool (Chrysler tool no. C-4579 or equivalent) on the clamp bridge **(see illustration)**. Tighten the tool until its jaws touch each other.

36   Release the crimping tool.

37   Install the CV joint (see Section 8).

38   Place the large end of the boot over the CV joint housing. Install and secure the clamp (see Steps 27 through 29).

**8**

# Notes

# Chapter 9  Brakes

## Contents

## Specifications

| | |
|---|---|
| Brake fluid type | See Chapter 1 |

### Disc brakes

| | |
|---|---|
| Brake pad wear limit | See Chapter 1 |
| Minimum disc thickness | See specifications cast into disc |
| Disc runout (maximum) | 0.004 inch |
| Hub runout | 0.003 inch |
| Disc thickness (parallelism) variation limit | 0.0005 inch |

### Drum brakes

| | |
|---|---|
| Brake shoe wear limit | See Chapter 1 |
| Drum | |
| Maximum diameter | See specifications cast into drum |
| Runout (maximum) | 0.006 inch |
| Out-of-round (maximum) | |
| In 30-degrees | 0.0025 inch |
| In 360-degrees | 0.0035 inch |

### Torque specifications

| | Ft-lbs (unless otherwise indicated) |
|---|---|
| Master cylinder-to-booster (or firewall) nuts | 17 |
| Power brake booster-to-firewall nuts | 17 |
| Caliper guide pin(s) | |
| ATE | 18 to 22 |
| Kelsey-Hayes | 25 to 35 |
| Caliper mounting bracket-to-steering knuckle bolts | |
| 1981 and 1982 | 70 to 100 |
| 1983 through 1989 | 130 to 190 |
| Brake hose-to-caliper inlet fitting bolt | 19 to 29 |
| Wheel cylinder-to-brake backing plate bolts | 75 in-lbs |

**9**

**1.2a ATE disc brake**

**1.2b Kelsey-Hayes single-pin disc brake**

**1.2c Kelsey-Hayes double-pin disc brake**

## 1   General information

*Refer to illustrations 1.2a, 1.2b and 1.2c*

All models are equipped with hydraulically operated disc front brakes. Rear drum brakes are standard on all models.

The front brakes use a single-piston, floating caliper design. Disc brake calipers from two manufacturers - ATE and Kelsey-Hayes - are used on the vehicles covered by this manual. They differ in design, so parts are not interchangeable. ATE calipers have two guide pins, while some Kelsey-Hayes calipers have two guide pins and some have only one guide pin **(see illustrations)**. 1981 and 1982 models are equipped with ATE calipers; 1983 through 1985 models are equipped with either ATE calipers or single-pin Kelsey-Hayes calipers; 1986 through 1988 models are equipped with either ATE calipers, Kelsey-Hayes single pin or Kelsey-Hayes double-pin calipers; 1989 models are equipped with either Kelsey-Hayes single pin or Kelsey-Hayes double-pin calipers.

The rear drum brakes are a leading/trailing design with automatic adjustment. 1981 and 1982 models share one design, while 1983 and later models are slightly different.

Front-wheel drive vehicles tend to wear the front brake pads at a faster rate than rear-drive vehicles. Consequently, it's very important to inspect the brake pads frequently to make sure they haven't worn to the point where the disc itself is scored or damaged. Note that the pad thickness limit on these models includes the metal portion of the brake pad, not just the lining material (see Chapter 1).

The hydraulic system consists of two separate circuits. The master cylinder has a separate section in the reservoir for each circuit. In the event of a leak or failure in one hydraulic circuit, the other circuit will remain operative.

All models are equipped with a cable-actuated parking brake, which operates the rear brakes, by expanding the brake shoes.

## 2   Disc brake pads - replacement

**Warning:** *Disc brake pads must be replaced on both front wheels at the same time - never replace the pads on only one wheel. Also, the dust created by the brake system may contain asbestos, which is harmful to your health. Never blow it out with compressed air and don't inhale any of it. An approved filtering mask should be worn when working on the brakes. Do not, under any circumstances, use petroleum-based solvents to clean brake parts. Use brake system cleaner only!*

1   Raise the front of the vehicle and support it securely on jackstands. Block the rear wheels and apply the parking brake, then remove the front wheels. **Note:** *If you're not sure what kind of disc brake you have, refer to illustrations 1.2a, 1.2b and 1.2c.* Wash the dust from the brake assembly with brake system cleaner.

### Single-pin Kelsey-Hayes caliper

*Refer to illustrations 2.2a, 2.2b, 2.3, 2.4 and 2.6*

2   Remove the caliper guide pin **(see illustration)**, swing up the lower end of the caliper and pull it off the caliper mounting bracket **(see illustration)**.

3   Support the caliper out of the way with a wire hanger **(see illustration)**. **Warning:** *Don't allow the caliper to hang by the brake hose!*

4   Detach the outer brake pad from the caliper mounting bracket **(see illustrations)**. Remove the anti-rattle spring from the bottom of the pad and install it on the new outer pad.

5   Remove the brake disc (see Section 4).

6   Detach the inner brake pad **(see illustration)**. Remove the anti-rattle spring from the top of the inner pad and install it on the new inner pad.

7   Inspect the caliper and caliper mounting bracket for wear, damage, rust and evidence of fluid leaks. If the caliper-to-bracket mating surfaces are rusty, clean them thoroughly with a wire brush (the caliper

2.2a  To get at the pads on a Kelsey-Hayes single-pin caliper, remove the guide pin . . .

2.3  Hang the caliper out of the way on a piece of wire - DO NOT let it hang by the brake hose!

2.6  Slide the inner pad off the mounting bracket, then remove the anti-rattle clip from the top of the pad and transfer it to the new pad

2.2b  . . . and pivot the caliper up off the mounting bracket (pry it loose from the bracket if necessary) - note the anti-rattle clip at the top of the caliper

2.4a  To remove the outer pad from a Kelsey-Hayes single-pin caliper, simply pull it straight off - then remove the anti-rattle spring clip at the bottom of the pad and transfer it to the new outer pad

must be able to move freely when the brakes are applied). Also inspect the brake disc (see Section 4).

8    Siphon some brake fluid from the master cylinder reservoir, or place rags or newspapers underneath the reservoir to catch the overflow that will occur when the piston is pushed back to make room for the new pads. Then use a piece of wood to carefully push the piston into the caliper bore far enough to provide clearance for the new pads.

9    Apply a thin film of high-temperature brake grease to the adapter-to-brake pad and caliper mating surfaces. **Caution:** *Don't get any grease on the pad lining material, gasket surface or brake disc.*

10    Remove the protective paper from the noise suppression gasket on both pads. Install the inner brake pad, making sure the anti-rattle spring is secure.

11    Install the brake disc (see Section 4).

12    Place the outer pad in position in the caliper mounting bracket. Make sure the anti-rattle spring is secure.

13    Slide the caliper into position over the pads and disc. Be sure the anti-rattle clip is engaged correctly.

**9**

**2.18 To get at the pads on a Kelsey-Hayes double-pin caliper, remove the two guide pins**

**2.19 Work the hold-down spring out from under the machined abutment and remove the caliper together with the pads**

14   Install the guide pin and tighten it to the torque listed in this Chapter's Specifications. Don't cross-thread the guide pin during installation.

15   Repeat Steps 2 through 14 for the other caliper.

16   Install the wheel and lug nuts, tightening them securely. Lower the vehicle and tighten the lug nuts to the torque listed in the Chapter 1 Specifications.

17   Pump the brake pedal several times to bring the pads into contact with the disc. Check the brake fluid level (see Chapter 1) and top it up, if necessary. Drive the vehicle in an isolated area and make several stops to wear off any foreign material on the pads and seat them on the disc.

## Double-pin Kelsey-Hayes caliper

*Refer to illustrations 2.18, 2.19, 2.20, 2.21, 2.26a and 2.26b*

18   Remove the caliper guide pins **(see illustration)**.

19   Pivot the bottom of the caliper away from the brake disc and lift it off **(see illustration)**, together with the brake pads. **Warning:** *Once the caliper is off, don't let it hang by the brake hose! Support it by hand while removing the pads, then hang it from the coil spring with a length of wire* **(see illustration 2.3)**.

20   Pry the outer pad away from the caliper **(see illustration)**.

21   Remove the inner pad by pulling it straight away from the piston **(see illustration)**.

22   Inspect the caliper and caliper mounting bracket for wear, damage, rust and evidence of fluid leaks. If the caliper-to-bracket mating surfaces are rusty, clean them thoroughly with a wire brush (the caliper

must be able to move freely when the brakes are applied). Also inspect the brake disc (see Section 4).

23   Siphon some brake fluid from the master cylinder reservoir, or place rags or newspapers underneath the reservoir to catch the overflow that will occur when the piston is pushed back to make room for the new pads. Then use a piece of wood to carefully push the piston into the caliper bore far enough to provide clearance for the new pads.

24   Apply a thin film of high-temperature brake grease to the adapter-to-brake pad and caliper mating surfaces. **Caution:** *Don't get any grease on the pad lining material, gasket surface or brake disc.*

25   Install the inner pad by pressing the retainer into the piston recess.

26   Select the correct outer pad for the side of the vehicle you're working on by referring to the identification marks **(see illustration)**. Remove the protective paper from the noise suppression gasket (if equipped) and install the pad on the caliper **(see illustration)**.

27   Install the caliper on the steering knuckle and position the hold-down spring under the steering knuckle abutment **(see illustration 2.19)**.

28   Repeat Steps 18 through 27 for the other caliper.

29   Perform Steps 16 and 17 to complete the installation.

**2.20 Pry the outer pad loose from the caliper with a screwdriver**

**2.21 To disengage the retainer spring (on the back of the inner pad) from the piston, pull the inner pad straight out**

**INBOARD SHOE ASSEMBLY
(RIGHT AND LEFT COMMON)**

**OUTBOARD SHOE ASSEMBLY
(RIGHT SIDE SHOWN)**

**2.26a** Inner pads on Kelsey-Hayes calipers are interchangeable; outer pads must be installed on the proper side of the vehicle - the pads are marked to indicate the correct side

**OUTBOARD SHOE ASSEMBLY**

**CALIPER**

**2.26b** Work the pad onto the caliper and engage the pad retainer spring with the caliper body

**2.30** Use two screwdrivers to lift the outer ends of the hold-down spring while lifting the center portion from the caliper

**2.31** Unscrew the caliper pins . . .

## ATE caliper

*Refer to illustrations 2.30, 2.31, 2.32, 2.33 and 2.34*

30   Pry off the caliper hold-down spring **(see illustration)**.

31   Loosen the caliper pins enough to permit removal of the caliper **(see illustration)**. It isn't necessary to pull them completely out of their bushings.

32   Lift the caliper off of the brake disc **(see illustration)**. The inner pad will remain with the caliper. Siphon some brake fluid from the master cylinder reservoir, or place rags or newspapers underneath the reservoir to catch the overflow that will occur when the piston is pushed back to make room for the new pads. Then use a piece of wood to carefully push the piston into the caliper bore far enough to provide clearance for the new pads.

33   Unsnap the inner pad from the caliper piston **(see illustration)**. Hang the caliper from the suspension spring using a piece of wire - don't let it hang by the brake hose.

34   Remove the outer pad from the the caliper adapter **(see illustration)**.

**2.32** Remove the caliper . . .

**2.33** . . . and pull the inner pad out to disengage it from the piston

**2.34** Remove the outer pad from the adapter

9

**3.2 Place some shop rags or newspapers under the brake hose inlet fitting bore, then plug it to prevent contamination right after you disconnect it**

**3.6 Place a piece of wood between the caliper and the piston, then force the piston out of the caliper bore with compressed air - be sure to keep your hands and fingers out of the way during this procedure**

**3.7 Use a screwdriver to pry the dust boot out of the cylinder bore**

35    Inspect the caliper for rust and leaking fluid. Also inspect the brake disc (see Section 4).

36    Attach the inner pad to the caliper by pressing the retainer into the piston recess.

37    Place the outer pad into position in the caliper adapter.

38    Install the caliper over the brake disc and pad.

39    Install the guide pins and tighten them to the torque listed in this Chapter's Specifications.

40    Install the hold-down spring.

41    Repeat Steps 30 through 40 for the other caliper.

42    Perform Steps 16 and 17 to complete the installation.

## 3   Brake caliper - removal, overhaul and installation

**Warning:** *Dust created by the brake system may contain asbestos, which is harmful to your health. Never blow it out with compressed air and don't inhale any of it. An approved filtering mask should be worn when working on the brakes. Do not, under any circumstances, use petroleum-based solvents to clean brake parts. Use brake system cleaner only!*

**Note:** *If an overhaul is indicated (usually because of fluid leakage), explore all options before beginning the job. New and factory-rebuilt calipers are available on an exchange basis, which makes this job quite easy. If you decide to rebuild the calipers, make sure a rebuild kit is available before proceeding. Always rebuild the calipers in pairs - never rebuild just one of them.*

### Removal

*Refer to illustration 3.2*

1    Loosen the wheel lug nuts, raise the front of the vehicle and support it securely on jackstands. Remove the front wheels.

2    **Note:** *Don't detach the brake hose from the caliper if you're only removing the caliper to gain access to other components.* If you're removing the caliper for overhaul, unscrew the brake hose inlet fitting bolt and detach the hose **(see illustration)**. Have a rag handy to catch spilled fluid and wrap a plastic bag tightly around the end of the hose to prevent fluid loss and contamination.

3    Remove the caliper guide pin(s) and detach the caliper from the vehicle (see Section 2).

### Overhaul

*Refer to illustrations 3.6, 3.7, 3.8, 3.9a, 3.9b, 3.9c, 3.9d, 3.14 and 3.15*

4    Remove the brake pads (see Section 2).

5    Clean the exterior of the caliper with brake system cleaner. Never use brake fluid, gasoline, kerosene or petroleum-based cleaning

**3.8 Remove the piston seal with a wood pencil or a plastic eating utensil so you don't damage the bore and seal groove**

solvents. Place the caliper on a clean workbench.

6    Position a wooden block or several shop rags in the caliper as a cushion, then use compressed air to remove the piston from the caliper **(see illustration)**. Use only enough air pressure to ease the piston out of the bore. If the piston is blown out, even with the cushion in place, it may be damaged. **Warning:** *Never place your fingers in front of the piston in an attempt to catch or protect it when applying compressed air - serious injury could result!*

7    Carefully pry the dust boot out of the caliper bore **(see illustration)**.

8    Using a wood or plastic tool, remove the piston seal from the groove in the caliper bore **(see illustration)**. Metal tools may damage the bore.

9    Remove the caliper bleeder screw. On double-pin calipers, remove the bushing sleeves. Remove and discard the caliper guide pin bushing(s). Discard all rubber parts **(see illustrations)**.

10    Clean the remaining parts with brake system cleaner.

11    Carefully examine the piston for nicks, burrs and excessive wear. If surface defects are present, the parts must be replaced.

12    Check the caliper bore in a similar way. Light polishing with crocus cloth is permissible to remove light corrosion and stains, but rust or pitting will require caliper replacement.

13    When reassembling the caliper, lubricate the bore and seal with

**3.9a  An exploded view of an ATE caliper**

ADAPTER

HOLD DOWN RETAINER

BOOT

SEAL

PISTON

PAD

PAD

PIN BUSHING

CALIPER

TEFLON SLEEVE

CALIPER PIN

**3.9b  An exploded view of a single-pin Kelsey-Hayes caliper**

OUTBOARD SHOE ASSEMBLY

INBOARD SHOE ASSEMBLY

ADAPTER

CALIPER PIN

DUST BOOT

SEAL

PISTON

CALIPER

BUSHING

**3.9c  An exploded view of a Kelsey-Hayes double-pin caliper**

SHOE ASSEMBLY (OUTBOARD)

SHOE ASSEMBLY (INBOARD)

PISTON

BLEEDER SCREW

CAP

BOLT

BUSHING

SLEEVE

SLEEVE

BUSHING

BOOT

SEAL

CALIPER

BOLT

**9**

**3.9d Grab the ends of the mounting pin bushings with needle-nose pliers and push them through the caliper ears with a twisting motion**

**3.14 When you install the piston, make sure it doesn't become cocked as you push it into its bore in the caliper**

**3.15 If the correct seal tool isn't available, use a hammer and a drift punch to tap around the edge until the dust boot is seated**

clean brake fluid. Position the seal in the caliper bore groove - make sure it isn't twisted.

14   Lubricate the piston with clean brake fluid, install it squarely in the bore and apply pressure to bottom it in the caliper **(see illustration)**.

15   Stretch the dust boot over the groove in the piston, then carefully seat it in the caliper bore **(see illustration)**.

16   Install the bleeder screw.

17   Install new caliper pin bushings and make sure they're centered in their bores. On double-pin calipers, install the bushing sleeves and make sure the bushings engage the sealing grooves in the sleeves.

## Installation

18   Inspect the caliper guide pin(s) for excessive corrosion. Replace them if necessary.

19   Clean the caliper and caliper mounting bracket contact surfaces with a wire brush, then apply a thin film of high-temperature brake grease to them.

20   Install the brake pads and caliper (see Section 2).

21   If it was detached, install the brake hose and inlet fitting bolt, using new copper washers, then tighten the bolt to the torque listed in this Chapter's Specifications.

22   If the line was disconnected, be sure to bleed the brakes (see Section 10).

23   Install the wheels and lower the vehicle. Tighten the lug nuts to the torque listed in the Chapter 1 Specifications.

**4.4a Make sure the lug nuts are in place and evenly tightened, then measure the disc runout with a dial indicator**

24   After the job has been completed, firmly depress the brake pedal a few times to bring the pads into contact with the disc.

25   Check brake operation before driving the vehicle in traffic.

## 4   Brake disc - inspection, removal and installation

1   Loosen the wheel lug nuts, raise the vehicle and support it securely on jackstands. Remove the wheel and reinstall the lug nuts to hold the disc in place. **Note:** *It will be necessary to install washers under the lug nuts to bear against the disc if the lug nuts don't contact the disc when tightened.*

2   Remove the brake caliper (see Section 2). It isn't necessary to disconnect the brake hose. After removing the caliper guide pin(s), suspend the caliper out of the way with a piece of wire. Don't let the caliper hang by the hose and don't stretch or twist the hose. On ATE and single-pin Kelsey-Hayes calipers, remove the outer brake pad from the caliper adapter.

## Inspection

*Refer to illustrations 4.4a, 4.4b, 4.5a and 4.5b*

3   Visually inspect the disc surface for scoring and other damage. Light scratches and shallow grooves are normal after use and may not affect brake operation, but deep score marks require disc removal and refinishing by an automotive machine shop. Be sure to check both sides of the disc. If pulsating has been noticed during application of the brakes, suspect disc runout.

4   To check disc runout, mount a dial indicator with the stem resting about 1/2-inch from the outer edge of the disc **(see illustration)**. Set the indicator to zero and turn the disc. The indicator reading should not exceed the maximum allowable runout listed in this Chapter's Specifications. If it does, the disc should be refinished by an automotive machine shop. **Note:** *Professionals recommend resurfacing of brake discs regardless of the dial indicator reading (to produce a smooth, flat surface that will eliminate brake pedal pulsations and other undesirable symptoms related to questionable discs). At the very least, if you elect not to have the discs resurfaced, deglaze them with sandpaper or emery cloth (use a swirling motion to ensure a non-directional finish)* **(see illustration)**.

5   The disc must not be machined to a thickness less than the minimum listed in this Chapter's Specifications. The minimum wear (or discard) thickness is also cast into the inside of the disc **(see illustration)**. The disc thickness can be checked with a micrometer **(see illustration)**. The disc should also be checked for thickness variations around the circumference with a micrometer, measuring at a number of points around the disc and comparing the results to Specifications. If it does not meet Specifications, it should be machined.

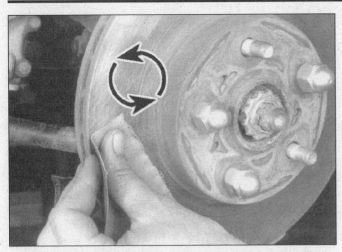

**4.4b  Using a swirling motion, remove the glaze from the disc surface with sandpaper or emery cloth**

**4.5a  The disc can be resurfaced by an automotive machine shop, provided the machining operation doesn't result in a disc thickness less than the minimum stamped on it**

## Removal

*Refer to illustrations 4.6a and 4.6b*

6    Remove the lug nuts you installed to hold the disc in place during inspection. The discs on some models are equipped with retaining washers to prevent them from slipping off while the caliper is removed; if the discs on your vehicle are so equipped, remove the washer **(see illustration)** and discard it. Slide the disc off the threaded studs **(see illustration)**.

## Installation

7    Place the disc in position over the threaded studs.
8    Install the caliper and brake pads (see Section 2). Tighten the caliper guide pin(s) to the torque listed in this Chapter's Specifications.
9    Install the wheel and lug nuts, then lower the vehicle to the ground. Tighten the lug nuts to the torque listed in the Chapter 1 Specifications.
10    Depress the brake pedal a few times to bring the brake pads into contact with the disc. Bleeding of the system isn't necessary unless the brake hose was disconnected from the caliper. Check the operation of the brakes carefully before driving the vehicle in traffic.

## 5    Drum brake shoes (1981 and 1982 models) - replacement

*Refer to illustrations 5.3, 5.4, 5.5, 5.6, 5.7a, 5.7b, 5.8, 5.15, 5.17 and 5.21*

**Warning:** *Drum brake shoes must be replaced on both wheels at the same time - never replace the shoes on only one wheel. Also, the dust created by the brake system may contain asbestos, which is harmful to your health. Never blow it out with compressed air and don't inhale any of it. An approved filtering mask should be worn when working on the brakes. Do not, under any circumstances, use petroleum-based solvents to clean brake parts. Use brake system cleaner only!*

**Caution:** *Whenever the brake shoes are replaced, the retractor and hold-down springs should also be replaced. Due to the continuous heating/cooling cycle that the springs are subjected to, they lose their tension over a period of time any may allow the shoes to drag on the drum and wear at a much faster rate than normal.*

1    Raise the rear of the vehicle, support it securely on jackstands and block the front wheels. Remove the rear wheels.
2    Remove the hub/brake drum assembly as described in Chapter 1, *Rear wheel bearing check, repack and adjustment*. If the drum won't pull off easily, refer to Section 6, Step 2.
3    Use brake system cleaner (only) to remove dust and brake fluid from the shoe assembly components **(see illustration)**.

**4.5b  Measure the disc thickness with a micrometer at several points around its circumference**

**4.6a  If the discs on your vehicle use retaining washers like this, cut them off and discard them**

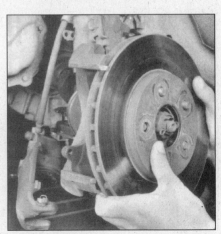

**4.6b  When you remove the disc, make sure you don't damage the threads on the wheel studs**

9

4    Disconnect the parking brake cable from the lever **(see illustration)**.

5    Remove the two lower brake shoe-to-anchor springs **(see illustration)**.

6    Remove the shoe hold-down springs by depressing them and sliding them off the pins **(see illustration)**.

7    Back off the adjuster screw assembly and remove it **(see illustrations)**.

8    Rotate the rear shoe forward and remove it, followed by the leading shoe **(see illustration)**.

9    Check the shoe linings to make sure they indicate full contact with the drum.

10    Check the drum for cracks, score marks and signs of overheating. Measure the inside diameter of the drum and compare it to the size stamped on the drum **(see illustration 6.13)**. Minor imperfections in the drum surface can be removed with fine emery paper. Deep score marks can be removed by having the drum resurfaced by an automotive machine shop (as long as the maximum diameter is not exceeded). Check the drum for runout. Replace the brake drum with a new one if it is not usable.

11    Check the brake springs for signs of discolored paint, indicating overheating, and distorted end coils. Replace them with new ones if necessary.

12    Check the adjuster screw assembly and threads for bent, corroded and damaged components. Replace the assembly if the screw threads are damaged or rusted. Clean the threads and lubricate them with lithium-based grease.

13    Check the wheel cylinder boots for damage and signs of leakage.

14    Rebuild or replace the wheel cylinder if there is any sign of

**5.3  Rear drum brake components (left side shown) (1981 and 1982 models)**

leakage around the boots **(see illustration 6.16)**.

15    Check for rough or rusted shoe contact areas on the backing plate, then lubricate the contact areas with high-temperature grease

**5.4  Pull the parking brake cable to the rear to disengage it from the lever**

**5.5  Hold the parking brake cable out of the way while disconnecting the shoe-to-anchor springs**

**5.6  Compress the hold-down springs and slide them off the pins**

**5.7a  Use a pair of pliers to hold the adjuster clip out of the way while backing off the adjuster screw, then . . .**

**5.7b  . . . disengage the adjuster clevis from the front shoe**

**5.8  Rotate the rear shoe and parking brake lever assembly forward to remove it from the backing plate**

5.15  Lubricate all of the shoe pivot and backing plate contact areas with high-temperature grease

5.17  Rotate the rear shoe and parking brake lever assembly into position in the wheel cylinder piston

5.21  Pull back the spring and attach the end of the cable to the lever

(see illustration).

16    Insert the upper return spring into the backing plate and install the leading shoe. Be sure to seat the ends securely in the wheel cylinder piston and anchor pivot.

6.2  Rear drum brake assembly - 1983 and later models (left side shown)

6.4a  Use pliers to detach the adjuster lever spring . . .

17    Install the trailing shoe return spring and then rotate the shoe and parking brake lever assembly to the rear, into position (see illustration). Seat the shoe ends in the anchor pivot and wheel cylinder.

18    Insert the adjuster screw assembly into the shoe notch, making sure the forward facing clevis of the screw is pointed down. Turn the adjusting star wheel until the screw is secure in the support.

19    Lightly lubricate the hold-down springs with high-temperature grease and install them.

20    Install the shoe-to-anchor springs.

21    Pull the parking brake cable housing spring back to expose the cable and attach it to the lever (see illustration).

22    Install the hub/drum assembly and the wheel. Repeat the procedure for the other wheel.

23    Adjust the brakes (see Chapter 1, Section 34).

24    Lower the vehicle and check the brake operation very carefully before placing the vehicle into normal service.

## 6    Drum brake shoes (1983 and later models) - replacement

*Refer to illustrations 6.2, 6.4a, 6.4b, 6.5, 6.6, 6.7, 6.8a, 6.8b, 6.9a, 6.9b, 6.10, 6.11, 6.13, 6.15, 6.16, 6.18, 6.19, 6.20, 6.27 and 6.28*

**Warning:** *Drum brake shoes must be replaced on both wheels at the same time - never replace the shoes on only one wheel. Also, the dust created by the brake system may contain asbestos, which is harmful to your health. Never blow it out with compressed air and don't inhale any of it. An approved filtering mask should be worn when working on the brakes. Do not, under any circumstances, use petroleum-based solvents to clean brake parts. Use brake system cleaner only!*

**Caution:** *Whenever the brake shoes are replaced, the retractor and hold-down springs should also be replaced. Due to the continuous heating/cooling cycle that the springs are subjected to, they lose their tension over a period of time any may allow the shoes to drag on the drum and wear at a much faster rate than normal.*

1    Raise the rear of the vehicle, support it securely on jackstands and block the front wheels. Remove the rear wheels.

2    Remove the hub/brake drum assembly (see Chapter 1, *Rear wheel bearing check, repack and adjustment*). If the drum won't slide off, you'll have to back off the automatic adjuster screw. Remove the rubber plug from the rear of the brake backing plate, then insert a screwdriver through the hole and use it to push the adjuster lever off the automatic adjuster (see illustration). Insert another screwdriver or brake adjusting tool and use it to turn the star wheel on the automatic adjuster screw until the drum will pull off.

3    Use brake system cleaner to remove dust and brake fluid from the shoe assembly components.

4    Remove the adjuster lever spring and adjuster lever (see illustrations).

**9**

6.4b ... and remove the adjuster lever

6.5 Back off the adjuster star wheel

6.6 Use needle-nose pliers to pull the cable from the
parking brake lever

6.7 Use a brake hold-down spring tool or pliers to depress the
hold-down spring and turn the retainer

5   Back off the adjuster screw star wheel **(see illustration)**.
6   Disconnect the parking brake cable with a pair of pliers **(see illustration)**.
7   Remove the hold-down springs by depressing them with a pair of pliers or a special tool and turning the retainer until the slot aligns with the flattened end of the pin, allowing removal **(see illustration)**.

8   Disengage the brake shoe assembly from the wheel cylinder at the top and the anchor plate at the bottom and remove it from the backing plate **(see illustrations)**.
9   Place the assembly on a work surface and remove the springs **(see illustrations)**.
10   Separate the shoes from the adjuster **(see illustration)**.

6.8a Pull the upper ends of the brake shoes away
from the wheel cylinder ...

6.8b ... then disengage the lower ends of the shoes
from the anchor plate

6.9a  Unhook the lower spring . . .

6.9b  . . . and use pliers to disengage the upper spring
from the shoes

6.10  Detach the adjuster from the shoes

6.11  Use a small screwdriver to pry the clip off the
parking brake lever post

11   Remove the parking brake lever retainer clip with a small screwdriver and transfer the lever to the new shoe **(see illustration)**.
12   Check the shoe linings to make sure they indicate full contact with the drum.
13   Check the drum for cracks, score marks and signs of overheating.

Measure the inside diameter of the drum (most auto parts stores will do this for you) and compare it to the size stamped on the drum **(see illustration)**. Minor imperfections in the drum surface can be removed with sandpaper or emery cloth. Deeper score marks can be removed by having the drum resurfaced by an automotive machine shop (as long as the maximum diameter is not exceeded). **Note:** *Professionals recommend resurfacing the drums whenever the shoes are replaced.*
14   Check the brake springs for signs of discolored paint, indicating overheating, and distorted end coils. It's a good idea to replace them as a matter of course.
15   Check the self-adjuster assembly and threads for bent, corroded and damaged components. Replace the assembly if the screw threads are damaged or rusted. Clean the threads and lubricate them with lithium-based grease **(see illustration)**.

6.13  The maximum allowable inside diameter of the
drum is stamped on it

OUTBOARD FORWARD     SELF ADJUSTER     OUTBOARD REAR

SELF ADJUSTER LEVER

6.15  Adjuster screw components

**9**

**6.16  Carefully peel back the wheel cylinder boots to check for brake fluid leakage**

**6.18  The brake shoe contact area on the backing plate must be smooth and lubricated with high-temperature grease**

16    Check the wheel cylinder boots for damage and signs of leakage **(see illustration)**.

17    Rebuild or replace the wheel cylinder if there is any sign of leakage around the boots (see Section 6).

18    Check for rough or rusted shoe contact areas on the backing plate, then lubricate the contact points with high-temperature grease **(see illustration)**.

19    Assemble the shoes over the adjuster and connect the return springs **(see illustration)**.

20    Place the assembly in position on the backing plate and insert the parking brake cable into the parking brake lever **(see illustration)**.

21    Spread the bottom spring enough to allow the lower ends of the shoes to be seated in the anchor plate.

22    Spread the top spring and seat the shoes in the wheel cylinder pistons.

23    Insert the pins through the backing plate from the rear and hold them in place while installing the hold-down springs and retainers.

24    Install the adjuster lever and connect the spring to it.

25    Turn the adjuster until the shoes are retracted enough to allow the drum to be reinstalled.

26    Install the hub/drum assembly and the wheel. Repeat the procedure for the other wheel.

27    Remove the rubber plug from the hole in the backing plate **(see illustration)**.

28    Insert a narrow screwdriver through the hole in the backing plate and turn the star wheel until the brake drags slightly as the wheel is turned **(see illustration)**.

29    Back off the star wheel until the wheel turns freely.

30    Repeat the adjustment on the opposite wheel.

31    Install the plugs in the backing plate access holes.

32    Adjust the parking brake.

33    Lower the vehicle and check the brake operation very carefully before placing the vehicle into normal service.

**6.19  Assemble the shoes, adjuster and springs prior to installation on the backing plate**

**6.20  Use pliers to insert the parking brake cable into the lever**

**6.27  Pry the rubber plug out of the adjusting hole with a screwdriver**

**6.28  Insert the screwdriver into the hole and turn the star wheel**

## 7 Wheel cylinder - removal, overhaul and installation

**Note:** *Before deciding to rebuild a wheel cylinder, make sure parts are available. It's sometimes more practical to simply replace the old wheel cylinder with a new or rebuilt unit instead of rebuilding it.*

### Removal

*Refer to illustration 7.4*

1    Raise the rear of the vehicle and support it securely on jack-stands, then block the front wheels. Remove the rear wheels.
2    Remove the rear hub/drum (see Chapter 1) and the brake shoes (see Section 6).
3    Unscrew the brake line fitting from the back of the wheel cylinder, using a flare-nut wrench, if available. Plug the hydraulic line to prevent excessive fluid loss and contamination.
4    Unbolt the wheel cylinder and remove it from the backing plate **(see illustration)**. Clean the backing plate and wheel cylinder mating surfaces.

### Overhaul

*Refer to illustration 7.5*

**Note:** *You'll need a clean place to work, clean rags, some newspapers, a wheel cylinder rebuild kit, a container of brake fluid and some brake system cleaner to perform a wheel cylinder overhaul.*

5    Remove the bleeder screw **(see illustration)** and check to make sure it is not obstructed.
6    Carefully pry the boots from the wheel cylinder and remove them.
7    Push in on one piston and force out the opposite piston, cups and spring with the cup expanders from the bore.
8    Clean the wheel cylinder, pistons and spring with brake system cleaner and dry them with filtered, unlubricated compressed air. **Warning:** *Do not, under any circumstances, use petroleum-based solvents or gasoline to clean brake parts.*
9    Check the cylinder bore and pistons for score marks and corrosion (pitting). Slight imperfections in the bore can be removed with fine crocus cloth (use a circular motion). Black stains on the cylinder walls are caused by the cups and will not impair brake operation. If the pistons or wheel cylinder bore are badly scored or pitted, replace the wheel cylinder.
10    Lubricate the components with clean brake fluid prior to installation.
11    With the cylinder bore coated with clean brake fluid, install the spring and cup expanders. Install the cups in each end of the cylinder. Make sure the open ends of the cups are facing each other.
12    Engage the boot on the piston and slide the assembly into the bore. Carefully press the boot over the cylinder end until it is seated.

**7.4 To detach the wheel cylinder from the brake backing plate, disconnect the brake line (tube) fitting and remove the two attaching bolts**

Repeat the procedure for the remaining boot and piston.
13    Install the bleeder screw.

### Installation

14    Apply RTV sealant to the wheel cylinder mating surface of the backing plate.
15    To install the wheel cylinder, hold it in position, install the mounting bolts and tighten them to the specified torque.
16    Unplug the brake line, insert it into the wheel cylinder fitting and carefully thread the flare nut into place. Once the nut is properly started, tighten it securely with a wrench (use a flare-nut wrench if available).
17    Install the brake shoes (see Section 6) and the hub/drum (see Chapter 1).
18    Bleed the brakes (see Section 10).
19    Install the wheels and lower the vehicle. Check the brake operation very carefully before placing the vehicle into normal service.

**9**

**7.5 An exploded view of a typical wheel cylinder assembly**

**8.2 To remove the master cylinder, disconnect the two brake line fittings (arrows) with a flare nut wrench . . .**

**8.3a . . . then remove the mounting nuts from the driver's side . . .**

## 8    Master cylinder - removal and installation

*Refer to illustrations 8.2, 8.3a and 8.3b*

**Note:** *The master cylinder installed on these vehicles cannot be rebuilt. If problems are encountered, replace it with a new unit.*

1    Place a container and several layers of newspaper under the master cylinder to catch spilled brake fluid.

2    Unscrew the brake line fittings **(see illustration)**, remove the lines and cap them. Use a flare-nut wrench, if available, to unscrew the nuts. Allow the fluid in the master cylinder to drain into the container.

3    Remove the mounting nuts and detach the master cylinder from the booster **(see illustrations)**. If you are installing a new master cylinder, it may be necessary to transfer the plastic fluid reservoir to the new master cylinder. To do so, first drain the reservoir, then place the aluminum portion of the master cylinder in a vise and use your hand (no tools) to gently pull the reservoir off while gently rocking it back and forth. Replace the two rubber grommets with new ones, put them in place in the master cylinder, lubricate them with clean brake fluid and press the reservoir back into place, using a rocking motion. Make sure the bottom of the reservoir touches the top of each grommet.

4    Every time the master cylinder is removed, the complete hydraulic system must be bled. The time required to bleed the system can be reduced if the master cylinder is filled with fluid and bench-bled before the master cylinder is installed on the vehicle.

5    Insert threaded plugs of the correct size into the cylinder outlet holes and fill both reservoirs with brake fluid. The master cylinder should be supported in a level manner so that brake fluid will not spill during the bench-bleeding procedure.

6    Loosen one plug at a time and push the piston assembly into the bore to force air from the master cylinder. To prevent air from being drawn back into the cylinder, the plug must be tightened before allowing the piston to return to its original position.

7    Since high pressure is not involved in the bench-bleeding procedure, an alternative to the removal and replacement of the plug with each stroke of the piston assembly is available. Before pushing in on the piston assembly, remove the plug, then depress the piston as described above. Before releasing the piston, however, instead of replacing the plug, simply put your finger tightly over the hole to keep air from being drawn back into the master cylinder. Wait several seconds for brake fluid to be drawn from the reservoir into the piston bore, then depress the piston again, removing your finger as the brake fluid is expelled. Be sure to put your finger back over the hole each time before releasing the piston. When the bleeding procedure is complete for that port, replace the plug and tighten it snugly before going on to the other port to repeat the procedure.

8    Stroke the piston three or four times for each outlet to ensure that all air has been expelled.

9    Refill the master cylinder reservoirs and install the cover assembly.

**Note:** *The reservoirs should only be filled to the top of the reservoir divider to prevent overflowing when the cover is installed.*

10    To install the master cylinder, hold it in position, align the pushrod and master cylinder piston and install the mounting nuts. Tighten the nuts to the torque listed in this Chapter's Specifications.

11    Install the lines and carefully start the fittings, taking care not to cross-thread them. After they have been started by hand, tighten them securely with a flare-nut wrench.

12    Fill the master cylinder reservoir and bleed the brakes.

## 9    Brake hoses and lines - inspection and replacement

*Refer to illustrations 9.4a and 9.4b*

1    About every six months, the flexible hoses which connect the steel brake lines with the rear brakes and the front calipers should be inspected for cracks, chafing of the outer cover, leaks, blisters and other damage.

2    Replacement steel and flexible brake lines are commonly available from dealer parts departments and auto parts stores. Do not, under any circumstances, use anything other than steel lines or approved flexible brake hoses as replacement items.

3    When installing the brake line, leave at least 3/4-inch clearance between the line and any moving or vibrating parts.

4    When disconnecting a hose and a line, loosen the fitting with a flare-nut wrench **(see illustration)**. Once the fitting has been loosened, the spring clip can be removed **(see illustration)**.

5    When connecting two hoses, use open-end wrenches on the hose ends. When connecting two hoses, make sure they're not bent, twisted or strained in any way.

6    Steel brake lines are usually retained at several points with clips. Always remove the clips before detaching a steel brake line. Always reinstall the clips (or new ones if the old ones are damaged) when replacing a brake line they provide support and keep the lines from vibrating, which can eventually break them.

7    After installing a line or hose, bleed the brakes (see Section 10).

## 10    Brake hydraulic system - bleeding

*Refer to illustration 10.8*

**Warning:** *Wear eye protection when bleeding the brake system. If the fluid comes in contact with your eyes, immediately rinse them with water and seek medical attention.*

**Note:** *Bleeding the hydraulic system is necessary to remove air that manages to find its way into the system when it's been opened during removal and installation of a hose, line, caliper, wheel cylinder or master cylinder.*

1    It'll probably be necessary to bleed the system at all four brakes if

8.3b . . . and passenger's side of the master cylinder - once the nuts are removed, lift the master cylinder off the booster

9.4a  To detach a metal brake line from the flexible hose, loosen the fitting with a flare-nut wrench . . .

9.4b . . . then pull off the retaining clip with pliers

10.8  When bleeding the brakes, push one end of a clear plastic tube onto the bleeder screw at the caliper or wheel cylinder and submerge the other end in a container of brake fluid; build up pressure in the lines with the brake pedal and open the bleeder screw - air expelled from the lines is visible as bubbles; when the bubbles disappear, you've bled the line to that caliper or wheel cylinder

11.4  Turn this nut to adjust the parking brake

air has entered the system due to low fluid level, or if the brake lines have been disconnected at the master cylinder.

2    If a brake line was disconnected only at a wheel, then only that caliper or wheel cylinder must be bled.

3    If a brake line was disconnected at a fitting located between the master cylinder and any of the brakes, that part of the system served by the disconnected line must be bled.

4    Remove any residual vacuum from the brake power booster by applying the brake several times with the engine off.

5    Remove the master cylinder reservoir cover and fill the reservoir with brake fluid. Reinstall the cover. **Note:** *Check the fluid level often during the bleeding operation and add fluid as necessary to prevent the fluid level from falling low enough to allow air into the master cylinder.*

6    Have an assistant on hand, as well as a supply of new brake fluid, a clear plastic container partially filled with clean brake fluid, a length of tubing (preferably clear) to fit over the bleeder screw and a wrench to open and close the bleeder screw.

7    Beginning at the right rear wheel, loosen the bleeder screw slightly, then tighten it to a point where it's snug but can still be loosened quickly and easily.

8    Place one end of the tubing over the bleeder screw and submerge the other end in brake fluid in the container **(see illustration)**.

9    Have your assistant pump the brakes slowly a few times to get pressure in the system, then hold the pedal down firmly.

10    While the pedal is held down, open the bleeder screw. Watch for

air bubbles to exit the submerged end of the tube. When the fluid flow slows, tighten the screw, then have your assistant release the pedal.

11    Repeat Steps 9 and 10 until no more air is seen leaving the tube, then tighten the bleeder screw and proceed to the left front wheel, the left rear wheel and the right front wheel, in that order, and perform the same procedure. Be sure to check the fluid in the master cylinder reservoir frequently.

12    Never use old brake fluid. It contains moisture which will deteriorate the brake system components and boil when the fluid gets hot.

13    Refill the master cylinder with fluid at the end of the operation.

14    Check the operation of the brakes. The pedal should feel solid when depressed, with no sponginess. If necessary, repeat the entire process. **Warning:** *Don't operate the vehicle if you're in doubt about the condition of the brake system.*

## 11   Parking brake - adjustment

9

*Refer to illustration 11.4*

1    The rear drum brakes must be in proper working order before adjusting the parking brake (see Section 5 or 6).

2    Block the front wheels to prevent vehicle movement, raise the rear of the vehicle and support it securely on jackstands. Release the parking brake.

3    Clean the cable adjuster threads with a wire brush and lubricate them with multi-purpose grease.

4    Loosen the adjusting nut **(see illustration)** until there's slack in the cable.

5    Have an assistant rotate the rear wheels to make sure they turn easily.

6    Tighten the adjusting nut until a slight drag can be felt when the rear wheels are turned. You may have to keep the adjuster rod from turning by holding it with a wrench or pair of locking pliers.

7    Loosen the nut until the rear wheels turn freely, then back it off an additional two full turns.

8    Apply and release the parking brake several times to make sure it operates properly. It must lock the rear wheels when applied and the wheels must turn easily, without dragging, when it's released.

9    Lower the vehicle.

## 12   Parking brake cables - removal and installation

1    Raise the rear of the vehicle and support it securely on jack-stands.

### *Front cable*

*Refer to illustrations 12.3 and 12.8*

2    Working under the vehicle, loosen the adjusting nut until there's slack in the cables **(see illustration 11.4)**.

3    Detach the rear end of the front cable from the connector that attaches it to the middle cable **(see illustration)**.

4    From inside the vehicle, remove the driver's side kick panel.

5    Pull up the forward end of the front cable and disconnect it.

6    Pinch the cable retainer with needle-nose pliers and pull it down through the cable retaining bracket.

7    Pull the cable assembly through the grommet in the hole in the floor.

8    Installation is the reverse of removal **(see illustration)**.

9    Adjust the parking brake (see Section 11).

**12.3 Once you've loosened the equalizer adjusting nut, detach the rear end of the front cable from this connector**

### *Rear cable*

*Refer to illustrations 12.14 and 12.15*

10    Remove the rear wheels and the hub/drum assemblies (see Chapter 1).

11    Back off the equalizer adjusting nut **(see illustration 11.4)** until the cable is slack.

12    Disconnect the rear brake cable from the brake shoe lever **(see illustration 6.6)**.

**12.8 Parking brake cable details**

**12.14 Using a hammer and punch, knock the cable lock loose from the brake cable support bracket on the trailing arm and detach the cable from the bracket**

**12.15 Pull forward on the rear cable to disconnect it from this connector**

13   Locate the retainer at the end of the rear cable, where it enters the brake shoe backing plate. Pinch this retainer with pliers (or use a small hose clamp) and pull the retainer through the backing plate.

14   Remove the cable lock from the brake cable support bracket on the trailing arm **(see illustration)** and detach the cable from the trailing arm assembly.

15   Disconnect the rear brake cable from the connector at the end of the middle cable **(see illustration)**.

16   The above procedure also applies to the other rear cable.

17   Installation is the reverse of removal **(see illustration 12.8)**.

18   Adjust the parking brake (see Section 11).

## 13   Power brake booster - check, removal and installation

### Operating check

1   Depress the brake pedal several times with the engine off and make sure there's no change in the pedal reserve distance.

2   Depress the pedal and start the engine. If the pedal goes down slightly, operation is normal.

### Airtightness check

3   Start the engine and turn it off after one or two minutes. Slowly depress the brake pedal several times. If the pedal goes down farther the first time but gradually rises after the second or third depression, the booster is airtight.

4   Depress the brake pedal while the engine is running, then stop the engine with the pedal depressed. If there's no change in the pedal reserve travel (distance between the pedal and the floor) after holding the pedal for 30 seconds, the booster is airtight.

### Removal and installation

*Refer to illustration 13.11*

5   Power brake booster units should not be disassembled. They require special tools not normally found in most service stations or shops. They're fairly complex and because of their critical relationship to brake performance it's best to replace a defective booster unit with a new or rebuilt one.

6   To remove the booster, first remove the brake master cylinder (see Section 8).

7   Disconnect the vacuum hose between the engine and the booster. Make sure you don't damage this hose when removing it from the booster fitting. **Caution:** *Disconnect the hose from the check valve on the booster; don't remove the check valve from the booster.*

8   Detach the brackets that secure the steel heater coolant tube to the dash panel and driver's side frame rail.

9   On vehicles with a manual transaxle, remove the clutch cable

mounting bracket. Also push aside the wiring harness on the shock tower. If you need more room, unplug the harness at the multi-connector on the firewall.

10   Working under the dash, position a small screwdriver between the center tang on the retainer clip and the pin in the brake pedal, then rotate the screwdriver enough to allow the retainer clip center tang to pass over the end of the brake pedal pin and pull it from the pin. Disconnect the pushrod from the pedal pin. Discard the retainer clip and use a new one on reassembly.

11   Remove the nuts and washers holding the brake booster to the firewall **(see illustration)**. You may need a light to see them, since they're up under the dash.

12   Slide the booster straight out until the studs clear the holes and lift it (along with any installed gaskets) out of the engine compartment.

13   Lubricate the bearing surfaces of the brake pedal pin and the tip of the pushrod with multi-purpose grease.

14   Install the booster, along with any previously installed gaskets. Connect the pushrod to the pedal pin and install a new retainer clip.

15   The remainder of installation is the reverse of the removal procedure. Tighten the booster mounting nuts to the torque listed in this Chapter's Specifications.

16   Adjust the brake light switch (see Section 14, Step 8).

**9**

**13.11 Power brake booster mounting details**

## 14   Brake light switch - check, adjustment and replacement

*Refer to illustration 14.1*

1    The brake light switch **(see illustration)** is located under the dash, at the upper end of the brake pedal assembly. A plunger on the switch is in constant contact with a striker at the top of the pedal assembly. When the pedal is depressed, the striker moves forward, releasing the plunger, which closes the circuit to the brake lights.

**14.1  Brake light switch installation details**

### Check

2    Use a test light to verify that there's voltage to the switch:
   a) *If there isn't, find the short or open and fix it (see Chapter 12).*
   b) *If there is voltage, proceed to the next Step.*

3    Now use the test light to verify that there's no voltage in the wire between the switch and the brake lights when the brake pedal is not depressed:
   a) *If there is, the switch is shorted or not adjusted correctly - replace it or adjust it.*
   b) *If there isn't, proceed to the next Step.*

4    Now depress the brake pedal and use the test light to verify that there's voltage in the wire between the switch and the brake lights:
   a) *If there is, the switch itself is functioning normally - the problem is somewhere between the switch and the brake lights.*
   b) *If there isn't, the switch is has an open - replace it (proceed to the next step).*

### Replacement

5    Unplug the electrical connector.
6    The retainer socket locks the switch into the mounting bracket, but if you pull on the switch with some force, the retainer socket will come free.
7    To install the new switch, insert the retainer socket through the switch mounting bracket and plug in the electrical connector.

### Adjustment

8    Push the switch forward as far as it will go. As you push the retainer socket through the hole in the bracket, it acts like a ratchet (it can be pushed into the bracket but it can't slip back). The brake pedal will move forward slightly.
9    Gently pull back on the brake pedal (very little movement is needed). This brings the plunger toward the switch until the brake pedal can't go any further. The switch then ratchets backward to the correct position. No further adjustment is necessary.

# Chapter 10
# Suspension and steering systems

## Contents

## Specifications

### Torque specifications

**Ft-lbs** (unless otherwise indicated)

### Front suspension

Balljoint clamp bolt/nut
| | |
|---|---|
| 1981 through 1983 | 50 |
| 1984 through 1989 | 70 |

Driveaxle/hub nut ............................................. See Chapter 8

Control arm pivot bolt nuts
Front pivot
| | |
|---|---|
| 1981 through 1985 | 105 |
| 1986 through 1989 | 95 |
| Rear pivot (stub strut) | 70 |

Stabilizer bar bolts (all) ....................................... 25

Strut assembly
Strut-to-steering knuckle nuts
| | |
|---|---|
| 1981 through 1983 | 45 plus 1/4-turn |
| 1984 on | 75 plus 1/4-turn |
| Upper mounting nuts | 20 |

Damper shaft nut
| | |
|---|---|
| 1987 and earlier | 60 |
| 1988 and 1989 | 55 |

**10**

## Rear suspension

| | |
|---|---|
| Trailing arm-to-hanger bracket mounting nuts | 40 |
| Track bar | |
| Pivot bolt at axle (lower end) | 70 |
| Pivot bolt at frame bracket (upper end) | 55 |
| Shock absorber mounting bolts/nuts | 45 |
| Spindle/brake assembly mounting bolts (drum and disc brakes) | 55 |

## Steering

| | |
|---|---|
| Power steering pump bolts | |
| Upper bolt (pivot bolt) | 30 |
| Lower bolt | 40 |
| Steering gear mounting bolts/nuts | 21 |
| Steering wheel retaining nut | 45 |
| Tie-rod end-to-steering knuckle nut | 38 |
| Wheel lug nuts | See Chapter 1 |

**1.1 Front suspension and steering components**

| | | | | | |
|---|---|---|---|---|---|
| 1 | Strut assembly | 4 | Control arm | 7 | Suspension arm stub strut |
| 2 | Control arm front pivot bolt | 5 | Stabilizer bar | 8 | Steering knuckle |
| 3 | Chassis crossmember | 6 | Steering gear | | |

## 1    General information

*Refer to illustrations 1.1 and 1.2*

Front suspension is by MacPherson struts. The steering knuckles are located by control arms and both control arms are connected by a stabilizer bar **(see illustration)**.

The rear suspension features a beam-type axle with coil springs, located by trailing arms and a track bar **(see illustration)**. Damping is handled by vertically mounted shock absorbers located between the axle and the chassis.

The rack-and-pinion steering gear is located behind the engine and actuates the steering arms which are integral with the steering knuckles. Power assist is optional and the steering column is designed to collapse in the event of an accident. **Note:** *These vehicles use a combination of standard and metric fasteners on the various suspension and steering components, so it would be a good idea to have both types of tools available when beginning work.*

Frequently, when working on the suspension or steering system components, you may come across fasteners which seem impossible to loosen. These fasteners on the underside of the vehicle are continually subjected to water, road grime, mud, etc., and can become rusted or frozen, making them extremely difficult to remove. In order to unscrew these stubborn fasteners without damaging them (or other components), be sure to use lots of penetrating oil and allow it to soak in for a while. Using a wire brush to clean exposed threads will also ease removal of the nut or bolt and prevent damage to the threads. Sometimes a sharp blow with a hammer and punch will break the bond between a nut and bolt threads, but care must be taken to prevent the punch from slipping off the fastener and ruining the threads. Heating the stuck fastener and surrounding area with a torch sometimes helps too, but isn't recommended because of the obvious dangers associated with fire. Long breaker bars and extension, or "cheater", pipes will increase leverage, but never use an extension pipe on a ratchet - the ratcheting mechanism could be damaged. Sometimes tightening the nut or bolt first will help to break it loose. Fasteners that require drastic

**1.2  Rear suspension components**

| 1 | Shock absorber | 2 | Coil spring | 3 | Rear axle beam | 4 | Track bar |

**2.3  Mark the position of the camber cam (arrow) in relation to the strut**

**2.5  Remove the bolt (arrow) and detach the brake hose bracket from the strut**

**2.6  Remove these three upper mounting nuts (arrows) - DO NOT remove the center nut!**

measures to remove should always be replaced with new ones.

Since most of the procedures dealt with in this Chapter involve jacking up the vehicle and working underneath it, a good pair of jackstands will be needed. A hydraulic floor jack is the preferred type of jack to lift the vehicle, and it can also be used to support certain components during various operations. **Warning:** *Never, under any circumstances, rely on a jack to support the vehicle while working on it. Whenever any of the suspension or steering fasteners are loosened or removed they must be inspected and, if necessary, replaced with new ones of the same part number or of original equipment quality and design. Torque specifications must be followed for proper reassembly and component retention. Never attempt to heat or straighten any suspension or steering components. Instead, replace any bent or damaged part with a new one.*

## 2  Strut assembly - removal and installation

*Refer to illustrations 2.3, 2.5, 2.6 and 2.11*

1    Loosen the front wheel lug nuts.
2    Raise the vehicle and support it securely on jackstands. Remove the front wheels.
3    Mark the position of the camber cam **(see illustration)**.
4    Remove the strut-to-steering knuckle nuts, bolts, cam and washer plate.
5    Disconnect the brake hose bracket from the strut **(see illustration)**.
6    Remove the upper mounting nuts **(see illustration)**, disengage the strut from the steering knuckle and detach it from the vehicle.

**10**

**2.11 Install a C-clamp to hold the knuckle and strut together while you align the camber cam, then tighten the knuckle-to-strut bolts and nuts**

7    Inspect the strut and coil spring assembly for leaking fluid, dents, damage and corrosion. If the strut is damaged, see Section 3.

8    To install the strut, place it in position with the studs extending up through the shock tower. Install the nuts and tighten them to the torque listed in this Chapter's Specifications.

9    Attach the strut to the steering knuckle, then insert the strut-to-steering knuckle bolts through the cam and washer plate. Install the nuts, but don't tighten them yet.

10    Attach the brake hose bracket to the strut.

11    Install a C-clamp on the strut and knuckle **(see illustration)**. Tighten it just enough to remove any looseness between the knuckle and strut. Align the marks you made on the cam and strut. Tighten the steering knuckle-to-strut bolts and nuts to the torque listed in this Chapter's Specifications.

12    Install the wheels and lower the vehicle.

## 3    Strut - replacement

*Refer to illustrations 3.4, 3.5 and 3.6*

**Note:** *You'll need a spring compressor for this procedure. Spring compressors are available on a daily rental basis at most auto parts stores or equipment yards.*

1    If the struts or coil springs exhibit the telltale signs of wear (leaking fluid, loss of damping capability, chipped, sagging or cracked coil springs), explore all options before beginning any work. The strut insert assemblies are not serviceable and must be replaced if a problem

**3.4 Install the spring compressor in accordance with the tool manufacturer's instructions and compress the spring until all pressure is removed from the upper spring seat**

develops. However, strut assemblies complete with springs may be available on an exchange basis, which eliminates much time and work. Whichever route you choose to take, check on the cost and availability of parts before disassembling your vehicle. **Warning:** *Disassembling a strut is potentially dangerous and utmost attention must be directed to the job, or serious injury may result. Use only a high-quality spring compressor and carefully follow the manufacturer's instructions furnished with the tool. After removing the coil spring from the strut, set it aside in a safe, isolated area.*

2    Remove the strut and spring assembly (see Section 2).

3    Mount the strut assembly in a vise. Line the vise jaws with wood or rags to prevent damage to the unit and don't tighten the vise excessively.

4    Install the spring compressor in accordance with the manufacturer's instructions **(see illustration)**. Compress the spring until you can wiggle the mount assembly and spring seat.

5    To loosen the damper shaft nut, hold the shaft with a box-end wrench while loosening the shaft nut with another box-end wrench **(see illustration)**.

6    Disassemble the strut assembly and lay out the parts in exactly the same order as shown **(see illustration)**. **Warning:** *When removing*

**3.5 To remove the damper shaft nut, hold the shaft with a box-end wrench and loosen the nut with another box-end wrench**

**3.6 An exploded view of the strut assembly**

**4.2  Put a back-up wrench on each nut (on top of control arm, not visible) and remove these retainer bolts (arrows) and retainers from both control arms**

**4.3  Remove these clamp bolts (arrows) and both clamps from the crossmember**

*the compressed spring, lift it off very carefully and set it in a safe place. Keep the ends of the spring away from your body.* **Note:** *Mark the spring so it can be reinstalled on the same side of the vehicle from which it was removed.*

7    Inspect all rubber parts for damage, cracking and hardness and replace as necessary.

8    Reassembly is the reverse of disassembly. Be careful not to damage the damper shaft or the strut will leak. When installing the spring, be sure the spring ends mesh with the spring anti-rotation stops provided by the spring upper and lower seats.

## 4    Stabilizer bar - removal and installation

*Refer to illustrations 4.2 and 4.3*

1    Loosen the front wheel lug nuts, raise the front of the vehicle, support it securely on jackstands and remove the front wheels.

2    Remove the stabilizer bar retainer bolts, nuts and retainers from the control arms **(see illustration)**.

3    Support the stabilizer bar and remove the stabilizer bar clamp bolts and clamps from the crossmember **(see illustration)**. Remove the stabilizer bar from the vehicle.

**5.5  Using a back-up wrench, remove the pinch bolt and nut for the balljoint stud clamp at the bottom of the steering knuckle, then pull the control arm down to separate the stud from the knuckle**

4    Check the bar for damage, corrosion and signs of twisting.

5    Check the clamps, bushings and retainers for distortion, damage and wear. Replace the inner bushings by prying them open at the split and removing them. Install the new bushings with the curved surface (early models) or external rib (later models) up and the split facing toward the front of the vehicle. The outer bushings can be removed by cutting them off or hammering them from the bar. Force the new bushings onto the end of the bar until 1/2-inch of the bar is protruding. Silicone spray lubricant will ease this process.

6    Attach the bar to the crossmember, then install the clamps, bolts and nuts, but don't tighten them completely yet.

7    Install the bushing retainers and bolts on the control arms, but don't tighten the bolts completely yet.

8    Raise the control arms to normal ride height and tighten the bolts to the torque listed in this Chapter's Specifications.

9    Install the wheels and lower the vehicle.

## 5    Control arm - removal, inspection and installation

*Refer to illustration 5.5*

1    Raise the front of the vehicle, support it securely on jackstands and remove the front wheels.

2    Disconnect the stabilizer bar from the control arms (see Section 4) and rotate the bar down, out of the way.

3    Remove the front pivot bolt and nut from the control arm **(see illustration 1.1)**.

4    Remove the rear pivot bolt and from the stub strut.

5    Remove the balljoint clamp pinch bolt and nut from the steering knuckle **(see illustration)**.

6    Pull the balljoint stud from the steering knuckle. **Caution:** *Do not move the steering knuckle/strut assembly out or you may separate the inner CV joint.*

7    Remove the control arm by pulling it forward and down.

8    Inspect the control arm for distortion and the bushings for wear, damage and deterioration. If the control arm is damaged or bent, replace it. If an inner pivot bushing or a balljoint are worn, have them replaced by a dealer service department or repair shop with the special tools necessary to do the job. **Note:** *Some bushings are not serviceable and the entire control arm must be replaced if the bushings are worn.*

9    Installation is the reverse of removal **(see illustration)**. Don't tighten the pivot bolts until the vehicle is at normal ride height.

10    After you've installed the wheels and lowered the vehicle so that its weight is on the suspension, tighten the pivot bolts to the torque listed in this Chapter's Specifications.

**10**

**6.1  An exploded view of a typical steering knuckle assembly and related components**

## 6   Steering knuckle, hub and bearing - removal, inspection and installation

### Removal

*Refer to illustration 6.1*

1    With the vehicle weight resting on the front suspension, remove the hub cap, cotter pin, nut lock and spring washer. Loosen, but do not remove, the front hub (driveaxle) nut and wheel lug nuts **(see illustration)**.

2    Raise the front of the vehicle, support it securely on jackstands and remove the front wheels.

3    Remove the driveaxle hub nut and washer.

4    Push the driveaxle in until it is free of the hub. It may be necessary to tap on the axle end with a brass drift and hammer to dislodge the driveaxle from the hub.

5    Remove the cotter pin and nut and use a puller to disconnect the tie-rod end from the steering knuckle (see Section 14).

6    Move the tie-rod out of the way and secure it with a piece of wire.

7    Disconnect the brake hose bracket from the strut by removing the bolt and retainer.

8    Remove the caliper and brake pads (see Chapter 9), then remove the caliper mounting bracket from the steering knuckle. Taking care not to twist the brake hose, hang the caliper out of the way in the wheel well with a piece of wire.

9    Remove the retainer washer (if equipped) from the wheel stud and pull off the brake disc.

10   Mark the position of the camber cam (see Section 2).

11   Remove the balljoint pinch bolt and nut and disengage the balljoint from the steering knuckle (see Section 5).

12   Remove the steering knuckle-to-strut bolts and nuts (see Section 2).

13   With the knuckle and hub assembly in the straight-ahead position, grasp it securely and pull it directly out and off the driveaxle splines. **Caution:** *Be careful not to pull the driveaxle out or you may disengage the inner CV joint.*

### Inspection

14   Place the assembly on a clean work surface and wipe it off with a lint-free cloth. Inspect the knuckle for rust, damage and cracks. Check the bearings by rotating them to make sure they move freely, without excessive noise or looseness. The bearings should be packed with an adequate supply of clean grease. **Note:** *Further disassembly will have to be left to your dealer service department or a repair shop because of the special tools required.*

**7.2  Try to lever the steering knuckle from side-to-side with a prybar or large screwdriver**

### Installation

15   Prior to installation, clean the CV joint seal and the hub grease seal with solvent (don't get any solvent on the CV joint boot). Lubricate the entire circumference of the CV joint wear sleeve and seal contact surface with multi-purpose grease (see Chapter 8).

16   Carefully place the knuckle and hub assembly in position. Align the splines of the axle and the hub and slide the hub into place.

17   Install the knuckle-to-strut bolts, camber cam, washer plate and nuts, followed by the balljoint pinch bolt and nut. Adjust the position of the camber cam (see Section 2) and tighten the nuts to the torque listed in this Chapter's Specifications.

18   Reattach the tie-rod end to the steering knuckle, tighten the nut and install a new cotter pin (see Section 13).

19   Install the brake disc, pads and caliper/adapter assembly (see Chapter 9).

20   Reattach the brake hose bracket to the strut.

21   Push the CV joint completely into the hub to make sure it is seated and install the washer and hub nut finger tight.

22   Install the wheels, hand tighten the lug nuts, lower the vehicle and tighten the wheel lug nuts to the torque specified in Chapter 1.

23   With an assistant applying the brakes, tighten the hub nut to the torque specified in Chapter 8. Install the spring washer, nut lock and a new cotter pin.

24   With the weight of the vehicle on the suspension, check the steering knuckle and balljoint nuts to make sure they are tightened properly.

8.2a An exploded view of typical rear suspension components

8.2b Support the rear axle with a jack before removing the shock absorber mounting bolts - if you don't, the coil spring, which is under a great deal of pressure, will snap the axle down violently

8.3a Remove the shock absorber upper mounting bolt and nut . . .

8.3b . . . then the lower mounting nut and bolt (arrow) and remove the shock absorber

25  Have the front end alignment checked and, if necessary, adjusted.

## 7  Balljoints - check and replacement

*Refer to illustration 7.2*

1  The suspension balljoints are designed to operate without freeplay.

2  To check for wear, place a prybar or large screwdriver between the control arm and the underside of the steering knuckle and try to lever the knuckle from side to side **(see illustration)**.

3  If there is any movement, the balljoint is worn and must be replaced with a new one. Remove the control arm (see Section 5) and take it to a dealer service department or automotive machine shop to have the old balljoint pressed out and a new one pressed in.

## 8  Rear shock absorbers and coil springs - removal, inspection and installation

### *Removal*

*Refer to illustrations 8.2a, 8.2b, 8.3a and 8.3b*

1  Raise the rear of the vehicle and support it securely on jack-stands.

2  Support the axle with a jack and remove the rear wheels **(see illustrations)**.

3  Remove the lower and upper shock mounting bolts **(see illustrations)** and detach the shock absorber.

4  If you wish to remove the coil springs, carefully lower the jack, supporting the axle until all compression is relieved and remove the coil spring.

**10**

## Inspection

5    With the shock upright, grasp it at each end and pump it in and out several times. The action should be smooth, with no binding or dead spots.

6    Check for fluid leakage. Replace the shock with a new one if it is leaking or if the action is rough. Always replace the shocks in pairs.

7    Inspect the jounce bumper at the upper end of the coil spring. If it's cracked or dried out, replace it: remove the two screws that attach the jounce bumper cup to the underside of the frame rail and remove it. Make sure the new cup fasteners are firmly tightened.

8    Check the springs for breakage, nicks and cracks. Replace the spring if you notice any of these conditions.

## Installation

9    To install the coil springs, make sure they're seated properly, then carefully raise the axle back into position with the jack.

10   Hold the shock in position and install the bolts. Tighten the upper bolt to the torque listed in this Chapter's Specifications. Lower the vehicle and tighten the lower bolt to the torque listed in this Chapter's Specifications.

---

### 9   Rear spindle - inspection, removal and installation

## Removal

1    Remove the rear hub/drum or disc (see Chapter 1, *Rear wheel bearing check, repack and adjustment*).

2    Clean the spindle and inspect the bearing contact surfaces for wear and damage.

3    The spindle should be replaced with a new one if it is bent, damaged or worn.

4    Disconnect the parking brake cable from the brake assembly (see Chapter 9).

5    Disconnect and plug the rear brake line at the wheel cylinder (see Chapter 9).

6    Remove the four backing plate mounting bolts and detach the brake assembly and spindle. The bolts may have Torx-type heads, which require a special tool for removal. Be sure to mark the location of any spindle shims.

## Installation

7    Place the shim(s) (if equipped), spindle and brake assembly in position, install the bolts and tighten them to the torque listed in this Chapter's Specifications, following a criss-cross pattern.

8    Connect the brake line and parking brake cable.

9    Install the hub/drum or disc (see Chapter 1), bleed the brakes and adjust the parking brake (see Chapter 9).

---

### 10   Track bar assembly - removal and installation

*Refer to illustration 10.3*

1    Loosen the rear wheel lug nuts, raise the vehicle, place it securely on jackstands and remove the rear wheels.

2    Raise the rear axle to normal ride height with a jack.

3    Support the track bar while you remove the track bar-to-axle pivot bolt and the track bar-to-frame pivot bolt **(see illustration)**.

4    Remove the track bar. Inspect the bushings for cracks and deterioration. A dealer service department or automotive machine shop can install new bushings in the track bar, if necessary.

5    Installation is the reverse of removal.

---

### 11   Rear axle assembly - removal and installation

*Refer to illustration 11.7*

1    Loosen the rear wheel lug nuts, raise the vehicle, place it securely on jackstands and remove the rear wheels.

2    Support the axle at the center with a floor jack.

**10.3  Remove the track bar pivot bolts (upper bolt shown)**

3    Disconnect the rear parking brake cables from the middle cable at the connectors, detach the retaining brackets and remove the cable retainer clips from the brackets on the trailing arms (see Chapter 9). Pull the rear cables through the holes in the trailing arms so they're clear of the axle assembly.

4    Disconnect the brake lines from the hoses at the trailing arm pivot points. Be prepared for fluid leakage.

5    Disconnect the lower ends of the shock absorbers (see Section 8) and the track bar (see Section 10). Support the lower end of the track bar with a piece of sturdy wire.

6    Carefully lower the axle assembly until the coil springs are no longer under compression, then remove the coil springs and isolators.

7    Support the forward ends of the trailing arms with stands and remove the pivot bolts **(see illustration)**.

8    Remove the axle assembly.

9    Inspect the pivot bushings. If they're cracked or dried out, replace them.

10   Installation is the reverse of removal. Be sure to bleed the brakes after the job is complete (see Chapter 9).

---

### 12   Steering wheel - removal and installation

*Refer to illustrations 12.3 and 12.4*

1    Disconnect the cable from the negative terminal of the battery.

2    Remove the center pad and disconnect the horn connectors.

3    Remove the steering wheel retaining nut and mark the relationship of the steering shaft and hub to simplify installation **(see illustration)**. On automatic transaxle models, remove the damper.

**11.7  To remove the pivot bolts for the trailing arms, remove the nuts (arrow) and drive the bolt through the bushing and bracket - it looks like the bolt will hit the body, but there's a small hole in the body behind the rubber flap on the right**

**12.3  After you've removed the steering wheel nut, mark the relationship of the steering wheel to the shaft to ensure proper alignment at reassembly**

**12.4  Use a bolt-type puller like this one to remove the steering wheel**

**13.2a  To disconnect the tie-rod end from the steering knuckle, remove the cotter pin and loosen the castle nut . . .**

4    Use a bolt-type puller to remove the steering wheel (**see illustration**). **Caution:** *Do not hammer on the shaft to remove the steering wheel.*

5    To install the wheel, align the mark on the steering wheel hub with the mark made on the shaft during removal and slip the wheel onto the shaft. Install the hub nut (and damper if removed) and tighten it to the torque listed in this Chapter's Specifications.

6    Connect the horn wires and install the center pad assembly.

7    Connect the negative battery cable.

## 13  Tie-rod ends - removal and installation

*Refer to illustration 13.2a, 13.2b, 13.3a and 13.3b*

1    Raise the front of the vehicle, support it securely on jackstands, block the rear wheels and set the parking brake. Remove the front wheels.

2    Remove the tie-rod-to-steering knuckle cotter pin, loosen the nut, then disconnect the tie-rod from the steering knuckle with a puller (**see illustrations**).

3    Loosen the jam nut (**see illustration**), mark the position of the tie-rod end on the inner tie-rod (**see illustration**), unscrew the tie-rod end and remove it.

4    To install the tie-rod end, thread it onto the rod to the marked position.

5    Connect the tie-rod end to the steering knuckle, install the nut and tighten it to the torque listed in this Chapter's Specifications.

**13.2b  . . . install a puller and separate the tie-rod end from the knuckle; note how the nut is still in place, loosened a few turns - this prevents the components from separating violently**

Install a new cotter pin. Now tighten the jam nut securely. Make sure the steering gear boot isn't twisted.

6    Have the front end alignment checked by a dealer service department or an alignment shop.

**13.3a  Using a back-up wrench on the tie-rod end, loosen the jam nut with another wrench . . .**

**13.3b  . . . then paint an alignment mark on the threads of the inner tie-rod to mark the position of the tie-rod end**

**14.4 Steering gear boot details**

## 14 Steering gear boots - replacement

*Refer to illustration 14.4*

1   Raise the vehicle and support it securely on jackstands.
2   Remove the tie-rod end (see Section 13).
3   Remove the boot clamps.
4   Mark the location of the breather tube, use a small screwdriver to lift the boot out of the groove in the steering gear and remove the boot **(see illustration).**

5   Prior to installation, lubricate the boot groove in the steering tie-rod with silicone-type grease.
6   Slide the new boot into position on the steering gear until it seats in the groove and install a new inner clamp. Make sure the breather tube fits securely in the boot.
7   Install the clamp(s).
8   Install the tie-rod end.
9   Lower the vehicle.
10   Have the front end alignment checked by a dealer service department or an alignment shop.

## 15 Steering gear - removal and installation

### *Removal*

*Refer to illustrations 15.3, 15.7, 15.8a and 15.8b*

1   Loosen the wheel lug nuts, raise the vehicle, support it securely on jackstands and remove the front wheels.
2   Disconnect the tie-rod ends from the steering knuckles (see Section 13).
3   Support the front crossmember with a jack **(see illustration).**
4   Remove the four bolts (early models) or three bolts and one nut (later models) holding the crossmember to the body.
5   Lower the jack and crossmember far enough to gain access to the U-joint between the steering input shaft and the intermediate shaft of the steering column.
6   Remove the boot that protects the U-joint. Mark the relationship of the U-joint to the intermediate shaft so it can be re-connected the same way. Remove the pinch bolt from the U-joint. Lower the crossmember a little farther to separate the U-joint from the intermediate shaft (the U-joint stays with the steering gear).

**15.3 Steering gear mounting details**

**15.7  Disconnect the two fluid line fittings indicated by arrows; leave the others connected**

7    On models with power steering, disconnect the lines (see illustration) and drain the fluid into a container.
8    Remove the steering gear mounting bolts and fluid line retaining clip bolt (see illustrations) and separate it from the crossmember by withdrawing it to the left side of the vehicle.

## Installation

9    Position the steering gear on the crossmember, install the steering gear mounting bolts and fluid line retaining clip bolt and tighten them securely.
10   Raise the crossmember and steering gear into position with the jack.
11   On power steering equipped models, reconnect the lines. Use new O-rings on the fittings.
12   Connect the U-joint to the intermediate shaft, aligning the marks made on disassembly.
13   Install the U-joint pinch bolt.
14   Install the U-joint boot.
15   Install the four crossmember bolts (early models) or three bolts and one nut (later models). Start with the right rear bolt or nut, which is the pilot that aligns the crossmember correctly, and tighten them securely.
16   Attach the tie-rod ends to the steering knuckles (see Section 14).
17   Install the front wheels and lower the vehicle.
18   On models with power steering, start the engine and bleed the steering system (see Section 17). While the engine is running, check for

**15.8b  . . . remove both mounting bolts on the passenger side (one is behind the steering gear) and detach the steering gear from the crossmember**

**15.8a  Remove the fluid line retainer clip bolt and both driver's side mounting bolts (one is behind the steering gear and not visible in this photo) . . .**

leaks at the hose connections.
19   Have the front end alignment checked by a dealer service department or an alignment shop.

## 16   Power steering pump - removal and installation

*Refer to illustration 16.2*
**Note:** *Metric fasteners are used on the power steering pump.*

## Removal

1    Open the hood and disconnect the two wires from the clutch cycling switch on the air conditioning compressor (if equipped).
2    Remove the drivebelt adjustment bolt (see illustration) from the front of the pump and (if equipped) the nut from the end hose bracket.
3    Raise the vehicle and support it securely on jackstands.
4    Disconnect the pump return hose and drain the fluid from the pump into a container.
5    While the pump is draining, remove the right side splash shield that protects the drivebelts.
6    Disconnect both hoses from the pump. Cap all open hose ends to prevent contamination.

**16.2  To detach the power steering pump from its mounting bracket, remove these three fasteners**

*1    Drivebelt adjustment bolt*
*2    Lower pivot bolt*
*3    Mounting stud nut*

**10**

7    Loosen the two lower pump mounting fasteners, a bolt and a stud nut, disconnect the drivebelt, then remove the fasteners.

8    To remove the pump, move it rearward to clear the mounting bracket, then remove the bracket. Rotate the pump clockwise until the pump pulley faces toward the rear of the vehicle and pull the pump up and out.

## Installation

9    Installation is the reverse of removal. Make sure the tab on the mounting bracket is in the lower left front mounting hole. Be sure to use new O-rings when you attach the hoses to the pump. Don't tighten the fasteners until you've adjusted the belt tension.

10    Adjust the belt to the proper tension (see Chapter 1) and tighten the fasteners.

11    Fill the pump with the specified fluid (see Chapter 1).

12    Start the engine, bleed the air from the system (see Section 17) and check the fluid level.

## 17   Power steering system - bleeding

1    The power steering system must be bled whenever a line is disconnected.

2    Check the fluid level in the reservoir; add the specified fluid to bring it up to the proper level (see Chapter 1 if necessary).

3    Start the engine and slowly turn the steering wheel several times from left to right and back again. Do not turn the wheel fully from lock to lock.

4    Check the fluid level, topping it up as necessary until it remains steady and no more bubbles appear in the reservoir.

**18.1  Metric tire size code**

## 18   Wheels and tires - general information

*Refer to illustration 18.1*

All vehicles covered by this manual are equipped with metric-size fiberglass or steel-belted radial tires **(see illustration)**. The installation of different size or other type tires may affect the ride and handling of the vehicle. Don't mix different types of tires, such as radials and bias belted, on the same vehicle; handling may be seriously affected. Always try to replace tires in pairs on the same axle. However, if only one tire is being replaced, be sure it's the same size, structure and tread design as the other. Because tire pressure has a substantial effect on handling and wear, the pressure in all tires should be checked at least once a month or before any extended trips (see Chapter 1).

Wheels must be replaced if they're bent, dented, leak air, have elongated bolt holes, are heavily rusted, out of vertical symmetry or if the lug nuts won't stay tight. Wheel repairs by welding or peening aren't recommended.

Tire and wheel balance is important to the overall handling, braking and performance of the vehicle. Unbalanced wheels can adversely affect handling and ride characteristics as well as tire life. Whenever a tire is installed on a wheel, the tire and wheel should be balanced by a shop with the proper equipment.

## 19   Front end alignment - general information

A front end alignment refers to the adjustments made to the front wheels so they're in proper angular relationship to the suspension and the ground. Front wheels that are out of proper alignment not only affect steering control, but also increase tire wear. The front end adjustments normally required are camber and toe-in.

Getting the proper front wheel alignment is a very exacting process in which complicated and expensive machines are necessary to perform the job properly. Because of this, you should have a technician with the proper equipment perform these tasks. We will, however, use this space to give you a basic idea of what's involved with front end alignment so you can better understand the process and deal intelligently with the shop that does the work.

Toe-in is the turning in of the front wheels. The purpose of a toe specification is to ensure parallel rolling of the front wheels. In a vehicle with zero toe-in, the distance between the front edges of the wheels will be the same as the distance between the rear edges of the wheels. The actual amount of toe-in is normally only a fraction of an inch. Toe-in adjustment is controlled by the positions of the tie-rod ends on the tie-rods. Incorrect toe-in will cause the tires to wear improperly by making them scrub against the road surface.

Camber is the tilting of the front wheels from vertical when viewed from the front of the vehicle. When the wheels tilt out at the top, the camber is said to be positive (+). When the wheels tilt in at the top the camber is negative (-). The amount of tilt is measured in degrees from vertical - this measurement is called the camber angle. This angle affects the amount of tire tread contacting the road and compensates for changes in the suspension geometry when the vehicle is cornering or traveling over an undulating surface.

Caster is the tilting of the top of the front steering axis from vertical. A tilt toward the rear is positive caster and a tilt toward the front is negative caster. Caster isn't adjustable on these vehicles.

# Chapter 11  Body

## Contents

## 1  General information

These models feature a "unibody" layout, using a floor pan with front and rear frame side rails which support the body components, front and rear suspension systems and other mechanical components. Certain components are particularly vulnerable to accident damage and can be unbolted and repaired or replaced. Among these parts are the body moldings, bumpers, the hood and trunk lids and all glass. Only general body maintenance practices and body panel repair procedures within the scope of the do-it-yourselfer are included in this chapter.

## 2  Body - maintenance

1  The condition of your vehicle's body is very important, because the resale value depends a great deal on it. It's much more difficult to repair a neglected or damaged body than it is to repair mechanical components. The hidden areas of the body, such as the wheel wells, the frame and the engine compartment, are equally important, although they don't require as frequent attention as the rest of the body.
2  Once a year, or every 12,000 miles, it's a good idea to have the underside of the body steam cleaned. All traces of dirt and oil will be removed and the area can then be inspected carefully for rust, damaged brake lines, frayed electrical wires, damaged cables and other problems. The front suspension components should be greased after completion of this job.

3  At the same time, clean the engine and the engine compartment with a steam cleaner or water-soluble degreaser.
4  The wheel wells should be given close attention, since undercoating can peel away and stones and dirt thrown up by the tires can cause the paint to chip and flake, allowing rust to set in. If rust is found, clean down to the bare metal and apply an anti-rust paint.
5  The body should be washed about once a week. Wet the vehicle thoroughly to soften the dirt, then wash it down with a soft sponge and plenty of clean soapy water. If the surplus dirt is not washed off very carefully, it can wear down the paint.
6  Spots of tar or asphalt thrown up from the road should be removed with a cloth soaked in solvent.
7  Once every six months, wax the body and chrome trim. If a chrome cleaner is used to remove rust from any of the vehicle's plated parts, remember that the cleaner also removes part of the chrome, so use it sparingly.

## 3  Vinyl trim - maintenance

Don't clean vinyl trim with detergents, caustic soap or petroleum-based cleaners. Plain soap and water works just fine, with a soft brush to clean dirt that may be ingrained. Wash the vinyl as frequently as the rest of the vehicle. After cleaning, application of a high-quality rubber and vinyl protectant will help prevent oxidation and cracks. The protectant can also be applied to weatherstripping, vacuum lines and rubber hoses, which often fail as a result of chemical degradation, and to the tires.

**11**

These photos illustrate a method of repairing simple dents. They are intended to supplement *Body repair - minor damage* in this Chapter and should not be used as the sole instructions for body repair on these vehicles.

1   If you can't access the backside of the body panel to hammer out the dent, pull it out with a slide-hammer-type dent puller. In the deepest portion of the dent or along the crease line, drill or punch hole(s) at least one inch apart . . .

2   . . . then screw the slide-hammer into the hole and operate it. Tap with a hammer near the edge of the dent to help 'pop' the metal back to its original shape. When you're finished, the dent area should be close to its original contour and about 1/8-inch below the surface of the surrounding metal

3   Using coarse-grit sandpaper, remove the paint down to the bare metal. Hand sanding works fine, but the disc sander shown here makes the job faster. Use finer (about 320-grit) sandpaper to feather-edge the paint at least one inch around the dent area

4   When the paint is removed, touch will probably be more helpful than sight for telling if the metal is straight. Hammer down the high spots or raise the low spots as necessary. Clean the repair area with wax/silicone remover

5   Following label instructions, mix up a batch of plastic filler and hardener. The ratio of filler to hardener is critical, and, if you mix it incorrectly, it will either not cure properly or cure too quickly (you won't have time to file and sand it into shape)

6   Working quickly so the filler doesn't harden, use a plastic applicator to press the body filler firmly into the metal, assuring it bonds completely. Work the filler until it matches the original contour and is slightly above the surrounding metal

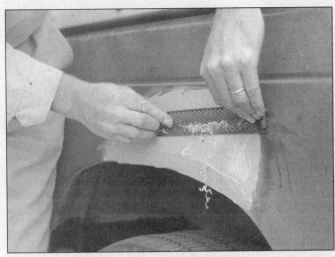

7  Let the filler harden until you can just dent it with your fingernail. Use a body file or Surform tool (shown here) to rough-shape the filler

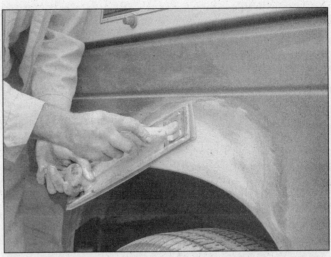

8  Use coarse-grit sandpaper and a sanding board or block to work the filler down until it's smooth and even. Work down to finer grits of sandpaper - always using a board or block - ending up with 360 or 400 grit

9  You shouldn't be able to feel any ridge at the transition from the filler to the bare metal or from the bare metal to the old paint. As soon as the repair is flat and uniform, remove the dust and mask off the adjacent panels or trim pieces

10  Apply several layers of primer to the area. Don't spray the primer on too heavy, so it sags or runs, and make sure each coat is dry before you spray on the next one. A professional-type spray gun is being used here, but aerosol spray primer is available inexpensively from auto parts stores

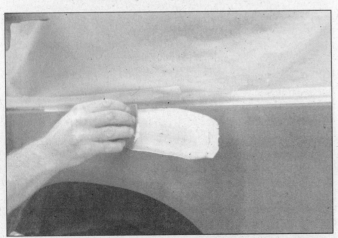

11  The primer will help reveal imperfections or scratches. Fill these with glazing compound. Follow the label instructions and sand it with 360 or 400-grit sandpaper until it's smooth. Repeat the glazing, sanding and respraying until the primer reveals a perfectly smooth surface

12  Finish sand the primer with very fine sandpaper (400 or 600-grit) to remove the primer overspray. Clean the area with water and allow it to dry. Use a tack rag to remove any dust, then apply the finish coat. Don't attempt to rub out or wax the repair area until the paint has dried completely (at least two weeks)

## 4   Upholstery and carpets - maintenance

1    Every three months remove the floormats and clean the interior of the vehicle (more frequently if necessary). Use a stiff whisk broom to brush the carpeting and loosen dirt and dust, then vacuum the upholstery and carpets thoroughly, especially along seams and crevices.

2    Dirt and stains can be removed from carpeting with basic household or automotive carpet shampoos available in spray cans. Follow the directions and vacuum again, then use a stiff brush to bring back the "nap" of the carpet.

3    Most interiors have cloth or vinyl upholstery, either of which can be cleaned and maintained with a number of material-specific cleaners or shampoos available in auto supply stores. Follow the directions on the product for usage, and always spot-test any upholstery cleaner on an inconspicuous area (bottom edge of a back seat cushion) to ensure that it doesn't cause a color shift in the material.

4    After cleaning, vinyl upholstery should be treated with a protectant. **Note:** *Make sure the protectant container indicates the product can be used on seats - some products may make a seat too slippery.* **Caution:** *Do not use protectant on vinyl-covered steering wheels.*

5    Leather upholstery requires special care. It should be cleaned regularly with saddlesoap or leather cleaner. Never use alcohol, gasoline, nail polish remover or thinner to clean leather upholstery.

6    After cleaning, regularly treat leather upholstery with a leather conditioner, rubbed in with a soft cotton cloth. Never use car wax on leather upholstery.

7    In areas where the interior of the vehicle is subject to bright sunlight, cover leather seating areas of the seats with a sheet if the vehicle is to be left out for any length of time.

## 5   Body repair - minor damage

### Repair of scratches

1    If the scratch is superficial and does not penetrate to the metal of the body, repair is very simple. Lightly rub the scratched area with a fine rubbing compound to remove loose paint and built up wax. Rinse the area with clean water.

2    Apply touch-up paint to the scratch, using a small brush. Continue to apply thin layers of paint until the surface of the paint in the scratch is level with the surrounding paint. Allow the new paint at least two weeks to harden, then blend it into the surrounding paint by rubbing with a very fine rubbing compound. Finally, apply a coat of wax to the scratch area.

3    If the scratch has penetrated the paint and exposed the metal of the body, causing the metal to rust, a different repair technique is required. Remove all loose rust from the bottom of the scratch with a pocket knife, then apply rust inhibiting paint to prevent the formation of rust in the future. Using a rubber or nylon applicator, coat the scratched area with glaze-type filler. If required, the filler can be mixed with thinner to provide a very thin paste, which is ideal for filling narrow scratches. Before the glaze filler in the scratch hardens, wrap a piece of smooth cotton cloth around the tip of a finger. Dip the cloth in thinner and then quickly wipe it along the surface of the scratch. This will ensure that the surface of the filler is slightly hollow. The scratch can now be painted over as described earlier in this section.

### Repair of dents

*See photo sequence*

4    When repairing dents, the first job is to pull the dent out until the affected area is as close as possible to its original shape. There is no point in trying to restore the original shape completely as the metal in the damaged area will have stretched on impact and cannot be restored to its original contours. It is better to bring the level of the dent up to a point which is about 1/8-inch below the level of the surrounding metal. In cases where the dent is very shallow, it is not worth trying to pull it out at all.

5    If the back side of the dent is accessible, it can be hammered out gently from behind using a soft-face hammer. While doing this, hold a block of wood firmly against the opposite side of the metal to absorb the hammer blows and prevent the metal from being stretched.

6    If the dent is in a section of the body which has double layers, or some other factor makes it inaccessible from behind, a different technique is required. Drill several small holes through the metal inside the damaged area, particularly in the deeper sections. Screw long, self tapping screws into the holes just enough for them to get a good grip in the metal. Now the dent can be pulled out by pulling on the protruding heads of the screws with locking pliers.

7    The next stage of repair is the removal of paint from the damaged area and from an inch or so of the surrounding metal. This is easily done with a wire brush or sanding disk in a drill motor, although it can be done just as effectively by hand with sandpaper. To complete the preparation for filling, score the surface of the bare metal with a screwdriver or the tang of a file or drill small holes in the affected area. This will provide a good grip for the filler material. To complete the repair, see the section on *filling and painting*.

### Repair of rust holes or gashes

8    Remove all paint from the affected area and from an inch or so of the surrounding metal using a sanding disk or wire brush mounted in a drill motor. If these are not available, a few sheets of sandpaper will do the job just as effectively.

9    With the paint removed, you will be able to determine the severity of the corrosion and decide whether to replace the whole panel, if possible, or repair the affected area. New body panels are not as expensive as most people think and it is often quicker to install a new panel than to repair large areas of rust.

10    Remove all trim pieces from the affected area except those which will act as a guide to the original shape of the damaged body, such as headlight shells, etc. Using metal snips or a hacksaw blade, remove all loose metal and any other metal that is badly affected by rust. Hammer the edges of the hole on the inside to create a slight depression for the filler material.

11    Wire brush the affected area to remove the powdery rust from the surface of the metal. If the back of the rusted area is accessible, treat it with rust inhibiting paint.

12    Before filling is done, block the hole in some way. This can be done with sheet metal riveted or screwed into place, or by stuffing the hole with wire mesh.

13    Once the hole is blocked off, the affected area can be filled and painted. See the following subsection on *filling and painting*.

### Filling and painting

14    Many types of body fillers are available, but generally speaking, body repair kits which contain filler paste and a tube of resin hardener are best for this type of repair work. A wide, flexible plastic or nylon applicator will be necessary for imparting a smooth and contoured finish to the surface of the filler material. Mix up a small amount of filler on a clean piece of wood or cardboard (use the hardener sparingly). Follow the manufacturer's instructions on the package, otherwise the filler will set incorrectly.

15    Using the applicator, apply the filler paste to the prepared area. Draw the applicator across the surface of the filler to achieve the desired contour and to level the filler surface. As soon as a contour that approximates the original one is achieved, stop working the paste. If you continue, the paste will begin to stick to the applicator. Continue to add thin layers of paste at 20-minute intervals until the level of the filler is just above the surrounding metal.

16    Once the filler has hardened, the excess can be removed with a body file. From then on, progressively finer grades of sandpaper should be used, starting with a 180-grit paper and finishing with 600-grit wet-or-dry paper. Always wrap the sandpaper around a flat rubber or wooden block, otherwise the surface of the filler will not be completely flat. During the sanding of the filler surface, the wet-or-dry paper should be periodically rinsed in water. This will ensure that a very smooth finish is produced in the final stage.

**9.2  Use a marking pen to outline the hinge plate and bolt heads**

**9.4  Hood details**

17   At this point, the repair area should be surrounded by a ring of bare metal, which in turn should be encircled by the finely feathered edge of good paint. Rinse the repair area with clean water until all of the dust produced by the sanding operation is gone.

18   Spray the entire area with a light coat of primer. This will reveal any imperfections in the surface of the filler. Repair the imperfections with fresh filler paste or glaze filler and once more smooth the surface with sandpaper. Repeat this spray-and-repair procedure until you are satisfied that the surface of the filler and the feathered edge of the paint are perfect. Rinse the area with clean water and allow it to dry completely.

19   The repair area is now ready for painting. Spray painting must be carried out in a warm, dry, windless and dust free atmosphere. These conditions can be created if you have access to a large indoor work area, but if you are forced to work in the open, you will have to pick the day very carefully. If you are working indoors, dousing the floor in the work area with water will help settle the dust which would otherwise be in the air. If the repair area is confined to one body panel, mask off the surrounding panels. This will help minimize the effects of a slight mismatch in paint color. Trim pieces such as chrome strips, door handles, etc., will also need to be masked off or removed. Use masking tape and several thicknesses of newspaper for the masking operations.

20   Before spraying, shake the paint can thoroughly, then spray a test area until the spray painting technique is mastered. Cover the repair area with a thick coat of primer. The thickness should be built up using several thin layers of primer rather than one thick one. Using 600-grit wet-or-dry sandpaper, rub down the surface of the primer until it is very smooth. While doing this, the work area should be thoroughly rinsed with water and the wet-or-dry sandpaper periodically rinsed as well. Allow the primer to dry before spraying additional coats.

21   Spray on the top coat, again building up the thickness by using several thin layers of paint. Begin spraying in the center of the repair area and then, using a circular motion, work out until the whole repair area and about two inches of the surrounding original paint is covered. Remove all masking material 10 to 15 minutes after spraying on the final coat of paint. Allow the new paint at least two weeks to harden, then use a very fine rubbing compound to blend the edges of the new paint into the existing paint. Finally, apply a coat of wax.

## 6   Body repair - major damage

1   Major damage must be repaired by an auto body shop specifically equipped to perform unibody repairs. These shops have the specialized equipment required to do the job properly.

2   If the damage is extensive, the body must be checked for proper alignment or the vehicle's handling characteristics may be adversely affected and other components may wear at an accelerated rate.

3   Due to the fact that all of the major body components (hood, fenders, etc.) are separate and replaceable units, any seriously

damaged components should be replaced rather than repaired. Sometimes the components can be found in a wrecking yard that specializes in used vehicle components, often at considerable savings over the cost of new parts.

## 7   Hinges and locks - maintenance

Once every 3000 miles, or every three months, the hinges and latch assemblies on the doors, hood and trunk should be given a few drops of light oil or lock lubricant. The door latch strikers should also be lubricated with a thin coat of grease to reduce wear and ensure free movement. Lubricate the door and trunk locks with spray-on graphite lubricant.

## 8   Windshield and fixed glass - replacement

Replacement of the windshield and fixed glass requires the use of special fast-setting adhesive/caulk materials and some specialized tools and techniques. These operations should be left to a dealer service department or a shop specializing in glass work.

## 9   Hood - removal, installation and adjustment

*Refer to illustrations 9.2, 9.4 and 9.10*
**Note:** *The hood is heavy and somewhat awkward to remove and install - at least two people should perform this procedure.*

### Removal and installation

1   Use blankets or pads to cover the cowl area of the body and the fenders. This will protect the body and paint as the hood is lifted off.

2   Scribe alignment marks around the bolt heads to insure proper alignment during installation (a permanent-type felt-tip marker also will work for this) **(see illustration).**

3   Disconnect any cables or wire harnesses which will interfere with removal.

4   Have an assistant support the weight of the hood. Remove the hinge-to-hood bolts **(see illustration).**

5   Lift off the hood.

6   Installation is the reverse of removal.

**11**

**9.10 Adjust the hood height by screwing the hood bumpers in or out**

**10.4 Hood cable details**

## Adjustment

7    Fore-and-aft and side-to-side adjustment of the hood is done by moving the hood in relation to the hinge plate after loosening the bolts.

8    Scribe or trace a line around the entire hinge plate so you can judge the amount of movement.

9    Loosen the bolts or nuts and move the hood into correct alignment. Move it only a little at a time. Tighten the hinge bolts or nuts and carefully lower the hood to check the alignment.

10    Adjust the hood bumpers on the radiator support so the hood is flush with the fenders when closed **(see illustration)**.

11    The safety catch assembly on the hood itself can also be adjusted fore-and-aft and side-to-side after loosening the bolts.

12    The hood latch assembly, as well as the hinges, should be periodically lubricated with white lithium-base grease to prevent sticking and wear.

## 10    Hood latch and cable - removal and installation

*Refer to illustration 10.4*

### Latch

1    Remove the bolts, detach the latch assembly, then use a screwdriver to detach the cable end.

2    Installation is the reverse of removal.

### Cable

3    For access to the cable-latch connection, either remove the latch or use a small screwdriver to pry out the push-in fasteners and detach the black plastic latch cover.

4    In the passenger compartment, remove the bolts and detach the hood release cable and handle assembly **(see illustration)**.

**11.1  Typical radiator grille details**

**11.2 Align the grille tab with this notch, then lower the grille into place**

5   Under the dash, remove the cable grommet from the firewall.
6   Connect a string or piece of wire to the engine compartment end of the cable, then detach the cable and pull it through the firewall into the passenger compartment.
7   Connect the string or wire to the new cable and pull it through the firewall into the engine compartment.
8   The remainder of installation is the reverse of removal.

## 11   Radiator grille - removal and installation

*Refer to illustrations 11.1 and 11.2*

1   Open the hood, remove the headlight bezels (earlier models), then remove the six retaining screws and detach the grille from the vehicle **(see illustration)**.
2   Align the tab with the notch in the radiator support and lower the grille into position **(see illustration)**.
3   Install the grille screws finger-tight, then install the headlight bezels (earlier models). Tighten the grille screws securely.

## 12   Front fender - removal and installation

*Refer to illustration 12.3*

1   Loosen the front wheel lug nuts. Raise the vehicle, support it securely on jackstands and remove the front wheel.
2   Disconnect the antenna and all light bulb electrical connectors and other components that would interfere with fender removal.
3   Remove the fender mounting bolts and nuts **(see illustration)**.
4   Detach the fender. It's a good idea to have an assistant support the fender while it's being moved away from the vehicle to prevent damage to the surrounding body panels.

FENDER SHIELD

FENDER ASSEMBLY

**12.3 Front fender details**

5   Installation is the reverse of removal.
6   Tighten all nuts, bolts and screws securely. Tighten the wheel lug nuts to the torque listed in the Chapter 1 Specifications.

## 13   Bumpers - removal and installation

*Refer to illustration 13.4*

1   If necessary for access, raise the vehicle and support it securely on jackstands.
2   Disconnect any wiring or other components that would interfere with bumper removal.
3   Support the bumper with a jack or have an assistant support the bumper as the bolts are removed.
4   Mark their locations, then remove the mounting bolts and detach the bumper **(see illustration)**.
5   Installation is the reverse of removal. Be sure to align the matchmarks.
6   Tighten the mounting bolts securely.
7   Install the bumper and any other components that were removed.

## 14   Door trim panel - removal and installation

*Refer to illustrations 14.2a, 14.2b, 14.5, 14.6, 14.8a and 14.8b*

1   Disconnect the negative cable from the battery.
2   Remove all door trim panel retaining screws and door pull/armrest assemblies **(see illustrations)**.

**13.4 Mark their locations, then remove the bolts**

**14.2a Remove the screws, pull the door handle out, lift the bezel off ...**

**14.2b ... then use a screwdriver to detach any electrical connectors**

11

14.5  Pry the clips at the corner free, pull out sharply on the panel to detach it from the door, then lift it up and off the door

14.6  Pull the watershield off very carefully, so it won't be torn

14.8a  Place the top of the trim panel in position . . .

3    On manual window models, remove the window crank screw, using an Allen wrench. On power window models, remove the screw, pry out the control switch assembly and unplug it.

4    Insert a putty knife between the trim panel and the door and disengage the retaining clips. Work around the outer edge until the panel is free.

5    Once all of the clips are disengaged, detach the trim panel, unplug any wire harness connectors and remove the trim panel from the vehicle (see illustration).

6    For access to the inner door, carefully peel back the plastic watershield (see illustration).

7    Prior to installation of the door panel, be sure to reinstall any clips in the panel which may have come out during the removal procedure and remain in the door itself.

8    Plug in the electrical connectors and place the panel in position in the door (see illustration). Press the trim panel into place until the clips are seated (see illustration).

9    Install the armrest/door pulls and the window switch or crank. Reconnect the battery negative cable.

14.8b  . . . then use the heel of your hand to seat the clips

## 15   Door - removal, installation and adjustment

Refer to illustrations 15.3a and 15.3b

1    Remove the door trim panel. Disconnect any electrical connectors and push them through the door opening so they won't interfere with door removal.

2    Place a jack under the door or have an assistant on hand to support it when the hinge bolts are removed. Note: If a jack is used, place a rag between it and the door to protect the door's painted surfaces.

3    Drive out the pins and carefully lift off the door (see illustrations).

4    Installation is the reverse of removal.

5    Following installation of the door, check the alignment and adjust it if necessary as follows:

15.3a  Typical front door hinge details

15.3b  Rear door hinge details

16.2  Typical front door latch details

---

a) *Up-and-down and forward-and-backward adjustments are made by carefully bending the hinges slightly, using a special tool (take the vehicle to a dealer service department or auto body repair shop).*

b) *The door lock striker can also be adjusted both up-and-down and sideways to provide positive engagement with the lock mechanism. This is done by loosening the mounting bolts and moving the striker as necessary.*

---

## 16   Door latch, lock cylinder and outside handle - removal and installation

*Refer to illustrations 16.2, 16.3, 16.7, 16.8 and 16.10*

1    Close the window completely and remove the door trim panel and watershield (see Section 14).

16.7  Insert an Allen wrench into the adjustment hole, loosen the screw and move the wrench up in the slot to remove the slack from the linkage

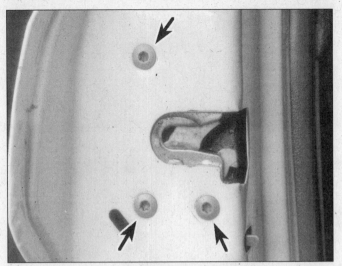

16.3  A Torx-head tool will be required to remove the door latch screws (arrows)

### Latch

2    Disconnect the link rods from the latch (see illustration).
3    Remove the three Torx-head mounting screws (see illustration). It may be necessary to use an impact-type screwdriver to loosen them.
4    Remove the latch from the door.
5    Place the latch in position and install the screws. Tighten the screws securely.
6    Connect the link rods to the latch.
7    Check the door to make sure it closes properly. Readjust the latch (by loosening the screws and moving it) as necessary until the door closes smoothly (with the door handle flush with the door). After installation, loosen the linkage adjusting screw by inserting a 5/32-inch Allen wrench through the adjustment hole in the end of the door (see illustration). Loosen the adjustment screw and push it up in the slot to remove all slack from the linkage, then tighten it.

### Lock cylinder

8    Disconnect the link, use a screwdriver to push off the retainer clip and withdraw the lock cylinder from the door (see illustration). Disconnect the link, push the retainer off with a screwdriver and remove the lock cylinder.
9    Installation is the reverse of removal.

16.8  Typical lock cylinder details

**11**

16.10  Typical outside door handle details

## Outside handle

10    Disconnect the outside handle (remote control) link from the latch, remove the mounting nuts and detach the handle from the door **(see illustration)**.

11    Place the handle in position, attach the link and install the nuts. Tighten the nuts securely.

## 17    Door window glass - removal, installation and adjustment

*Refer to illustrations 17.2, 17.4 and 17.10*

1    Remove the door trim panel and watershield (see Section 14).

## Front door

2    Lower the glass enough to provide access and remove the three mounting nuts **(see illustration)**.

3    Lower the window mechanism completely and disengage the glass.

4    Remove the outer glass weatherstrip by pulling it up and out of the door **(see illustration)**.

5    Lift the glass up and out of the door toward the outside of the window opening.

6    Install the glass by lowering it into door and seating it in the regulator mechanism.

7    Install the nuts and bolts finger tight, raise the glass until it seats in the channel at the top of the door, then tighten the nuts and bolts securely.

17.4  Grasp the weatherstrip and pull it up and out of the door

17.2  Lower the glass for access, then remove the three retaining nuts

8    Lower the glass and seat the weatherstripping, align the clips and press them into place. Install the door trim panel.

## Rear door

9    Remove the end seals from the door.

10    Remove the fixed vent window support bracket and detach the division channel-to-door inner panel brackets **(see illustration)**.

11    Remove the door glass run weatherstrip.

12    Remove the screw from the top of the division channel and remove the fixed glass.

13    Detach the clips and remove the outside weatherstripping.

14    Raise the division channel, door glass and drive arm assembly, rotate it 90-degrees and lift it out through the glass opening.

15    Installation is the reverse or removal.

## 18    Door window regulator - removal and installation

1    Remove the door trim panel and watershield (see Section 14).

## Flex-drive regulator

*Refer to illustration 18.3*

2    Move the glass attachment to the door access hole and remove the glass-to-drive arm bolt.

3    Drill out the rivets securing the regulator to the door **(see illustration)**.

4    Rotate the regulator and flex drive assembly and withdraw it from the door through the access hole.

5    Installation is the reverse of removal. Make sure the flex drive is clean and well lubricated with multi-purpose grease before installation. Tighten the nuts and screws evenly to prevent the possibility of binding.

## Gear-type regulator

*Refer to illustration 18.7*

6    Prop the window glass in the fully up position. **Caution:** *The window glass must be in the full-up position throughout the entire procedure.*

7    Drill out the retaining rivets, detach the regulator arm and remove the regulator from the door **(see illustration)**.

8    Install the regulator by placing it in position, and connecting the arm to the lift plate.

DIVISION CHANNEL

FIXED GLASS OR PLUG

SUPPORT BRACKET

END SEAL

DIVISION BRACKETS

FLEX DRIVE REGULATOR

TAB

GLASS RUN WEATHERSTRIP

GLASS

END SEAL

DRIVE ARM

GLASS ATTACHMENT

**17.10 Rear door window glass details**

RIVET

**18.7 Gear-type regulator details**

## 19 Center console - removal and installation

*Refer to illustration 19.3*

1    Disconnect the negative battery cable.

2    Pry out the retainers and remove the carpet from both sides of the console (if equipped).

3    Remove the mounting screws **(see illustration)**.

4    Lift the console up sufficiently for access to the wiring and unplug the connectors.

FRONT DOOR GLASS CHANNEL

POWER WINDOW REGULATOR (FLEX DRIVE)

GLASS RUN

**18.3 Typical flex drive window regulator installation details**

CENTER ARM REST

CONSOLE

BRACKET MANUAL TRANS.

BRACKET AUTO TRANS.

**19.3 Center console details**

11

**20.3 Draw around the bolt heads with a marking pen so the trunk lid can be installed in the same position**

5    On manual transaxles, unscrew the shift knob.
6    On automatic transaxles, it may be necessary to disconnect the shift cable to allow clearance so the console can be removed.
7    Remove the console.
8    Installation is the reverse of removal.

## 20   Trunk lid - removal, installation and adjustment

*Refer to illustration 20.3*
1    Open the trunk lid and cover the edges of the trunk compartment with pads or cloths to protect the painted surfaces when the lid is removed.
2    Disconnect any cables or electrical connectors attached to the trunk lid that would interfere with removal.
3    Use a marking pen to make alignment marks around the hinge bolt mounting flanges **(see illustration)**.
4    While an assistant supports it's weight, remove the hinge bolts from both sides and lift the trunk lid off.
5    Installation is the reverse of removal. **Note:** *When reinstalling the trunk lid, align the hinge bolt flanges with the marks made during removal.*
6    After installation, close the lid and see if it's in proper alignment with the surrounding panels. Fore-and-aft and side-to-side adjustments of the lid are controlled by the position of the hinge bolts in the slots. To adjust it, loosen the hinge bolts, reposition the lid and retighten the bolts.
7    The height of the lid in relation to the surrounding body panels when closed can be adjusted by loosening the lock striker bolts, repositioning the striker and retightening the bolts.

## 21   Liftgate - removal, installation and adjustment

*Refer to illustration 21.4*
1    Open the liftgate and cover the upper body area around the opening with pads or cloths to protect the painted surfaces when the liftgate is removed.
2    Unplug all electrical connectors and pull the wire harness out of the liftgate (tie string or wire to the cables so they can be pulled back into the body when the liftgate is reinstalled).
3    Paint or scribe alignment marks around the liftgate hinge flanges.
4    While an assistant supports the liftgate, remove the clips and pins and detach the support struts **(see illustration)**.
5    Remove the hinge bolts and detach the liftgate from the vehicle.
6    Installation is the reverse of removal. Be extremely careful with the wire harness when threading it back into the liftgate or you could cut it on a metal edge.
7    After installation, close the liftgate and make sure it's in proper alignment with the surrounding body panels.
8    If the liftgate needs to be adjusted, loosen the hinge bolts slightly,

**21.4 Liftgate prop details**

**22.3a Cluster bezel attachment details**

gently close the liftgate and verify that it's centered (the striker should center it). Then carefully open the liftgate and retighten the hinge bolts.

## 22   Instrument cluster bezel - removal and installation

*Refer to illustrations 22.3a and 22.3b*
1    On column shift models, place the shift lever in position 1.
2    On tilt steering models, lower the steering wheel to its lowest position.
3    Remove the six screws and detach the bezel from the clips **(see illustrations)**. A small pick with a bent end (available at auto parts stores) makes the job of detaching these clips easier. Insert the tool into the gap between the bezel and surrounding dash panel, rotate the end of the tool behind the bezel until you have a good purchase and pull out sharply to detach the clips. Work around the outer circumference until all of the clips are detached, then lift the bezel off.
4    Place the bezel in position and push it into place until any clips are seated and install the screws.

## 23   Dashboard panels - removal and installation

### *Lower trim bezel*

*Refer to illustration 23.2*
1    Remove the instrument cluster bezel (see Section 22).
2    Remove the screws and detach the trim bezel from the dashboard **(see illustration)**.
3    Installation is the reverse of removal.

**22.3b  This tool (available at auto parts stores) makes the job of detaching the bezel clips easier - simply insert it between the bezel and the dashboard, rotate it to get a good purchase on the bezel and pull out**

**23.2  Typical lower trim bezel details**

## Steering column cover

*Refer to illustration 23.4*

4    Detach the clips and lower the cover from the dashboard **(see illustration)**.
5    Installation is the reverse of removal.

## Glove box

*Refer to illustration 23.7*

6    Open the glove box and detach the retainer strap (if equipped).
7    Remove the glove box retaining screws, detach the glove box and remove it from the dashboard **(see illustration)**.
8    Installation is the reverse of removal.

## 24  Steering column cover - removal and installation

1    Disconnect the negative battery cable.
2    Remove the screws and detach the lower half of the column cover.
3    Unscrew the steering column tilt lever and remove the upper half of the cover.

## 25  Mirrors - removal and installation

*Refer to illustrations 25.1 and 25.4*

## Interior

1    Use a Phillips head screwdriver to remove the set screw, then slide the mirror up off the button on the windshield **(see illustration)**.
2    Installation is the reverse of removal.

LOWER STEERING COLUMN COVER

CLIP

**23.4  Typical lower steering column cover details**

INSTRUMENT PANEL

GLOVE BOX

GLOVE BOX RETAINER

MOUNTING SCREW

**23.7  Typical glove box details**

WINDSHIELD

MIRROR

BUTTON

**25.1  The interior mirror fits over a button on the glass and is held in position by a screw**

11

**25.4 Exterior mirror details**

## Exterior

3    If equipped with power mirrors, remove the door trim panel (see Section 14).

4    Remove the screws and detach the mirror knob and bezel **(see illustration)**.

5    Remove the nuts and detach the mirror from the door.

6    Installation is the reverse of removal.

## 26  Wheelhouse splash shields - removal and installation

*Refer to illustration 26.2*

1    Apply the parking brake. Loosen the wheel lug nuts, raise the front of the vehicle and support it securely on jackstands. Remove the wheel(s).

2    The wheelhouse splash shield is retained by plastic (tree-type) fasteners, which generally aren't reusable after removal. Carefully pry the fasteners out with pliers or wire cutters **(see illustration)**.

3    After all the fasteners have been removed, detach the splash shield.

4    To install the splash shield, hold it in position and install the new plastic fasteners.

**26.2 Typical wheelhouse splash shield details**

## 27  Seats - removal and installation

*Refer to illustration 27.2*

### Front

1    Move the seat forward.

2    Remove the seat track nuts, then move the seat to the rear and remove the bolts at the front **(see illustration)**. Unplug any electrical connectors attached to the seat.

3    Lift the seat from the vehicle.

4    Installation is the reverse of removal.

### Rear

5    Remove the two seat cushion-to-floor bolts and lift the seat cushion out of the vehicle.

6    Remove the two bolts from the bottom of the seat back, detach the seat belts, then lift the seat back out.

7    Installation is the reverse of removal.

**27.2 Typical front seat details**

# Chapter 12
# Chassis electrical system

## Contents

## 1   General information

The electrical system is a 12-volt, negative ground type. Power for the lights and all electrical accessories is supplied by a lead/acid-type battery which is charged by the alternator.

This Chapter covers repair and service procedures for the various electrical components not associated with the engine. Information on the battery, alternator, distributor and starter motor can be found in Chapter 5. **Warning:** *When working on the electrical system, disconnect the negative battery cable from the battery to prevent electrical shorts and/or fires.*

## 2   Electrical troubleshooting - general information

A typical electrical circuit consists of an electrical component, any switches, relays, motors, fuses, fusible links or circuit breakers related to the component and the wiring and connectors that link the component to both the battery and the chassis. To help pinpoint an electrical circuit problem, wiring diagrams are included at the end of this Chapter.

Before tackling any troublesome electrical circuit, first study the appropriate wiring diagrams to get a complete understanding of what makes up that individual circuit. Trouble spots, for instance, can often be narrowed down by noting if other components related to the circuit are operating properly. If several components or circuits fail at one time, chances are the problem is in a fuse or ground connection, because several circuits are often routed through the same fuse and ground connections.

Electrical problems usually stem from simple causes, such as loose or corroded connections, a blown fuse, a melted fusible link or a bad relay. Visually inspect the condition of all fuses, wires and connections in a problem circuit before troubleshooting it.

If testing instruments are going to be utilized, use the diagrams to plan ahead of time where to make the necessary connections to accurately pinpoint the trouble spot.

The basic tools needed for electrical troubleshooting include a circuit tester or voltmeter (a 12-volt bulb with a set of test leads can also be used), a continuity tester (which includes a bulb, battery and set of test leads) and a jumper wire, preferably with a circuit breaker incorporated, which can be used to bypass electrical components. Before attempting to locate a problem with test instruments, use the wiring diagram(s) to decide where to make the connections.

### Voltage checks

Voltage checks should be performed if a circuit isn't functioning properly. Connect one lead of a circuit tester to either the negative battery terminal or a known good ground. Connect the other lead to a connector in the circuit being tested, preferably nearest to the battery or fuse. If the bulb of the tester lights, voltage is present, which means the part of the circuit between the connector and the battery is problem free. Continue checking the rest of the circuit in the same fashion. When you reach a point where no voltage is present, the problem lies between that point and the last test point with voltage. Most of the time the problem can be traced to a loose connection. **Note:** *Keep in mind that some circuits receive voltage only when the ignition key is in the Accessory or Run position.*

### Finding a short

One method of finding a short in a circuit is to remove the fuse and connect a test light or voltmeter in its place to the fuse terminals. There should be no voltage present in the circuit. Move the wiring harness from side-to-side while watching the test light. If the bulb lights, there's a short to ground somewhere in that area, probably where the insulation has rubbed through. The same test can be performed on each component in the circuit, even a switch.

### Ground check

Perform a ground test to check whether a component is properly grounded. Disconnect the battery and connect one lead of a self-powered test light, known as a continuity tester, to a known good ground. Connect the other lead to the wire or ground connection being tested. If the bulb lights, the ground is good. If the bulb doesn't light, the ground is no good.

### Continuity check

A continuity check is done to determine if there are breaks in a circuit - if it's capable of passing electricity properly. With the circuit off (no power in the circuit), a self-powered continuity tester can be used to check it. Connect the test leads to both ends of the circuit (or to the "power" end and a good ground) - if the test light comes on the circuit is passing current properly. If the light doesn't come on, there's a break (open) somewhere in the circuit. The same procedure can be used to test a switch by connecting the continuity tester to the switch terminals. With the switch on, the test light should come on.

### Finding an open circuit

When diagnosing for possible open circuits, it's often difficult to locate them by sight because oxidation or terminal misalignment are hidden by the connectors. Merely wiggling a connector on a sensor or in the wiring harness may correct the open circuit condition. Remember this when an open is indicated when troubleshooting a circuit. Intermittent problems may also be caused by oxidized or loose connections. Electrical troubleshooting is simple if you keep in mind that all electrical circuits are basically electricity running from the battery, through the wires, switches, relays, fuses and fusible links to each electrical component (light bulb, motor, etc.) and to ground, where it's passed back to the battery. Any electrical problem is an interruption in the flow of electricity to and from the battery.

---

### 3    Fuses - general information

*Refer to illustrations 3.1 and 3.3*

The electrical circuits of the vehicle are protected by a combination of fuses, circuit breakers and fusible links. The fuse block is located under the instrument panel on the left side of the dashboard **(see illustration)**. For access, grasp the lower steering column cover securely and detach it (see Chapter 11).

Each of the fuses is designed to protect a specific circuit, and the various circuits are identified on the fuse panel itself.

Miniaturized fuses are employed in the fuse block. These compact fuses, with blade terminal design, allow fingertip removal and replacement. If an electrical component fails, always check the fuse first. A blown fuse is easily detected with a test light - if voltage is available on one side of the fuse but not the other, it's blown (the circuit must be energized for this check). You can also visually inspect the element for evidence of damage **(see illustration)**.

Be sure to replace blown fuses with the correct type. Fuses of

**3.1  The fuse block is located under the left side of the instrument panel - this is a typical fuse block component layout**

**3.3  The fuses can be easily checked visually to determine if they are blown**

different ratings are physically interchangeable, but only fuses of the proper rating should be used. Replacing a fuse with one of a higher or lower value than specified is not recommended. Each electrical circuit needs a specific amount of protection. The amperage value of each fuse is molded into the fuse body.

If the replacement fuse immediately fails, don't replace it again until the cause of the problem is isolated and corrected. In most cases, the cause will be a short circuit in the wiring caused by a broken or deteriorated wire.

---

### 4    Fusible links - general information

*Refer to illustrations 4.2a and 4.2b*

Some circuits are protected by fusible links. The links are used in circuits which are not ordinarily fused, such as the ignition circuit.

Although the fusible links appear to be a heavier gauge than the wires they're protecting, the appearance is due to the thick insulation **(see illustration)**. All fusible links are several wire gauges smaller than the wire they're designed to protect. Fusible links can't be repaired, but a new link of the same size wire can be installed. The procedure is as follows:

a) *Disconnect the negative cable from the battery.*
b) *Disconnect the fusible link from the wiring harness.*
c) *Cut the damaged fusible link out of the wire just behind the connector.*
d) *Strip the insulation back approximately 1-inch **(see illustration)**.*
e) *Position the connector on the new fusible link and crimp it into place.*
f) *Use rosin core solder at each end of the new link to obtain a good connection.*
g) *Use plenty of electrical tape around the soldered joint. No wires should be exposed.*
h) *Connect the negative battery cable. Test the circuit for proper operation.*

**4.2a The fusible links (arrow) are located in the engine compartment adjacent to the battery**

**4.2b Typical fusible link repair details**

**8.2 Unplug the electrical connector from the dimmer switch**

## 5 Circuit breakers - general information

Circuit breakers protect components such as power windows, power door locks and headlights. Some circuit breakers are located in the fuse box **(see illustration 3.1)**. On some models the circuit breaker resets itself automatically, so an electrical overload in the circuit will cause it to fail momentarily, then come back on. If the circuit doesn't come back on, check it immediately. Once the condition is corrected, the circuit breaker will resume its normal function. Some circuit breakers may have a button on top and must be reset manually.

## 6 Relays - general information

Several electrical accessories in the vehicle utilize relays to transmit current to the component **(see illustration 3.1)**. If the relay is defective, the component won't operate properly.

If a faulty relay is suspected, it can be removed and tested by a dealer service department or a repair shop. Defective relays must be replaced as a unit.

## 7 Turn signal and hazard flashers - check and replacement

### *Turn signal flasher*

1    The turn signal flasher, a small canister-shaped unit located in the fuse block under the instrument panel, flashes the turn signals **(see illustration 3.1)**. On later models the turn signal and hazard flasher are combined into one unit. This unit is usually coded yellow for easy identification.
2    When the flasher unit is functioning properly, an audible click can be heard during its operation. If the turn signals fail on one side or the other and the flasher unit doesn't make its characteristic clicking sound, a faulty turn signal bulb is indicated.
3    If both turn signals fail to blink, the problem may be due to a blown fuse, a faulty flasher unit, a broken switch or a loose or open connection. If a quick check of the fuse box indicates the turn signal fuse has blown, check the wiring for a short before installing a new fuse.
4    To replace the flasher, simply detach it from its electrical connector and plug in the new one.
5    Make sure the replacement is identical to the original. Compare the old one to the new one before installing it.
6    Installation is the reverse of removal.

### *Hazard flasher*

7    The hazard flasher, a small canister-shaped unit located in the fuse block under the dash, flashes all four turn signals simultaneously when activated. On later models the hazard flasher unit is incorporated with the turn signal flasher into one unit (see Step 1).
8    The hazard flasher is checked just like the turn signal flasher (see Steps 2 and 3).
9    To replace the hazard flasher, pull it out of the fuse block, harness or relay module.
10    Make sure the replacement is identical to the original. Compare the old one to the new one before installing it.
11    Installation is the reverse of removal.

## 8 Headlight dimmer switch - check and replacement

*Refer to illustrations 8.2, 8.3 and 8.6*

**12**

### *Check*

1    Remove the steering column cover.
2    Unplug the electrical connector from the switch **(see illustration)**.

3    Use an ohmmeter to check the continuity between the switch terminals. There should be continuity between the B and H terminals with the switch in the high beam position and the B and L terminals in the low beam position **(see illustration)**. If there isn't, replace the switch.

## Replacement

4    Remove the two bolts and lower the switch from the steering column.
5    Place the new switch in position and install the mounting bolts finger tight.
6    Insert an adjustment pin fabricated from a piece of wire. Push the switch to the rear to take up the slack in the actuator control rod, then tighten the bolts securely **(see illustration)**.
7    Remove the pin, plug in the connector and install the steering column cover.

## 9    Turn signal/hazard warning switch - check and replacement

*Refer to illustrations 9.4, 9.5, 9.10a, 9.10b, 9.10c and 9.12*
1    The turn signal switch is located at the top end of the steering column and is operated by the multi-function control stalk. The hazard warning switch is mounted under the turn signal switch, next to the ignition key light.

## Check

2    Disconnect the negative cable from the battery.
3    Remove the steering column lower cover.
4    Unplug the turn signal switch electrical connector **(see illustration)**.
5    Use an ohmmeter or self-powered test light to check for continuity between the indicated switch connector terminals **(see illustration)**.
6    Replace the turn signal or hazard switch if the continuity is not as specified.

## Replacement

7    Disconnect the negative battery cable, then remove the steering wheel (see Chapter 10).
8    Detach the wiring harness trough from the steering column.
9    Unplug the electrical connector **(see illustration 9.4)**.

**8.3  Terminal continuity guide for a typical electrical connector of the headlight dimmer switch**

10    Install a lock plate removal tool, depress the lock plate, remove the retaining ring and remove the lock plate **(see illustrations)**. Remove the hazard warning knob and ignition key lamp.

**8.6  An exploded view of a typical dimmer switch assembly - you can fabricate your own adjustment pin using a piece of coat hanger or paper clip, or use proper size drill bits**

**9.4  Details of the steering column electrical connectors**

11  Remove the wiper/washer switch pivot screw, leaving the control stalk in place.

12  Remove the three screws and detach the turn signal switch **(see illustration)**. Carefully pull the wiring harness out through the top of the steering column.

13  Installation is the reverse of removal, remembering to lubricate the steering shaft contact surfaces with multi-purpose grease and to make sure the dimmer switch rod is located securely in the pocket of the control stalk.

## 10  Wiper/washer switch -check and replacement

*Refer to illustrations 10.5, 10.14 and 10.15*

1  These models are equipped with a multi-function lever located on the left side of the steering column which controls the wiper/washer, turn signal and dimmer switches mounted on the steering column.

### *Check*

2  Disconnect the negative cable from the battery.

3  Remove the steering column lower cover.

4  Unplug the electrical connector **(see illustration 9.4)**.

5  Use an ohmmeter or self-powered test light to check for continuity between the switch terminals at the electrical connector **(see illustration)**.

6  Replace the wiper/washer switch if the continuity is not as specified.

### *Replacement*

7  Perform the procedures in Steps 2 and 3, then remove the

steering wheel (see Chapter 10).

8  Install a lock plate removal tool, depress the lock plate, remove the retaining ring and remove the lock plate **(see illustrations 9.10a, 9.10b and 9.10c)**. Remove the hazard warning knob and ignition key lamp.

9  Detach the wiring harness trough from the steering column.

10  Unplug the electrical connector **(see illustration 9.4)**.

11  Remove the housing cover screws and pull the cover off.

12  Pull the switch hider out for access.

13  On intermittent wiper or cruise control equipped models, remove the two screws and detach the switch from the stalk, then remove the

### SWITCH CONTINUITY CHART

| Turn Signal Switch | | | |
|---|---|---|---|
| Switch Position: | Left | Neutral | Right |
| Continuity Between: | 7 and 4 | 10 and 9 | 7 and 5 |
| Continuity Between: | 7 and 8 | 10 and 8 | 7 and 9 |
| Continuity Between:* | 21 and 23 | — | 22 and 21 |
| Continuity Between: | 10 and 9 | — | 10 and 8 |
| **Hazard Warning Switch** | | | |
| Switch Position: | Off | | On |
| Continuity Between: | 10 and 9 | | 6 and 4 |
| Continuity Between: | 10 and 8 | | 6 and 5 |
| Continuity Between: | — | | 6 and 8 |
| Continuity Between: | — | | 6 and 9 |
| *Cornering Lamps Only | | | |

**9.5  Turn signal and hazard switch continuity chart**

**9.10a  On tilt column models, install a lock plate removal tool to depress the lock plate . . .**

**9.10b . . . remove the retaining ring from the steering shaft . . .**

**9.10c . . . and remove the lock plate**

STEERING SHAFT BEARING

STEERING COLUMN LOCK HOUSING

TURN SIGNAL SWITCH

SHAFT BEARING HOUSING

**9.12  Typical turn signal switch mounting details**

### INTERMITTENT WIPE SWITCH CONTINUITY CHART

| SWITCH POSITION | CONTINUITY BETWEEN |
|---|---|
| OFF | L and $P_2$ |
| DELAY | $P_1$ and $I_1$<br>R and $I_1$*<br>$I_2$ and G |
| LOW | $P_1$ and L |
| HIGH | $P_1$ and H |

*Resistance at maximum delay position should be between 270,000 ohms and 330,000 ohms.
*Resistance at minimum delay position should be zero with ohmmeter set on the high ohm scale.

**10.5  Wiper/washer switch continuity check chart - continuity should be as specified in the four switch positions**

**12**

**10.14  Rotate the stalk to align the slot with the pin and pull it out**

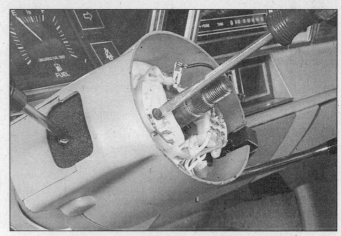

**10.15  Remove the wiper/washer switch pivot screw**

wiper knob from the end of the stalk.
14   Rotate the control stalk fully clockwise, align the slot and pin, then pull the stalk out **(see illustration)**.
15   Remove the screws and detach the wiper switch **(see illustration)**.
16   Installation is the reverse of removal.

## 11   Ignition switch - check and replacement

*Refer to illustrations 11.1 and 11.3*
1    The ignition switch is located on the steering column and is actuated by a rod attached to the key lock cylinder **(see illustration)**.

### Check

2    Remove the switch (see Steps 5 through 8).
3    Use an ohmmeter or self-powered test light and the accompanying diagram to check for continuity between the switch terminals **(see illustration)**.
4    If the switch does not have correct continuity, replace it.

### Replacement

5    Disconnect the negative cable from the battery.
6    Insert the key into the lock cylinder and turn it to the Acc position.
7    Remove the steering column cover (see Chapter 11). On some models it may be necessary to remove the bolts or nuts and lower the steering column for access to the switch.

8    Unplug the electrical connector, remove the bolts, then detach the switch from the actuator rod and lower it from the steering column.
9    Installation is the reverse of removal. With the switch in the Lock position engage it to the actuator rod, then push up on the switch to remove any slack from the rod before fully tightening the bolts.

## 12   Headlight - replacement

*Refer to illustrations 12.1 and 12.2*
1    Remove the screws and detach the bezel **(see illustration)**.
2    Remove the headlight retainer screws **(see illustration)**. Don't disturb the adjustment screws.
3    Detach the retainer, pull the headlight out, unplug the electrical connector and remove the headlight assembly.
4    Installation is the reverse of removal.

**IGNITION SWITCH CONNECTOR
LOOKING INTO SWITCH**

**11.1  The ignition switch is located on the top right side of the steering column**

| WIRE CAVITY | WIRE COLOR | APPLICATION |
|---|---|---|
| 1 | YELLOW | STARTER RELAY |
| 2 | DARK BLUE | IGNITION RUN/START |
| 3 | GRAY/BLACK | BRAKE WARNING LAMP |
| 4 | PINK/BLACK | IGNITION SWITCH BATTERY FEED |
|   | PINK OR PINK/WHITE |  |
| 5 | BLACK/ORANGE OR BLACK/TAN | RUN ACCESSORY |
| 6 | BLACK OR BLACK/WHITE | ACCESSORY |
| 7 | RED | IGNITION SWITCH BATTERY FEED |

**11.3  Ignition switch continuity chart**

12.1 Headlight bezel details

PARK, TURN SIGNAL AND SIDE MARKER BEZEL

SCREWS

ADJUSTING SCREWS

SCREWS

SCREW

GRILLE PANEL

SPRING

RETAINER

12.2 Remove the headlight retainer screws, making sure not to disturb the adjusting screws

## 13  Headlights - adjustment

**Warning:** *The headlights must be aimed correctly. If adjusted incorrectly, they could temporarily blind the driver of an oncoming vehicle and cause an accident or seriously reduce your ability to see the road. The headlights should be checked for proper aim every 12 months and any time a new headlight is installed or front end body work is performed. The following procedure is only an interim step to provide temporary adjustment until the headlights can be adjusted by a properly equipped shop.*

1    Headlights have two spring loaded adjusting screws, one on the top controlling up-and-down movement and one on the side controlling left-and-right movement **(see illustration 12.2)**.
2    This procedure requires a blank wall 25 feet in front of the vehicle and a level floor.
3    Position masking tape vertically on the wall in reference to the vehicle centerline and the centerlines of both headlights.
4    Position a horizontal tape line in reference to the centerline of all

the headlights. **Note:** *It may be easier to position the tape on the wall with the vehicle parked only a few inches away.*
5    Adjustment should be made with the vehicle sitting level, the gas tank half-full and no unusually heavy load in the vehicle.
6    Starting with the low beam adjustment, position the high intensity zone so it's two inches below the horizontal line and two inches to the right of the headlight vertical line. Adjustment is made by turning the top adjusting screw clockwise to raise the beam and counterclockwise to lower the beam. The adjusting screw on the side should be used in the same manner to move the beam left or right.
7    With the high beams on, the high intensity zone should be vertically centered with the exact center just below the horizontal line. **Note:** *It may not be possible to position the headlight aim exactly for both high and low beams. If a compromise must be made, keep in mind that the low beams are the most used and have the greatest effect on driver safety.*
8    Have the headlights adjusted by a dealer service department or service station at the earliest opportunity.

**12**

**14.1a  Remove the turn signal bulb housing by rotating counterclockwise and withdrawing it**

**14.1b  Push the bulb in and rotate it to remove it**

**14.2  Pull the side marker bulb holder counterclockwise and withdraw it, then pull the bulb straight out**

## 14   Bulb replacement

### Turn signal/parking/side marker/ lights

*Refer to illustrations 14.1a, 14.1b and 14.2*

1    Remove the headlight bezel **(see illustration 12.1)** and detach the bulb by rotating it counterclockwise and pull it out **(see illustrations)**. To remove the bulb from the holder, push the bulb in, turn it counterclockwise and pull it out.

2    The side marker bulb housing is removed the same way as in the previous step, but the bulb can be pulled straight out of the holder **(see illustration)**.

3    Installation is the reverse of removal.

### Tail light

#### Sedan

4    Open the trunk lid for access to the tail light housing.

5    Turn the bulb holder counterclockwise and remove it from the back of the housing. Push in and rotate the turn signal, stop and tail light bulbs counterclockwise to remove them from the holder.

6    Installation is the reverse of removal.

#### Station wagon

*Refer to illustration 14.7*

7    Open the liftgate, remove the nuts and detach the tail light housing **(see illustration)**.

8    Turn the bulb holder counterclockwise and remove it from the back of the housing. Push in and rotate the bulbs counterclockwise to remove them from the holder.

9    Installation is the reverse of removal.

**14.7  On station wagon models, the tail light housing lower nuts are accessible from below the bumper**

### Center high-mounted brake light

*Refer to illustrations 14.10 and 14.11*

#### Sedan

10    Pry off the cover, remove the screws and detach the bulb holder. Pull the bulb holder out and replace the bulb by pulling it straight out **(see illustration)**.

#### Station wagon

11    Open the tailgate. Remove the screws and pry off the housing cover. Pull the bulb socket out and replace the bulb by pulling it straight out **(see illustration)**.

12    Installation is the reverse of removal.

CENTER HIGH-MOUNTED BRAKE LIGHT
PUSH FASTENERS
COVER
BULB
SOCKET
ADAPTER

**14.10  Sedan model center high mounted brake light details**

SIDE MARKER LAMP
HIGH-LINE
PREMIUM
CORNERING LAMP ASSEMBLY
PARK AND TURN LAMP

**14.11  Station wagon center high mounted brake light details**

DECK LID

VIEW IN DIRECTION OF ARROW Y

BULB

SOCKET AND CABLE ASSEMBLY

LAMP ASSEMBLY

LENS

ATTACHING SCREW

SOCKET AND CABLE ASSEMBLY

LENS

BULB

LIFTGATE

ATTACHING SCREW

LAMP ASSEMBLY

VIEW IN DIRECTION OF ARROW Z

**14.16 License plate bulb removal details**

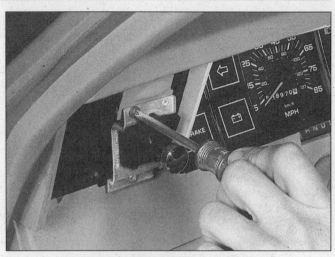

**15.2 Remove the headlight switch screws . . .**

### License plate light

*Refer to illustration 14.16*

16    Remove the screws and detach the license lamp assembly, then remove the bulbs by pulling straight out **(see illustration)**.
17    Installation is the reverse of removal.

### Dome light

18    Pry the dome lamp lens off.
19    Grasp the bulb securely and pull it from the socket.
20    Installation is the reverse of removal.

### 15    Headlight switch - removal and installation

*Refer to illustrations 15.2, 15.3, 15.4 and 15.5*

1    Disconnect the negative battery cable.
2    Remove the lower trim bezel (see Chapter 11). Remove the three screws and pull the switch from the dash panel **(see illustration)**.
3    Carefully pull the switch out of the dash and unplug the electrical connector **(see illustration)**.
4    Press the release button on the side of the switch and withdraw the switch knob and shaft **(see illustration)**.
5    Remove the nut holding the switch on the mounting plate **(see illustration)**.
6    Remove the nut, detach the switch from the mounting plate then remove the switch.
7    Installation is the reverse of removal.

### Instrument cluster lights

13    To gain access to the instrument cluster illumination lights, the instrument cluster will have to be removed (see Section 19). The bulbs can then be removed and replaced from the rear of the cluster.
14    Rotate the bulb counterclockwise to remove it.
15    Installation is the reverse of removal.

**15.3 . . . then pull the switch out and unplug the connector using a rocking motion**

**15.4 Depress the headlight switch button (arrow) while withdrawing the knob and stem**

**15.5 Unscrew the escutcheon mounting nut**

**12**

**16.4a  Remove the instrument panel cover . . .**

**16.3  Radio mounting details**

---

**16   Radio and speakers - removal and installation**

## Radio

*Refer to illustrations 16.3, 16.4a, 16.4b and 16.5*

1   Disconnect the negative battery cable from the battery.
2   Remove the instrument cluster bezel (see Chapter 11).
3   Remove the two mounting screws, pull the radio out far enough to allow the connectors to be unplugged, then remove the radio from the dash **(see illustration)**.

## Speakers

4   On instrument panel mounted speakers, remove the instrument panel top cover, then remove the screws, detach the speaker and

unplug it **(see illustrations)**.
5   On door-mounted speakers, remove the door trim panel (see Chapter 11), remove the retaining screws and unplug the speaker **(see illustration)**.
6   Installation is the reverse of removal.

---

**17   Antenna - removal and installation**

*Refer to illustrations 17.3a, 17.3b and 17.3c*

1   Remove the radio from the dash.
2   Unplug the antenna cable from the back of the radio.
3   Use a small open-end wrench to unscrew the antenna mast, then remove the cap nut and lift off the upper adapter and gasket **(see illustrations)**.
4   Working under the vehicle, remove the three plastic rivets from the rear edge of the inner fender splash shield and pull the shield away for access to the antenna.
5   Detach the antenna from the fender and remove it from the vehicle.
6   Installation is the reverse of removal.

**16.4b  . . . and then the speaker**

**16.5  Door-mounted speaker details**

**17.3a  Unscrew the antenna mast with a small wrench**

**17.3b  Use needle-nose pliers to unscrew the cap nut - be careful, the pliers can easily slip and scratch the fender**

**17.3c  Lift the adapter off the fender**

## 18   Windshield wiper motor - check and replacement

*Refer to illustration 18.9*

### Check

1    If the wiper motor does not run at all, first check the fuse block for a blown fuse (see Section 3).
2    Check the wiper switch (see Section 10).
3    Turn the ignition switch and wiper switch on.
4    Connect a jumper wire between the wiper motor and ground, then retest. If the motor works now, repair the ground connection.
5    If the wipers still don't work, turn on the wipers and check for voltage at the motor connector. If there's voltage, remove the motor and check it off the vehicle with fused jumper wires from the battery. If the motor now works, check for a binding linkage. If the motor still doesn't work, replace it.
6    If there's no voltage at the motor, the problem is in the switch or wiring.

### Replacement

7    Disconnect the negative cable from the battery.
8    Mark their locations, remove the nuts and detach the wiper arms.
9    Unplug the wiper motor electrical connector and remove the mounting bolts **(see illustration)**.
10    Hold the motor drive crank with a wrench, remove the crank nut and detach the crank, then lift the motor out.
11    Installation is the reverse of removal.

**18.9  Typical wiper motor installation details**

RIGHT WIPER BLADE

RIGHT WIPER ARM

LEFT WIPER BLADE

LEFT WIPER ARM

LINKS AND PIVOT ASSEMBLY

LINK

CRANK MOUNTING NUT

DRIVE CRANK

WIPER MOTOR COVER ASSEMBLY

MOTOR MOUNTING NUT

WIPER MOTOR ASSEMBLY

WIPER MOTOR ASSEMBLY

LINKS AND PIVOT ASSEMBLY

PIVOT MOUNTING SCREW

VIEW IN DIRECTION OF ARROW Z

VIEW IN CIRCLE Y

**12**

## 19  Instrument cluster - removal and installation

*Refer to illustration 19.3*

1    Disconnect the negative cable from the battery.
2    Remove the cluster bezel (see Chapter 11).
3    Remove the cluster mounting screws. Pull the assembly out and disconnect the electrical connectors and speedometer cable **(see illustration)**.
4    Installation is the reverse of removal.

## 20  Instrument panel - removal and installation

*Refer to illustration 20.10*

1    Disconnect the negative battery cable. Refer to Chapter 11 and remove the instrument cluster bezel, steering column cover and the dashboard panels.
2    Remove the left and right side cowl and scuff plate panels. On some models it may be necessary to remove the A-pillar covers.
3    Remove the hood release handle.
4    Remove the center floor console (see Chapter 11).
5    Remove the radio and heater/air conditioner controls.
6    Disconnect the PRND21 cable from the steering column. Remove the two nuts retaining the steering column to the support brace and lower the column.
7    Unplug the instrument panel bulkhead electrical connector.
8    Disconnect the heater/air conditioner electrical and vacuum lines.
9    Remove the instrument panel top cover.

**19.3 Disconnect the speedometer cable and electrical connectors from the instrument cluster**

10    Loosen the left and right hand instrument panel pivot screws **(see illustration)**.
11    Remove the screws attaching the instrument panel to the cowl.
12    Roll the instrument panel back for access and unplug any remaining electrical connectors.
13    With an assistant supporting the weight, remove the pivot screws, then remove the instrument panel from the vehicle.
14    Installation is the reverse of removal.

**20.10 Typical instrument panel details**

21.3a Unscrew the speedometer cable at the coupling (if equipped) or . . .

## 21 Speedometer cable - removal and installation

*Refer to illustrations 21.3a and 21.3b*

### Removal

1 Disconnect the negative battery cable.
2 Remove the instrument cluster (see Section 19) and lower steering column cover (see Chapter 11).
3 Disconnect the cable at the transaxle coupling in the engine compartment by unscrewing the collar **(see illustrations)**.
4 In the passenger compartment, pull the speedometer cable and grommet out through the instrument panel and remove it from the vehicle.

### Installation

5 Route the cable through the instrument panel, making sure not to kink it and to seat the grommet securely.
6 Connect the cable to the coupling or transaxle and install the instrument cluster.

## 22 Horn - check and replacement

*Refer to illustrations 22.6 and 22.7*
**Note:** *Check the fuse and relay before beginning electrical diagnosis* (see Section 3).

22.6 Horn tone adjustment details

21.3b . . . at the transaxle

### Check

1 If the horn will not sound, release the parking brake, place the transaxle selector in Park or Neutral and observe the brake warning light on the dash as you start the engine. If the light does not go on, the steering column (and consequently the horn switch) isn't grounded properly to the instrument panel.
2 If the brake light glows but the horn still doesn't sound, unplug the horn connector and check for a blown fuse (see Section 3). Should the new fuse blow out when the horn button is pushed, there is a short in the horn assembly itself or between the fuse block and the horn.
3 If the fuse is good and the horn still doesn't sound, unplug the connector at the horn and connect a test lamp lead. Ground the other lead and observe whether the lamp lights when the horn button is pushed. If it does, the horn is either faulty or improperly grounded. To check the horn for proper grounding, connect a wire between the battery negative cable and the horn bracket, making sure to scratch through the paint. If the horn still doesn't sound, replace the horn relay with a new one (see Section 3).
4 If the horn sounds continuously, replace the relay. If the horn still sounds, detach the steering wheel hub cover and make sure the horn contact wire isn't shorting out against the hub.
5 To adjust the horn tone, first determine which horn needs adjustment. The low-tone horn is on the right side of the radiator support and the high-tone on the right side shield. Unplug the horn that isn't being adjusted.
6 Connect the horn to the positive battery terminal and a remote starter switch and ammeter in series **(see illustration)**.
7 With the remote starter switch depressed, the ammeter should read between 4.5 and 5.5 amps. To adjust, turn the adjusting screw clockwise to increase, or counterclockwise to decrease, the current **(see illustration)**. Check the horn for satisfactory tone and current draw after each adjustment.

### Replacement

8 Unplug the electrical connector(s) and remove the mounting bolt.
9 Installation is the reverse of removal.

22.7 Turn the horn adjusting screw to vary the tone

**12**

CABLE RETAINING CLIP

THROTTLE BODY

THROTTLE LEVER

SPEED CONTROL CABLE

BATTERY TRAY

BRACKET

VACUUM HOSE

BATTERY TRAY

Z

SPEED CONTROL SERVO

VIEW IN DIRECTION OF ARROW Z

**23.1  Cruise control system component layout**

## 23  Cruise control system - description and check

*Refer to illustration 23.1*

1    The cruise control system maintains vehicle speed with servo motor located near the battery in the engine compartment, which is connected to the throttle linkage by a cable. The system consists of the servo motor, brake switch, clutch switch, control switches and associated wiring and vacuum hoses **(see illustration).** Some features of the system may require special testers and diagnostic procedures which are beyond the scope of the home mechanic. Listed below are some general procedures that may be used to locate common problems.

2    Locate and check the fuse (see Section 3).

3    Have an assistant operate the brake lights while you check their operation (voltage from the brake light and (if equipped) clutch switch deactivates the cruise control).

4    If the brake lights don't come on or don't shut off, correct the problem and retest the cruise control. Check the clutch switch (Chapter 8).

5    Visually inspect the vacuum hose connected to the servo and check the control linkage between the cruise control servo and the throttle linkage and replace as necessary.

6    Cruise controls use a speed sensing devices and on these models the speed sensor pickup is located in the transaxle. Inspect the speedometer cable for kinks or damage that would prevent it from turning freely. Remove the bolt and detach the sensor, rotate the sensor and check that it turns easily.

7    Test drive the vehicle to determine if the cruise control is now working. If it isn't, take it to a dealer service department or an automotive electrical specialist for further diagnosis and repair.

## 24  Power window system - description and check

1    The power window system operates the electric motors mounted in the doors which lower and raise the windows. The system consists

of the control switches, the motors, glass mechanisms (regulators) and associated wiring.

2    The windows can be lowered and raised from the master control switch by the driver or by remote switches located at the individual windows. Each window has a separate motor which is reversible. The position of the control switch determines the polarity and therefore the direction of operation. Some systems are equipped with relays that control current flow to the motors.

3    Each motor is equipped with a separate circuit breaker in addition to the fuse or circuit breaker protecting the whole circuit. This prevents one stuck window from disabling the whole system.

4    The power window system will only operate when the ignition switch is ON. In addition, when activated the window lockout switch at the master control switch disables the switches at the passenger's window also. Always check these items before troubleshooting a window problem.

5    These procedures are general in nature, so if you can't find the problem using them, take the vehicle to a dealer service department.

6    If the power windows don't work at all, check the fuse or circuit breaker.

7    If only the rear windows are inoperative, or if the windows only operate from the master control switch, check the rear window lockout switch for continuity in the unlocked position. Replace it if it doesn't have continuity.

8    Check the wiring between the switches and fuse panel for continuity. Repair the wiring, if necessary.

9    If only one window is inoperative from the master control switch, try the other control switch at the window. **Note:** *This doesn't apply to the drivers door window.*

10    If the same window works from one switch, but not the other, check the switch for continuity.

11    If the switch tests OK, check for a short or open in the wiring between the affected switch and the window motor.

12    If one window is inoperative from both switches, remove the trim panel from the affected door and check for voltage at the motor while the switch is operated.

13  If voltage is reaching the motor, disconnect the glass from the regulator (see Chapter 11). Move the window up and down by hand while checking for binding and damage. Also check for binding and damage to the regulator. If the regulator is not damaged and the window moves up and down smoothly, replace the motor. If there's binding or damage, lubricate, repair or replace parts, as necessary.

14  If voltage isn't reaching the motor, check the wiring in the circuit for continuity between the switches and motors. You'll need to consult the wiring diagram for the vehicle.

15  Test the windows after you are done to confirm proper repairs.

## 25  Power door lock system - description and check

1  The power door lock system operates the door lock actuators mounted in each door. The system consists of the switches, actuators, relays and associated wiring. Diagnosis can usually be limited to simple checks of the wiring connections and actuators for minor faults which can be easily repaired.

2  Power door lock systems are operated by bi-directional solenoids located in the doors. The lock switches have two operating positions: Lock and Unlock. These switches activate a relay which in turn connects voltage to the door lock solenoids. Depending on which way the relay is activated, it reverses polarity, allowing the two sides of the circuit to be used alternately as the feed (positive) and ground side.

3  Some vehicles may have anti-theft systems incorporated into the power locks. If you are unable to locate the trouble using the following general steps, consult a dealer service department or other repair shop.

4  Always check the circuit protection first. On these models the battery voltage passes through the 20 amp mini-fuse (F-1) in the engine compartment power distribution center to the 15 amp fuse (number 8) in the fuse block.

5  Operate the door lock switches in both directions (Lock and Unlock) with the engine off. Listen for the faint click of the relay operating.

6  If there's no click, check for voltage at the switches. If no voltage is present, check the wiring between the fuse block and the switches for shorts and opens.

7  If voltage is present but no click is heard, test the switch for continuity. Replace it if there's no continuity in both switch positions.

8  If the switch has continuity but the relay doesn't click, check the wiring between the switch and relay for continuity. Repair the wiring if there's no continuity.

9  If the relay is receiving voltage from the switch but is not sending voltage to the solenoids, check for a bad ground at the relay case. If the relay case is grounding properly, replace the relay.

10  If all but one lock solenoid operates, remove the trim panel from the affected door (see Chapter 11) and check for voltage at the solenoid while the lock switch is operated. One of the wires should have voltage in the Lock position; the other should have voltage in the unlock position.

11  If the inoperative solenoid is receiving voltage, replace the solenoid.

12  If the inoperative solenoid isn't receiving voltage, check for an open or short in the wire between the lock solenoid and the relay.

**Note:** *It's not uncommon for wires to break in the portion of the harness between the body and door (opening and closing the door fatigues and eventually breaks the wires).*

## 26  Power seats - description and check

1  Power seats allow you to adjust the position of the seat with little effort. These models feature a six-way seat that goes forward and backward, up and down and tilts forward and backward. The seats are powered by three reversible motors mounted in one housing that are controlled by switches on the side of the seat. Each switch changes the direction of seat travel by reversing polarity to the drive motor.

2  Diagnosis is a simple matter, using the following procedures.

3  Look under the seat for any object which may be preventing the seat from moving.

4  If the seat won't work at all, check the circuit breaker in the fuse block (see Section 3).

5  With the engine off to reduce the noise level, operate the seat controls in all directions and listen for sound coming from the seat motors.

6  If the motor doesn't work or make noise, check for voltage at the motor while an assistant operates the switch.

7  If the motor is getting voltage but doesn't run, test it off the vehicle with jumper wires. If it still doesn't work, replace it.

8  If the motor isn't getting voltage, remove the switch check for voltage. If there's no voltage at the switch, check the wiring between the fuse block and the switch. If the switch is OK, check for a short or open in the wiring between the switch and motor.

9  Test the completed repairs.

## 27  Rear window defogger - check and repair

*Refer to illustrations 27.4 and 27.13*

1  The rear window defogger consists of a number of horizontal elements baked onto the glass surface.

2  Small breaks in the element can be repaired without removing the rear window.

### *Check*

3  Turn the ignition switch and defogger system switches On.

4  Ground the negative lead of a voltmeter to terminal B and the positive lead to terminal A **(see illustration)**.

5  The voltmeter between 10 and 15 volts. If the reading is lower, there is a poor ground connection.

6  Contact the negative lead to a good body ground. The reading should stay the same.

7  Connect the negative lead to terminal B, then touch each grid line at the mid-point with the positive lead.

8  The reading should be approximately six volts. If the reading is 0, there is a break between mid-point "C" and terminal "A".

9  A 10 to 14 volt reading is an indication of a break between mid-point "C" and terminal B. Move the lead toward the break; the voltage will change when the break is crossed.

### *Repair*

10  Repair the break in the line using repair kit recommended specifically for this purpose, such as Mopar Repair Kit No. 4267922 (or equivalent). Included in this kit is plastic conductive epoxy.

11  Prior to repairing a break, turn off the system and allow it to de-energize for a few minutes.

12  Lightly buff the element area with fine steel wool, then clean it thoroughly with rubbing alcohol.

**27.4  Rear window defogger test points**

**12**

BREAK          GRID LINE

MASKING TAPE

**27.13  To repair a broken grid, first apply a strip of tape to either side of the grid to mask off the area**

13   Use masking tape to mask off the area of repair **(see illustration)**.
14   Mix the epoxy thoroughly, according to the instructions on the package.
15   Apply the epoxy material to the slit in the masking tape, overlapping the undamaged area about 3/4-inch on either end.
16   Allow the repair to cure for 24 hours before removing the tape and using the system.

## 28   Wiring diagrams - general information

*Refer to illustration 28.4*

Since it isn't possible to include all wiring diagrams for every year covered by this manual, the following diagrams are those that are typical and most commonly needed.

Prior to troubleshooting any circuit, check the fuses, fusible links

| WIRE COLOR CODE CHART | | | | | |
|---|---|---|---|---|---|
| COLOR CODE | COLOR | STANDARD TRACER COLOR | COLOR CODE | COLOR | STANDARD TRACER CODE |
| BK | BLACK | WT | PK | PINK | BK OR WH |
| BR | BROWN | WT | RD | RED | WT |
| DB | DARK BLUE | WT | TN | TAN | WT |
| DG | DARK GREEN | WT | VT | VIOLET | WT |
| GY | GRAY | BK | WT | WHITE | BK |
| LB | LIGHT BLUE | BK | YL | YELLOW | BK |
| LG | LIGHT GREEN | BK | * | WITH TRACER | |
| OR | ORANGE | BK | | | |

**28.4  Wiring diagram color code chart**

and circuit breakers (if equipped) to make sure they're in good condition. Make sure the battery is properly charged and check the cable connections (see Chapter 1).

When checking a circuit, make sure that all connectors are clean, with no broken or loose terminals. When unplugging a connector, do not pull on the wires. Pull only on the connector housings themselves.

Refer to the accompanying table and legend for the wire color codes applicable to your vehicle **(see illustration)**.

**Starting system wiring diagram (typical 2.6L carbureted engine)**

**Starting system wiring diagram (typical 2.2/2.5L carbureted engine)**

**12**

**Starting system wiring diagram (typical fuel-injected engine) (2 of 2)**

**Starting system wiring diagram (typical fuel-injected engine) (1 of 2)**

**Ignition switch wiring diagram (typical fuel-injected engine)**

**Ignition switch wiring diagram (typical carbureted engine)**

**12**

**Charging system wiring diagram (typical 2.2/2.5L carbureted engine) (2 of 2)**

**Charging system wiring diagram (typical 2.2/2.5L carbureted engine) (1 of 2)**

Charging system wiring diagram (typical 2.6L carbureted engine) (2 of 2)

Charging system wiring diagram (typical 2.6L carbureted engine) (1 of 2)

Charging system wiring diagram (typical fuel-injected engine) (2 of 2)

Charging system wiring diagram (typical fuel-injected engine) (1 of 2)

Typical front end lighting system wiring diagram (1 of 2)

Typical horn system wiring diagram

Typical headlight switch wiring diagram

Typical front end lighting system wiring diagram (2 of 2)

Typical turn signal and hazard/hazard flasher system wiring diagram (2 of 2)

Typical turn signal and hazard/hazard flasher system wiring diagram (1 of 2)

**12**

**Typical interior lighting system wiring diagram (1 of 2)**

**Typical interior lighting system wiring diagram (1 of 2)**

Typical heater system wiring diagram

Typical windshield wiper system wiring diagram

12

Typical heater and air conditioning system wiring diagram (2 of 2)

Typical heater and air conditioning system wiring diagram (1 of 2)

Typical power door lock wiring diagram (2 of 2)

Typical power door lock wiring diagram (1 of 2)

**12**

Typical rear lighting wiring diagram (2 of 2)

Typical rear lighting wiring diagram (1 of 2)

Typical fuel injection system wiring diagram (2 of 4)

Typical fuel injection system wiring diagram (1 of 4)

**12**

**Typical fuel injection system wiring diagram (4 of 4)**

**Typical fuel injection system wiring diagram (3 of 4)**

# Index

# Haynes Automotive Manuals

**ACURA**
*1776 Integra & Legend '86 thru '90

**AMC**
Jeep CJ - see JEEP (412)
694 Mid-size models, Concord, Hornet, Gremlin & Spirit '70 thru '83
934 (Renault) Alliance & Encore '83 thru '87

**AUDI**
615 4000 all models '80 thru '87
428 5000 all models '77 thru '83
1117 5000 all models '84 thru '88

**AUSTIN**
Healey Sprite - see MG Midget (265)

**BMW**
*2020 3/5 Series not including diesel or all-wheel drive models '82 thru '92
276 320i all 4 cyl models '75 thru '83
632 528i & 530i all models '75 thru '80
240 1500 thru 2002 except Turbo '59 thru '77
348 2500, 2800, 3.0 & Bavaria '69 thru '76

**BUICK**
Century (FWD) - see GM (829)
*1627 Buick, Oldsmobile & Pontiac Full-size (Front wheel drive) '85 thru '95
Buick Electra, LeSabre and Park Avenue; Oldsmobile Delta 88 Royale, Ninety Eight and Regency; Pontiac Bonneville
1551 Buick Oldsmobile & Pontiac Full-size (Rear wheel drive)
Buick Estate '70 thru '90, Electra'70 thru '84, LeSabre '70 thru '85, Limited '74 thru '79 Oldsmobile Custom Cruiser '70 thru '90, Delta 88 '70 thru '85,Ninety-eight '70 thru '84 Pontiac Bonneville '70 thru '81, Catalina '70 thru '81, Grandville '70 thru '75, Parisienne '83 thru '86
627 Mid-size Regal & Century '74 thru '87
Regal - see GENERAL MOTORS (1671)
Skyhawk - see GENERAL MOTORS (766)
Skylark '80 thru '85 - see GM (38020)
Skylark '86 on - see GM (1420)
Somerset - see GENERAL MOTORS (1420)

**CADILLAC**
*751 Cadillac Rear Wheel Drive all gasoline models '70 thru '93
Cimarron - see GENERAL MOTORS (766)

**CHEVROLET**
*1477 Astro & GMC Safari Mini-vans '85 thru '93
554 Camaro V8 all models '70 thru '81
866 Camaro all models '82 thru '92
Cavalier - see GENERAL MOTORS (766)
Celebrity - see GENERAL MOTORS (829)
625 Chevelle, Malibu, El Camino '69 thru '87
449 Chevette & Pontiac T1000 '76 thru '87
Citation - see GENERAL MOTORS (38020)
*1628 Corsica/Beretta all models '87 thru '95
274 Corvette all V8 models '68 thru '82
*1336 Corvette all models '84 thru '91
1762 Chevrolet Engine Overhaul Manual
704 Full-size Sedans Caprice, Impala, Biscayne, Bel Air & Wagons '69 thru '90
Lumina - see GENERAL MOTORS (1671)
Lumina APV - see GM (2035)
319 Luv Pick-up all 2WD & 4WD '72 thru '82
626 Monte Carlo all models '70 thru '88
241 Nova all V8 models thru '79
*1642 Nova/Geo Prizm front wheel drive '85 thru '92
420 Pick-ups '67 thru '87 - Chevrolet & GMC, all V8 & in-line 6 cyl, 2WD & 4WD '67 thru '87; Suburbans, Blazers & Jimmys '67 thru '91
*1664 Pick-ups '88 thru '95 - Chevrolet & GMC, all full-size models '88 thru '95; Blazer & Jimmy '92 thru '94; Suburban '92 thru '95; Tahoe & Yukon '95
*831 S-10 & GMC S-15 Pick-ups '82 thru '93
*1727 Sprint & Geo Metro '85 thru '94
*345 Vans - Chevrolet & GMC, V8 & in-line 6 cylinder models '68 thru '95

**CHRYSLER**
2114 Chrysler Engine Overhaul Manual
*2058 Full-size Front-Wheel Drive '88 thru '93
K-Cars - see DODGE Aries (723)
Laser - see DODGE Daytona (1140)
*1337 Chrysler & Plymouth Mid-size front wheel drive '82 thru '93;
Rear-wheel Drive - see DODGE Rear-wheel Drive (2098)

**DATSUN**
402 200SX all models '77 thru '79
647 200SX all models '80 thru '83
228 B-210 all models '73 thru '78
525 210 all models '78 thru '82
206 240Z, 260Z & 280Z Coupe '70 thru '78
563 280ZX Coupe & 2+2 '79 thru '83
300ZX - see NISSAN (1137)
679 310 all models '78 thru '82
123 510 & PL521 Pick-up '68 thru '73
430 510 all models '78 thru '81
372 610 all models '72 thru '76
277 620 Series Pick-up all models '73 thru '79
720 Series Pick-up - see NISSAN (771)
376 810/Maxima all gas models, '77 thru '84
Pulsar - see NISSAN (876)

**DODGE**
400 & 600 - see CHRYSLER Mid-size (1337)
*723 Aries & Plymouth Reliant '81 thru '89
1231 Caravan & Plymouth Voyager Mini-Vans all models '84 thru '95
699 Challenger/Plymouth Saporro '78 thru '83
Challenger '67-'76 - see DODGE Dart (234)
236 Colt all models '71 thru '77
610 Colt/Plymouth Champ (front wheel drive) all models '78 thru '87
*1668 Dakota Pick-ups all models '87 thru '93
234 Dart, Challenger/Plymouth Barracuda & Valiant 6 cyl models '67 thru '76
*1140 Daytona & Chrysler Laser '84 thru '89
*545 Omni & Plymouth Horizon '78 thru '90
*912 Pick-ups all full-size '74 thru '91
*556 Ram 50/D50 Pick-ups & Raider and Plymouth Arrow Pick-ups '79 thru '93
2098 Dodge/Plymouth/Chrysler rear wheel drive '71 thru '89
*1726 Shadow/Plymouth Sundance '87 thru '93
*1779 Spirit & Plymouth Acclaim '89 thru '95
*349 Vans - Dodge & Plymouth '71 thru '91

**EAGLE**
Talon - see Mitsubishi Eclipse (2097)

**FIAT**
094 124 Sport Coupe & Spider '68 thru '78
273 X1/9 all models '74 thru '80

**FORD**
*1476 Aerostar Mini-vans '86 thru '94
788 Bronco and Pick-ups '73 thru '79
*880 Bronco and Pick-ups '80 thru '95
268 Courier Pick-up all models '72 thru '82
2105 Crown Victoria & Mercury Grand Marquis '88 thru '94
1763 Ford Engine Overhaul Manual
789 Escort/Mercury Lynx '81 thru '90
*2046 Escort/Mercury Tracer '91 thru '95
*2021 Explorer & Mazda Navajo '91 thru '95
560 Fairmont & Mercury Zephyr '78 thru '83
334 Fiesta all models '77 thru '80
754 Ford & Mercury Full-size, Ford LTD & Mercury Marquis ('75 thru '82); Ford Custom 500,Country Squire, Crown Victoria & Mercury Colony Park ('75 thru '87); Ford LTD Crown Victoria & Mercury Gran Marquis ('83 thru '87)
359 Granada & Mercury Monarch '75 thru '80
773 Ford & Mercury Mid-size, Ford Thunderbird & Mercury Cougar ('75 thru '82); Ford LTD & Mercury Marquis ('83 thru '86); Ford Torino,Gran Torino, Elite, Ranchero pick-up, LTD II, Mercury Montego, Comet, XR-7 & Lincoln Versailles ('75 thru '86)
*654 Mustang & Mercury Capri incl. Turbo Mustang, '79 thru '93; Capri, '79 thru '86
357 Mustang V8 all models '64-1/2 thru '73
231 Mustang II 4 cyl, V6 & V8 '74 thru '78
649 Pinto & Mercury Bobcat '75 thru '80
1670 Probe all models '89 thru '92
*1026 Ranger/Bronco II gas models '83 thru '93
*1421 Taurus & Mercury Sable '86 thru '94
*1418 Tempo & Mercury Topaz '84 thru '94
1338 Thunderbird/Mercury Cougar '83 thru '88
*1725 Thunderbird/Mercury Cougar '89 and '93
344 Vans all V8 Econoline models '69 thru '91
*2119 Vans full size '92 thru '95

**GENERAL MOTORS**
*829 Buick Century, Chevrolet Celebrity, Olds Cutlass Ciera & Pontiac 6000 all models '82 thru '93
*1671 Buick Regal, Chevrolet Lumina, Oldsmobile Cutlass Supreme & Pontiac Grand Prix front wheel drive '88 thru '95
*766 Buick Skyhawk, Cadillac Cimarron, Chevrolet Cavalier, Oldsmobile Firenza Pontiac J-2000 & Sunbird '82 thru '94
38020 Buidk Skylar, Chevrolet Citation, Olds Omega, Pontiac Phoenix '80 thru '85
1420 Buick Skylark & Somerset, Olds Achieva, Calais & Pontiac Grand Am '85 thru '95
*2035 Chevrolet Lumina APV, Oldsmobile Silhouette & Pontiac Trans Sport '90 thru '94
General Motors Full-size Rear-wheel Drive - see BUICK (1551)

**GEO**
Metro - see CHEVROLET Sprint (1727)
Prizm - see CHEVROLET Nova (1642)
*2039 Storm all models '90 thru '93
Tracker - see SUZUKI Samurai (1626)

**GMC**
Safari - see CHEVROLET ASTRO (1477)
Vans & Pick-ups - see CHEVROLET (420, 831, 345, 1664)

**HONDA**
351 Accord CVCC all models '76 thru '83
1221 Accord all models '84 thru '89
2067 Accord all models '90 thru '93
*42013 Accord all models '94 thru '95
160 Civic 1200 all models '73 thru '79
633 Civic 1300 & 1500 CVCC '80 thru '83
297 Civic 1500 CVCC all models '75 thru '79
1227 Civic all models '84 thru '91
2118 Civic & del Sol '92 thru '95
*601 Prelude CVCC all models '79 thru '89

**HYUNDAI**
*1552 Excel all models '86 thru '94

**ISUZU**
*1641 Trooper & Pick-up, all gasoline models Pick-up, '81 thru '93; Trooper, '84 thru '91

**JAGUAR**
*242 XJ6 all 6 cyl models '68 thru '86
*478 XJ12 & XJS all 12 cyl models '72 thru '85

**JEEP**
*1553 Cherokee, Comanche & Wagoneer Limited all models '84 thru '93
412 CJ all models '49 thru '86
*50025 Grand Cherokee all models '93 thru '95
*1777 Wrangler all models '87 thru '94

**LINCOLN**
2117 Rear Wheel Drive all models '70 thru '95

**MAZDA**
648 626 (rear wheel drive) '79 thru '82
*1082 626 & MX-6 (front wheel drive) '83 thru '91
267 B Series Pick-ups '72 thru '93
370 GLC (rear wheel drive) '77 thru '83
757 GLC (front wheel drive) '81 thru '85
*2047 MPV all models '89 thru '94
Navajo - see FORD Explorer (2021)
460 RX-7 all models '79 thru '85
*1419 RX-7 all models '86 thru '91

**MERCEDES-BENZ**
*1643 190 Series 4-cyl gas models, '84 thru '88
346 230, 250 & 280 6 cyl sohc '68 thru '72
983 280 123 Series gas models '77 thru '81
698 350 & 450 all models '71 thru '80
697 Diesel 123 Series '76 thru '85

**MERCURY**
See FORD Listing

**MG**
111 MGB Roadster & GT Coupe '62 thru '80
265 MG Midget & Austin Healey Sprite Roadster '58 thru '80

**MITSUBISHI**
*1669 Cordia, Tredia, Galant, Precis & Mirage '83 thru '93
*2097 Eclipse, Eagle Talon & Plymouth Laser '90 thru '94
*2022 Pick-up & Montero '83 thru '95

**NISSAN**
1137 300ZX all models incl. Turbo '84 thru '89
*1341 Maxima all models '85 thru '91
*771 Pick-ups/Pathfinder gas models '80 thru '95
876 Pulsar all models '83 thru '86
*982 Sentra all models '82 thru '94
*981 Stanza all models '82 thru '90

**OLDSMOBILE**
Bravada - see CHEVROLET S-10 (831)
Calais - see GENERAL MOTORS (1420)
Custom Cruiser - see BUICK (1551)
*658 Cutlass '74 thru '88
Cutlass Ciera - see GM (829)
Cutlass Supreme - see GM (1671)
Delta 88 - see BUICK Full-size RWD (1551)
Delta 88 Brougham - see BUICK Full-size: FWD (1551), RWD (1627)
Delta 88 Royale - see BUICK (1551)
Firenza - see GENERAL MOTORS (766)
Ninety-eight Regency - see BUICK Full-size RWD (1551), FWD (1627)
Omega - see GENERAL MOTORS (38020)
Silhouette - see GENERAL MOTORS (2035)

**PEUGEOT**
663 504 all diesel models '74 thru '83

**PLYMOUTH**
Laser - see MITSUBISHI Eclipse (2097)
Other PLYMOUTH titles, see DODGE

**PONTIAC**
T1000 - see CHEVROLET Chevette (449)
J-2000 - see GENERAL MOTORS (766)
6000 - see GM (829)
Bonneville - see Buick Full-size FWD (1627), RWD (1551)
Bonneville Brougham - see Buick (1551)
Catalina - see Buick Full-size (1551)
1232 Fiero all models '84 thru '88
555 Firebird V8 models except Turbo '70 thru '81
867 Firebird all models '82 thru '92
Full-size Front Wheel Drive - see BUICK Oldsmobile, Pontiac Full-size FWD (1627)
Full-size Rear Wheel Drive - see BUICK Oldsmobile, Pontiac Full-size RWD (1551)
Grand Am - see GM (1420)
Grand Prix - see GM (1671)
Grandville - see Buick (1551)
Parisienne - see BUICK (1551)
Phoenix - see GM (38020)

**PORSCHE**
*264 911 all Coupe & Targa models except Turbo & Carrera 4 '65 thru '89
239 914 all 4 cyl models '69 thru '76
397 924 all models incl. Turbo '76 thru '82
*1027 944 all models incl. Turbo '83 thru '89

**RENAULT**
141 5 Le Car all models '76 thru '83
Alliance & Encore - see AMC (934)

**SAAB**
247 99 all models including Turbo '69 thru '80
*980 900 including Turbo '79 thru '88

**SATURN**
*2083 Saturn all models '91 thru '94

**SUBARU**
237 1100, 1300, 1400 & 1600 '71 thru '79
*681 1600 & 1800 2WD & 4WD '80 thru '89

**SUZUKI**
*1626 Samurai/Sidekick/Geo Tracker '86 thru '95

**TOYOTA**
1023 Camry all models '83 thru '91
*92006 Camry all models '92 thru '95
935 Celica Rear Wheel Drive '71 thru '85
*2038 Celica Front Wheel Drive '86 thru '92
1139 Celica Supra all models '79 thru '92
361 Corolla all models '75 thru '79
961 Corolla rear wheel drive models '80 thru '87
*1025 Corolla front wheel drive models '84 thru '92
636 Corolla Tercel all models '80 thru '82
360 Corona all models '74 thru '82
532 Cressida all models '78 thru '82
313 Land Cruiser all models '68 thru '82
*1339 MR2 all models '85 thru '87
304 Pick-up all models '69 thru '78
*656 Pick-up all models '79 thru '95
*2048 Previa all models '91 thru '93
2106 Tercel all models '87 thru '94

**TRIUMPH**
113 Spitfire all models '62 thru '81
322 TR7 all models '75 thru '81

**VW**
159 Beetle & Karmann Ghia '54 thru '79
238 Dasher all gasoline models '74 thru '81
*884 Rabbit, Jetta, Scirocco, & Pick-up gas models '74 thru '91 & Convertible '80 thru '92
451 Rabbit, Jetta & Pick-up diesel models '77 thru '84
082 Transporter 1600 all models '68 thru '79
226 Transporter 1700, 1800, 2000 '72 thru '79
084 Type 3 1500 & 1600 '63 thru '73
1029 Vanagon air-cooled models '80 thru '83

**VOLVO**
203 120, 130 Series & 1800 Sports '61 thru '73
129 140 Series all models '66 thru '74
*270 240 Series all models '76 thru '93
400 260 Series all models '75 thru '82
*1550 740 & 760 Series all models '82 thru '88

**TECHBOOK MANUALS**
2108 Automotive Computer Codes
1667 Automotive Emissions Control Manual
482 Fuel Injection Manual, 1978 thru 1985
2111 Fuel Injection Manual, 1986 thru 1994
2069 Holley Carburetor Manual
2068 Rochester Carburetor Manual
10240 Weber/Zenith/Stromberg/SU Carburetor
1762 Chevrolet Engine Overhaul Manual
2114 Chrysler Engine Overhaul Manual
1763 Ford Engine Overhaul Manual
1736 GM and Ford Diesel Engine Repair
1666 Small Engine Repair Manual
10355 Ford Automatic Transmission Overhaul
10360 GM Automatic Transmission Overhaul
1479 Automotive Body Repair & Painting
2112 Automotive Brake Manual
2113 Automotive Detailing Manual
1654 Automotive Eelectrical Manual
1480 Automotive Heating & Air Conditioning
2109 Automotive Reference Manual & Illustrated Dictionary
2107 Automotive Tools Manual
10440 Used Car Buying Guide
2110 Welding Manual

**SPANISH MANUALS**
98905 Códigos Automotrices de la Computadora
98915 Inyección de Combustible 1986 al 1994
99040 Chevrolet & GMC Camionetas '67 al '87 Incluye Suburban, Blazer & Jimmy '67 al '91
99041 Chevrolet & GMC Camionetas '88 al '95 Incluye Suburban '92 al '95, Blazer & Jimmy '92 al '94, Tahoe y Yukon '95
99075 Ford Camionetas y Bronco '80 al '94
99125 Toyota Camionetas y 4-Runner '79 al '95